T0335886

Managing Big Data in Cloud Computing Environments

Zongmin Ma
Nanjing University of Aeronautics and Astronautics, China

A volume in the Advances in Systems Analysis,
Software Engineering, and High Performance
Computing (ASASEHPC) Book Series

An Imprint of IGI Global

Published in the United States of America by
    Information Science Reference (an imprint of IGI Global)
    701 E. Chocolate Avenue
    Hershey PA, USA 17033
    Tel: 717-533-8845
    Fax: 717-533-8661
    E-mail: cust@igi-global.com
    Web site: http://www.igi-global.com

Library of Congress Cataloging-in-Publication Data

Names: Ma, Zongmin, 1965- editor.
Title: Managing big data in cloud computing environments / Zongmin Ma, editor.
Description: Hershey, PA : Information Science Reference, [2016] | Includes
  bibliographical references and index.
Identifiers: LCCN 2015046880| ISBN 9781466698345 (hardcover) | ISBN
  9781466698352 (ebook)
Subjects: LCSH: Cloud computing. | Big data.
Classification: LCC QA76.585 .M356 2016 | DDC 004.67/82--dc23 LC record available at http://lccn.loc.gov/2015046880

This book is published in the IGI Global book series Advances in Systems Analysis, Software Engineering, and High Performance Computing (ASASEHPC) (ISSN: 2327-3453; eISSN: 2327-3461)

British Cataloguing in Publication Data
A Cataloguing in Publication record for this book is available from the British Library.

All work contributed to this book is new, previously-unpublished material. The views expressed in this book are those of the authors, but not necessarily of the publisher.

For electronic access to this publication, please contact: eresources@igi-global.com.

Advances in Systems Analysis, Software Engineering, and High Performance Computing (ASASEHPC) Book Series

Vijayan Sugumaran
Oakland University, USA

ISSN: 2327-3453
EISSN: 2327-3461

MISSION

The theory and practice of computing applications and distributed systems has emerged as one of the key areas of research driving innovations in business, engineering, and science. The fields of software engineering, systems analysis, and high performance computing offer a wide range of applications and solutions in solving computational problems for any modern organization.

The **Advances in Systems Analysis, Software Engineering, and High Performance Computing (ASASEHPC) Book Series** brings together research in the areas of distributed computing, systems and software engineering, high performance computing, and service science. This collection of publications is useful for academics, researchers, and practitioners seeking the latest practices and knowledge in this field.

COVERAGE

- Engineering Environments
- Performance Modelling
- Virtual Data Systems
- Parallel Architectures
- Computer Networking
- Metadata and Semantic Web
- Storage Systems
- Distributed Cloud Computing
- Network Management
- Software Engineering

IGI Global is currently accepting manuscripts for publication within this series. To submit a proposal for a volume in this series, please contact our Acquisition Editors at Acquisitions@igi-global.com or visit: http://www.igi-global.com/publish/.

Titles in this Series

For a list of additional titles in this series, please visit: www.igi-global.com

Emerging Research Surrounding Power Consumption and Performance Issues in Utility Computing
Ganesh Chandra Deka (Regional Vocational Training Institute (RVTI) for Women, India) G.M. Siddesh (M S Ramaiah Institute of Technology, Bangalore, India) K. G. Srinivasa (M S Ramaiah Institute of Technology, Bangalore, India) and L.M. Patnaik (IISc, Bangalore, India)
Information Science Reference • copyright 2016 • 460pp • H/C (ISBN: 9781466688537) • US $215.00 (our price)

Advanced Research on Cloud Computing Design and Applications
Shadi Aljawarneh (Jordan University of Science and Technology, Jordan)
Information Science Reference • copyright 2015 • 388pp • H/C (ISBN: 9781466686762) • US $205.00 (our price)

Handbook of Research on Computational Simulation and Modeling in Engineering
Francisco Miranda (Instituto Politécnico de Viana do Castelo and CIDMA of University of Aveiro, Portugal) and Carlos Abreu (Instituto Politécnico de Viana do Castelo, Portugal)
Engineering Science Reference • copyright 2016 • 824pp • H/C (ISBN: 9781466688230) • US $420.00 (our price)

Intelligent Applications for Heterogeneous System Modeling and Design
Kandarpa Kumar Sarma (Gauhati University, India) Manash Pratim Sarma (Gauhati University, India) and Mousmita Sarma (SpeecHWareNet (I) Pvt. Ltd, India)
Information Science Reference • copyright 2015 • 407pp • H/C (ISBN: 9781466684935) • US $255.00 (our price)

Achieving Enterprise Agility through Innovative Software Development
Amitoj Singh (Chitkara University, Punjab, India)
Information Science Reference • copyright 2015 • 349pp • H/C (ISBN: 9781466685109) • US $225.00 (our price)

Delivery and Adoption of Cloud Computing Services in Contemporary Organizations
Victor Chang (Computing, Creative Technologies and Engineering, Leeds Beckett University, UK) Robert John Walters (Electronics and Computer Science, University of Southampton, UK) and Gary Wills (Electronics and Computer Science, University of Southampton, UK)
Information Science Reference • copyright 2015 • 519pp • H/C (ISBN: 9781466682108) • US $225.00 (our price)

Emerging Research in Cloud Distributed Computing Systems
Susmit Bagchi (Gyeongsang National University, South Korea)
Information Science Reference • copyright 2015 • 446pp • H/C (ISBN: 9781466682139) • US $200.00 (our price)

www.igi-global.com

701 E. Chocolate Ave., Hershey, PA 17033
Order online at www.igi-global.com or call 717-533-8845 x100
To place a standing order for titles released in this series, contact: cust@igi-global.com
Mon-Fri 8:00 am - 5:00 pm (est) or fax 24 hours a day 717-533-8661

Editorial Advisory Board

Table of Contents

Detailed Table of Contents

Section 1
Foundational Issues in Big Data Management in Cloud Computing Environments

Jaroslav Pokorny, Charles University, Czech Republic
Bela Stantic, Griffith University, Australia

The development and extensive use of highly distributed and scalable systems to process Big Data have been widely considered. New data management architectures, e.g. distributed file systems and NoSQL databases, are used in this context. However, features of Big Data like their complexity and data analytics demands indicate that these concepts solve Big Data problems only partially. A development of so called NewSQL databases is highly relevant and even special category of Big Data Management Systems is considered. In this work we will discuss these trends and evaluate some current approaches to Big Data processing, identify the current challenges, and suggest possible research directions.

Ahmet Artu Yıldırım, Utah State University, USA
Dan Watson, Utah State University, USA

Major Internet services are required to process a tremendous amount of data at real time. As we put these services under the magnifying glass, It's seen that distributed object storage systems play an important role at back-end in achieving this success. In this chapter, overall information of the current state-of–the-art storage systems are given which are used for reliable, high performance and scalable storage needs in data centers and cloud. Then, an experimental distributed object storage system (CADOS) is introduced for retrieving large data, such as hundreds of megabytes, efficiently through HTML5-enabled web browsers over big data – terabytes of data – in cloud infrastructure. The objective of the system is to minimize latency and propose a scalable storage system on the cloud using a thin RESTful web service and modern HTML5 capabilities.

Chapter 3

With IoT era, development raises several significant research questions in terms of system architecture, design and improvement. For example; the requirement of virtual resource utilization and storage capacity necessitates making IoT applications smarter; therefore, integrate the IoT concept with cloud computing will play an important role. This is crucial because of very large amounts of data that IoT is expected to generate. The Cloud of Things (CoT) is used to connect heterogeneous physical things to the virtual domain of the cloud. Despite its numerous advantages, there are many research challenges with utilization of CoT that needs additional consideration. These include high complexity, efficiency, improving reliability, and security. This chapter introduces CoT, its features, the applications that use CoT. CoT, like all other networked functions, is vulnerable to security attacks. The security risks for CoT are listed and described. The security requirements for CoT are identified and solutions are proposed to address the various attacks on CoT and its components.

Chapter 4

Cloud computing technology is a modern emerging trend in the distributed computing technology that is rapidly gaining popularity in network communication field. Despite the advantages that the cloud platforms bolstered, it suffers from many security issues such as secure communication, consumer authentication, and intrusion caused by attacks. These security issues relevant to customer data filtering and lost the connection at any time. In order to address these issues, this chapter, introduces an innovative cloud computing cryptographic environment, that entails both Quantum Cryptography-as-service and Quantum Advanced Encryption Standard. CCCE poses more secure data transmission channels by provisioning secret key among cloud's instances and consumers. In addition, the QCaaS solves the key generation and key distribution problems that emerged through the online negotiation between the communication parties. It is important to note that the CCCE solves the distance limitation coverage problem that is stemmed from the quantum state property.

Chapter 5

Big Data is driving radical changes in traditional data analysis platforms. To perform any kind of analysis on such voluminous and complex data, scaling up the hardware platforms becomes impending. With the entire buzz surrounding Big Data; it is being collected at an unprecedented scale. Big Data has potential to revolutionize much more than just research. Loading large data-sets is often a challenge. Another shift of this Big Data processing is the move towards cloud computing. As many communities begin to rely on cloud based data management, large shared data goes up extensively. Analysis of such large data on distributed processing system or cloud is a bit difficult task to handle. The aim of this chapter is to provide a better understanding of the design challenges of cloud computing and analytics of big data on it. The challenge is related to how a large extent of data is being harnessed, and the opportunity is related to how effectively it is used for analyzing the information from it.

Section 2
Managing Big Data of Special Types in Cloud Computing Environments

Chapter 6

Berkay Aydin, Georgia State University, USA
Vijay Akkineni, Georgia State University, USA
Rafal A Angryk, Georgia State University, USA

With the ever-growing nature of spatiotemporal data, it is inevitable to use non-relational and distributed database systems for storing massive spatiotemporal datasets. In this chapter, the important aspects of non-relational (NoSQL) databases for storing large-scale spatiotemporal trajectory data are investigated. Mainly, two data storage schemata are proposed for storing trajectories, which are called traditional and partitioned data models. Additionally spatiotemporal and non-spatiotemporal indexing structures are designed for efficiently retrieving data under different usage scenarios. The results of the experiments exhibit the advantages of utilizing data models and indexing structures for various query types.

Chapter 7

Wei Yan, Liaoning University, China

Parallel queries of k Nearest Neighbor for massive spatial data are an important issue. The k nearest neighbor queries (kNN queries), designed to find k nearest neighbors from a dataset S for every point in another dataset R, is a useful tool widely adopted by many applications including knowledge discovery, data mining, and spatial databases. In cloud computing environments, MapReduce programming model is a well-accepted framework for data-intensive application over clusters of computers. This chapter proposes a parallel method of kNN queries based on clusters in MapReduce programming model. Firstly, this chapter proposes a partitioning method of spatial data using Voronoi diagram. Then, this chapter clusters the data point after partition using k-means method. Furthermore, this chapter proposes an efficient algorithm for processing kNN queries based on k-means clusters using MapReduce programming model. Finally, extensive experiments evaluate the efficiency of the proposed approach.

Chapter 8

Katarina Grolinger, Western University, Canada
Emna Mezghani, Université de Toulouse, France
Miriam A. M. Capretz, Western University, Canada
Ernesto Exposito, Université de Toulouse, France

Decision-making in disaster management requires information gathering, sharing, and integration by means of collaboration on a global scale and across governments, industries, and communities. Large volume of heterogeneous data is available; however, current data management solutions offer few or no integration capabilities and limited potential for collaboration. Moreover, recent advances in NoSQL, cloud computing, and Big Data open the door for new solutions in disaster data management. This chapter presents a Knowledge as a Service (KaaS) framework for disaster cloud data management (Disaster-CDM), with the objectives of facilitating information gathering and sharing; storing large amounts of disaster-related data; and facilitating search and supporting interoperability and integration. In the Disaster-CDM approach NoSQL data stores provide storage reliability and scalability while service-oriented architecture achieves flexibility and extensibility. The contribution of Disaster-CDM is demonstrated by integration capabilities, on examples of full-text search and querying services.

Chapter 9

Zongmin Ma, Nanjing University of Aeronautics and Astronautics, China
Li Yan, Nanjing University of Aeronautics and Astronautics, China

The Resource Description Framework (RDF) is a model for representing information resources on the Web. With the widespread acceptance of RDF as the de-facto standard recommended by W3C (World Wide Web Consortium) for the representation and exchange of information on the Web, a huge amount of RDF data is being proliferated and becoming available. So RDF data management is of increasing importance, and has attracted attentions in the database community as well as the Semantic Web community. Currently much work has been devoted to propose different solutions to store large-scale RDF data efficiently. In order to manage massive RDF data, NoSQL ("not only SQL") databases have been used for scalable RDF data store. This chapter focuses on using various NoSQL databases to store massive RDF data. An up-to-date overview of the current state of the art in RDF data storage in NoSQL databases is provided. The chapter aims at suggestions for future research.

Section 3
Two Application Scenarios of Big Data Management in Cloud Computing Environments

Chapter 10

Tomayess Issa, Curtin University, Australia
Yuchao Duan, Curtin University, Australia
Theodora Issa, Curtin University, Australia
Vanessa Chang, Curtin University, Australia

Cloud Computing become a significant factor in E-commerce and E-business processes and will reduce negative IT impacts on the environment without compromising the needs of future generations. This chapter aim to examine the attitudes of Chinese Organizations towards Cloud Computing adoption. This chapter provides an answer to the question: "What are the advantages and disadvantages of Cloud Computing adoption in Chinese organizations?" The answer was sought by means of an online survey of (N=121) respondents. The survey results revealed the Chinese position regarding the cloud movement, its strengths and weaknesses, the threats posed by Cloud Computing in China, and the specific advantages and disadvantages of this new technology that Chinese organizations and research communities should embrace for the realization of future cloud systems.

Chapter 11

K. Palanivel, Pondicherry University, India

S Kuppuswami, Kongu Engineering College, India

Information and Communication Technology (ICT) is one of the fast growing industries that facilitate many latest services to the users and therefore, the number of users is increasing rapidly. The usage of ICT and its life cycle produce hazardous substances that need to be addressed in efficient and green ways. The adoption of green computing involves many improvements and provide energy-efficiency services for data centers, power management and cloud computing. Cloud computing is a highly scalable and cost-effective infrastructure for running Web applications. However, the growing demand of Cloud infrastructure has drastically increased the energy consumption of data centers, which has become a critical issue. Hence, energy-efficient solutions are required to minimize the impact of Cloud environment. E-learning methodology is an example of Green computing. Thus, it is proposed a Green Cloud Computing Architecture for e-Learning Applications that can lower expenses and reduce energy consumption.

Preface

In recent years, advances in Web technology and the proliferation of sensors and mobile devices connected to the Internet have resulted in the generation of immense data sets available on the Web that need to be processed and stored. Cloud computing has emerged as a paradigm that promises to meet these requirements. Cloud computing is an extremely successful paradigm of service oriented computing, and has revolutionized the way computing infrastructure is abstracted and used. Three most popular cloud paradigms include: Infrastructure as a Service (IaaS), Platform as a Service (PaaS), and Software as a Service (SaaS).

Cloud computing is associated with service provisioning and these services are based on processing and analysis of huge volume of data. Big data management in cloud computing environments is hereby proposed in recent years. It should be noted that big data management in cloud computing environments need information interoperations in a right way. At this point, explicit knowledge management can play a critical role in cloud computing. Viewed from this point, a new cloud paradigm named Knowledge as a Service (KaaS) is emerging. It is very critical to deal with the worth information for effective problem solving and decision making. It is especially true when a variety of data types and users' requirements as well as large volumes of data are available. The techniques of data and knowledge management in cloud computing environments are challenging today's database and information systems, and meanwhile promote their evolution.

The research, development and application of data and knowledge management in cloud computing environments are receiving increasing attention. By means of cloud computing technology, massive data and knowledge can be managed effectively and efficiently to support various problem solving and decision making. Data and knowledge management in cloud computing environments are the fields which must be investigated by academic researchers together with developers. Nowadays the research and development of big data management in cloud computing environments are receiving increasing attention. Some key techniques of data management in cloud computing environments are investigated by researchers all around the world on the one hand. On the other hand, massive data in many application domains are managed and analyzed in cloud computing environments.

This book covers a fast-growing topic in great depth and focuses on technologies and applications of big data management in cloud computing environments. It aims to provide a single record of current advances in big data management in cloud computing environments. The objective of the book is to provide state of the art information to academics, researchers and industry practitioners who are involved or interested in the study, use, design and development of advanced and emerging information technologies with ultimate aim to empower individuals and organizations in building competencies for exploiting the opportunities of the data and knowledge society. The book presents the latest results in technology research, design implementation and application development of big data management in cloud computing environments. The chapters of the book have been contributed by different authors and provide possible solutions for the different types of technological problems.

This book, which consists of eleven chapters, is organized into three major sections. The first section contains the first five chapters. The next four chapters comprise the second section. The third section consists of the final two chapters.

The first section discusses several foundational issues in big data management in cloud computing environments. Let us look at these issues.

The development and extensive use of highly distributed and scalable systems to process Big Data have been widely considered. As a result, new data management architectures (e.g. distributed file systems and NoSQL databases) are used in this context. However, features of Big Data like their complexity and data analytics demands indicate that these concepts solve Big Data problems only partially. A development of so called NewSQL databases is highly relevant and even special category of Big Data Management Systems is considered. Jaroslav Pokorny and Bela Stantic discuss these trends and evaluate some current approaches to Big Data processing. They further identify the current challenges and suggest possible research directions in Big Data processing.

Ahmet Artu Yildirim and Dan Watson concentrate on cloud-aware distributed object storages in Internet services. They first present overall information of the current state-of –the-art storage systems which are used for reliable, high performance and scalable storage needs in data centers and cloud. On the basis, they introduce a novel distributed object storage system (CADOS) for retrieving big data efficiently through HTML5-enabled web browsers over big data in cloud infrastructure. The objective of the system is to minimize latency and propose a scalable object storage system on the cloud using a thin RESTful web service and modern HTML5 capabilities.

The Cloud of Things (CoT) is used to connect heterogeneous physical things to the virtual domain of the cloud. Bashar Alohali demonstrate the creation of CoT system faces many challenges and risks linked with specific technical and network characteristics of things. Bashar Alohali particularly discusses the security threats and available solutions that are connected with resource-constrained nature of CoT devices, and further addresses new security requirements that tackle the issue of CoT network. Finally it is advocated to investigate the issue of CoT architecture deployment and implementation focusing on specific features of IoT (Internet of Things) integration with cloud computing services.

Omer K. Jasim *et al.* introduce an innovative cloud computing cryptographic environment (CCCE), which entails both Quantum Cryptography-as-service (QCaaS) and Quantum Advanced Encryption Standard (QAES). CCCE poses more secure data transmission channels by provisioning secret key among cloud's instances and consumers. In addition, the QCaaS solves the key generation and key distribution problems that emerged through the online negotiation between the communication parties. Note that the CCCE solves the distance limitation coverage problem that is stemmed from the quantum state property. Also the CCCE reveals a higher secure data transmission comparing to others cloud security systems.

Big Data is driving radical changes in traditional data analysis platforms. Cloud Computing appears as an ideal solution for the efficient management and analysis of big data streams. However, there are many limitations and barriers in such effectiveness, especially in the light of the remote and local data movement overhead (network messages, memory and storage accesses). After critically analyzing the several cloud-based big data solutions available on the market, positioning them in the different phases of a well-established data value chain, Madhavi Arun Vaidya tries to highlight the potential, the urgent challenges to be faced and the early results related to the development of data-intensive applications distributed across multiple cloud-based data centres.

The second section deals with the issues of managing big data of special types in cloud computing environments.

In order to store massive spatiotemporal datasets, Berkay Aydin, Vijay Akkineni and Rafal A Angryk investigate the important aspects of non-relational (NoSQL) databases for storing large-scale spatio-temporal trajectory data. They propose two main data storage schemata for storing trajectories, which are called traditional and partitioned data models. In addition, to efficiently retrieve data under different usage scenarios, they design spatiotemporal and non-spatiotemporal indexing structures. The results of the experiments exhibit the advantages of utilizing the proposed data models and indexing structures for various query types.

Wei Yan concentrates on parallel queries of k Nearest Neighbor (kNN) for massive spatial data in cloud computing environments. They propose a parallel method of kNN queries based on clusters in MapReduce programming model. They first propose a partitioning method of spatial data using Voronoi diagram and then cluster the data point after partition using k-means method. They furthermore propose an efficient algorithm for processing kNN queries based on k-means clusters using MapReduce programming model. Extensive experiments evaluate the efficiency of the proposed approaches.

In the domain of disaster management, large volume of heterogeneous data is gathered and integrated by means of collaboration on a global scale and across governments, industries, and communities. Katarina Grolinger *et al.* propose a Knowledge as a Service (KaaS) framework for disaster cloud data management (Disaster-CDM), with the objectives of facilitating information gathering and sharing; storing large amounts of disaster-related data; and facilitating search and supporting interoperability and integration. In the Disaster-CDM approach, NoSQL data stores provide storage reliability and scalability while service-oriented architecture achieves flexibility and extensibility. They demonstrate the contribution of Disaster-CDM by integration capabilities, on examples of full-text search and querying services.

Chapter 9

The Resource Description Framework (RDF) is a model for representing information resources on the Web. With the widespread acceptance of RDF as the de-facto standard recommended by W3C (World Wide Web Consortium) for the representation and exchange of information on the Web, a huge amount of RDF data is being proliferated and becoming available. To manage massive RDF data, NoSQL ("not only SQL") databases have been used for scalable RDF data store. Zongmin Ma and Li Yan provide an up-to-date overview of the current state of the art in RDF data storage in NoSQL databases. They aim at suggestions for future research.

The third section presents two application scenarios of big data management in cloud computing environments.

Aiming to examine the attitudes of Chinese Organizations towards Cloud Computing adoption, Tomayess Issa *et al.* provides an answer to the question: "What are the advantages and disadvantages of Cloud Computing adoption in Chinese organizations?" The answer is sought by means of an online survey of (N = 121) respondents. Their survey results reveal the Chinese position regarding the cloud movement, its strengths and weaknesses, the threats posed by Cloud Computing in China, and the specific advantages and disadvantages of this new technology that Chinese organizations and research communities should embrace for the realization of future cloud systems.

K. Palanivel proposes a cloud-oriented green computing architecture for eLearning applications (COGALA). The COGALA consists of client, client-oriented green cloud middleware and green broker. The green cloud middleware provides the client a tool to better manage the distribution of tasks to cloud with the least carbon emission and other relevant decision criteria. The middleware is composed of a user interface application and a windows service. This architecture provides incentives to both users and providers to use and deliver the most "Green" services, respectively. K. Palanivel also discusses the implication of the proposed solution for future research directions to enable cloud-oriented green computing.

Acknowledgment

The editor wishes to thank all of the authors for their insights and excellent contributions to this book and would like to acknowledge the help of all involved in the collation and review process of the book, without whose support the project could not have been satisfactorily completed. Most of the authors of chapters included in this book also served as referees for chapters written by other authors. Thanks go to all those who provided constructive and comprehensive reviews.

A further special note of thanks goes to all the staff at IGI Global, whose contributions throughout the whole process from inception of the initial idea to final publication have been invaluable. Special thanks also go to the publishing team at IGI Global. This book would not have been possible without the ongoing professional support from IGI Global.

The idea of editing this volume stems from the initial research work that the editor did in past several years. The research work of the editor was supported by the *National Natural Science Foundation of China* (61370075 & 61572118).

Zongmin Ma
Nanjing University of Aeronautics and Astronautics, China
October 2015

Section 1
Foundational Issues in Big Data Management in Cloud Computing Environments

Chapter 1
Challenges and Opportunities in Big Data Processing

Jaroslav Pokorny
Charles University, Czech Republic

Bela Stantic
Griffith University, Australia

ABSTRACT

The development and extensive use of highly distributed and scalable systems to process Big Data have been widely considered. New data management architectures, e.g. distributed file systems and NoSQL databases, are used in this context. However, features of Big Data like their complexity and data analytics demands indicate that these concepts solve Big Data problems only partially. A development of so called NewSQL databases is highly relevant and even special category of Big Data Management Systems is considered. In this work we will discuss these trends and evaluate some current approaches to Big Data processing, identify the current challenges, and suggest possible research directions.

INTRODUCTION

Big Data is often characterized by its volume which exceeds the normal range of databases in practice. For example, web clicks, social media, scientific experiments, and datacenter monitoring belong among data sources that generate vast amounts of raw data every day. An interesting characteristic of Big Data is its processing, i.e. Big Data computing. In last years, just Big Data processing is an issue of the highest importance, particularly so called *Big Analytics*. Big Analytics is another buzzword denoting a combination of Big Data and Advanced Analytics. J. L. Leidner (R&D at Thomson Reuters) in the interview with R. V. Zicari (ODMS.org, 2013) emphasizes that buzzwords like "Big Data" do not by themselves solve any problem – they are not magic bullets. He gives an advice how to tackle and solve any problem. There is need to look at the input data, specify the desired output, and think hard about whether and how you can compute the desired result, which is basically nothing but "good old" computer science.

The recent advances in new hardware platforms, methods, algorithms as well as new software systems support Big Data processing and Big Analytics.

DOI: 10.4018/978-1-4666-9834-5.ch001

Effective use of systems incorporating Big Data in many application scenarios requires adequate tools for storage and processing such data at low-level and analytical tools on higher levels. Moreover, applications working with Big Data are both transactional and analytical. However, they require usually different architectures.

Big Analytics is the most important aspect of Big Data computing mainly from a user's point of view. Unfortunately, large datasets are expressed in different formats, e.g., relational, XML, textual, multimedia or RDF, which may cause difficulties in their processing by data mining algorithms. Also, increasing either data volume in a repository or the number of users of this repository requires more feasible solution of scaling in such dynamic environments than it is offered by traditional database architectures.

Clearly, Big Analytics is done also on big amounts of transaction data as extension of methods used usually in technology of data warehouses (DW). Generally DW technology is focused on structured data in comparison to much richer variability of Big Data as it is understood today. Therefore, analytical processing of Big Data Analytics requires not only new database architectures but also new methods for integrating and analyzing heterogeneous data.

Big Data storage and processing are essential for cloud services. This reinforces requirements on the availability and scalability of computational resources offered by cloud services.

Users have a number of options associated with above mentioned issues. For storing and processing large datasets they can use:

- Traditional parallel database systems (shared nothing architectures),
- Distributed file systems and Hadoop technologies,
- Key-value datastores (so called NoSQL databases),
- New database architectures (e.g., NewSQL databases).

In particular, three last categories are not mutually exclusive and can and they should co-exist in many enterprises.

The NoSQL and NewSQL databases present themselves as data processing alternatives that can handle huge volumes of data and provide the required scalability. NoSQL databases are a type of databases which were initiated by Web companies in early 2000s. NewSQL databases are aiming to provide the scale-out advantages of NoSQL databases often on commodity hardware and maintain the transactional data consistency guarantees of traditional relational DBMS. They are also compatible with SQL. Especially, *massively parallel analytic databases* play an important role here. Algorithms supporting Big Analytics are presented on the top of these systems or they are a native part of their implementation.

The chapter is an attempt to cover principles and core features of these systems and to associate them to main application areas of Big Data processing and management in practice, particularly in relation to Big Analytics. We also focus in more extent on challenges and opportunities associated with Big Data.

BACKGROUND

The fundamental concept of generating data has changed recently, in the past, several main sources have been generating data and all others have been consuming data. However, today all of us are both generating data and also consumers of this shared data. Usually we talk about the Big Data when the dataset size is beyond the ability of the current system to collect, process, retrieve and manage the data. (Manyika et al., 2011) describes Big Data as large pools of unstructured and structured data that can be captured, communicated, aggregated, stored, and analyzed. Big Data are now becoming part of every sector and function of the global economy. Data created both inside corporations and outside the firewall via the Web, mobile devices, IT infrastructure and other sources increases exponentially each year (Kelly, 2014).

Web plays a prominent role towards shifting to the Big Data paradigm. The textual Web content is a source that people want to easily consult and search. Challenges in this area include primarily document summarization, personalized search, sentiment analysis, and recommender systems. The social structures formed over the Web, mainly represented by the online social networking applications such as Facebook, LinkedIn and Twitter, contribute intensively to Big Data. Typically, the interactions of the users within a social networking platform form large and dynamic graph structures. Use cases identified for Big Data in enterprises include risk modelling, fraud detection, customer analysis, effectiveness of marketing campaigns, etc.

In general, Big Data come mainly from these contexts:

- Large data collections in traditional DWs or databases,
- Enterprise data of large, non-Web-based companies working with internet transactions,
- Data from large Web companies providing social networking and media,
- Data generated and/or transferred through mobile devices,
- Data streams generated by remote sensors and other IT hardware,
- Data archives from e-science (computational biology, bioinformatics, genomics, and astronomy).

A typical feature of Big Data is the absence of a schema characterization, which makes difficulties when we want to integrate heterogeneous datasets.

Big Data Characteristics

Big Data are most often characterized by several V's:

- **Volume:** Data scale in the range of TB to PB and even more. The big volume is not only storage issue but also influences a Big Analytics. Not only data samples, but often all data are captured for analysis.
- **Velocity:** Both how quickly data is being produced and how quickly the data must be processed to meet demand (e.g., streaming data).
- **Variety:** Data is in many format types – structured, unstructured, semistructured, text, media, etc. Data does not come only from business transactions, but also from machines, sensors and other sources, making it much more complex to manage.
- **Veracity:** Managing the reliability and predictability of inherently imprecise data.

The first three V's have been introduced by Gartner in (Laney, 2001), the V associated with Veracity has been added by D. Snow in his blog (Snow, 2012). Both Variety and Velocity are actually working against the Veracity of the data. They decrease the ability to cleanse the data before analyzing it and making decisions.

The fifth V was introduced by Gamble and Goble (2011):

- **Value:** Indicates if the data is worthwhile and has value for business.

Data value vision includes creating social and economic added value based on the intelligent use, management and re-uses of data sources with a view to increase business intelligence (BI).

Several other V's have been mentioned in literature:

- **Visualization:** Visual representations and insights for decision making,
- **Variability:** The different meanings/contexts associated with a given piece of data,
- **Volatility:** How long the data is valid and how long should it be stored (at what point specific data is no longer relevant to the current analysis).

An actual question is whether some V's are really definitional and not only confusing. For example, veracity expresses a quality of any data; it is not a definitional property of Big Data. When we use the Gartner's definition "Big data is high-volume, -velocity and -variety information assets that demand cost-effective, innovative forms of information processing for enhanced insight and decision making", we simply see that the 3 V's are only 1/3 of the definition! The second part of the definition addresses the challenges we face to take the best of infrastructure and technology capabilities. Sometimes also other characteristics (not only V's) are assigned to Big Data, associated not only to logic complexity and transactions complexity. It seems that a common definition of Big Data is still unclear (Stuart & Barker, 2013).

Big Data Processing and Big Analytics

Big analytics is a genuine leap forward and a clear opportunity to realize enormous gains in efficiency, productivity, revenue, and profitability. It is process of analyzing large amounts and different types of data to uncover hidden patterns, correlations and other useful information. Big analytics could accomplish much more than what can be done with smaller datasets. For example, Big Analytics allows move beyond linear approximation models towards complex models of greater sophistication because small datasets often limit our ability to make accurate predictions and assessments. Additionally, Big Data significantly improves the ability to locate and analyze the impact of rare events that might escape detection in smaller data sets. Access to larger datasets, affordable high-performance hardware, and new powerful analytical tools provide means for better accuracy in predictions. As data is becoming more and more complex its analysis is also becoming increasingly complex. To exploit this new resource, we need to scale both infrastructures and standard data management techniques. Now the problem with data volume is it's speed (velocity) not only size. Big Data processing involves interactive processing and decision support processing of *data at rest*, and real-time processing of *data in motion*. The former can be warehoused in a relatively traditional way or stored and processed by inexpensive systems, e.g., NoSQL databases. The latter is usually performed by Data Stream Management Systems. Time is an integral dimension of data in a stream which influences it's processing, i.e., the analyst cannot reanalyze the data after it is streamed. A velocity also can be a problem, since the value of the analysis (and often of the data) decreases with time. If several passes are required, the data has to be put into a DW where additional analysis can be performed.

Big Analytics is about turning information into knowledge using a combination of existing and new approaches. Related technologies include:

- Data management (uncertainty, query processing under near real-time constraints, information extraction, explicitly managed time dimension),
- New programming models,
- Machine learning and statistical methods,
- Complex systems architectures, and
- Information visualization.

Big Data is often mentioned only in context with BI; however, not only BI developers but also e-scientists analyze large collections of data. A challenge for computer specialists or data scientists is to provide these people with tools that can efficiently perform complex analytics considering the special nature of Big Data. It is important to emphasize that Big Analytics does not involve only the analysis and modelling phase because noisy context, heterogeneity, and interpretation of results are also necessary to be taken into account. All these aspects influence scalable strategies and algorithms, therefore, more effective preprocessing steps (filtering and integration) and advanced parallel computing environments are needed.

Besides these rather classical themes of mining Big Data, other interesting issues have appeared in last years, e.g., entity resolution and subjectivity analysis. The latter includes sentiment analysis and opinion mining as topics using information retrieval and Web data analysis. A particular problem is finding sentiment-based contradictions at a large scale and to characterize them. Graph pattern matching is commonly used in social network analysis, where the graph can involve billions of users and hundreds billions links. In any case the main problems of current data mining techniques applied on Big Data are related to their inadequate scalability and parallelization.

MAIN FOCUS OF THE CHAPTER

First we describe two types of database architectures in this context: the traditional universal one and Hadoop-like implementing MapReduce framework. Then we present a short overview of NoSQL technology, particularly data models, architectures, and some representatives of NoSQL databases. We also focus on some issues connected with transaction processing with these tools. Then we discuss issues related to Big Data storage and processing with NoSQL and Hadoop, particularly with respect to Big Analytics. The next section presents recent architectures usable for Big Data: Big Data Management Systems, NewSQL databases, and NoSQL databases with ACID transactions. In the last two sections, we identify open problems associated with Big Data that represent a challenge for software engineering methods development and a research in the Big Data storage and processing area. Several conclusions finalize the chapter.

From the Universal DBMS Architecture to Hadoop

In Table 1 we show the well-known *universal DBMS architecture* (Härder, 2005) based on a mapping model consisting from five abstraction layers. In the most general version the architecture is encapsulated together with use of the SQL language in L5. Same model can be used in the case of distributed databases for every node of a network together with a *connection layer* responsible for communication, adaptation, or mediation services. Also, a typical shared nothing parallel relational DBMS can be described by this architecture. Layers L1-L4 are present usually at each machine in a cluster. A typical property of the universal architecture is that users can see only the outermost (SQL) layer.

In any case, associated database technologies both centralized and distributed were found not well suited for Web-scale data management of sources generating Big Data. Perhaps the most important problem is a hard scalability of traditional DBMSs in Web environment. A *vertical scaling* (called also *scale-up*), i.e. adding more CPU and more memory to each node or even new expensive big servers, was replaced by database partitioning across multiple cheap machines added dynamically to a network. In vertical scaling the data resides on a single node and scaling is done through the use of multi-cores, etc., i.e. spreading the load between the CPU and RAM resources of that single machine.

So-called *horizontal scaling* (also *scale-out*) can apparently ensure scalability in a more effective and cheaper way. Data is distributed horizontally in the network into groups of rows via consistent hashing or range partitioning based on ranges of a partition key in the case of tabular data. These groups stored into different segments may be located on different servers. A vertical data partitioning or combinations of both styles are being used as well. *Sharding* is just another name for horizontal partitioning. Horizontal data distribution enables to divide the computation into concurrently processed tasks. The advantage of this approach is the effective processing of range queries, because adjacent keys often reside in the same node.

To place multiple partitions on different machines is easier for NoSQL to implement because there is no enforcement of integrity except in the application. A sharding uses the shared nothing model, i.e., each server has its own data and processor. However, "database sharding" cannot provide high scalability at large scale due to the inherent complexity of the interface and ACID guarantees mechanisms. Multiple databases are unified even at application layer in this case. On the other hand, MPP (Massively Parallel Processing) can be used, i.e. a single DBMS with distributed storage.

Sharding scales well for both reads and write, but it has not to be transparent, i.e. application needs to be partition-aware. Thus, it is necessary to manage parallel access in the application.

A typical layered architecture of open source software Hadoop (The Apache Software Foundation, 2014a) often used in NoSQL environment has also a three-layer model but it looks a little differently.

Table 1. The five-layered DBMS mapping hierarchy

	Level of Abstraction	**Objects**	**Auxiliary Mapping Data**
L5	non-procedural access or algebraic access	tables, views, rows	logical schema description
L4	record-oriented, navigational approach	records, sets, hierarchies, networks	logical and physical schema description
L3	records and access path management	physical records, access paths	free space tables, DB-key translation tables
L2	propagation control	segments, pages	buffers, page tables
L1	file management	files, blocks	directories

The number of layers in the universal architecture is often reduced to the usual three-layer model.

The distributed file system considered here, i.e. *Hadoop Distributed File System* (HDFS) (Shvachko, Kuang, Radia, & Chansler, 2010), distinguishes from traditional network file systems (e.g., in UNIX). It uses file partitioning and replications. In additions to HDFS, Hadoop uses the highly scalable data-intensive MapReduce platform (Dean & Ghemawat, 2008). On the top of HDFS there is, e.g., the NoSQL database HBase (The Apache Software Foundation, 2014b). Complexity of tasks for data processing in such architectures is minimized using programming languages, like MapReduce. Obviously the approach is not easily realizable for arbitrary algorithm and arbitrary programming language. MapReduce, inspired by functional programming, enables to implement, e.g., multiplication of sparse matrices by a vector in a natural way. On the other hand, an effective implementation of the relational operation join in MapReduce requires special approach both in data distribution and indexing (Rajaman & Ullman, 2011). Also, the execution techniques used by MapReduce systems are suboptimal for analysis tasks such as iterative machine learning, and graph processing. Figure 1, based on the work of Borkar, Carey, & Li (2012), documents this architecture.

One remarkable difference of the Hadoop software stack from the universal DBMS architecture is that we can access data by three different sets of tools in particular layers. The middle layer Hadoop MapReduce system serves for batch analytics with Hadoop M/R jobs. HBase is available as a key-value layer (see the next section) with get/put operations as input. Finally, high-level languages HiveQL (Thusoo et al., 2009), PigLatin (Gates et al., 2009), and Jaql (Beyer et al., 2011) are for some users at disposal at the outermost layer. The SQL-like language HiveQL enables non-procedural data analytics (with constructs SELECT-FROM-GROUP-BY) without detailed programming. Jaql is a declarative scripting language for analyzing large semistructured datasets. The use of declarative languages reduces code size by orders of magnitude and enables distributed or parallel execution. PigLatin is not declarative; programs are series of assignments similar to an execution plan of a relational database.

NOSQL DATABASES

For storing and processing some Big Data datasets NoSQL databases are often used. NoSQL means "not only SQL" or "no SQL at all", that makes this category of databases very diverse. NoSQL solutions starting in development from late 90s provide simpler scalability and improved performance comparing to traditional relational databases, see, e.g., (Hecht & Jablonski, 2011; Pokorny, 2011; Moniruzzaman & Hossain, 2013; Gudivada, Rao, & Raghavan, 2014). We shortly elaborate their data models, identify abilities of transaction processing, and index techniques used in their implementations.

Figure 1. The three-layered Hadoop software stack

	Level of abstraction	Data processing		
L5	non-procedural access	HiveQL/PigLatin/Jaql		
L2-L4	record-oriented, navigational approach	Hadoop MapReduce Dataflow Layer	M/R jobs	
	records and access path management		Get/Put Ops	
	propagation control		HBase Key-Value Store	
L1	file management	Hadoop Distributed File System		

Data Models Used in NoSQL Databases

What is principal in classical approaches to databases – a (logical) data model – is in NoSQL databases described rather intuitively, without any formal fundamentals. The NoSQL terminology is also very diverse and a difference between conceptual and database view of data is mostly blurred.

The simplest NoSQL databases called *key-value stores* (or *big hash tables*) contain a set of couples (key, value). A key uniquely identifies a value (typically string, but also a pointer, where the value is stored). Even, a value can be a collection of couples (name, value), e.g., in Redis (Redis, 2014). This means that the data access operations, typically get and put, have only a key as the address argument. Though very efficient and scalable, the disadvantage of such too simple data model can be essential for such databases. On the other hand, NULL values are not necessary, since in all cases these databases are schema-less.

In a more complex case, NoSQL database stores combinations of couples (name, value) collected into collections, i.e. rows addressed by a key. Then we talk about *column NoSQL databases* whose column-oriented data structure accommodates multiple attributes per key. New columns can be added to these collections. There is even further level of structure, e.g., in CASSANDRA (The Apache Software Foundation, 2014c), called *super-columns*, where a column contains nested (sub)columns. Data access is improved by using column names in operations get, insert and delete.

The most general data models belong to *document-oriented NoSQL databases*. They are same as key-value stores but pair each key with an arbitrarily complex data structure reminding as a document. The JSON (JavaScript Object Notation) format is usually used for presentation of such data structures. JSON is a binary and typed data model which supports the data types list, map, date, Boolean as well as numbers of different precisions. JSON is similar to XML but it is smaller, faster and easier to parse than XML. CouchDB (The Apache Software Foundation, 2014d) is based on JSON. MongoDB (MongoDB, Inc., 2014) uses BSON (Binary JSON). Its types are a superset of JSON types. Querying document data is possible by other means than just a key (selection and projection over results are possible). Unlike simple key-value stores, both keys and values are fully searchable in document databases.

We can observe that all the data models are in principle key-valued. The three categories considered distinguish mainly in possibilities of aggregation of (key, value) couples and accessing the values. In general NoSQL databases can be classified in the categoires contained in Table 2.

Graph databases are considered as a special category of NoSQL databases. They offer graph-partitioning strategies for large data, graph query languages designed for particular types of graph data, and efficient evaluation of queries (graph traversals, sub-graph and super-graph queries, and graph similarity evalua-

Table 2. Basic categories of NoSQL databeses

Category	Representatives
Key-Value Stores	SimpleDB (Amazon Web Services, 2014a), Redis, Memcached (Dormando, 2014), Dynamo (Amazon Web Services, 2014b), Voldemort (GitHub, Inc., 2014)
Column-Oriented	BigTable (Chang et al., 2009), HBase, Hypertable (Hypertable Inc., 2014), CASSANDRA, PNUTS (Cooper, 2008)
Document-Oriented	MongoDB, CouchDB
Graph Databases	Neo4j (Neo Technology, Inc., 2014), InfoGrid (Netmesh Inc., 2014)

tion). Although the graphs have properties, these DBMSs are optimized for relationships, i.e. traversing and not for querying. Some of them are also usable for storage and processing of Big Graphs. Neo4j is an open-source, highly scalable, robust native graph database that stores data in a graph. InfoGrid is primarily focused on social network analysis.

A special attention needs to be focused on operational part of NoSQL databases. A typical NoSQL API enables only a reduced access given by CRUD operations – create, read, update, delete, e.g.

- **get(key):** extract the value given a key
- **put(key, value):** create or update the value given its key
- **delete(key):** remove the key and its associated value
- **execute(key, operation, parameters):** invoke an operation to the value (given its key) which is a special data structure (e.g., List, Set, Map, ..., etc.).
- **multi-get(key1, key2, .., keyN)**

Some NoSQL databases are *in-memory databases*, which mean that the data is stored in computer's memory to achieve faster access. The fastest NoSQL data stores such as Redis and Memcached entirely serve from memory. This trend is supported by hardware achievements in last years. Modern servers nowadays can possess large main memory capability that can size up to 1 Terabytes (TB) and more. As memory accesses are at least 100 times faster than disk, keeping data in main memory becomes an interesting design principle to increase the performance of data management systems. On the other hand, Redis and Memcached do not implement any partitioning strategy and leave it to the client to devise one.

NoSQL databases described in the list of well-maintained Web site (Edlich, 2014) include at least 150 products including so called soft NoSQL databases like object-oriented, XML, and others.

Querying NoSQL Databases

In many cases the NoSQL API offers access to low-level data manipulation and selections methods (CRUD operations). Queries capabilities are often limited so queries can be expresses in a simple way. The same holds for some restricted variants of SQL used in NoSQL databases. NoSQL database systems are often highly optimized for retrieval and appending operations and mostly offer little functionality beyond record storage (e.g., key–value stores). The simplicity of CRUD operations in API of NoSQL databases implies that a functionality requiring more complex structures and dealing with these structures must be implemented in the client application interacting with the database, particularly in a key-value store.

On the other hand, there are some exclusions in querying in document-oriented and column-oriented categories. MongoDB offers SQL-like query language; similarly Cassandra uses a high-level language CQL. In MongoDB, the db.collection.find() method retrieves documents from a collection. It is possible to specify equality conditions, IN operator, logical connectives AND, OR, matching array elements, and more complex combinations of these criteria. Find queries can be combined with some aggregation functions, like, e.g., count(). MongoDB does not support joins.

Some possibilities of querying are provided by MapReduce using map and reduce functions. For example, supposing a collection of documents, then the map is applied on each document to filter out irrelevant documents and to emit data for all documents of interest. Emitted data is sorted in groups to reduce for aggregation, or is the final result. This approach is procedural, i.e. it is a programming and not writing queries.

Transaction Processing

A special attention in NoSQL database community is devoted to data consistency. Transaction processing in traditional relational DBMS is based on ACID properties. We call consistency in such databases *strong consistency*. In practice, ACID properties are hard to achieve, moreover, they are not always required, particularly *C*. In context of NoSQL databases ACID properties are not implemented fully, databases can be only *eventually consistent* or *weakly consistent*.

In distributed architectures we consider the triple of requirements including consistency (*C*), availability (*A*) and partitioning tolerance (*P*), shortly CAP.

- *Consistency* means that whenever data is written, everyone who reads from the database will always see the latest version of the data. The notion is different from one used in ACID.
- *Availability* means that we can always expect that each operation terminates in an intended response. High availability is usually accomplished through large numbers of physical servers acting as a single database through data sharing between various database nodes and replications. Traditionally, the requirement to have a server/process available 99.999% of time. For a large-scale node system, there is a high probability that a node is either down or that there is a network partitioning.
- *Partition Tolerance* means that the database still can be read from and written to when parts of it are completely inaccessible, i.e. in the case of a network partition. That is write and read operations are redirected to available replicas when segments of the network become disconnected.

If we look on the CAP theorem formulated by Brewer (2000) and formally proved by Gilbert & Lynch (2002), then we see that for any system sharing the data it is impossible to guarantee simultaneously all of these three properties. Particularly, in Web applications based on horizontal scaling it is necessary to decide between *C* and *A*, i.e. two basic situations can occur:

1. Strong consistency is a core property and *A* is maximized. The advantage of strong consistency, which reminds ACID transactions, means to develop applications and to manage data services in more simple way. On the other hand, complex application logic has to be implemented, which detects and resolves inconsistency.
2. *A* is prioritized and *C* is maximized. Priority of *A* has rather economic justification. Unavailability of a service can imply financial losses. In an unreliable system, based on the CAP theorem, *A* cannot be guaranteed. For any *A* increasing it is necessary to relax *C*. Corporate cloud databases prefer *C* over *A* and *P*.

Table 3 shows how different NoSQL databases solve these problems. By design, most graph databases are ACID compliant.

Table 3. Consistency and Availability preferences

CP	Redis, BigTable, HBase, Hypertable, MongoDB
AP	Dynamo, Voldemort, CASSANDRA, Memcached, PNUTS, CouchDB, SimpleDB

A recent transactional model used in Web distributed replicated databases uses properties *BASE* (*Basically Available*, *Soft state*, *Eventually consistent*) (Pritchett, 2008). The availability in BASE corresponds to availability in CAP theorem. An application works basically all the time (basically available), does not have to be consistent all the time (soft state) but the storage system guarantees that if no new updates are made to the object eventually (after the inconsistency window closes) all accesses will return the last updated value. When no updates occur for a long period of time, eventually all updates will propagate through the system and all the nodes will be consistent. For a given accepted update and a given node, eventually either the update reaches the node or the node is removed from service. For example, SimpleDB acknowledges a client's write before the write has propagated to all replicas. It offers even a range of consistency options.

In principle, if we abandon strong consistency we can reach better availability, which will highly improve database scalability. It can be in accordance to database practice where ACID transactions are also required only in certain use cases, however, not all data need to be treated at the same level of consistency. For example if we consider automated teller machines, in their design, A has a priority to C, but of course with a certain risk. Also, MongoDB provides strong consistency and guarantees ACID operations at the document level, which tends to be sufficient for most applications. Similarly, in online social networking services a certain amount of data errors is tolerable.

If we analyze NoSQL databases, we identify more sophisticated approaches to consistency:

- Tunable consistency (e.g., in CASSANDRA),
- Configurable consistency (e.g., CP or AP in Oracle NoSQL database (Oracle, 2014a)).

A tunable consistency means that the application developer can influence its degree. For any given read or write operation, the client application decides how consistent the requested data should be. This enables to use CASSANDRA in applications with real time transaction processing.

By taking into account evaluations of the CAP theorem we can observe that a design of a distributed system requires a deeper approach dependent on the application and technical conditions. For Big Data computing with, e.g., of datacenter networking, failures in the network are minimized. Then we can reach both high C and P with a high probability. On the other hand, the practice has shown that discussed problems have not to be so critical. Brewer (2012) wrote that the CAP theorem has been widely misunderstood. CAP prohibits only a tiny part of the design space: perfect availability and consistency in the presence of partitions, which are rare. Bailis et al. (2013) introduce so called Highly Available Transactions (HAT), i.e. guarantees that do not suffer unavailability during system partitions or incur high network latency. They demonstrate that many weak replica consistency models from distributed systems are both HAT-compliant and simultaneously achievable with several ACID properties.

Basically NoSQL can be used for non-relational, distributed systems that do not attempt to provide ACID guarantees.

Indexing

NoSQL databases are generally based on the key-value store model which efficiently supports the single-key index and can respond to queries in milliseconds. To achieve this performance, different NoSQL databases utilize different indexing methods. For example, CouchDB has a B-tree index which is a bit different to the original. While it maintains all of the important properties, it adds Multi-Version Concurrency Control and an append-only design. B-trees are used to store the main database file as well as view indexes. One database is one B-tree, and one view index is one B-tree. MongoDB provides different types of indexes for different purposes and different types of content. *Single field indexes* only include data from a single field of the documents in a collection. They are applicable on fields at the top level of a document and on fields in sub-documents. A *compound index* includes more than one field of the documents in a collection. Also supported are *multikey indexes*, which support efficient queries against array fields. To improve efficiency, an index can be created as sparse and in this case the indexes will not include documents that do not have the indexed field.

However, numerous applications require multi-dimensional queries, which NoSQL databases do not support efficiently. Some solutions of NoSQL database that respond to multi-dimensional query are MapReduce and Table-Scan but they are inefficient and costly, especially when the selectivity of the query request is low. Multi-dimensional index technology has been extensively studied in traditional DBMSs. However, they cannot meet the increasingly requirements of scalability, high I/O throughput in the context of Big Data, therefore distributed *multi-dimensional index* for Big Data management on cloud platform management has been introduced. Indexes can be generally grouped into two categories according to the associated distributed storage architecture:

- Peer-to-Peer system: Several methods have been proposed in the literature including (Wu et al., 2009) who proposed a general index framework with global and local indexes. The local index is built on local data while the index framework selects nodes from local indexes by a respective cost model and organizes them together to form the global index. There is the RT-CAN proposal which employs R-trees for local indexes (Wang et al., 2010) and is based on CAN (Ratnasamy et al., 2001) protocol, while QT-Chord has a local index based on a quad tree (Ding et al., 2011).
- Master-slave style: EMINC is a two-layered index with R-Tree for a global index which is stored in master node, while slave nodes local data are indexed with K-d tree (Zhang et al., 2009). MD-HBase utilizes Z-order curve and K-d tree or Quad-Tree (Nishimura et al., 2011). EDMI in the global layer employs K-d tree to partition entire space into many subspaces and the local layer contains a group of Z-order prefix R-trees related to one subspace (Wang et al., 2010).

BIG DATA WITH NoSQL AND HADOOP

In this section we analyze pros and cons of tools discussed in the previous two sections and show possibilities of some current approaches. A lot of NoSQL databases are built on top of the Hadoop core, i.e. their performance depends on M/R jobs. It means these sections are not independent.

Usability of NoSQL Databases

Usability of NoSQL databases is closely related to unusual and often inappropriate phenomena of these tools:

- Have little or no use for data modelling, i.e., developers generally do not create a logical model,
- Database design is rather query driven,
- Data is unconstrained,
- Have only few facilities for ad-hoc query and analysis and even a simple query requires significant programming expertise.
- There is no standard query language,
- Some of them are more mature than others, but each of them is trying to solve similar problems,
- Migration from one such system to another is complicated.

Although belonging to one category, two NoSQL tools can be very different. For example, CouchDB uses a low-level query language, and scalability through replications. Mongo owns a rich, declarative query language, and its scalability is achieved through sharding.

There are two types of NoSQL databases: OLAP-like and OLTP- like. The former are useful for complex analytical processing on relatively large amount of data with read/throughput optimization. This includes applications which do not require transactional semantics, e.g., address books, blogs, serving pages on high-traffic websites, delivering streaming media or managing data as typically occurs in social networking applications. Content management systems also fall to this category. NoSQL are appropriate here also for indexing a large number of documents. The latter uses not only reads but also updates/writes and needs transaction support mostly on relatively small amount of data.

Key-value stores are ideally suited to lightning-fast, highly-scalable retrieval of the values needed for application tasks like managing user profiles or sessions or retrieving product names.

Column-oriented databases provide distributed data storage appropriate especially for versioned data because of their time-stamping functions. Then they are appropriate for large-scale, batch-oriented data processing including sorting, parsing, and data conversion. In context of Big Analytics, Column-oriented NoSQL databases can perform exploratory and predictive analytics, however, they are not suitable for the majority of DW/BI applications, or even for many traditional web-based applications.

Document databases are good for storing and managing Big Data-size collections of literal documents, like text documents, email messages, and XML documents. They are also good for storing sparse data in general, that is irregular (semistructured) data that would require an extensive use of NULL values in a relational DBMS.

Graph databases are very good for storing information about the relationships between objects in cases when relationship between two objects in the database is at least as important as the objects themselves.

NoSQL are inadvisable for applications requiring enterprise-level functionality (ACID, security, and other features of relational DBMS technology). In turn they provide a good platform for Big Analytics, e.g., for analyzing high-volume, real time data. For example, Web log analysis and Web-site click streams analysis belong to high parallelizable problems which can be addressed with NoSQL databases. There are a number of reasons to justify this possibility:

- Enforcing schemas and row-level locking as in relational DBMS unnecessarily over-complicate these applications,
- Mobile computing makes transactions at large scale technically infeasible,
- Absence of ACID properties allows significant acceleration and decentralization of NoSQL databases.

For example, HBase enables fast analytical queries, but on column level only. Also commonly used BI tools do not provide connectivity to NoSQL.

An interesting question is how important are NoSQL DBMSs in the database world. An answer can be found on the DB-Engines ranking server (solid IT, 2015) where, e.g., in April 2015, 259 systems are ranked. The top ten popular DBMSs include well-known relational systems like Oracle, MySQL, etc., but also three NoSQL MongoDB, Cassandra, and Redis on the 4th, 8th, and 10th place, respectively.

Big Data is often associated with a cloud computing. But cloud computing means only computing resources that are delivered as a service, typically over the Internet. A significant feature of cloud computing is the capability to deliver both software and hardware resources as services in a scalable way. NoSQL databases used in such environments are mostly sufficient for storage and processing of Big Data used there. However, as we consider more complex cloud architectures, NoSQL should not be the only option in the cloud. In consequence, it increases requirements on a general architecture of cloud computational environment, i.e. on ability to run on commodity heterogeneous servers, as most cloud environments are based on them.

Usability of Hadoop

MapReduce is still very simple technique compared to those used in the area of distributed databases. MapReduce is well suited for applications that analyze elements of a large dataset independently; however, applications whose data access patterns are more complex must be built using several invocations of the Map and Reduce steps. The performance of such design is dependent on the overall strategy as well as the nature and quality of the intermediate data representation and storage. For example, e-science applications involve complex computations, which pose new challenges to MapReduce systems. As scientific data is often skewed and the runtime complexity of the reducer task is typically high, the resulted data processing M/R jobs may be not too effective. MapReduce is also not appropriate for ad hoc analyses but rather for organized data processing.

There are many other reasons against MapReduce. For example, big velocity is one of many cases where MapReduce and Hadoop cannot fit to the "on-line" speed requirements. Often it is not possible to wait for a batch job on Hadoop to complete because the input data would change before we get any result from the processing process. The first-generation Big Analytics platforms like Hadoop lack an essential feature for Big Graph Analytics - iteration (or equivalently, recursion). Iteration is hardly achieved in NoSQL based on Hadoop MapReduce. The MapReduce programming model is not ideal for expressing many graph algorithms. Consequently, some modifications like HaLoop framework (Bu, Howe, Balazinska, & Ernstm, 2012) occur now which support iteration.

A more radical solution offers a flexible dataflow-based execution model that can express a wide range of data access and communication. An example is Pregel system (Malewicz et al., 2010) viewing its data as a graph and supporting large-scale iterative processing. Each node of the graph corresponds roughly to a task.

Problems with NoSQL concern their whole architecture. Stonebraker (2014) points out, that the Hadoop stack has a poor performance except where the application is "trivially parallel". Also, it has no indexing and it has very inefficient joins in Hadoop layer, additionally, it is "sending the data to the query" and not "sending the query to the data". Another example is Couchbase (Couchbase, 2014) which replicates the whole document if only its small part is changed.

Despite NoSQL are becoming dominant for Big Analytics they still have a lot disadvantages, e.g., a heavy computational model, low-level information about data processed, etc. There are exceptions, e.g., the Apache's library Mahout (The Apache Software Foundation, 2014e) which is implemented on top of Hadoop, brings very effective automated machine learning and data mining algorithms to find hidden trends and otherwise unthought-of or unconsidered ideas. In the Big Data world NoSQL databases dominate rather for operational capabilities, i.e. interactive workloads where data is primarily captured and stored. Analytical Big Data workloads, on the other hand, tend to be addressed by parallel database systems and MapReduce.

TOWARDS NEW ARCHITECTURES FOR BIG DATA PROCESSING

To address *Big Analytics* challenges, a new generation of scalable data management technologies has emerged in the last years. We describe so called Big Data Management Systems, NewSQL DBMSs, and NoSQL databases with transactions.

Big Data Management Systems

A *Big Data Management System* (BDMS) is a highly scalable platform which supports requirements of Big Data processing. A representative of BDMS is ASTERIX system (Vinayak, Borkar, Carey, & Li, 2012). It is fully parallel, able to store, access, index, query, analyze, and publish very large quantities of semistructured data. Its architecture shown in Figure 2 is similar to one presented in Figure 1, but with own Hyracks layer in the bottom to which manages parallel data computations, the Algebrics algebra layer in the middle, and the topmost ASTERIX system layer – a parallel information management system. ASTERIX QL (Behm et al., 2011) is composable language reminding of XQuery and using fuzzy joins appropriate for analytical purposes. The Asterix software stack includes also a Hadoop compatibility layer, Pregelix software for graph analytics, and other useful facilities.

Oracle Big Data Appliance (Oracle, 2014b) classified also among BDBSs. It includes two components:

Figure 2. The Asterix software stack

	Level of abstraction	Data processing				
L5	non-procedural access	Asterix QL				
L2-L4	algebraic approach	ATERIX DBMS	HiveQL, Piglet			
			Other HLL Compilers	M/R jobs	Pregel job	
		Algebrics Algebra Layer	Hadoop M/R compatability		Pregelix	Hyracks jobs
L1	file management	Hyracks Data-parallel Platform				

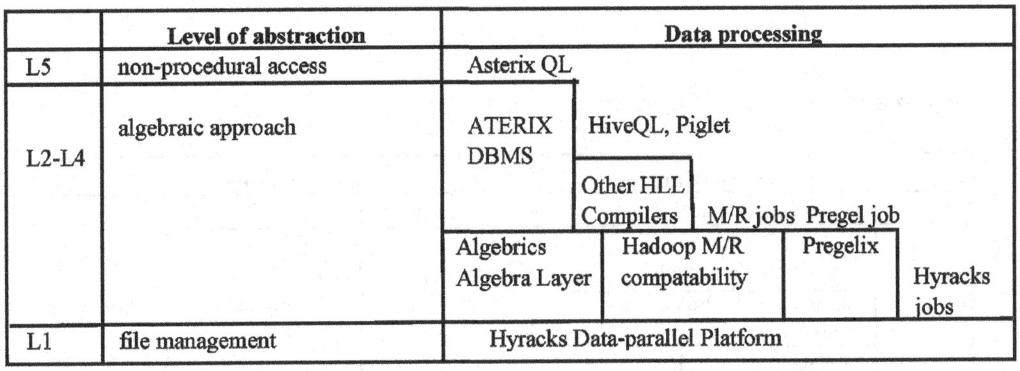

- Oracle Big Data SQL combining data from Oracle DB, Hadoop and NoSQL in a single SQL query; enables to query and analyze data in Hadoop and NoSQL,
- Oracle Big Data Connectors for simplifying data integration and analytics of data from Hadoop.

Its platform contains Oracle Exadata Database Machine and Oracle Exalytics Business Intelligence Machine.

The third representative of BDMS is Lily (NGDATA, 2014) integrating Apache Hadoop, HBase, Apache Solr (The Apache Software Foundation, 2014f) - enterprise search platform based on the popular full-text search engine Lucene), and machine learning (see Figure 3).

NewSQL Databases

A category of parallel DBMSs called *NewSQL databases* (451 Research, 2011) is characterized by the following properties:

- Are designed to scale out horizontally on shared nothing machines,
- Partitioning is transparent,
- Still provide ACID guarantees,
- Applications interact with the database primarily using SQL (with joins),
- Employ a lock-free concurrency control,
- Provide higher performance than available from the traditional systems.

NewSQL DBMSs can be categorized in the following way:

- General purpose pure relational DBMS: ClustrixDB (Clustrix, 2014), NuoDB (NuoDB, Inc., 2014), VoltDB (VoltDB, Inc., 2014),
- Google's hybrids: Spanner (Corbett et al., 2012) and F1 (Shute et al., 2012),
- Hadoop-relational hybrids: HadoopDB (HadoopDB Team - Yale University, 2009) – a parallel database with Hadoop connectors, Vertica[29],
- Supporting more data models: FoundationDB (Hewlett-Packard Development Company, L.P., 2014), OrientDB (Orient Technologies LTD, 2014), Postgres NoSQL (EnterpriseDB Corporation, 2014).

Figure 3. The three-layered Lily software stack

	Level of abstraction	Data processing		
L5	non-procedural access	M/R jobs	HiveQL	
L2-L4	record-oriented, navigational approach	Hadoop MapReduce	HBase Key-Value Store	Solr
	records and access path management			
	propagation control			
L1	file management	Hadoop Distributed File System		

Particularly NuoDB is appropriate for clouds. It is interesting that NuoDB stores its data into a key-value store. Spanner uses semirelations, i.e. each row has a name (i.e. always there is a primary key), versions, and hierarchies of tables. F1 is built on Spanner which provides synchronous cross-datacenter replication and strong consistency. Its authors characterize F1 as a fault-tolerant globally-distributed OLTP OLAP database. F1 includes a fully functional distributed SQL query engine. OrientDB has a document, key-value, and graph databases functionality. Postgres NoSQL owns native data types JSON and HSTORE in SQL. Remind that data type HSTORE enables to store key/value pairs within a single column.

Very different is also the approach of these DBMS to SQL. For example, VoltDB has a larger number of restrictions of SQL. It is not possible to use the HAVING clause, self-joins are not allowed, all joined tables must be partitioned over the same value. A special NewSQL tool is ScalArc iDB (ScaleArc, 2014) - a high performance SQL Accelerator appropriate for both for cloud and datacenters. Some NewSQL databases, e.g., MySQL Cluster and ClustrixDB use transparent sharding.

NewSQL provides performance and scalability not comparable with traditional DBMS and with Hadoop as well. For example, a comparison of Hadoop and Vertica shown that query times for Hadoop were a lot slower (1–2 orders of magnitude) (Pavlo et al., 2009).

A lot of success of some NewSQL solutions lies in new database architectures based on MPP (e.g., ClustrixDB and Vertica), but often even on massively parallel analytic databases. Technologies like columnar storage are often used there (e.g., Vertica). In memory data processing approach is used, e.g., in the MySQL-like database MemSQL (MemSQL Inc., 2014) and VoltDB. For example, MemSQL belongs to the fastest NewSQL tools in data loading and query execution times.

Most representatives of NewSQL are suitable for real-time analytics. But in general their performance is still a problem (Stantic & Pokorný, 2014). New alternatives for Big Analytics with NewSQL include:

- HadoopDB (combines parallel database with Map Reduce),
- MemSQL, VoltDB (automatic cross-partition joins),
- ClustrixDB (for transaction processing and real-time analytics).

There are attempts of shipping to No Hadoop DBMSs in which the MapReduce layer is eliminated. Details of their comparison with NewSQL databases can be found in the more recent paper (Grolinger, Higashino, Tiwari, & Capretz, 2013).

NoSQL Databases with ACID Transactions

The last new generation of NoSQL databases we mention are NoSQL databases with ACID transactions. Many NoSQL designers are therefore exploring a return to transactions with ACID properties as the preferred means of managing concurrency for a broad range of applications. Using tailored optimizations, designers are finding that implementation of ACID transactions need not sacrifice scalability, fault-tolerance, or performance.

These DBMSs

- Maintain distributed design, fault tolerance, easy scaling, and a simple, flexible base data model,
- Extend the base data models of NoSQL,
- Are CP systems with global transactions.

A good example of such DBMS is a key-value FoundationDB with scalability and fault tolerance (and an SQL layer). Oracle NoSQL Database provides ACID complaint transactions for full CRUD operations, with adjustable durability and consistency transactional guarantees. Spanner is also NoSQL which can be considered as NewSQL as well. MarkLogic (MarkLogic Corp., 2014) is a NoSQL document database with JSON storage, HDFS, and optimistic locking. The distributed graph database OrientDB guarantees also ACID properties.

FUTURE RESEARCH DIRECTIONS

Considering BI as Analytics 1.0 and methods used by online companies like Google, Yahoo, and Facebook as Analytics 2.0, the development comes on towards a new wave of complex Big Analytics - Analytics 3.0, which are able to predict future not just provide valuable information from data. Traditional data mining techniques, already widely applied in the layer (3) to extract frequent correlations of values from both structured and semistructured datasets in BI, are interesting solutions for Big Analytics, too, but they have to be extended and accommodated. Today's main challenges for research in Big Data and Big Analytics area include:

- Improving the quality and scalability of data mining methods. Indeed, the processes of query composition - especially in the absence of a schema - and the presentation and interpretation of the obtained answers may be non-trivial.
- Transforming the content into a structured format for later analysis as much data today is not natively in structured format.
- Improving performance of related applications and shipping to NoHadoop DBMSs, where MapReduce layer will be eliminated.

The second challenge means not only the integration step but also it concerns filtering and more effective representation of Big Data. For example, in a Big Data project working with digital sky surveys we can move with data transformations from TB data to dozens GB (Yaghob, Bednárek, Kruliš, & Zavoral, 2014).

The last but not least challenge concerns role of man in Big Analytics. So far the mining process is guided by the analyst or the data scientist, where depending on the application scenario he/she determines the portion of data where/from the useful patterns can be extracted. A better approach would be the automatic mining process and to extract approximate, synthetic information on both the structure and the contents of large datasets. This seems to be the biggest challenge in Big Data.

CONCLUSION

Efficient data storage and processing in a database style is only first assumption for Big Analytics. We have seen that NoSQL databases partially contribute to this goal. But their diversity and different properties contribute to key problems with application of them in practice:

- Choosing the right product, design of appropriate architecture for a given class of applications,
- Ensuring skilled developers of applications to be at disposal.

Edlich (2012) even suggests choosing a NoSQL database after answering about 70 questions in 6 categories, and building a prototype. Similarly, Grolinger, Higashino, Tiwari, & Capretz (2013) emphasize that although NoSQL and NewSQL data stores deliver powerful capabilities, the large number and immense diversity of available solutions make choosing the appropriate solution for the problem at hand especially difficult.

Despite of the fact that some companies offer reference models for Big Data, no common one is at disposal now. Such a model should contain layers for:

1. Data,
2. Integration,
3. Analytics, and
4. A layer for predictive and prescriptive analysis on the top.

In this chapter we discussed layers (1) and (3) and their strong mutual correlation. The problem increases for more complex architectures. Hadoop, NoSQL and massively parallel analytic databases are not mutually exclusive. Kelly (2014) believes the three approaches are complementary to each other and can and should co-exist in many enterprises. The evolution of information architectures to include Big Data will likely provide the foundation for a new generation of enterprise infrastructure (Manoj, 2013).

ACKNOWLEDGMENT

This chapter was supported by Czech Science Foundation (the grant No. P103/13/08195S).

REFERENCES

451 Research. (2011). *NoSQL, NewSQL and Beyond: The drivers and use cases for database alternatives.* Retrieved from http://451research.com/report-long?icid=1651

Amazon Web Services. (2014a). *Amazon SimpleDB.* Retrieved from http://aws.amazon.com/simpledb/

Amazon Web Services. (2014b). *Amazon DynamoDB.* Retrieved from http://aws.amazon.com/dynamodb/

Bailis, P., Davidson, A., Fekete, A., Ghodsi, A., Hellerstein, J. M., & Stoica, I. (2013). Highly Available Transactions: Virtues and Limitations (Extended Version). *PVLDB*, *7*(3), 181–192.

Behm, A., Borkar, V. R., Carey, R. M., Grover, J., Li, Ch., Onose, N., & Tsotras, V. J. et al. (2011). ASTERIX: Towards a Scalable, Semistructured Data Platform for Evolving-world Models. *Distributed and Parallel Databases*, *29*(3), 185–216. doi:10.1007/s10619-011-7082-y

Beyer, K., Ercegovac, V., Gemulla, R., Balmin, A., Eltabakh, M., Kanne, C.-Ch., & Shekita, E. J. et al. (2011). Jaql: A scripting language for large scale semistructured data analysis. *PVLDB, 4*(12), 1272–1283.

Borkar, V., Carey, M.-J., & Li, Ch. (2012). Inside "Big Data management": ogres, onions, or parfaits? *Proceedings of EDBT Conference*, Berlin, Germany (pp. 3-14).

Brewer, E. A. (2000). Towards robust distributed systems. *Paper presented at PODC 2000*, Portland, Oregon.

Brewer, E. A. (2012). CAP twelve years later: How the 'rules' have changed. *Computer, 45*(2), 22–29. doi:10.1109/MC.2012.37 PMID:24976642

Bu, Y., Howe, Y., Balazinska, M., & Ernstm, M. D. (2012). The HaLoop approach to large-scale iterative data analysis. *The VLDB Journal, 21*(2), 169–190. doi:10.1007/s00778-012-0269-7

Chang, F., Dean, J., Ghemavat, S., Hsieh, W.C., Wallach, D.A., Burrows, M.,… Gruber, R.E. (2008). Bigtable: A Distributed Storage System for Structured Data. *Journal ACM Transactions on Computer Systems*, 26(2).

Clustrix. (2014). *Clustrix*. Retrieved from http://www.clustrix.com/

Cooper, B.F., Ramakrishnan, R., Srivastava, U., Silberstein, A., Bohannon, Ph., Jacobsen, H.A.,… Zemeni, R. (2008). PNUTS: Yahoo!'s hosted data serving platform. *Journal PVLDB* 1(2), 1277-1288.

Corbett, J. C., Dean, J. C., Epstein, M., Fikes, A., Frost, Ch., & Furman, J. J., …Woodford, D. (2012). Spanner: Google's Globally-Distributed Database. *Proceedings of 10th USENIX Symposium on Operation Systems Design and Implementation (OSDI 2012)*, Hollywood.

Couchbase. (2014). *Couchbase*. Retrieved from http://www.couchbase.com/

Dean, D., & Ghemawat, S. (2008). MapReduce: Simplified Data Processing on Large Clusters. *Communications of the ACM, 51*(1), 107–113. doi:10.1145/1327452.1327492

Ding, L., Qiao, B., Wang, G., & Chen, C. (2011). An efficient quad-tree based index structure for cloud data management. In: Proceedings of WAIM 2011, LNCS, Vol. 6897, pp. 238–250.

Dormando (2014). *Memcached*. Retrieved from http://memcached.org/

Edlich, S. (2012). *Choose the "Right" Database and NewSQL: NoSQL Under Attack Retrieved.* from http://www.infoq.com/presentations/Choosing-NoSQL-NewSQL

Edlich, S. (2014). *NoSQL*. Retrieved from http://nosql-database.org/

Enterprise, D. B. Corporation (2014). NoSQL for the Enterprise. Retrieved from http://www.enterprisedb.com/nosql-for-enterprise

Foundation, D. B. (2014). *FoundationDB - Key-Value Store*. Retrieved from https://foundationdb.com/

Gamble, M., & Goble, C. (2011). Quality, Trust and Utility of Scientific Data on the Web: Toward a Joint model. *Proceedings of WebSci'11 Conference*, Koblenz, Germany. doi:10.1145/2527031.2527048

Gates, A., Natkovich, O., Chopra, S., Kamath,P., Narayanamurthy, S.M., Olston, Ch.,…Sristava, U. (2009). Building a high level dataflow system on top of MapReduce: The pig experience. *PVLDB, 2*(2), 1414–1425.

Gilbert, S., & Lynch, N. (2002). Brewer's conjecture and the feasibility consistent, available, partition-tolerant web services. *ACM SIGACT News, 33*(2), 51–59. doi:10.1145/564585.564601

GitHub, Inc. (2014). *Project Voldemort - a distributed database.* Retrieved from http://www.project-voldemort.com/voldemort/

Grolinger, K., Higashino, W.A., Tiwari, A., & Capretz, M.A.M. (2013). Data management in cloud environments: NoSQL and NewSQL data stores. *Journal of Cloud Computing: Advances, Systems and Applications, 2*(22).

Gudivada, V. N., Rao, D., & Raghavan, V. V. (2014). NoSQL Systems for Big Data Management. (SERVICES). *Proceedings of the 2014 IEEE World Congress on Services* (pp. 190–197). doi:10.1109/SERVICES.2014.42

Hadoop, D. B. Team - Yale University (2009). *HadoopDB - An Architectural Hybrid of MapReduce and DBMS Technologies for Analytical Workloads.* Retrieved from http://db.cs.yale.edu/hadoopdb/hadoopdb.html

Härder, T. (2005). DBMS Architecture – the Layer Model and its Evolution. *Datenbank-Spektrum, 13,* 45–57.

Hecht, R., & Jablonski, S. (2011). NoSQL evaluation: A use case oriented survey. *Proceedings 2011 Int Conf Cloud Serv Computing* (pp. 336–341). doi:10.1109/CSC.2011.6138544

Hewlett-Packard Development Company. L.P. (2014). *HP Vertica Analytics Platform.* Retrieved from http://www.vertica.com/

Hypertable Inc. (2014). *Hypertable.* Retrieved from http://hypertable.org/

Kelly, J. (2014). Big Data: Hadoop, Business Analytics and Beyond. *Wikibon.* Retrieved from http://wikibon.org/wiki/v/Big_Data:_Hadoop,_Business_Analytics_and_Beyond

Laney, D. (2001). 3D data management: Controlling data volume, velocity and variety. Meta Group, Gartner. Retrieved from http://blogs.gartner.com/doug-laney/files/2012/01/ad949-3D-Data-Management-Controlling-Data-Volume-Velocity-and-Variety.pdf

Malewicz, G., Austern, M. H., Bik, A. J. C., Dehnert, J. C., Horn, I., Leiser, N., & Czajkowski, G. (2010). Pregel: A System for Large-scale Graph Processing. *Proceedings of the /PODS,* Indianapolis, IN, USA.

Manoj, P. (2013). Emerging Database Models and Related Technologies. *International Journal of Advanced Research in Computer Science and Software Engineering, 3*(2), 264–269.

Manyika, J., Chui, M., Brown, B., Bughin, J., Dobbs, R., Roxburgh, Ch., & Byers, A. H. (2011). Big data: the next frontier for innovation, competition, and productivity. McKinsey Global Inst. Retrieved from http://www.mckinsey.com/insights/business_technology/big_data_the_next_frontier_for_innovation

MarkLogic Corp. (2014). *MarkLogic*. Retrieved from http://www.marklogic.com/

MemSQL Inc. (2014). *MemSQL*. Retrieved from http://www.memsql.com/

Mongo, D. B. Inc. (2014). *MongoDB*. Retrieved from https://www.mongodb.org/

Moniruzzaman, A. B. M., & Hossain, S. A. (2013). NoSQL Database: New Era of Databases for Big data Analytics - Classification, Characteristics and Comparison. *International Journal of Database Theory and Application*, 6(4), 1–14.

Neo Technology, Inc. (2014). *Neo4j*. Retrieved from http://www.neo4j.org/

Netmesh Inc. (2014). *InfoGrid – the Web Graph Database*. Retrieved from http://infogrid.org/trac/

NGDATA. (2014). *Lily*. Retrieved from http://www.lilyproject.org/lily/index.html

Nishimura, S., Das, S., Agrawal, D., & Abbadi, A. E. (2011). MD-HBase: A scalable multidimensional data infrastructure for location aware services. In: Proceedings of the 2011 IEEE 12th Int. Conf. on Mobile Data Management - Volume 01, IEEE Computer Society Washington, pp. 7–16.

Nuo, D. B. Inc. (2014). *NuoDB*. Retrieved from http://www.nuodb.com/

ODMS. org. (2013). Big Data Analytics at Thomson Reuters. Interview with Jochen L. Leidner. Retrieved from http://www.odbms.org/blog/2013/11/big-data-analytics-at-thomson-reuters-interview-with-jochen-l-leidner/

Oracle (2014a). *Oracle NoSQL Database*. Retrieved from http://www.oracle.com/technetwork/database/database-technologies/nosqldb/overview/index.html

Oracle (2014b). *Big Data Appliance X4-2*. Retrieved from http://www.oracle.com/technetwork/database/bigdata-appliance/overview/index.html

Orient Technologies, L. T. D. (2014). *OrientDB*. Retrieved from http://www.orientechnologies.com/orientdb/

Pavlo, A., Paulson, E., Rasin, A., Abadi, D., DeWitt, D. J., Madden, S., & Stonebraker, M. (2009). A Comparison of Approaches to Large-Scale Data Analysis. *Proceedings of SIGMOD/PODS'09*, Providence, RI, USA. doi:10.1145/1559845.1559865

Pokorny, J. (2011). NoSQL Databases: A step to database scalability in Web environment. *Int J Web Info Syst*, 9(1), 69–82. doi:10.1108/17440081311316398

Pritchett, D. (2008). BASE: An ACID alternative. *ACM Queue; Tomorrow's Computing Today*, 6(3), 48–55. doi:10.1145/1394127.1394128

Rajaman, A., & Ullman, J. D. (2011). *Mining of Massive Datasets*. Cambridge University Press. doi:10.1017/CBO9781139058452

Ratnasamy, S., Francis, P., Handley, M., Karp, R. M., & Shenker, S. (2001). A scalable content addressable network. In: *Proceedings of SIGCOMM*, ACM, pp. 161–172.

Redis. (2014) *Redis*. Retrieved from http://redis.io/

ScaleArc. (2014). *ScaleArc*. Retrieved from http://scalearc.com/

Shute, J., Vingralek, R., Samwel, B., Handy, B., Whipkey, Ch., Rollins, E.,… Apte, H. (2013). F1 A Distributed SQL Database That Scales. *PVLDB,* 6(11), 1068-1079.

Shvachko, K., Kuang, H., Radia, S., & Chansler, R. (2010). The Hadoop Distributed File System, *Proceedings of 2010 IEEE 26th Symposium on Mass Storage Systems and Technologies (MSST)*, Lake Tahoe, Nevada, USA doi:10.1109/MSST.2010.5496972

Snow, D. (2012). *Dwaine Snow's Thoughts on Databases and Data Management*. Retrieved from http://dsnowondb2.blogspot.cz/2012/07/adding-4th-v-to-big-data-veracity.html

solid IT (2014). *DB-engines*. Retrieved from http://db-engines.com/en/ranking

Stantic, B., & Pokorný, J. (2014). Opportunities in Big Data Management and Processing. *Frontiers in Artificial Intelligence and Applications*, 270, 15–26.

Stonebraker, M. (2014). *No Hadoop: The Future of the Hadoop/HDFS Stack*. Retrieved from http://istc-bigdata.org/index.php/no-hadoop-the-future-of-the-hadoophdfs-stack/

Stuart, J., & Barker, A. (2013). Undefined By Data: A Survey of Big Data Definitions. *CoRR*, abs/1309.5821. Retrieved from http://arxiv.org/pdf/1309.5821v1.pdf

The Apache Software Foundation. (2014a). *Hadoop*. Retrieved from http://hadoop.apache.org/

The Apache Software Foundation. (2014b). *Apache HBase*. Retrieved from https://hbase.apache.org/

The Apache Software Foundation. (2014c). *Cassandra*. Retrieved from http://cassandra.apache.org/

The Apache Software Foundation. (2014d). *Apache CouchDB™*. Retrieved from http://couchdb.apache.org/

The Apache Software Foundation. (2014e). *Mahout*. Retrieved from http://mahout.apache.org/

The Apache Software Foundation. (2014e). Mahout. Retrieved from http://mahout.apache.org/

The Apache Software Foundation. (2014f). *Apache Solr™ 4.10*. Retrieved from http://lucene.apache.org/solr/

Thusoo, A., Sarma, J. S., Jain, N., Shao, Z., Chakka, P., Anthony, S., & Murthy, R. et al. (2009). Hive - a warehousing solution over a map-reduce framework. *PVLDB*, 2(2), 1626–1629.

Vinayak, R., Borkar, V., Carey, M.-J., & Li, Ch. (2012). Big data platforms: What's next? *ACM Cross Road*, 19(1), 44–49. doi:10.1145/2331042.2331057

Volt, D. B. Inc. (2014). *VoltDB*. Retrieved from http://voltdb.com/

Wang, J., Wu, S., Gao, H., Li, J., & Ooi, B. C. (2010). Indexing multi-dimensional data in a cloud system. In: *Proceedings of SIGMOD*, ACM, pp. 591–602.

Wu, S. & Wu, K. (2009). An indexing framework for efficient retrieval on the cloud. IEEE Data Engineering Bulletin, 01/2009, 32:75-82.

Yaghob, J., Bednárek, D., Kruliš, M., & Zavoral, F. (2014). Column-oriented Data Store for Astrophysical Data. *Proceedings of 25th International Workshop on Database and Expert Systems Applications*, Munich, Germany.

Zhang, X., Ai, J., Wang, Z., Lu, J., & Meng, X. (2009). An efficient multi-dimensional index for cloud data management. In *Proceedings of CloudDB* (pp. 17–24). ACM.

KEY TERMS AND DEFINITIONS

Big Analytics: A set of methods, algorithms, and tools to analyze a mix of structured, semi-structured and unstructured data in search of valuable business information and insights.

Big Data: Any collection of data sets so large and complex that it becomes difficult to process them using traditional data processing applications.

Hadoop: An open source software project that enables the distributed processing of large data sets across clusters of commodity servers.

NoSQL Databases: Databases mostly addressing some of the points: being non-relational, distributed, open-source and horizontally scalable.

Scalability: The ability of a system, network, or process to handle a growing amount of work in a capable manner or its ability to be enlarged to accommodate that growth.

Transaction Processing: A style of computing that divides work into individual, indivisible operations, called transactions.

Universal DBMS Architecture: An architecture based on a mapping model consisting from five abstraction layers.

Chapter 2
A Cloud-Aware Distributed Object Storage System to Retrieve Large Data via HTML5-Enabled Web Browsers

Ahmet Artu Yıldırım
Utah State University, USA

Dan Watson
Utah State University, USA

ABSTRACT

Major Internet services are required to process a tremendous amount of data at real time. As we put these services under the magnifying glass, It's seen that distributed object storage systems play an important role at back-end in achieving this success. In this chapter, overall information of the current state-of-the-art storage systems are given which are used for reliable, high performance and scalable storage needs in data centers and cloud. Then, an experimental distributed object storage system (CADOS) is introduced for retrieving large data, such as hundreds of megabytes, efficiently through HTML5-enabled web browsers over big data – terabytes of data – in cloud infrastructure. The objective of the system is to minimize latency and propose a scalable storage system on the cloud using a thin RESTful web service and modern HTML5 capabilities.

INTRODUCTION

With the advent of the Internet, we have faced with a need to manage, store, transmit and process big data in an efficient fashion to create value for all concerned. There have been attempts to alleviate the problems emerged due to the characteristics of big data in high-performance storage systems that have existed for years such as: Distributed file systems: e.g., NFS (Pawlowski et al., 2000), Ceph (Weil et

DOI: 10.4018/978-1-4666-9834-5.ch002

al., 2006), XtreemFS (Hupfeld et al., 2008) and Google File System (Ghemawat et al., 2003); Grid file systems: GridFTP (Allcock et al., 2005) and recently object-oriented approach to the storage systems (Factor et al., 2005).

As an emerging computing paradigm, cloud computing refers to leasing of hardware resources as well as applications as services over the Internet in an on-demand fashion. Cloud computing offers relatively low operating costs that the cloud user no longer needs to provision hardwares according to the predicted peak load (Zhang et al., 2010) via on-demand resource provisioning that comes with pay-as-you-go business model. In realization of this elasticity, virtualization is of significant importantance where hypervisors run virtual machines (VMs) and share the hardware resources (e.g. CPU, storage, memory) between them on the host machine. This computing paradigm provides a secure, isolated environment that operational errors or malicious activity occurred in one VM do not affect directly the execution of another VM on the same host. Virtualization technology also enables the cloud providers to further cut the spendings through live migration of VMs to underutilized physical machines without downtime in a short time (Clark et al., 2005), thus, maximize resource utilization.

The notion of an object in the context of storage is a new paradigm introduced in (Gibson et al., 1997). An object is a smallest storage unit that contains data and attributes (user-level or system-level). Contrary to the block-oriented operations that perform on the block level, object storage provides the user higher-level of abstraction layer to create, delete and manipulate objects (Factor et al., 2005). Backends of most object storage systems maximize throughput by means of caching and distributing the load over multiple storage servers, and ensuring fault-tolerance by file replication on data nodes. Thus, they share similar characteristics with most high-performance data management systems, such as fault-tolerance and scalability.

Modern web browsers have started to come with contemporary APIs with the introduction of the fifth revision of the HTML standard (HTML5) to enable complex web applications that provide a richer user experience. However, despite a need on client-side, web applications still are not taking advantage of HTML5 to deal with big data. In regards to the server-side, object storage systems are complex to build and to manage its infrastructure.

We introduce an experimental distributed object storage system for retrieving relatively bigger data, such as hundreds of megabytes, efficiently through HTML5-enabled web browsers over big data – terabytes of data – using an existing online cloud object storage system, Amazon S3, to transcend some of the limitations of online storage systems for storing big data and to address further enhancements.

Existing systems exhibit the capability of managing high volumes of data, retrieving larger size resources from a single storage server might cause an inefficient I/O due to unparalleled data transfer at the client-side and underutilized network bandwidth. The main objective of the implemented system is to minimize latency via data striping techniques and propose a scalable object storage system on top of an existing cloud-based object storage system. For the client side, we implemented a Java Script library that spawns a set of web workers – which is introduced with HTML5 to create separate execution streams on web browsers – to retrieve the data chunks from the storage system in parallel. We aim to increase the data read rates on the web browser by utilizing full Internet bandwidth. Our approach is also capable of handling data loss by automatically backing up the data on a geographically distinct data center. The proposed distributed object storage system handles a common error gracefully, such as if a disaster takes place in the data center that might result in data inaccessibility, the implemented client detects this issue and then starts retrieving the data from the secondary data center. We discuss advantages and disadvantages of using the proposed model over existing paradigms in the chapter.

The remainder of this chapter is organized as follows. In Section 2, we discuss high performance storage systems; distributed file systems, grid file systems, object storage systems and common storage models to handle big data. Then in Section 3, we introduce cloud-aware distributed object system (CADOS) and present its architecture, CADOS library and performance measurements. Finally, we present our conclusions in Section 4.

HIGH PERFORMANCE STORAGE SYSTEMS

Distributed File Systems

Distributed file systems provide access to geographically distributed files over POSIX-compliant interface or API. The advantage of using distributed file systems comes from their fault-tolerance, high-performance, highly scalable data retrieval by following replication and load balancing techniques. Variety of distributed file systems have been used for decades and especially on data centers, high-performance computing centers and cloud computing facilities as backend storage providers.

Lustre file system (Wang et al., 2009) is an object-based file system that composed of three software components: Metadata servers (MDSs) to provide metadata of the file system such as directory structure, file names, access permissions; object storage servers (OSSs) that stores file data objects and functions as block devices; and clients that access the file system over POSIX-compliant file system interface, such as open(), read(), write() and stat().

Figure 1. Lustre file system

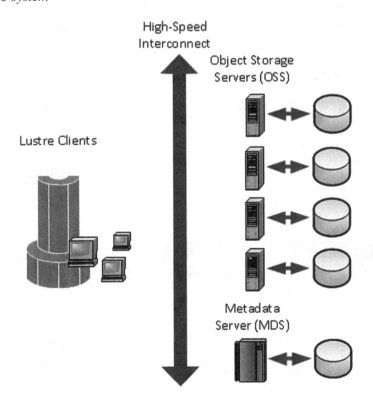

In Lustre, the high performance is achieved by the employing striping technique where the segments of the file are spread across multiple OSSs and then the client starts reading each data segment in parallel directly from OSSs. This goal of this approach is to minimize the disk load over the disks and to achieve high utilization of the bandwidth of underlying interconnect. The number of stripes for a file highly affects the performance of the data retrieval, but it also increases the possibility of data loss in case any object storage server is failed. The other important factor is that MSD might be considered a single point of failure where all the data becomes inaccessible over the object storage servers when MSD fails. To achieve high-availability of metadata, multiple OSS nodes can be configured as failover nodes to serve as metadata server. Moreover, OSS nodes can also function as a failover pair for high-availability of block devices.

Ceph (Weil et al., 2006) is a distributed file system that provides high performance, reliability, and scalability. Ceph is following the same paradigm like Lustre File System by separating data and metadata management. A special-purpose data distribution function called CRUSH is used to assign objects to heterogeneous and dynamic clusters of unreliable object storage devices (OSDs). In order to prevent overloading of the metadata cluster, Ceph utilizes a novel metadata cluster architecture based on Dynamic Subtree Partitioning (Roselli et al., 2000) that adaptively and intelligently distributes responsibility for managing the file system directory hierarchy among multiple of MDSs where the client sees the object storage cluster as a single logical object store and namespace. Ceph follows a stochastic approach by randomly distributing the data over OSDs. In data distribution and data location, Ceph uses a hash function to map the objects of the file into placement groups (PGs), in turn, placement groups are assigned to OSDs using CRUSH. Thus in data placement, it does not rely on any block or object list metadata. This approach is depicted in Figure 2.

With the advent of Apache Hadoop library (White, 2009), a distributed file system tailored for the map-reduce computations is of necessity for processing large data sets where Hadoop applications mostly need a write-once-read-many access model for files. To address this model, the Hadoop Distrib-

Figure 2. Ceph data distribution among multiple OSDs

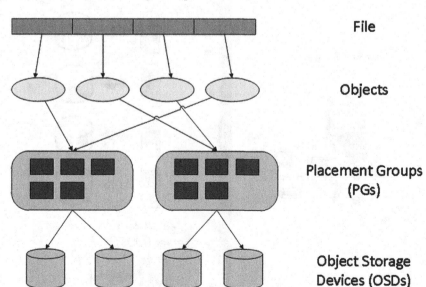

uted File System (HDFS) (Shvachko et al., 2010) locates the data near the application that operates on. This approach minimizes network congestion for extensive reading operations and increases the overall throughput of the system. An HDFS cluster consists of a single NameNode that manages the file system namespace and file accesses, and multiple DataNodes where data are spread across the DataNodes in a striping fashion. HDFS replicates file blocks to provide fault tolerance.

Other distributed file systems can be found in (Hupfeld et al., 2008), (GlusterFS, 2014), (MooseFS, 2014) and (Ghemawat et al., 2003).

Grid File Systems

Grid (Ferreira et al., 2003) is the federation of a number of heterogeneous, geographically disperse systems where shares various types of resources such as CPU, storage and software resources. Grid file systems create an illusion of a single file system by utilizing many storage systems where reliability, high-speed data access and a secure sharing mechanism are of the important factors in design.

GridFTP (Allcock et al., 2005) is the extension to the File Transfer Protocol (FTP) to be a general-purpose mechanism for secure, reliable, high-performance data movement. Thus, apart from the features supported by FTP, it provides a framework with additional capabilities such as multiple data channels for parallel data transfer, partial file transfer, failure detection, server side processing and striped data transfer for faster data retrieval over the grid. For secure file operations, GridFTP supports GSS-API, for Grid Security Infrastructure (GSI) and Kerberos authentication bindings.

The Gfarm Grid file system (Tatebe et al., 2010) is designed to share files across multiple geographically distributed storage centers. High I/O performance through parallelism, security, scalability across a large number of storages in wide area and reducing the cost of metadata management has taken into account in designing such a file system. Gfarm consists of gfmd (metadata server) for namespace, replica

Figure 3. Typical grid file system in Wide, storage with red color depicts metadata server; other storages are data servers

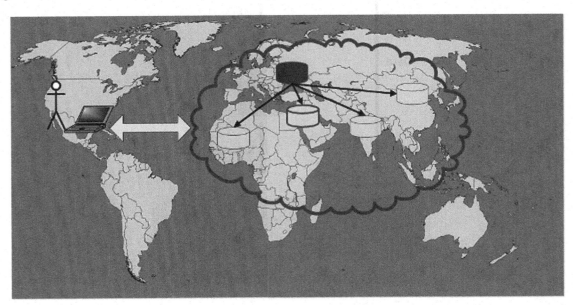

catalog, host information and process information and multiple of gfsd (I/O servers) for file access. In design, gfmd caches all metadata in memory for performance and monitoring concerns for all I/O servers. To prevent corrupted metadata in case of a client application crash, close() operations are carried out by the file system nodes.

Object Storage Systems

An object has higher-level of data abstraction than block data storage that consists of both data and attributes including user and system-defined attributes. As one of the distinctive properties of an object, metadata is stored and recoverable with the object's data and it provides secure data sharing mechanism, mostly on distributed and scalable storage systems (Factor et al., 2005).

Figure 4 shows the illustration of the object storage system. Manager nodes provide the metadata and key to client nodes that in turn use this key to access the object storage devices (OSDs) directly for secure data access. The main advantage of using an object storage system in performance when compared to block-based storage system clients can not suffer from queuing delays at the server (Mesnier et al., 2003).

Online cloud-based object storage systems are gaining popularity due to the need for handling elastic storage demands, ready-to-use and relatively easy APIs, durability and initiating business with minimum start-up costs. Although it is not a standard practice, we see most of online object storage systems le-

Figure 4. Object storage system

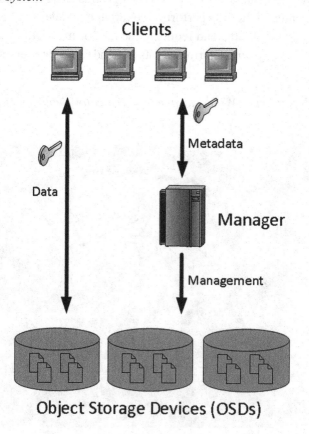

verage the use of Restful (Pautasso et al., 2008) web APIs because of its lightweight infrastructure and widespread adoption of programming languages and APIs. Although at the backend of the cloud-based storage systems might utilize high-performance distributed object storage systems, the major advantage of the cloud storages come from the elastic usage of object storage from the customer perspective. Thus, cloud-based object storage systems give the illusion of infinite storage capacity where the cloud users have the opportunity to adjust their allotted storage capacity as the demand varies.

Amazon Simple Storage Service (S3) (AmazonS3, 2014) enables the user to store objects in a container, named bucket, which has a unique name to access later using HTTP URLs via Amazon API and physically mapped to a geographic region. The service complies with the pay-as-you-go charging model of utility computing. Today, many companies start their business over cloud-based object storage systems with minimum investment for storage needs, including a popular personal cloud storage service, Dropbox, which is known to use Amazon S3 to store users' personal data (Drago et al., 2012). That creates a different charging model for companies where online object storage systems charge a company per HTTP request to store, access, delete and manipulate data over the cloud and per GB per month. However, its integration with science applications is criticized and recommendations are given to reduce the usage costs (Palankar et al., 2008). Other cloud-based storage systems can be found in (GoogleCloudStorage, 2014), (Pepple, 2011), (Wilder, 2012), (OracleNimbula, 2014) and (Nurmi et al., 2009).

RADOS (Weil et al., 2007) aims a scalable and reliable object storage service, built as part of the Ceph (Weil et al., 2006) distributed file system. In design, each object corresponds to a file to be stored on an Object Storage Device (OSD). I/O operations are managed by Ceph OSD Daemons such as reading/writing of an object including globally unique object id, metadata with name/value pairs and binary data. To eliminate the single point of failure and performance purposes, clients interact with Ceph OSD Daemons directly to retrieve metadata using CRUSH algorithm. CRUSH provides location information of an object without need of central lookup table (Weil et al., 2006). Ceph OSD Daemons replicates the objects on other Ceph nodes for data safety and high availability.

Storage Systems for Big Data

Internet age comes with the vast amount of data that requires efficient storage and processing capabilities. To alleviate this issue, we discuss data storage systems which are tailored to store and process big data effectively. While general-purpose RDBMSs are still a viable option in handling and analyzing structural data, they suffer from a variety of problems, including performance and scalability issues when it comes to big data. To increase the performance of DBMS for big data storage needs, partitioning the data across several sites and paying big license fees for enterprise SQL DBMS might be the two possible options (Stonebraker, 2010), however they are not even without disadvantages such as inflexible data management, high system complexity, high operational and management costs and limited scalability.

NoSQL Databases

The complexity of analyzing data via SQL queries has severe performance degradations in cloud computing, especially demand on multi-table association query (Han et al., 2011). Thus, NoSQL databases (e.g. (Anderson et al., 2010), (Chodorow, 2013) and (ApacheHBase, 2014)) change the data access

Figure 5. Cloud-based online object storage system

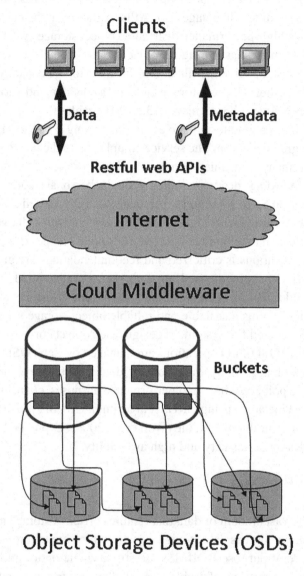

model with Key-value format where a value corresponds to a Key. That design leads to simpler model that enables faster query speed than relational databases, mass storage support, high concurrency and high scalability (Jing et al., 2011). The key features of NoSQL database are listed by (Cattell, 2011):

1. Capability to scale horizontally by adding database nodes when necessary, because of its "shared nothing" nature
2. Support for data replication and distribution over many database nodes
3. Easier API and protocol to store, delete and manipulate data when compared to SQL bindings
4. To provide high performance in reading and writing data, weaker concurrency model than the ACID transactions of RDBMSs

5.   Efficient usage of distributed indexing and memory for data storage
6.   The ability to add user attributes dynamically; associated with data records

Column-Oriented Databases

Most row-oriented relational databases are not optimized for reading large amount of data and in performing operations such as aggregate operations (e.g. *max, min, sum, average*) that are widely used in generating reports. These operations might potentially result in performance problems on row-based databases in the big data analysis because of irrelevant data load that leads to high disk seek time and ineffective cache locality. Contrary to row-based approach, column-oriented databases store the records in a column fashion where each column value is located on the disk contiguously, as illustrated in Figure 6. Thus, column-based databases perform better in locating the group of columns with minimum seek time, as stated in (Stonebraker et al., 2005), (Idreos et al., 2012), (Harizopoulos et al., 2006) and (Chang et al., 2008). Furthermore, because the same type of data are stored together, high data compression can be achieved using variety of compression schemes (D. Abadi et al., 2006).

C-Store (Stonebraker et al., 2005) physically stores a collection of columns sorted on some attribute(s). It is referred as "projections" if the groups of columns are sorted on the same attribute. Thus, when multiple attributes are used, redundant copies of the columns may exist on multiple projections that might lead to the data explosion in space. However, this problem can be alleviated to some degree with proper using of strong compression techniques. C-Store aims to provide read-optimized database system toward ad-hoc querying of large amounts of data, contrary to most relational DBMSs that are write-optimized. In design, C-Store follows a hybrid paradigm by combining a read-optimized column store (RS) and an update/insert-oriented writeable store (WS), connected by a tuple mover that performs batch movement of records from WS to RS. Thus, queries access data in both storage systems.

Bigtable (Chang et al., 2008) is a distributed column-based database where the data key is generated using three parameters which are strings of row and column, and timestamp of the input. Then Bigtable returns the corresponding data where it behaves similar to a distributed hash table. Bigtable maintains the data in lexicographic order by row string and the data is partitioned according to the row

Figure 6. Record locality illustration for row-based database (left), and column-based database (right)

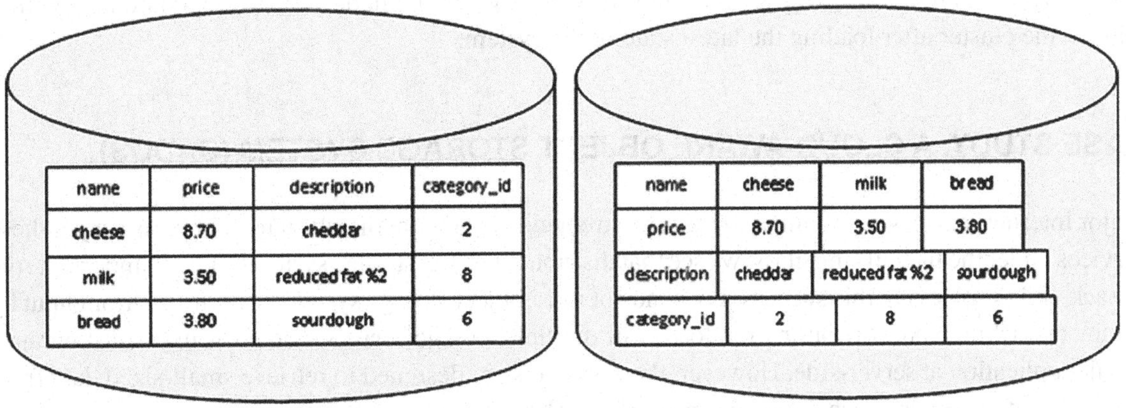

range, called a tablet. By incorporating the timestamp value, Bigtable gains the ability to store multiple versions of the same data. For faster retrieval of the tablets, Bigtable takes advantage of a three-level hierarchy analogous to B+-tree.

However, disadvantages of column-oriented databases are listed below(D. J. Abadi, 2007):

- This model might not be convenient if multiple columns are read in parallel that might lead to increased disk seek time.
- At each record insertion, multiple distinct locations on disk have to be updated; this might lead to increased cost of I/O operation.
- CPU cost can be significant in the reconstruction of a tuple by grouping values from multiple columns into a row-store style tuple.

NewSQL Databases

In on-line transaction processing (OLTP), we mostly face with repetitive and short-lived transaction execution whose performance depends on the I/O performance (Kallman et al., 2008). In recent years, researchers have begun to seek efficient ways to outperform legacy database systems. As the RAM capacities increase, the technique of storing partitions of data on the RAM of shared-nothing machines is more applicable than ever. NewSQL databases are designed by taking advantage of some modern techniques such as data sharding, data replication and distributed memory database and offer scalable and high performance solution to disk-based legacy database systems. NewSQL databases provide an object oriented database language that is considered easier to learn than the standard SQL language (Kumar et al., 2014).

H-Store (Kallman et al., 2008) divides database into partitions where each partition is replicated and resides in main memory. The H-Store system relies on distributed machines that share no data to improve the overall performance of database operations.

VoltDB (Stonebraker et al., 2013) demonstrates a main-memory based DBMS that horizontally partition tables into shards and stores the shards in the cluster of nodes. The database is optimized based on the frequency of transaction types. As the paper states, vast majority of transactions can be efficiently performed using a single shard on a single node independent of other nodes and shards such as retrieval of a phone number of a particular person. VoltDB achieves high availability via replication. A VoltDB cluster can continue to run until K nodes fail. However, when the node becomes operational again, it joins to the cluster after loading the latest state of the system.

CASE STUDY: A CLOUD-AWARE OBJECT STORAGE SYSTEM (CADOS)

Major Internet services are required to process a tremendous amount of data at real time. As we put these services under the magnifying glass, we see that distributed object storage systems play an important role at back-end in achieving this success. Backends of most object storage systems maximize throughput by means of caching and distributing the load over multiple storage servers, and ensuring fault-tolerance by file replication at server-side. However, these systems are designed to retrieve small-sized data from large-scale data centers, such as photos on Facebook (Beaver et al., 2010) and query suggestions in Twitter (Mishne et al., 2012), designed specifically to meet the high demand of Internet services.

We introduce an experimental distributed object storage system for retrieving relatively bigger data, such as hundreds of megabytes, efficiently through HTML5-enabled web browsers over big data – terabytes of data – in cloud infrastructure. The objective of the system is to minimize latency and propose a scalable object storage system. While the existing systems exhibit the capability of managing high volumes of data, retrieving a resource with higher sizes from a single storage server might cause an inefficient I/O due to unparalleled data transfer over web browsers that load data from one host only. Our approach is designed to alleviate this problem via the use of parallel data retrieval at client side unlike the existing paradigm. Data are stored over the implemented distributed object storage system in a striped way in cloud storage servers where common errors are handled gracefully.

With the advent of the fifth revision of the HTML standard, modern web browsers have started to come with contemporary APIs to enable complex web applications that provide a richer user experience. Our approach takes advantage of modern HTML 5 APIs in order to retrieve large resource by transferring its data chunks from multiple storage servers in parallel by circumventing same-origin policy of the web, and then merging data chunks efficiently at client-side. By this way, the proposed approach might offload data preparation phase out of storage servers and provide an efficient resource retrieval way by approaching a web application to the modern distributed client using scalable web services and backend system.

The implemented cloud-aware distributed object storage system (CADOS) leverages online cloud storage system, Amazon S3; but transcends data size limitations and retrieves data in parallel via HTML5-enabled web browser. Although the storage system is using Amazon S3 for storing data, it's not bound to the specific cloud environment in design. The benefits of the implemented storage system are listed below:

1. Data striping is a technique that advocates data partitioning across multiple storage nodes and then clients can retrieve stripes in parallel directly communicating with storage nodes. We used this technique to go beyond the file size limitation of the underlying cloud storage and gain high performance.
2. Disaster recovery is a phenomenon that in case of a disaster on the data center such as earthquake or nuclear disaster. If data become inaccessible for some reason, the software system starts serving backup data to avoid interruption of system and data loss. CADOS automatically backups the objects on a data center which is geographically distant from the source.
3. Although the storage system can be used by various types of clients, we designed a system, particularly for modern web applications that take advantage of HTML5 features and desire to be capable to perform big data operations including data analysis, retrieval and uploading over the web browser.

Design Overview

CADOS consists of two software components; a Restful web service (CADOS server) that provides URLs of data segments in JSON format, object metadata and, upon an upload request, dynamic data portioning; and a Java Script library (CADOS client) running on the web browser to upload the selected file, to retrieve the data segments in parallel and to merge the segments onto a file over RAM.

Figure 7 illustrates a typical data retrieval process from a web browser using high performance data storage system. (1) Web browser firstly requests the web page from a web server and then web server returns the HTML content (2). To speed-up the loading speed of web pages, set of files such as images

Figure 7. Typical high performance data retrieval on Internet

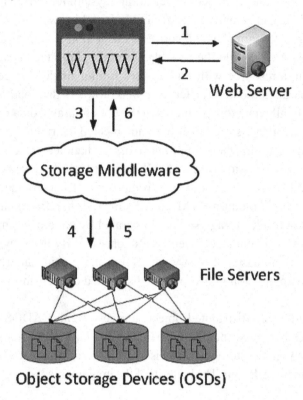

are hosted on file servers that prevents the overloading of the web server. In the 3rd step, web application starts requesting the files using URL addresses of the files from storage middleware. The storage architecture might be simply set up with one file server, but might also take advantage of parallel file system for low latency. Finally, storage middleware efficiently returns data to the web browser. Additionally, to further reduce disk operations, data caching can be employed between storage middleware and web browser that given file id as a key, cached data is located via distributed hash table (Beaver et al., 2010).

While this approach performs well, because of same-origin policy that restricts a file or scripts to be loaded from different origins, for example when the web application tries to load the resource whose URL differs from the web site URL (e.g. port, protocol or host). To work around this policy, we enabled the cross-origin resource sharing (CORS) in Amazon S3 that allowed us to load file stripes from different domains.

Figure 8 illustrates the CADOS design. In the loading event of the web page, CADOS JavaScript library spawns a number of web workers; a set of slave web workers that perform data retrieval, and a master web worker that orchestrates slave web workers. A web worker is a new feature coming with HTML5 standard. Analogous to threads in operating systems, this feature allows a user to create concurrent execution streams by running a JavaScript code in the background. After the web browser retrieves the content of the web page (1), instead of connecting directly to the storage system, it connects to the CADOS server (3) where master web worker fetches the URL list of file segments (4), and then fairly

Figure 8. CADOS design

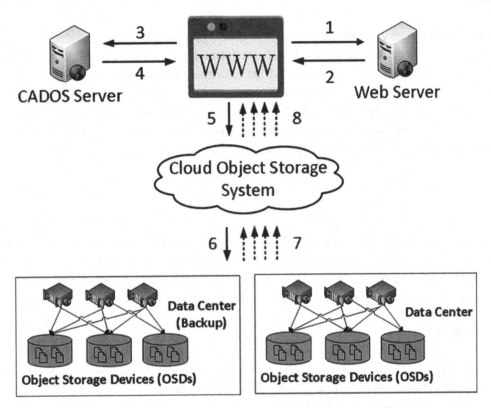

distributes the URLs among slave web workers. This list contains the temporary URLs of the file stripes located in the cloud object storage system. Then, each slave web workers starts retrieving file segments asynchronously from the source data center. If the URL is inaccessible, slave web worker connects to CADOS server to obtain the secondary URL of the file segment and then starts again to fetch the data segment from a backup data center which is physically distant from the source data center for disaster recovery. As the retrieval of the file segment finishes, slave workers send message to the master web worker, and then the master web worker stores the pointer of the data segment and merges them into a blob. To avoid copying operation between the master web worker and slave web workers, web workers pass the pointer of the data, not the data itself.

File upload operations are performed over CADOS server as well. Thus, this approach is potentially a bottleneck for multiple clients. To alleviate this problem, we used asynchronous data uploading techniques on the server where the upload operation is assigned to one of the threads in the thread pool of the web server. To achieve scalability, multiple upload servers can be utilized, or the upload operations can be offloaded to cloud storage servers that is performed via HTTP post method using uniquely generated signed URL, like the approach applied in data retrieval. Because high-performance and scalability in upload operations are not focused in this study, we will study further enhancements of data uploading in future research.

Data Indexing

Object storage systems are complex systems that require high-speed data management system to handle the vast amount of object attributes. In CADOS, we take advantage of PostgreSQL (Stonebraker and Rowe, 1986) database to store the object and stripe information. *Namespace* technique is widely used to prevent the name conflict of objects with the same name. Each object in CADOS is accessed via well-defined namespace paths. The object path column is represented via a ltree structure (ltree, 2015) in order to support hierarchical tree-like structure in an efficient way. This structure allows us to use regular-expression-like patterns in accessing the object attributes.

Security

One of the distinctive propertes of the object storage systems is the security that enables the system to share resources over the Internet. CADOS is applying 'Signed URL' approach using the Amazon S3 feature that the object has a fixed expiration time to be retrieved from the cloud object storage system. Once the object URL is generated for temporary use, it's guaranteed to be never generated again. The benefit of using this technique that the URL can be shared between many clients.

CADOS Client

CADOS library is a JavaScript library that separate execution streams (web workers) retrieve file segments in parallel through HTML5 capabilities. The working of the web workers is illustrated in Figure 9. The master web worker communicates with CADOS server using AJAX, which is an asynchronous technique to send data to or receive from a server (Garrett, 2005), and obtains the list of URLs to file segments that reside on the cloud object storage (1). All the communication between the master web worker and slave web workers are made in a message-passing fashion. At (2), master web worker distributes the URL list of the data segments across the slave web workers that are created in the loading event on the web page. *onmessage* is an event handler that is called when the message is posted to the corresponding web worker. In *onmessage* handler of the slave web workers, unique IDs of URLs are posted to the slave web worker, then each slave web worker starts retrieving data segments from the cloud object storage, again, by means of AJAX communication technique (3). As the slave web worker finishes the retrieval of the data segment, it posts the data pointer and corresponding index to the master web worker (4). Index of the data segment is used to locate the data segment on the main cache created by the master web worker. Because the data is passed to the master web worker using pointers, there is no data copy overhead. Once all the slave workers finish data retrieval operations, the master web worker writes out the cache to the hard disk (5). The downside of this technique the total amount of retrieved data is limited by the RAM capacity of a user's machine, although we anticipate this feature to be introduced in the future as a part of the HTML standard with the introduction of the File API: Writer draft (W3C, 2015). To work around this issue, another solution, which is a specific API to Google Chrome browsers, is chrome.fileSystem API (GoogleChrome, 2015).

Figure 9. Demonstration of web worker pool in CADOS client

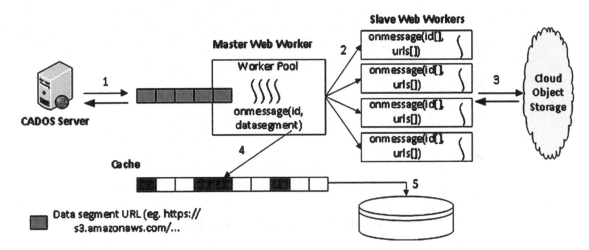

Data Loading Benchmarks

We conducted experiments to measure the read rates (MB/s) on a single machine with respect to varying number of slave workers and stripe size. We purposely used wireless router that provides speeds of up to 60 Mbps that is common in today's home and business networks. The datasets used in the experiments were synthetically generated and the stripes of which were uploaded into Amazon S3 storage by CADOS upon file upload request of the web browser.

We see that the stripe size highly affects throughput, thus this parameter needs to be calibrated based on the target computing environment and network bandwidth. However, note that, there is also trade-off that as the stripe size decreases, the number of HTTP requests per object increases that might lead to higher cost using a public cloud, which is true for Amazon S3 as of writing this chapter. Figure 10 (left) shows the read rate performance where stripe size is 5 MB. Throughput is limited by the network bandwidth of the client (web browser). It shows that we obtain 41% performance gain at most when 2 slave web workers are utilized with respect to serial data retrieval. However, the performance reached saturation after 2 slave web workers with slightly less performance gain. Then we increased the stripe size to 20 MB that the result is shown in Figure 10 (right). The results show that we obtained the maximum throughput when we utilize 3 slave web workers with 3.38 MB/s read rate. On the other hand, we obtained worse data read rates as we go further in stripe size over 20 MB.

CONCLUSION

In this chapter, we overview the software storage systems, particularly to handle big data via distributed file system, grid file systems, object storage systems and relatively new storage paradigms such as No-

Figure 10. Data read rate (MB/s), stripe size is 5 MB

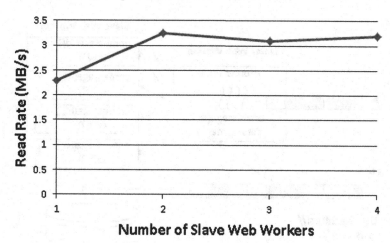

Figure 11. Data read rate (MB/s), stripe size is 20 MB

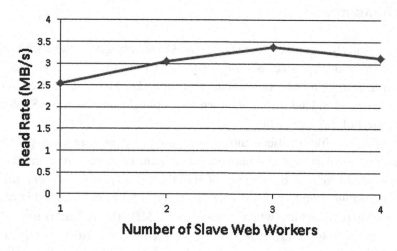

SQL, NewSQL and column-oriented databases. The objective of the storage systems is to deliver the data with low latency and secure by following data sharding techniques such as data striping, which promises data reliability, availability and system scalability.

With the advent of the Internet, realization of the high-available and high-performance storage systems is of necessity to meet the clients' demands, for example, high demands of user images in Facebook, a tremendous amount of tweets per second in Twitter or even in a private cloud for enterprise needs. Object storage systems differ from the block-based storage systems with the capabilities to provide secure data sharing between clients, and ability in dynamically adding user and system type attributes. While an objects might be mapped to a file on a file system, this is considered a paradigm shift in storage design and a higher-level of view over block-based storages.

Cloud computing promises elastic resource provision in all three layers of a cloud: Infrastructure-as-a-Service (IaaS), Platform-as-a-Service (PaaS) and Software-as-a-Service (SaaS). Cloud-based object storage systems with their own security model, handling of elastic storage demands, ready-to-use and relatively easy APIs, and data durability gains attention on public and private cloud users. We introduce a cloud-aware object storage system (CADOS) that leverages an existing on-line object storage system, but further delivers faster data retrieval for HTML5-enabled web applications by loading data segments in parallel via web workers; works around the object size limitation of the underlying cloud storage system; and recovers data automatically from the backup data center in case of disaster. Read rate experiments show that we obtain nearly 40% higher read rates on one machine, that the segments of the file are retrieved in parallel, and merged on the client side over the web browser. In future research, we will study to enhance the scalability in writing the file segments to the cloud object storage system. Moreover, because the replicates of the file segments are stored in a geographically distinct data center, the system will direct the user to the nearest data center for faster data retrieval. We believe that the implemented system conveys important I/O design ideas to further achieve high-throughput on data retrieval/upload for modern web applications.

REFERENCES

Abadi, D., Madden, S., & Ferreira, M. (2006). Integrating compression and execution in column-oriented database systems. *Paper presented at the Proceedings of the 2006 ACM SIGMOD international conference on Management of data*, Chicago, IL, USA. doi:10.1145/1142473.1142548

Abadi, D. J. (2007). *Column Stores for Wide and Sparse Data.* Paper presented at the CIDR.

Allcock, W., Bresnahan, J., Kettimuthu, R., Link, M., Dumitrescu, C., Raicu, I., & Foster, I. (2005). The Globus Striped GridFTP Framework and Server *Proceedings of the 2005 ACM/IEEE Conference on Supercomputing* (p. 54). Washington, DC, USA: IEEE Computer Society. doi:10.1109/SC.2005.72

AmazonS3. (2014). Retrieved from http://aws.amazon.com/documentation/s3/

Anderson, J. C., Lehnardt, J., & Slater, N. (2010). *CouchDB: the definitive guide.* O'Reilly Media, Inc.

ApacheHBase. (2014). http://hbase.apache.org/

Beaver, D., Kumar, S., Li, H. C., Sobel, J., & Vajgel, P. (2010). Finding a Needle in Haystack: Facebook's Photo Storage *Proceedings of the 9th USENIX Conference on Operating Systems Design and Implementation* (pp. 1-8). Vancouver, BC, Canada: USENIX Association.

Cattell, R. (2011). Scalable SQL and NoSQL data stores. *SIGMOD Record, 39*(4), 12–27. doi:10.1145/1978915.1978919

Chang, F., Dean, J., Ghemawat, S., Hsieh, W. C., Wallach, D. A., Burrows, M., & Gruber, R. E. et al. (2008). Bigtable: A Distributed Storage System for Structured Data. *ACM Transactions on Computer Systems, 26*(2), 1–26. doi:10.1145/1365815.1365816

Chodorow, K. (2013). *MongoDB: the definitive guide.* O'Reilly Media, Inc.

Clark, C., Fraser, K., Hand, S., Hansen, J. G., Jul, E., Limpach, C., . . . Warfield, A. (2005). Live Migration of Virtual Machines *Proceedings of the 2Nd Conference on Symposium on Networked Systems Design & Implementation* (Vol. 2, pp. 273-286). Berkeley, CA, USA: USENIX Association.

Drago, I., Mellia, M., Munafo, M. M., Sperotto, A., Sadre, R., & Pras, A. (2012). Inside dropbox: understanding personal cloud storage services. *Paper presented at the Proceedings of the 2012 ACM conference on Internet measurement conference*, Boston, Massachusetts, USA. doi:10.1145/2398776.2398827

Factor, M., Meth, K., Naor, D., Rodeh, O., & Satran, J. (2005). Object storage: the future building block for storage systems Local to Global Data Interoperability - Challenges and Technologies, 2005 (pp. 119-123).

Ferreira, L., Berstis, V., Armstrong, J., Kendzierski, M., Neukoetter, A., Takagi, M., & Hernandez, O. (2003). *Introduction to grid computing with globus*. IBM Corporation, International Technical Support Organization.

Garrett, J. J. (2005). Ajax: A new approach to web applications.

Ghemawat, S., Gobioff, H., & Leung, S.-T. (2003). The Google File System. *SIGOPS Oper. Syst. Rev., 37*(5), 29–43. doi:10.1145/1165389.945450

Gibson, G. A., Nagle, D. F., Amiri, K., Chang, F. W., Feinberg, E. M., Gobioff, H., & Zelenka, J. et al. (1997). File Server Scaling with Network-attached Secure Disks *Proceedings of the 1997 ACM SIGMETRICS International Conference on Measurement and Modeling of Computer Systems* (pp. 272-284). Seattle, Washington, USA: ACM. doi:10.1145/258612.258696

Gluster, F. S. (2014). Retrieved from http://www.gluster.org/

GoogleChrome. (2015). chrome.fileSystem. Retrieved from https://developer.chrome.com/apps/fileSystem

GoogleCloudStorage. (2014). Retrieved from https://cloud.google.com/storage/#pricing-calc

Han, J., Song, M., & Song, J. (2011, May 16-18). A Novel Solution of Distributed Memory NoSQL Database for Cloud Computing. *Paper presented at the 2011 IEEE/ACIS 10th International Conference on Computer and Information Science (ICIS)*.

Harizopoulos, S., Liang, V., Abadi, D. J., & Madden, S. (2006). Performance tradeoffs in read-optimized databases. *Paper presented at the Proceedings of the 32nd international conference on Very large data bases*, Seoul, Korea.

Hupfeld, F., Cortes, T., Kolbeck, B., Stender, J., Focht, E., Hess, M., & Cesario, E. et al. (2008). The XtreemFS architecture—a case for object-based file systems in Grids. *Concurrency and Computation, 20*(17), 2049–2060.

Idreos, S., Groffen, F., Nes, N., Manegold, S., Mullender, S., & Kersten, M. (2012). MonetDB: Two decades of research in column-oriented database architectures. *Bulletin of the IEEE Computer Society Technical Committee on Data Engineering, 35*(1), 40–45.

Jing, H., Haihong, E., Guan, L., & Jian, D. (2011, October 26-28). *Survey on NoSQL database. Paper presented at the 2011 6th International Conference on Pervasive Computing and Applications (ICPCA)*.

Kallman, R., Kimura, H., Natkins, J., Pavlo, A., Rasin, A., Zdonik, S., & Abadi, D. J. et al. (2008). Hstore: A high-performance, distributed main memory transaction processing system. *Proceedings of the VLDB Endowment, 1*(2), 1496–1499. doi:10.14778/1454159.1454211

Kumar, R., Gupta, N., Maharwal, H., Charu, S., & Yadav, K. (2014). Critical Analysis of Database Management Using NewSQL. International Journal of Computer Science and Mobile Computing, May, 434-438.

Ltree (2015). Retrieved from http://www.postgresql.org/docs/9.1/static/ltree.html

Mesnier, M., Ganger, G. R., & Riedel, E. (2003). Object-based storage. *Communications Magazine, IEEE, 41*(8), 84–90. doi:10.1109/MCOM.2003.1222722

Mishne, G., Dalton, J., Li, Z., Sharma, A., & Lin, J. (2012). Fast Data in the Era of Big Data: Twitter's Real-Time Related Query Suggestion Architecture. *CoRR, abs/1210.7350.*

Moose, F. S. (2015). Retrieved from http://www.moosefs.org/

Nurmi, D., Wolski, R., Grzegorczyk, C., Obertelli, G., Soman, S., Youseff, L., & Zagorodnov, D. (2009). The eucalyptus open-source cloud-computing system. *Paper presented at the 9th IEEE/ACM International Symposium on Cluster Computing and the Grid CCGRID'09.* doi:10.1109/CCGRID.2009.93

OracleNimbula. (2014). Retrieved from http://www.oracle.com/us/corporate/acquisitions/nimbula/index.html

Palankar, M. R., Iamnitchi, A., Ripeanu, M., & Garfinkel, S. (2008). Amazon S3 for science grids: a viable solution? *Paper presented at the Proceedings of the 2008 international workshop on Data-aware distributed computing*, Boston, MA, USA. doi:10.1145/1383519.1383526

Pautasso, C., Zimmermann, O., & Leymann, F. (2008). Restful web services vs. "big"' web services: making the right architectural decision. *Paper presented at the Proceedings of the 17th international conference on World Wide Web*, Beijing, China. doi:10.1145/1367497.1367606

Pawlowski, B., Shepler, S., Beame, C., Callaghan, B., Eisler, M., Noveck, D., & Thurlow, R. et al. (2000). The NFS version 4 protocol. *Proceedings of the 2nd International System Administration and Networking Conference (SANE 2000).*

Pepple, K. (2011). *Deploying OpenStack.* O'Reilly Media, Inc.

Roselli, D., Lorch, J. R., & Anderson, T. E. (2000). A comparison of file system workloads. *Paper presented at the Proceedings of the annual conference on USENIX Annual Technical Conference*, San Diego, California.

Shvachko, K., Hairong, K., Radia, S., & Chansler, R. (2010, May 3-7). *The Hadoop Distributed File System.* Paper presented at the 2010 IEEE 26th Symposium on Mass Storage Systems and Technologies (MSST).

Stonebraker, M. (2010). SQL databases v. NoSQL databases. *Communications of the ACM, 53*(4), 10–11. doi:10.1145/1721654.1721659

Stonebraker, M., Abadi, D. J., Batkin, A., Chen, X., Cherniack, M., Ferreira, M., . . . Zdonik, S. (2005). C-store: a column-oriented DBMS. *Paper presented at the Proceedings of the 31st international conference on Very large data bases*, Trondheim, Norway.

Stonebraker, M., & Rowe, L. A. (1986). The design of Postgres: Vol. 15. *No. 2* (pp. 340–355). ACM.

Stonebraker, M., & Weisberg, A. (2013). The VoltDB Main Memory DBMS. *IEEE Data Eng. Bull.*, *36*(2), 21–27.

Tatebe, O., Hiraga, K., & Soda, N. (2010). Gfarm Grid File System. *New Generation Computing*, 28(3), 257–275. doi:10.1007/s00354-009-0089-5

W3C. (2015). File API: Writer. Retrieved from http://dev.w3.org/2009/dap/file-system/file-writer.html

Wang, F., Oral, S., Shipman, G., Drokin, O., Wang, T., & Huang, I. (2009). Understanding Lustre file-system internals. *Oak Ridge National Lab technical report. ORNL. U. S. Atomic Energy Commission*, *TM-2009*(117).

Weil, S. A., Brandt, S. A., Miller, E. L., Long, D. D. E., & Maltzahn, C. (2006). Ceph: A Scalable, High-performance Distributed File System *Proceedings of the 7th Symposium on Operating Systems Design and Implementation* (pp. 307-320). Seattle, Washington: USENIX Association.

Weil, S. A., Brandt, S. A., Miller, E. L., & Maltzahn, C. (2006). CRUSH: controlled, scalable, decentralized placement of replicated data. *Paper presented at the Proceedings of the 2006 ACM/IEEE conference on Supercomputing*, Tampa, Florida. doi:10.1109/SC.2006.19

Weil, S. A., Leung, A. W., Brandt, S. A., & Maltzahn, C. (2007). RADOS: a scalable, reliable storage service for petabyte-scale storage clusters. *Paper presented at the Proceedings of the 2nd international workshop on Petascale data storage: held in conjunction with Supercomputing '07*, Reno, Nevada. doi:10.1145/1374596.1374606

White, T. (2009). *Hadoop: the definitive guide: the definitive guide*. O'Reilly Media, Inc.

Wilder, B. (2012). *Cloud Architecture Patterns: Using Microsoft Azure*. O'Reilly Media, Inc.

Zhang, Q., Cheng, L., & Boutaba, R. (2010). Cloud computing: State-of-the-art and research challenges. *Journal of Internet Services and Applications*, *1*(1), 7–18. doi:10.1007/s13174-010-0007-6

KEY TERMS AND DEFINITIONS

Big Data: Data that takes an excessive amount of time/space to store, transmit, and process using available resources.

Cloud Computing: A computing paradigm that refers to leasing of hardware resources as well as applications as services over the Internet in an on-demand fashion.

Data Striping: A technique that applies data partitioning across multiple storage nodes that provides high throughput in data access.

Distributed File Systems: File systems that provide access to geographically distributed files over POSIX-compliant interface or API.

Grid: A federation of a number of heterogeneous, geographically dispersed systems that share various types of resources such as CPU, storage and software resources.

Object: A storage unit that consists of both data and attributes including user and system-defined attributes.

Chapter 3
Security in Cloud of Things (CoT)

Bashar Alohali
Liverpool John Moores University, UK

ABSTRACT

With IoT era, development raises several significant research questions in terms of system architecture, design and improvement. For example; the requirement of virtual resource utilization and storage capacity necessitates making IoT applications smarter; therefore, integrate the IoT concept with cloud computing will play an important role. This is crucial because of very large amounts of data that IoT is expected to generate. The Cloud of Things (CoT) is used to connect heterogeneous physical things to the virtual domain of the cloud. Despite its numerous advantages, there are many research challenges with utilization of CoT that needs additional consideration. These include high complexity, efficiency, improving reliability, and security. This chapter introduces CoT, its features, the applications that use CoT. CoT, like all other networked functions, is vulnerable to security attacks. The security risks for CoT are listed and described. The security requirements for CoT are identified and solutions are proposed to address the various attacks on CoT and its components.

INTRODUCTION

Through the years, the era of information technology and pervasiveness of digital technologies have showed an exponential growth. The rising number of technological improvements offers a wealth of new services. Recently, Internet of Things (IoT) has attracted attention since it involves several applications, including smart grid, control systems, remote healthcare, smart mobility, traffic flow management and so on. In addition, it is expected to grow in terms of its deployment as well as its applicability in various application areas. The term IoT was coined by Kevin Ashton in 1999, which meant any entity that has a chip placed inside it or addressable on a network with an IP-address and can connect to wireless or wired network infrastructure (Gratton, 2013). These are everyday objects with ubiquitous connectivity and communicating and operating constantly. The use of IoT leads to a smart world with ubiquitous computing and provides services that enables remote access and intelligent functionality (Chaouchi,

DOI: 10.4018/978-1-4666-9834-5.ch003

2013). IoT enables real-time analysis of data flows that could improve efficiency, reliability and economy of systems. For example, connecting all appliances in the smart house can save electricity by efficient monitoring. Thus, IoT provides convenience in day-to-day living and makes an intelligent use of resources in a home (Parwekar, 2011).

CoT represents an important extension of IoT. CoT refers to the virtualization of IoT infrastructure to provide monitoring and control. IoT deployments typically generate large amounts of data that require computing as well as storage. A cloud infrastructure that can provide these resources can effectively offload the computing and storage requirements within the IoT network to the cloud. An added benefit is the ability to virtualize the underlying IoT infrastructure to provide monitoring and control from a single point. An application using IoT could therefore become a smart application. A CoT connects heterogeneous appliances to the virtual cloud domain. Both tangible and intangible objects (home appliances, sensor-based and network-enabled) and surrounding people can be integrated on a network or into a set of networks (Sun, Zhang, & Li, 2012).

CoT suggests a model consisting of a set of services (or commodities) that are delivered just like the traditional commodities. In other words, CoT can provide a virtual infrastructure which can integrate analytic tools, monitoring devices and visualization platforms (Parwekar, 2011). Moreover, CoT is a recent technological breakthrough that can enable end-to-end service provisioning for users and businesses to directly access applications on demand from anywhere, anytime (Sun et al., 2012). The emerging CoT services will enable a new generation and intelligent use of a collection of applications that will be fed with real time and analysis.

CoT, as a connected universe of things, can become a tangible reality in the future. Connected devices and things, ranging from sensors to public transport, will send huge of data that should be effectively managed and processed. However, cyber-attacks on critical infrastructure, recently, have highlighted security as a major requirement for CoT. A compromise of the CoT can have drastic effects, sometimes nation-wide and on people's lives. So, a CoT infrastructure should be secure. This chapter will present an overview of some of the concepts related to CoT. After introducing CoT, it continues to present the architecture and the applications of CoT. In addition, the security requirements for the CoT are discussed and the security challenges are highlighted. Specifically, the threats to the CoT are discussed. The chapter concludes with a discussion on the existing security solutions and a mention of the open research issues.

BACKGROUND

Overview of CoT

IoT on which CoT is based, is a new IT paradigm that describes an imagined reality of trillions of things connected to each other. It is transmitting valuable data that is stored, processed and analyzed by computers to control and addresses all sorts of human activities, ranging from healthcare, road traffic, emergency management, retail, crime prevention, lighting, energy and power and/or transportation. IoT is closely linked with the concepts of "smart city", "ubiquitous computing" (Vasseur & Dunkels, 2010), and other paradigms that describe new technological reality in which sensors and microcontrollers are embedded in various things and integrated into human living. This results in increased comfort and security. IoT unites several individual technologies, including machine-to-machine (M2M), supervisory control and data acquisition (SCADA), a system designed for industrial remote monitoring & control of equipment, wireless sensor networks (WSN) and radio-frequency identification (RFID). All these systems and technologies have diverse and complex functionalities that include monitoring, sensing, tracking, locating, alerting, scheduling, controlling, protecting, logging, auditing, planning, maintenance, upgrading, data mining, trending, reporting, decision support, back office applications, and others (Gubbi, Buyya, Marusic, & Palaniswami, 2013).

One of the main differences of IoT paradigm from machine-to-machine technologies (M2M) technologies is remote sensing (McGrath & Scanaill, 2013). Its significance on prospective creation of complex and all-embracing network architecture with its unique protocols, storage capacities, software applications and users is similar to the Internet.

The main idea behind cloud computing is that cloud providers offer a shared access to multiple users to physical computing infrastructure and software. Cloud computing formed into three different service scopes, namely, Infrastructure as a Service (IaaS), Platform as a Service (PaaS) and Software as a Service (SaaS) (Kifayat, Merabti, & Shi, 2010). These models may be deployed as a private, public, and community or hybrid clouds. From the technological viewpoint, key characteristics of cloud technologies, such as on-demand service, broad network access, resource pooling, rapid elasticity and measured service are enabled by virtualization process. Through virtualization single system images may be created from cluster machine infrastructure, which provides a unified user interface and efficient utilization of resources. Virtualization in cloud services is enabled by middleware. Given its huge storage, computing and sharing capabilities IT clouds are regarded as enablers for implementation of IoT networks. Cloud of Things is a real-world mixture between IoT paradigm and cloud technology. Both of them have three layers - IoT includes devices, connection and management (DCM) layers, whereas cloud computing has SaaS, PaaS and IaaS (SPI) layers (see Figure 1). IoT can be organized as Intranet of Things, Extranet of Things or Internet of Things, as clouds can be deployed as private, public or hybrid clouds.

However, these successful examples of technology application, implementation of the CoT require further transformation of cloud technologies. In fact, current storage infrastructure and file, systems

Figure 1. Components of cloud computing

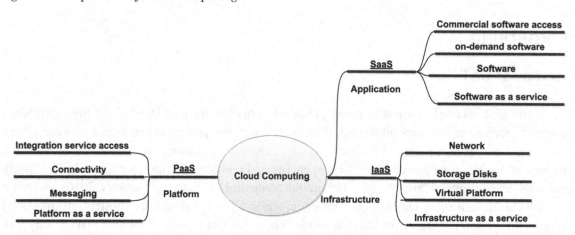

cannot be used in IoT context that will require processing, analysis and response to sensitive data that handles dynamic real-world infrastructures and processes. In this view, considerations of security and protection become fundamental in the CoT framework.

CoT has a potential of integrating a large number of connected devices; including GPSs, mobile phones, broadband, TV and outgrow the number of human subscribers in a cloud. Therefore, implementation of cloud based on IoT paradigm requires the development of complex infrastructure and software architecture to fit with IoT characteristic and requirements. Currently, M2M connectivity, data storage, processing and interchange with other machines are limited, because the majority of IoT devices exist in Intranet and Extranet. M2M is normally regulated by systems that focus on connectivity and monitoring, rather than data sharing and data interchange with other machines. Few IoT networks are currently accessible on the Internet and most of the projects have been experimental (Parwekar, 2011).

Architectural Elements of CoT

The elements of the CoT architecture are presented in this section. They are mentioned using a high level taxonomy to help in identifying and defining the components required by CoT. It requires three components that can enable continuous ubiquitous computing:

1. Hardware consisting of embedded communication hardware, sensors and actuators,
2. Middleware which is responsible for 'on demand' storage and computing tools for data analytics
3. Visualization and analysis tools that are user-friendly and available on different platforms and for different applications (Distefano, Merlino, & Puliafito, 2012).

Figure 2. System architecture for the CoT

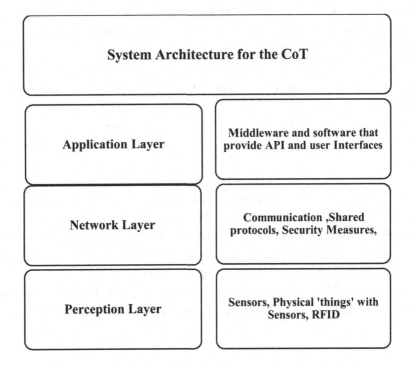

This section briefly discusses a few enabling technological developments in these categories that make up the 3 components indicated above.

Hardware

The first CoT architectural element is the Radio Frequency IDentification (RFID). RFID act as an e-barcode providing a capability to automatically identify anything that they are attached to. RFID "tags" are of two types – inactive tags and active tags. Inactive tags are not powered with a battery but they utilize the power from the RFID reader's interrogation signal. Such tags are typically used in the Retail and Supply-Chain Management sector. An example that can be given to explain this procedure better are the applications used in transportation, such as the registration stickers or the replacement of tickets. RFID active tags are powered from their own battery and are able to initiate communication. Such tags are used in port containers to monitor the movement of cargo (Hwang, Dongarra, & Fox, 2013). Sensors are similar to active RFIDs but they have better onboard storage and computing capability.

Another necessary architectural element of CoT is Wireless Sensor Networks (WSNs). They are cost-effective, efficient and low power, miniature electronic devices used in remote sensing applications. WSN components include WSN hardware, a WSN communication stack, a WSN middleware and a secure data aggregation (Emary & Ramakrishnan, 2013). WSNs consist of a large number of intelligent sensors and can collect, process and analyze the distribution of valuable data and information that are gathered in a variety of environments. Specifically, the data from the sensors are shared between sensor nodes and thereafter sent to a centralized (or distributed) system for analysis. However, the technical challenges that must be addressed in order to exploit WSNs' huge potential are multidisciplinary and substantial in nature.

WSN core hardware is a node consisting of power supply, multiple sensor interfaces and Analogue/Digital convertors, a transceiver and processing units. The sensors interconnect into a WSN in an ad-hoc mode and applications ride over the network. On a sensor, the MAC layer predominantly used is the IEEE 802.15.4. The network layer, in recent past, is moving towards an IP based implementation such as 6LoWPAN and ZigBee over IP. WSN nodes communicate with each other to propagate information to an aggregation/storage point in the network (also termed as "gateway"). They can use either a single-hop path or a multi-hop path to reach such a point in the network. Routing protocols are necessary to route data to the destination. The aggregation point could provide the connecting link to the Internet. The WSN, therefore, becomes a sub-network connected to the Internet.

Middleware

WSN middleware is a mechanism that is necessary to combine the sensor network infrastructure and the Service Oriented Architecture (SOA) to provide an independent access to other heterogeneous sensor resources. To achieve this, a platform-independent middleware is needed. One leading example is the Open Sensor Web Architecture (OSWA) which is developed upon a uniform set of standard data representations and operations (Emary & Ramakrishnan, 2013).

The fourth component of WSN is the secure data aggregation methodology that is required to ensure that the data collected by the several sensors are reliable. This component is necessary for WSNs as they are open to several malicious attacks that can cause node failures. In such an event, the impact of the node failures must be minimal and the rest of the WSN must continue to function. Hence, the WSN must have the capability to heal itself and ensure secure and authentic data over the network.

Addressability is a requirement since each device/sensor requires to be uniquely addressed (Zhou, 2013). Thus, addressing is another architectural element of CoT. This mechanism allows the network to uniquely identify millions of devices and control remote devices through the Web. The features that must be taken into account in order to develop and implement a unique address are the scalability, the persistence, the reliability and the uniqueness. In other words, the target here is every single connected element to the network must be identified by its identity, functionality, and location.

Data Storage, Analytics, and Visualization

The data storage and analytics is one of the most important architectural elements of CoT as the development of an unprecedented amount of data is compulsory in this emerging field. In other words, as mentioned above the data gathered within the CoT must be stored and used intelligently for smart actuation and monitoring purposes. This can be achieved through the development of various Artificial Intelligence (AI) algorithms (such as novel fusion algorithms), which will be centralized based on the need. These algorithms, in combination with temporal machine learning methodologies based on evolutionary algorithms, should make sense of the data gathered as well as must be able to achieve automated decision making.

The last CoT architectural element relates with visualization which is crucial for a CoT application as it allows a better interaction between the end-user and the environment/s. The visualization must be attractive and easy for the end-user to fully benefit from the CoT revolution. Luckily, this is achieved through the years since most information is provided in meaningful ways to consumers. Raw data is processed and converted into knowledge. This knowledge helps in fast decision-making, especially in applications where the decision-making is automated and is in real-time. The meaningful information extraction from raw data is non-trivial. Raw data, along with event detection information is generated according to the needs of the users (Chao, 2012).

CoT Applications

CoT involves several applications that can be classified based on the network availability type, heterogeneity, repeatability coverage, scale, user involvement and impact. Thus, CoT applications can be categorized into 4 application domains:

1.   Personal and home,
2.   Enterprise,
3.   Utilities and
4.   Mobile

Personal and Home

This concerns the information gathered by the sensor from the ambience of a home or from that of a personal space such as a body area network (BAN). Only those who own the network use the data that is collected. For example, nowadays it is possible for a smartphone with iOS, Android or Windows Phone operating system to communicate with the several interfaces (Bluetooth, Bluetooth LE, Wi-Fi) for interconnecting sensors that measure physiological parameters. In addition to this, applications can allow the control of home equipment such as fridges, air conditioners, lighting, and other appliances providing an ease of energy and functional management of a home. This involves customers in the CoT revolution (Zhou, 2013). Such applications could use Twitter-like approach where the individual 'things' in the house could periodically tweet the readings that could be easily followed from anywhere by developing a TweetOT (Gubbi et al., 2013). However, such services require a common framework for using the cloud for information access. The security requirements for these services would require a new approach to provide privacy, authentication secrecy and integrity.

Enterprise

Enterprise-based applications mainly relate with businesses and deals with the NoT (Network of Things) within a business environment. The data and the information gathered by these networks are selectively released and their owners only use them. For instance, the data generated and gathered by an application to keep track of the number of residents within a building (for environmental reasons), is utilized by the environment control agency. A light sensor can automate this counting/monitoring activity and feed the data into a larger system that controls the environment. The same input can also be extrapolated to track resident movement from a security functional requirement. Similarly, the sensors can be enhanced to perform additional sensing functions and the application can be enhanced to provide this functionality. The CoT approach provides this application/implementation with the flexibility of making changes to parts of the system (adding areas of coverage) or changing the devices, enhancing the functionality of the application and so on.

Utilities

CoT applications, such as the one mentioned above, introduce users to a smarter environment that can provide security, convenience and automation. The term "Smart Cities" has gained relevance in this context and there are various test beds that are being implemented as proof-of-concept. The bases of the Smart City implementations are CoT based applications in various domains. Such applications, both large and small scale, have been implemented and tested on test bed infrastructure for the last few years. The test beds consist of several subsystems and involve multiple focus (user) groups with an objective to share the collected data. Some of the applications address larger community issues such as pollution, health and well being and transportation (Gubbi et al., 2013). These applications are also used for the safety and physical security. An example is a surveillance application that can help identify intrusions/ illegal access and identify wary activities, both with and without visual sensors such as cameras.

The need for service optimization is another driver for CoT based applications. Applications are used by several utility organizations mainly to manage their resources, to optimize their services, e.g. Cost of Electricity delivery vs profit margin. Such a CoT application predominantly works at the front-end on the sensing infrastructure and requires interworking with other applications at the back-end to cooperatively deliver the service optimization targeted for. Usually, such networks are used by large businesses (on a national scale) that have the resources for large network infrastructure. A typical example is networks labeled as critical infrastructure, such as power generation and distribution grids, water distribution grids, transportation networks, railroad network, Logistics and so on. With resource optimization, CoT applications are deemed to enhance environment friendliness – efficient use of power/water and delivery, pollution monitoring and control, etc., are typical applications that enhance environment friendliness. (Bandyopadhyay & Sen, 2011).

Mobility

The final CoT application deals with the mobility (such as transportation and traffic) (Gubbi et al., 2013). In fact, urban traffic is what causes the traffic noise pollution as well as the degradation of the air quality. In addition, the traffic congestion, the supply-chain efficiencies and the productivity are directly related and can result in high-costs due to delays and delivery schedule failures. Therefore, CoT application for mobility uses multi-dynamic traffic information that provides the capability for better planning and improved scheduling. Large-scale WSNs are used to feed the sensed information to such applications that are used for the online control of travel times, queue lengths and noise emissions. The CoT application replaces the existing automated physical systems, comprising networks of inductive loop vehicle detectors, to monitor and sense the traffic data.

CoT applications can be enhanced by the implementation of scenario-based models that attempt to plan and design mitigation and alleviation plans. The availability of Bluetooth devices affects the penetration of such applications in a number of smart products such as the smartphones and the navigation systems (GPS) (Zhou, 2013). Bluetooth devices release signals with a nomadic media access ID number that can be read by Bluetooth sensors within a particular coverage area enabling the movement identification of devices. If this is also complemented by other data sources i.e. bus GPS, then problems such as vehicle travel time on motorways would be addressed, as these applications would be able to provide accurate and reliable real time transport information.

Another important application in mobile CoT domain is logistics management dealing with the efficient transportation planning and scheduling. It involves monitoring the items being transported. The monitored items are sensed and the data is fed into the large-scale, back-end network that includes other sensing networks such as a transportation-monitoring network. The monitored items physically transit through various physical locations and the sensing network feeds the item's location information to the back-end network that does the tracking.

In summary, we observe that CoT based applications have implementations across several application domains. They often form elements of the front-end network and communicate with a large-scale back-end network to provide a service. They have helped to make services both efficient as well as innovative and in almost all cases provide a means of replacing existing infrastructure with greener solutions. A distinctive feature of these applications is overall cost reductions and increased revenue margins. Consequently, it is expected that the proliferation of such applications will only increase.

CoT for a Smart Grid

Smart grid is considered as an intelligent network of meta-systems and subsystems to provide energy cost-effectively and reliably. Figure 3 illustrates the communication network of a smart grid. It has a hierarchical structure, comprising three areas, Home Area Network (HAN), Neighbor Area Network

Figure 3. CoT for a smart grid

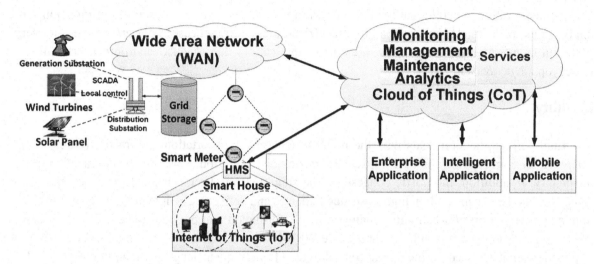

(NAN) or Field Area Network (FAN) and Wide Area Network (WAN). Smart Grids derive benefit from the fact that homes can be automated using ubiquitous computing and such automation can help in energy monitoring. It is the embedded Internet of things that provide several services linked to physical devices or resource monitors and enable the management of energy consumption of devices and appliances (Xi, Jianming, Xiangzhen, Limin, & Yan, 2011). The occupant expects to be able to monitor and control various systems in a home using a Home Management System, a typical CoT application. The operation is based on real-time data and two-way communication with renewable power generation (Alohali, Merabti, & Kifayat). One of the main purposes of smart home is to adapt to the movements of green, energy saving, environment-friendly concepts that have emerged in recent years.

There are many applications involved with smart home, including demand response, dynamic pricing, system monitoring, cold-load pick-up, and the mitigation of greenhouse gas emissions (Karnouskos, 2013). CoT for HAN is expected to play an important role in smart grids. The obvious benefits of deploying a CoT based on smart grid are improved storage, computing offload from the sensors and devices and faster access via the Internet (Karnouskos, 2013).

The following are the summarized benefits of utilizing CoT on a smart grid:

- Better-quality storage ability, memory, and maintenance of the resources.
- Reduced energy consumption of devices.
- Real time control and fast, extensive analytics.
- Capability to support several platforms and OS.

Security Challenges of CoT

The infrastructure for a CoT is built using the combination of IoT levels (intranet, extranet or internet) and cloud computing. CoT security, therefore, has a similar set of security threats, vulnerabilities and objectives. Primarily, the data exchange between elements of the CoT need to be checked for their integrity and kept private. In addition, the data itself requires to be checked for validity and freshness.

Apart from this, there is the factor of security provided by the Cloud service provider, within the cloud infrastructure, which includes data storage, data access and data isolation. The impact of failure of hardware or a potential service breakdown due to security reasons (malicious intrusions) is intense on a community, especially if it is in relation to a CoT deployed as a Critical Infrastructure (Electricity, Water, Gas, Telecom, Healthcare, etc.).

Connected things are resource-limited devices with reduced storage capacity and energy, which makes them vulnerable to a number of potential attacks and risks. This means that sensitive data may be blocked and manipulated. Avoiding requires that Security be addressed as part of the basic design of a service deployed as a CoT application. In order to improve things' against attacks new security protocols, encryption methods and algorithms are being developed taking into consideration memory and computing limitations of connected devices. Several such schemes already exist in the context of security in WSNs and could possibly be adapted to the CoT scenario requirements. Security architecture of CoT should also address the issue of fault tolerance, since device failures may be quite common in CoT system. Filtering bogus and manipulated data and securing data identity are critical tasks for robust CoT security system (Aazam, Khan, Alsaffar, & Eui-Nam, 2014).

Connected devices generate large volumes of data that should be transmitted, processed and managed. In a focused CoT, data management is primarily realized by cloud computing systems. Therefore, the security of this data depends on security measures undertaken by cloud service providers. Data security in cloud systems depends on protection of virtualization process and safe allocation and reallocation of resources. Recall that the Cloud is made up of shared as well as distributed computing and storage resources. The hypervisor and virtual machine should be organized/configured sufficiently to prevent data exposure when resources are reallocated from one virtual machine (VM) to another. Data security may be also compromised by the malicious traffic going from one VM to another. In order to avoid this risk, traffic monitoring and firewalls between VMs may be used as effective counter-measures. Another technique is segregation and isolation of different VMs classes from each other (Cucurull & Guasch, 2014). Anomaly detection is used to monitor behavior and detect deviations. Those deviating the agreed code of conduct are either debarred from further use or quarantined. This helps to prevent potential security incidents.

In addition to the security concerns mentioned so far, there are a few distinct to CoT. These security challenges originate from the features of embedded computer devices, RFID, networks and M2M communication. The key challenges and obstacles to practical security of CoT and available technology solutions are outlined below:

1. **Dynamic Activity Cycle:** Security challenges of CoT are linked with a difference of roles and functions that may be realized by connected devices. They may be a waste in some situations and active in others (Gál et al., 2014). They may transmit data immediately to cloud servers or to other devices. Things may just receive data from other devices serving as an intermediary storage capacity in the network. The variability of roles played by connected devices, which are frequently different from CRUD tasks made by computers, makes it necessary to develop new security approaches and techniques address these challenges (Oh & Kim, 2014).

2. **Heterogeneous Interactions:** The domain of connected devices is extremely heterogeneous, because different manufacturers with different standards, protocols and technical requirements make many of them. So, it is unlikely that all home devices fit homogeneity and interoperability

criteria achieved in the computer industry; the standards are evolving. This is especially true for device network's points of connection with external networks, such as Internet. This connection frequently requires gateways or proxies, which makes end-to-end communication problematic. Different protocols and technical features of connected devices make it necessary to implement qualitatively new cryptographic algorithms that lightweight and offer an end-to-end secure communication channel (Sharma et al., 2014).

3. **Anti-Virus Provision:** In classic computer networks, PCs are normally protected from malware and attacks by advanced and memory-consuming anti-virus suites (Shon, Cho, Han, & Choi, 2014). Provision of connected devices with such anti-virus protection is a challenge due to memory and computing power constraints of CoT.

4. **Small Packets Vulnerability:** Connected devices are normally built based on IEEE 802.15.4 standard created for low-rate wireless personal area network (LR-WPANs). The standard supports 127-byte packets at the physical layer (Saha & Sridhar, 2012). This architecture may cause fragmentation of large packets of security protocols, which results in opening of new attack, especially for DoS attacks. The implications of these attacks may be particularly adverse in case of key exchange messaging by connected devices (Chaouchi, 2013).

Attacks on CoTs

Attackers with different motives and skills can take advantage of the security weaknesses of the cloud of things, and can cause various levels of damage to the network. Attackers at the top level include online hackers, terrorists, employee's opponents, or users, and so on. Thus with developments in the security of networks and computers, we are currently facing more and more complex and advanced attacks and threats. In this section, we will describe and discuss attacks and threats as they relate to CoTs. However, the majority of these attacks are related to those that apply to traditional networks. We will briefly illustrate attacks, which are dangerous and can potentially tend towards significant harm to the network.

1. **Denial of Service (DoS):** DoS is defined as stopping the system or network from providing normal service. It involves an attack that reduces or removes a network's capacity to execute its expected function through hardware failures/crashes, software bugs, resource (memory/computing) exhaustion, malicious broadcasting of high-energy signals or complex interaction between these points. CoT is especially vulnerable to DoS attacks due to the small memory, processing and power limitations of devices. These attacks may only be noticed after the service is blocked or becomes unavailable due to memory or battery exhaustion (Medaglia & Serbanati, 2010).

2. **Jamming:** Things in CoT are also especially vulnerable to electromagnetic interference based on the same frequency-band signals as in the attacked devices. This attack is known as jamming and is typically prevented by anti-jamming (Chen & Gong, 2012).

3. **Brute-Force Attack:** A brute-force attack usually involves an exhaustive key search, where an adversary goes against any block cipher in a search for the key. In general, cryptanalysis on the key leads to an exhaustive key search attack in which every possible combination of bits in the key is tried in turn (Smith & Marchesini, 2007). This can lead to compromise of the communication

of an entire network. Therefore, the stronger the key is, the greater the key length and the longer it will take for the attacker to discover the valid key and decrypt the message. However, long keys impact both storage and computing on the embedded devices and therefore the design of the security mechanisms require to strike a fine balance between the security objectives and the limited resources available on the devices.

4. **Replay Attack:** This is where an attacker can capture the network traffic and resend the packets at a later time to obtain unauthorized entry to the resources. In a common method of replay attack, a malicious user can eavesdrop on communications and resend old packets again multiple times in order to spoof information or gain access/trust to/of another device. It can also waste node or system resources (Miri, 2013) thereby inducing a mild DoS as well.

5. **Malware:** CoT devices may also be attacked by malware that includes viruses, Trojan horses, worms and other programs that are designed to damage the appliance. Penetration of these threats into the network is usually addressed by antivirus software and firewalls, at the perimeter.

Security Methods for Cloud of Things

The existing methods of securing the cloud of things include using the private cloud with enterprise parameter, content encryption, session containers, cloud access brokers and runtime security visualization.

Table 1.

Private Clouds	Content Encryption	Session Containers	Cloud Access Brokers	Runtime Security Visualization
Involve establishing a virtual infrastructure inside currently existing corporate firewall	Designed to ensure that cloud resident content is not retrievable through plain text by ATP malware	Secures the public clouds by making the user to initiate a relatively secure connection that maintains end-to-end closure as opposed to HTML5	Involves the use of a broker, which monitors the authentication path from users and provide enhanced security	Involve the dynamic establishment of runtime security visualization. Reasoning being, the storage and other computing infrastructure are embedded on in virtual runtime systems and that makes security systems be embedded too.
Accessible to only authenticated users	Works only if the underlying algorithm cannot be broken and are based strong ciphers	Supports multiple personas	Allows flexible integration of emerging security capacities	Provide a virtual WAF to protect an HTTP application
Provides easy access to members yet restrictive	Ensures significant data secrecy and have malware resistance platform	Session containers provides client system data wipe that ensures the user data is not retrieved by another user	Provide passive security observation that may be desirable to the users. It also offers active security measure in that it accesses the proxies in active mode.	Benefits include providing security for dynamic objects and handle different assets at a go

SECURITY REQUIREMENTS

CoT and the networks it hosts need a multi-layered approach to security starting at powering up. The security requirements must be addressed through the device's entire lifecycle. In this section, a general and brief review about security requirement in CoTs is presented.

1. Confidentiality

Confidentiality is one of the primary aims of security. One of the best ways to achieve confidentiality, data integrity and non-repudiation of communication is by encrypting data and establishing a shared secret key among nodes. In cryptography, the most crucial and challenging step is key management. Key management is a critical challenge, and to obtain proper security, the key's length should be sufficiently long to meet the security objectives and at the same time not drain the embedded system's resources. Furthermore, the key's lifetime should fit with the security requirement. A keying relationship can be used to facilitate cryptographic mechanisms in CoT communication.

Cryptographic techniques make use of two types of keys, either symmetric or asymmetric. Symmetric cryptography relies on a shared secret key between two nodes to enable secure communication. Asymmetric cryptography applies a pair of keys per node, a private key and a public key. The public key is used for encryption and can be published. The private key is used for decryption and is known only to the node and no one else. From a computational point of view, asymmetric cryptography requires many orders of magnitude more resources than symmetric cryptography (Stavroulakis & Stamp, 2010). In general, key management involves the following four sorts of keys: one-time session symmetric keys, public keys, private keys and passphrase-based symmetric keys. The session keys are used once and are generated for each new message. The public keys are used in asymmetric encryption. On the other hand, private keys are also used in asymmetric encryption. Passphrase-based keys are used to protect private keys. A single node can have multiple public or private key pairs (Alfred J. Menezes, Oorschot, & Vanstone, 1996).

2. Secure Booting

Secure booting deals with the integrity and the authenticity of the software packages on the devices that can be verified by using cryptographically generated digital signatures (Chandramouli, Iorga, & Chokhani, 2014). The digital signature must be attached to the software to ensuring that only the particular software is authorized to run on that device. Although the foundation of trust has been already established, CoT devices still need protection from several run-time threats and/or malicious purposes.

3. Access Control

Access control involves the application of various forms of access control and resource. These controls are usually built into the device's operating system, therefore limiting the device component's privileges in accessing only the resources needed in order to do only their assigned tasks. However, in the case where a component is compromised, this security requirement (access control) can assure that the intruder has minimal access to other system components as possible. The least privilege's principle commands that only the minimal access expected to perform a function should be endorsed to minimize the effectiveness and efficiency of any security breach (A Younis, Kifayat, & Merabti, 2014).

CoT devices also need a firewall mainly to control traffic, which will terminate at the cloud device. Therefore, firewalling is another one crucial security requirement for CoT (Zhou, 2013). The firewall and deep packet check capability have unique protocols that can direct how such devices can communicate to each other. At the same time, these tools have the strength to identify malicious payloads hiding in non-IT protocols (daCosta, 2013).

4. Authentication

When a device is plugged into the network, it must be able to authenticate itself prior to receiving or transmitting data and information (Swaminatha & Elden, 2003). This is necessary embedded devices do not have end-users sitting behind computers, waiting to type the identifications required to access the network (Bhattasali, Chaki, & Chaki, 2013). Thus, in order for the devices to access a network, they must automatically and correctly identify their credentials, securely, prior to authorization by using several machine authentication techniques.

5. Privacy

One of the most security concerns in CoT relates to privacy. Privacy attacks may target individual privacy (identification of a user's location, private information and preferences) and group privacy. To improve privacy protection, which is especially crucial as more things carrying sensitive user data enter the CoT, privacy-enhancing technologies may be utilized (Rosado, Mellado, & Piattini, 2013).

6. Updates and Patches

The final security requirement concerns the updates and patches. When the device is in operation it should start to receive software updates and patches to work properly. The devices must be ready to authenticate the patches which are received from their operators (Amies & Alex Amies, 2012). However, this authentication must not damage the functional safety of the device. This is critical when multiple devices in the field are performing crucial operations and are dependent on security patches to defend against vulnerability that escapes into the wild. Therefore, both the software updates and the security patches must be provided in a way so that they can save the limited bandwidth and the periodic connectivity of an embedded device and reduce the possibility of compromising functional safety.

A SECURE SCHEME FOR CLOUD OF THINGS (CoT)

Figure 4 details the network model elements and how they communicate. The IoTs consists of devices that are grouped into two. One group is prepared for devices that require basic operation (basically one-way communication) and is called Group 1. The other is reserved for devices that can be monitored

Box 1.

Pre-deployment Phase

1. *Assign a unique ID to every appliances in Group 1 and Group 2 and the two group leaders*

2. ### In Group 2:
    a. *Assign a unique group key to group leader of Group 2. This group key is shared with all appliances in the group*
    b. *Use the group key and the ID of the device to generate a unique key for each appliances in Group 2*

3. ### In Group 1:
    a. *Assign a unique key to the group leader for Group 1*
    b. *Assign the same key to every appliances in Group1*
    c. *Assign the shared key provided by the CoT*

4. ### Group Leaders 1, 2:
    a. *Assign the group key shared with the group*
    b. *Assign a different group key shared by the CoT*

5. ### CoT
    a. *Register the unique IDs of the Group 1, Group 2 appliances and the group leaders in the CoT*
    b. *Share a unique group key with the group leaders*
    c. *Share a unique key with all appliances in Group 1*

and controlled, thus requiring two-way communication, and is termed Group 2. Each group has a group leader with which the appliances in each group interconnect. The group leaders connect with the cloud of things (CoT).

CoT has access for monitored data from the appliances in the IoTs and can send control commands to the devices. Smart phones access the CoT via the Internet. The utility provider also uses a cloud infrastructure for its services. Any data regarding the IoTs is sourced from the CoT. The group leaders communicate with the cloud using a public data network such as the Internet via wired broadband links. The IoTs appliances in each group, as well as and each group leader, will communicate using technologies like ZigBee or WiFi. The objective of our solution is to provide effective resources for secure communication.

Given the functionality and interaction mentioned, the functional security requirements are as follows:

1. The IoTs appliances must be physically secured to the greatest extent possible. Physical compromise of a device cannot be permitted and can cause the loss of functionality of portion of the network.
2. The data sent or received should be protected sufficiently to prevent sniffing packets on the wireless channels from decrypting the data.

Figure 4. The network model

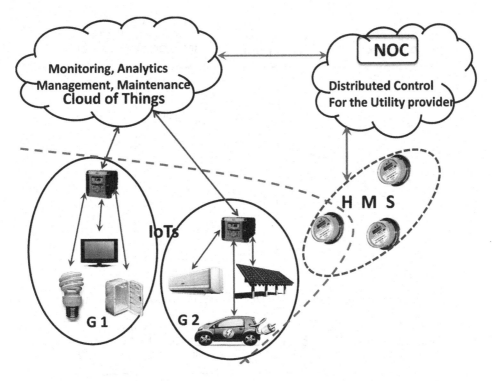

The assumptions made for designing the solution are:

1. The IoT devices in the two groups, as well as both group leaders, use unicast communication.
2. The group leaders are trusted devices.
3. The CoT interface is registered with the group leaders.
4. The appliances in each group are connected as a tree with the appliances as leaf nodes.
5. An attacker could eavesdrop on all traffic or replay messages since the IoTs uses wireless technologies.
6. Time stamps are applied for data freshness testing.
7. The devices are tamper-resistant; any attempt to manipulate the device to access stored information will result in that information being destroyed and the device becomes inactive.

Symmetric key cryptography is installed for secure interaction between the appliances in each group and each group leader as well as for interaction between the group leaders and the cloud. The objectives of the scheme are to provide a means for secure data exchange among the communicating components of each of the groups with CoT. The scheme benefits from the following points – all data is encrypted, the encryption key changes with time, the encryption key distribution is secure and the limitation of resources on the IoTs are considered.

The security scheme works as follows: The communication between the CoT and the appliances in the groups are shown in the Figures 5, 6. In Group 1, the communication is between the CoT and the appliance and is typically in the form of ON/OFF commands. The CoT first forms the data, D, to be sent to the appliance in Group 1. Recall that the data to the appliance in Group 1 is sent via group leader 1

Figure 5. CoT to Group 1 device interaction via the Group Controller 1

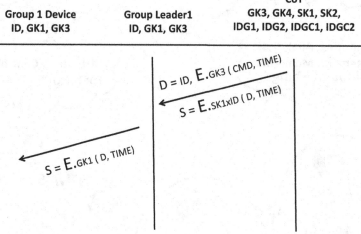

Figure 6. CoT to Group 2 device and Group 2 device to CoT interaction via the Group Controller 2

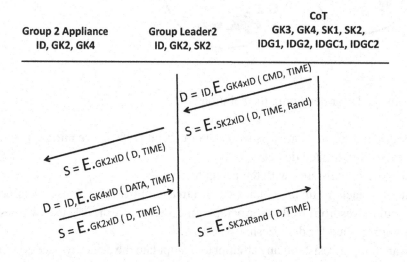

(GL1). The CoT generates a triplet of the ID of the Group 1 appliance, the command text for the appliance and a time stamp. The command and the time stamp are privately sent to the appliance in Group 1 via GL1. Therefore, the command and time stamp are encrypted using the symmetric key shared between the CoT and the appliance in Group 1(Figure 5), Group Key 3 (GK3). This message is now packaged and destined to GL1, which is the next immediate recipient. A triplet of D, a time stamp and the ID of GL1 is formed. D and the time stamp need to be encrypted for privacy. The CoT generates an encryption key using the shared key with GL1, SK1 and the ID of GL1. D and the time stamp are encrypted using the generated key and sent to GL1.

GL1 determines that the message has arrived from the CoT. It now generates the decryption key using the shared key with the CoT, SK1 and its ID and decrypts the message. If the message is successfully decrypted, it verifies the time to confirm that the value is greater than the earlier value it received from the CoT. It then reads D to identify the ID of the Group 1 appliance to which the message is designated. GL1 then sends the message to the appliance by encrypting D and its time stamp using the shared key with the Group 1 appliance, GK1. On receiving this message, the Group 1 appliance decrypts the message using GK1 to retrieve D, verifies the time stamp, decrypts D using the shared key with CoT, GK3, retrieves the time stamp, validates it and then takes the command sent by the CoT.

In Group 2 (Figure 6), the communication is from the CoT to the Group 2 appliance via the GL2. The data packaging is similar to that for Group 1 devices, except for the addition of a random number generated by the CoT. GL2 registers the random value, which is used with SK2 to generate a key for sending data to the CoT. When the Group 2 appliance asks to send data to the CoT, the same two-step process is followed. Applying the random value confirms that the key is refreshed each time the CoT receives some data.

Open Research Issues for Securing CoT

The security challenges and research open issues concerning CoT are the reliability in privacy and security, the efficiency in participatory sensing, the data analytics (or data mining), the quality of service and the Geographic Information Services (GIS)-based visualization. The final goal of CoT is the ability to deploy smart objects, get them to interact with similar smart object networks as well as Internet infrastructure, seamlessly. An extension of this is to be able to deploy sensor-based networks and be able to run multiple applications over them. These applications should be able to use the infrastructure, both interchangeably as well as concurrently. Standardization plays an important role in the realizing such an objective, given the heterogeneous nature of the devices and their operations.

1. Reliable Secure Reprogrammable Networks and Privacy

Reliable security and privacy are major concerns for the networks, especially if they are deployed on a large scale. A network or service, when vulnerable will be attacked causing the network to have inoperative parts as well as harbor the possibility of invalid data being injected into the network, leading to undesirable consequences. The three main architectural elements of CoT, which are the cloud, the RFID and WSN, are highly vulnerable to such attacks. Therefore, a primary line of defense in protecting these networks against the data exploitation is the cryptography (Bhattasali et al., 2013).

Cryptography is an effective and efficient solution as it can use cryptographic methodologies that can ensure the data confidentiality, integrity and authenticity. Embedded systems often need to update/ upgrade the software that they run as part of the CoT application. Such updates are centrally "pushed" onto the devices. These must be applied to all nodes in the network. CoT adopts a secure reprogramming protocol, which allows the nodes to authenticate every single code update resulting in the prevention of potentially malicious installations. Addressing these issues of secure reprogramming and insider attacks is a potential area of research.

The security issues in the cloud, is somewhat similar to the re-programming problem. The data, within the cloud, moves across virtual hosts and these hosts themselves can move between several locations (servers/data centres). The means to ensure data privacy across the cloud is an active research area and continues to address this issue. Particularly, this issue holds a higher risk in the database-based applications that involve personal information.

2. Efficient Participatory Sensing

CoT indicates the development and use of efficient participatory sensing platforms mainly to reduce the sensing costs. In addition to this, the participatory sensing can give the nearest indication concerning environmental parameters experienced by the end-users. In other words, these platforms derive from the environmental data gathered by the end-users that form a social currency (Wang et al., 2009). This is also, at times, associated with the term "crowd sensing".

The consequence of this phenomenon is that the more timely data that are generated to be directly compared with the available data through a fixed infrastructure sensor network. In either case, the importance here is for the end-users to be able to give an experience feedback in regards to a given environmental parameter. Unfortunately however, the end-users meet difficulties to do this and these limitations might place a new implication on the reference data role offered by a fixed infrastructure CoT as a backbone (Wang et al., 2009).

If one were to attempt to rely on the crowd-sensed data alone, it limits the ability to produce significant information and data for policy decisions. Addressing these problems in terms of security, reliability of data as well as data analytics within a mobile cloud (formed in an ad-hoc manner with smartphones, for example) are current areas of research.

3. Data Analytics (or Data Mining)

CoT uses a complex sensing environment. Extracting useful data, transforming that data into knowledge is a challenge. Data availability is asynchronous and has a varied time and spatial resolution. This makes the data extraction a reasonably tough challenge. In addition, data validity has to be continuously established. Research studies that have been conducted in the recent past have adopted methodologies using light learning methods that allowed data anomalies and pre-defined events to be extracted through the use of supervised and unsupervised learning. Then, there is the issue of simultaneously learning events, activities and their representations at multiple levels of complexity (Qian, Ruicong, Qi, Yan, & Weijun, 2010; Shen, Liu, & Wang, 2010).

4. Proper Security Risk Mitigation

Mitigating possible security threats is critical to creating a relatively secure and effectivity among CIOs and CISOs, which facilitate migration of applications and data to the cloud-computing platform. Most of the existing data, applications and systems possess variable security thresholds. In a way of example, web, social and mobile systems can be migrated to the virtual server without similar level of security concerns compared to the highly regulated information or sensitive applications. The decision as to whether a product, application or service is for the cloud server depends on the kind of data or application at hand, the service level agreement and the associated security environment. Therefore, the decision to migrate to the clouds primarily depends on the data sensitivity and the degree of security the cloud provider is offering, especially in public clouds. Business organizations must therefore establish whether the overall value achieved offset the risk when making the decision to go clouds in their data storage and management.

5. Adequate Understanding of the Cloud Service Provider

Many companies are facing the challenge in adequately understanding the cloud service provider before to getting the environment. Some providers may not be aware of the data security requirements that the customer requires. Therefore, the cloud service providers need comprehensive auditing to confirm how secure they are. However, few institutions having the auditing capacity currently exist in the market; hence, most organizations blindly enter into agreements to move to the clouds without considering the security implications their actions may impose on their data. The technology arena and the government should research and develop clear regulations for the cloud service providers. Additionally, proper policies relating to data breach in the cloud of things need clear statement to secure the cloud users.

Quality of Service

Taking into consideration that CoT is comprised of several heterogeneous networks that provide multiple services, there are multiple traffic types within the network. It is essential that this single network is able to support all the types of traffic (and therefore all applications on the network) without quality of service compromise. There are two application classes: i) the bandwidth and delay sensitive inelastic traffic such as the traffic monitoring and ii) the delay tolerant elastic traffic such as the monitoring of weather parameters at low sampling rates. All the traffic has to be securely delivered and their temporal characteristics have to be maintained end-to-end. However, due to the segments that often constitute 'gaps' in resource guarantee, it is not easy to provide quality of service guarantees in wireless networks (El-Sayed, Mellouk, George, & Zeadally, 2008).

As a result of these, the quality of service in cloud computing is an open research issue requiring more and more attention and research as the data and tools continuously become available on clouds (A Vouk, 2008).

GIS-Based Visualization

In many cases, CoT directly relates with new display technologies as well. Therefore, as long as these display technologies emerge, creative visualization will be enabled. Touch-based interfaces have given the opportunity to end-users to navigate the data better than even before, as well as the ability to directly operate with the display objects. However, the data arising from the ubiquitous computing (such as CoT) is not always ready for handling and consumption using visualization platforms, therefore they have to undergo further processing. This phenomenon makes the entire situation very complex for heterogeneous spatial and temporal data (Zhou, 2013).

Thus, there is a need for new visualization schemes which must be able to represent the heterogeneous sensors in a 3D landscape that varies temporally (Ren, Tian, Zhang, & Zhang, 2010). Finally, another challenge that emerges concerning the visualization of data gathered within CoT is that these data are usually geographically-related and are sparsely distributed in the cloud (Ning, 2013) and, therefore to cope with this, a framework based on Internet GIS is required (Ren et al., 2010).

CONCLUSION

The concept of the Internet of Things (IoT) is an interconnection of distinguishable objects and defines a thing within the Internet or similar IP structure. The things refer to physical objects, such as home appliances, medical devices, intelligent devices and so on. Those things are enhanced with computing and communication technology and have the ability to interconnect and communicate through embedded RFID chips, barcodes, sensors, or other networks. The Cloud of Thing (CoT) is a conceptual model used by Internet of Things (IoT) that provides smart things functions as process of analyzing, developing, controlling and maintaining of multiple applications (Seong Hoon & Daeyoung, 2013). It is combination between IoT paradigm and modern cloud technology. However, current storage infrastructure and file, systems cannot be used in IoT that will require processing, analysis and response to sensitive data that handles huge real-world infrastructures and processes. Therefore, considerations of security and protection become critical related with the specific technical characteristics of CoT things, networks and cloud technologies compatible with IoT architecture.

This chapter demonstrated the creation of CoT system faces many challenges and risks linked with specific technical and network characteristics of things. In particular, security threats and available solutions connected with resource-constrained nature of CoT devices were discussed and new security requirements that tackle the issue of CoT network were addressed. The future research should address the issue of CoT architecture deployment and implementation focusing on specific features of IoT integration with cloud computing services.

RECOMMENDATIONS

In order to achieve the goal of world cloud ecosystem, the stakeholders in the ICT sector needs to enact policies that embed the cloud computing in the global market and the business environment. The policies should further ensure timely address of issues affecting the cloud of things and encourage the business sector to embrace the new computing platform. To achieve the above, the global ICT stakeholders should consider implementing the following recommendations:

First, the ICT should intensify the progress in cloud research. The current clouds are based on the broader domain of computing utility, which overlap into other associated domains that are a result of several years of research and development. Consequently, there is significant risk that the research and development in the ICT sector may be repeated as opposed to being improved in the cloud computing. Therefore, the progress in the cloud computing field research should specifically focus on the cloud computing and the challenges currently affecting it. In other words, holistic approach is necessary to facilitate collaboration and use of results between associated domains such as grids, high performing computing and web services.

Two, the industry and research should concentrate on concerns facilitates long-term relevance. Therefore, any short term measures in research poses the risk of obsolesce in the near future instead of spearheading diversification and essential realization in the cloud of things capability. To avoid the ambiguity of the long-term relevance, the commercial interest needs to be clear in indicating the benefit and significant impact of such a long-term investment in the cloud-computing field.

Three, the ICT stakeholders need to facilitate smooth transition to the cloud of things arena. Many developers do not get enough support to test the possible cloud computing applications and services. That implies that we already have the cloud computing yet the necessary tools of trading are lacking. Similarly, the trading organizations also find it quite difficult to migrate their data to the clouds because of the security challenge. Evidently, the ICT sector has a lot more work to do in making the transition work.

Lastly, Cloud of things stakeholders need to encourage the establishment and adoption of standards. This will ensure that the developers of cloud applications, the cloud service providers and other parties offering cloud related services adhere to specific standards. That give confidence to the general public and other participants that the cloud computing is safe for use. Both the large scale SMEs and the Large-scale players will have equal platform to compete in cloud service provision.

REFERENCES

Aazam, M., Khan, I., Alsaffar, A. A., & Eui-Nam, H. (2014, January 14-18). Cloud of Things: Integrating Internet of Things and cloud computing and the issues involved. *Paper presented at the 2014 11th International Bhurban Conference on Applied Sciences and Technology (IBCAST)*.

Alohali, B., Merabti, M., & Kifayat, K. A New Key Management Scheme for Home Area Network (HAN) In Smart Grid.

Amies, A., Sluiman, H., Guo Tong, Q., & Ning Liu, G. (2012). Developing and Hosting Applications on the Cloud. IBM Press/Pearson.

Bandyopadhyay, D., & Sen, J. (2011). Internet of Things: Applications and Challenges in Technology and Standardization. *Wireless Personal Communications, 58*(1), 49–69. doi:10.1007/s11277-011-0288-5

Bhattasali, T., Chaki, R., & Chaki, N. (2013, December 13-15). Secure and trusted cloud of things. *Paper presented at the 2013 Annual IEEE India Conference (INDICON)*.

Chandramouli, R., Iorga, M., & Chokhani, S. (2014). *Cryptographic Key Management Issues and Challenges in Cloud Services*. Springer. doi:10.1007/978-1-4614-9278-8_1

Chao, L. (2012). *Cloud Computing for Teaching and Learning: Strategies for Design and Implementation*. Information Science Reference. doi:10.4018/978-1-4666-0957-0

Chaouchi, H. (2013). *The Internet of Things: Connecting Objects*. Wiley. doi:10.1002/9781118600146

Chen, L., & Gong, G. (2012). *Communication System Security*. Taylor & Francis.

Cucurull, J., & Guasch, S. (2014). *Virtual TPM for a secure cloud: fallacy or reality? daCosta, F. (2013). Rethinking the Internet of Things: A Scalable Approach to Connecting Everything*. Apress.

Distefano, S., Merlino, G., & Puliafito, A. (2012, July 4-6). Enabling the Cloud of Things. *Paper presented at the 2012 Sixth International Conference on Innovative Mobile and Internet Services in Ubiquitous Computing (IMIS)*.

El-Sayed, H., Mellouk, A., George, L., & Zeadally, S. (2008). Quality of service models for heterogeneous networks: overview and challenges. *Annals of telecommunications, 63*(11-12), 639-668. doi:10.1007/s12243-008-0064-z

Emary, I. M. M. E., & Ramakrishnan, S. (2013). *Wireless Sensor Networks: From Theory to Applications.* Taylor & Francis. doi:10.1201/b15425

Gál, Z., Almási, B., Dabóczi, T., Vida, R., Oniga, S., Baran, S., & Farkas, I. (2014). *Internet of Things: application areas and research results of the FIRST project.*

Gratton, D. A. (2013). *The Handbook of Personal Area Networking Technologies and Protocols.* Cambridge University Press. doi:10.1017/CBO9780511979132

Gubbi, J., Buyya, R., Marusic, S., & Palaniswami, M. (2013). Internet of Things (IoT): A vision, architectural elements, and future directions. *Future Generation Computer Systems, 29*(7), 1645–1660. doi:10.1016/j.future.2013.01.010

Hwang, K., Dongarra, J., & Fox, G. C. (2013). *Distributed and Cloud Computing: From Parallel Processing to the Internet of Things.* Elsevier Science.

Karnouskos, S. (2013, February 25-28). Smart houses in the smart grid and the search for value-added services in the cloud of things era. *Paper presented at the 2013 IEEE International Conference on Industrial Technology (ICIT).*

Kifayat, K., Merabti, M., & Shi, Q. (2010). Future security challenges in cloud computing. *International Journal of Multimedia Intelligence and Security, 1*(4), 428–442. doi:10.1504/IJMIS.2010.039241

McGrath, M. J., & Scanaill, C. N. (2013). *Sensor Technologies: Healthcare, Wellness and Environmental Applications.* Apress. doi:10.1007/978-1-4302-6014-1

Medaglia, C., & Serbanati, A. (2010). An Overview of Privacy and Security Issues in the Internet of Things. In D. Giusto, A. Iera, G. Morabito, & L. Atzori (Eds.), *The Internet of Things* (pp. 389–395). Springer New York. doi:10.1007/978-1-4419-1674-7_38

Menezes, A., van Oorschot, P., & Vanstone, S. (1996). Handbook of Applied Cryptography.

Miri, A. (2013). *Advanced Security and Privacy for RFID Technologies.* Information Science Reference. doi:10.4018/978-1-4666-3685-9

Ning, H. (2013). *Unit and Ubiquitous Internet of Things.* Taylor & Francis. doi:10.1201/b14742

Oh, S. W., & Kim, H. S. (2014). Decentralized access permission control using resource-oriented architecture for the Web of Things. *Paper presented at the 2014 16th International Conference on Advanced Communication Technology (ICACT).* doi:10.1109/ICACT.2014.6779062

Parwekar, P. (2011, September 15-17). From Internet of Things towards cloud of things. *Paper presented at the 2011 2nd International Conference on Computer and Communication Technology (ICCCT).*

Ren, L., Tian, F., Zhang, X., & Zhang, L. (2010). DaisyViz: A model-based user interface toolkit for interactive information visualization systems. *Journal of Visual Languages and Computing, 21*(4), 209–229. doi:10.1016/j.jvlc.2010.05.003

Rosado, D. G., Mellado, D., & Piattini, M. (2013). *Security Engineering for Cloud Computing: Approaches and Tools*. Information Science Reference. doi:10.4018/978-1-4666-2125-1

Saha, D., & Sridhar, V. (2012). *Next Generation Data Communication Technologies: Emerging Trends*. Information Science Reference. doi:10.4018/978-1-61350-477-2

Seong Hoon, K., & Daeyoung, K. (2013, June 28-July 3). Multi-tenancy Support with Organization Management in the Cloud of Things. *Paper presented at the 2013 IEEE International Conference on Services Computing (SCC)*.

Sharma, S., Shuman, M. A. R., Goel, A., Aggarwal, A., Gupta, B., Glickfield, S., & Guedalia, I. D. (2014). Context aware actions among heterogeneous internet of things (iot) devices: Google Patents.

Shon, T., Cho, J., Han, K., & Choi, H. (2014). Toward Advanced Mobile Cloud Computing for the Internet of Things: Current Issues and Future Direction. *Mobile Networks and Applications, 19*(3), 404–413. doi:10.1007/s11036-014-0509-8

Smith, S., & Marchesini, J. (2007). *The Craft of System Security*. Pearson Education.

Stavroulakis, P., & Stamp, M. (2010). *Handbook of Information and Communication Security*. Springer. doi:10.1007/978-3-642-04117-4

Sun, E., Zhang, X., & Li, Z. (2012). The internet of things (IOT) and cloud computing (CC) based tailings dam monitoring and pre-alarm system in mines. *Safety Science, 50*(4), 811–815. doi:10.1016/j.ssci.2011.08.028

Swaminatha, T. M., & Elden, C. R. (2003). *Wireless Security and Privacy: Best Practices and Design Techniques*. Addison-Wesley.

Vasseur, J. P., & Dunkels, A. (2010). *Interconnecting Smart Objects with IP: The Next Internet*. Elsevier Science.

Vouk, A. (2008). Cloud computing–issues, research and implementations. *CIT. Journal of Computing and Information Technology, 16*(4), 235–246. doi:10.2498/cit.1001391

Wang, Y., Lin, J., Annavaram, M., Jacobson, Q. A., Hong, J., Krishnamachari, B., & Sadeh, N. (2009). A framework of energy efficient mobile sensing for automatic user state recognition. *Paper presented at the Proceedings of the 7th international conference on Mobile systems, applications, and services*, Kraków, Poland. doi:10.1145/1555816.1555835

Xi, C., Jianming, L., Xiangzhen, L., Limin, S., & Yan, Z. (2011, October 14-16). Integration of IoT with smart grid. *Paper presented at the IET International Conference on Communication Technology and Application (ICCTA 2011)*.

A Younis, Y., Kifayat, K., & Merabti, M. (2014). An access control model for cloud computing. *Journal of Information Security and Applications*.

Zhou, H. (2013). *The Internet of Things in the Cloud: A Middleware Perspective*. Taylor & Francis.

KEY TERMS AND DEFINITIONS

Asymmetric Cryptography: Also known as public-key cryptography, asymmetric cryptography is a model of cryptography whereby a pair of keys is used in the encryption and decryption of a message for safe transfer. One key is used to encrypt a message, and all intended recipients can get the decryption key from a public database.

Data Mining: This involves analyzing Big Data in the search for patterns or relationships between variables.

Field Area Network (FAN): This is a combination of Neighborhood Area Networks and local devices, attached to a Field Area Router that offers a backhaul WAN interface.

Home Area Network (HAN): This is a network that is set up within a home. It entails a connection between digital devices, multiple computers, to telephones, televisions, home security systems, and other smart appliances wired into the network.

Internet of Things: This is a scenario where people, animals and other objects have unique identifiers, and are able to transfer data over a network without the need for human-to-computer or human-to-human interaction.

Neighbor Area Network (NAN): This is an offshoot of Wi-Fi hotspots and other wireless local area networks (WLANs) that enable users to share one access point to connect to the internet.

Secure Booting: This is a standard that was developed to make sure that a computer system boots only with a software that is trusted by the device manufacturer.

Virtualization: This is the creation of a virtual version of a computer hardware platforms, network resources, and even operating systems.

Wide Area Network (WAN): This is a telecommunications network covering a wide area, of a half mile or a mile radius.

Chapter 4
CCCE:
Cryptographic Cloud Computing Environment Based On Quantum Computations

Omer K. Jasim
Al-Ma'arif University College, Iraq

El-Sayed M. El-Horbaty
Ain Shams University, Egypt

Safia Abbas
Ain Shams University, Egypt

Abdel-Badeeh M. Salem
Ain Shams University, Egypt

ABSTRACT

Cloud computing technology is a modern emerging trend in the distributed computing technology that is rapidly gaining popularity in network communication field. Despite the advantages that the cloud platforms bolstered, it suffers from many security issues such as secure communication, consumer authentication, and intrusion caused by attacks. These security issues relevant to customer data filtering and lost the connection at any time. In order to address these issues, this chapter, introduces an innovative cloud computing cryptographic environment, that entails both Quantum Cryptography-as-service and Quantum Advanced Encryption Standard. CCCE poses more secure data transmission channels by provisioning secret key among cloud's instances and consumers. In addition, the QCaaS solves the key generation and key distribution problems that emerged through the online negotiation between the communication parties. It is important to note that the CCCE solves the distance limitation coverage problem that is stemmed from the quantum state property.

INTRODUCTION

In this era, computing is categorized according to their usage pattern. Parallel Computing, Sequential Computing, and Distributed Computing are a well-known form of computing technologies (Sunita & Seema, 2013). In general, distributed computing involved in many communication systems to solve a large scale communication problems. The growing of high-speed broadband networks and the rapid growth of the Internet changed the network communication way. Thus, the new trends of distributed computing

DOI: 10.4018/978-1-4666-9834-5.ch004

technology require integration between distributed computing systems and networking communication systems (Aidan, Hans, Patrick, and Damian, 2012). This integration allows computer networks to be involved in a distributed computing environment as full participants in other sharing computing resources such as CPU capacity and memory/disk space.

Emerging trends in distributed computing paradigm include grid computing, utility computing and cloud computing (Sunita & Seema, 2013). These emerging distributed computing together with the development of networking technologies are changing the entire computing paradigm toward a new trend in distributed computing. This chapter describes the emerging technology in distributed computing which known as cloud computing.

Cloud computing is a specialized form of grid and utility computing, and that takes grid computing style when the dynamic connection service and the virtual resources service are available through the internet. In addition, any cloud architecture consisting of many layers (Service Platform Infrastructure layers-SPI) such as the infrastructure as a service (IaaS), the platform as a service (PaaS), the Software as a Service (SaaS) and some others collectively as a services (*aaS). These services layers offer numerous roles as reducing the hardware costs, providing the reliability of each consumer and provisioning resources on-demand (Chander & Yogesh, 2013; Mohammad, John, & Ingo, 2010).

SPI layers and Service Level Agreements (SLA) provide communication between cloud services provider (CSP) and consumers using cloud networks. Since cloud computing environment is a virtual and dynamic, it requires a scalable hardware that supports the virtualization technology and data transformation remotely. Data transformations remotely expose the whole cloud environment to various attacks (Faiza, 2012; Mather & Kumaraswamy, 2012). Therefore, a secure communication is an essential prerequisite for opening cloud environment as a robust and feasible solution (Kumaraswamy, 2012). Many distinct cloud security groups discussed the security vulnerabilities in the cloud computing and classified the possible vulnerabilities into cloud characteristics-related and security controls- related (Omer, Safia, El-Sayed & Abdel-Badeeh, 2014).

Despite different groups try to solve the security challenges in cloud computing, many gaps and threads are still uncovered or handled. Accordingly, the cryptographic tools are installed and developed in many cloud computing environments. These tools require a long-term secret key to guaranteeing the encryption/decryption process, which in turn, considered a valuable target for various attacks (Doelitzsch, Reich, Kahl & Clarke, 2011).

In the cloud computing environment, deploying such long-secret key for any modern encryption algorithm (symmetric or asymmetric) ensures the data confidentiality (prevention of unauthorized disclosure of information), integrity (change in the data), and availability (readiness of correctional services) (CSA, 2012, Omer, Safia, El-Sayed & Abdel-Badeeh, 2013). Despite the solvable problems based such long secret key, the key management and distribution problems still disclosed.

Quantum Key Distribution (QKD) addresses these problems in distributed computing and negotiation mechanism. It can preserve data privacy when users interact with remote computing centers remotely (Doelitzscher, Reich, Knahl & Clarke, 2011; Dabrowski, Mills, & orphan, 2011).

This chapter presents a robust cloud cryptographic environment that completely depends on quantum computations and a newly developed symmetric encryption algorithm. In addition, this chapter introduces an innovative CCCE, which poses more secured data transmission by provisioning secret key among cloud's instances based on QCaaS layer. Finally, this chapter solves the distance limitation coverage problem, by measures the randomness of qubits based on the NIST and DIEHARD test suite algorithms (Juan S., 2012; Andrew, Juan, James, Miles, Elaine and Stefan, 2013).

The rest of the chapter is organized as follows; Section 2 surveys the existing methods for cloud computing security issues such privacy, confidentiality, and key management. The background of cloud computing related-technologies, cloud security precautions, standard cloud cryptographic models, modern cloud cryptographic algorithms, and QKD technology are given in Section 3. Section 4 presents in details the CCCE development and the basic software/hardware requirements. QCaaS is explained in Section 5. Section 6 discusses in details the main building block of CCCE. CCCE phases are illustrated in Section6.

Section7 presents the CCCE characteristics and analysis. Finally, Section 8 shows the conclusion and future work.

RELATED WORKS

This section shows the literature survey correlated with the cloud data privacy, confidentiality and cloud key management.

Cloud Data Privacy and Confidentiality

Despite different studies' attempts to solve the security problem in cloud communications, many gaps and threads are still uncovered or handled. Accordingly, numerous efforts have been exerted in order overcome such gaps.

Wang et al. (2012) introduced the anonymity based method for achieving the cloud privacy. In which, the anonymity algorithm has processed the data and the output released to the cloud provider. The anonymous output is split into different tables or parts and stored on multiple service providers' storages. If the user needs to restore the meaningful information, he/she has to get all the parts or tables. Two cases have been manipulated in this study:

- **Case 1:** if one service provider aggregates the meaningful contents depending on collecting the service from other services and providing data to the consumers'. Here, there is no preservation of privacy because the aggregating service provider may read or leak the information.
- **Case 2:** if the consumers have to aggregate themselves, then they have to contact multiple service providers, which will reduce the efficiency of the service on-demand.

Itani et al. (2012) proposed the privacy-as-a-services (PaaS) model, in which, the contents are divided into two parts: sensitive and non-sensitive. Sensitive data are encrypted based on the modern encryption algorithm, but a non-sensitive data kept as plain. In general, sensitive data is decrypted by the consumer with the shared secret key between consumer and the CSP. Here, the service providers are maintaining the key in tamper-resistance device/memory with the help of the trusted third party then it is again like the standard cloud scenario.

Stephen et al. (2013) proposed the model based on obfuscation mechanism for the cloud infrastructure and ultimately based on assigned VMs. This model setups the encryption key for each trusted consumer and encrypted all the consumer-data stored in the cloud. In this model, the data goes out of the VM will be encrypted to avoid the network sniffing by CSP or others. This model is very efficient if the data are posted and accessed by a single person. Otherwise, the consumer faced the same problem mentioned in the previous model (Syam, Subramanian & Thamizh., 2010). In addition, if the consumer is posting the content as on-demand for end-users, decryption key and de-obfuscation procedure need to be setup with each one. Otherwise, it is not feasible for them to read the data. The foible of this model summarizes in case of increasing the number of end users, the key revocation and re-distribution between the data owner and end-user stilled uncover.

Emmanuel et al. (2013) described a data security system in cloud computing based DES algorithm to secure consumer and cloud server. The security architecture of the system was developed by using DES- Cipher Block Chaining (CBC), which eliminates the data stolen. However, DES algorithm hacked by many attackers such as man-in-the-middle attack, side channel attack, and Differential Power Analysis (DPA) in which the key expansion phase is exploited in the DES structure.

Doelitzscher et al. (2011) identified the abuse of cloud resources, lack of security monitoring in cloud infrastructure and the defective isolation of shared resources as focal points to be managed. They also focused on the lack of flexibility of intrusion detection mechanisms to handle virtualized environments and suggesting the use of special security tools associated with the business flow modeling through security SLAs. In addition, the analysis of the highest security concerns is also based on publications from CSA, ENISA, and NIST, without offering a detail quantitative compilation of security risks and areas of concern. Table 1 summarizes the characteristics of the surveyed cloud security studies by describing the innovative security model, cloud operating environment, security issues, and weaknesses.

Finally, we can conclude that the cryptographic mechanism is an essential field for the cloud security process. In addition, due to the dynamic characteristics of cloud technology there are many challenges regarding the securing for communications. These challenges lie in the existence of a robust security model that guarantees a trusted data transformation.

Key Management

In order to achieve the cloud data privacy and confidentiality (mentioned above), the efficiency of key management and re-keying with consumers is vital for cloud cryptographic process. Hence, this section reviews the existing models related to the key management between consumers and CSP in order to achieve the privacy and confidentiality.

Table 1. Characteristics of the cloud data privacy studies

Authors	Innovative Model	Cloud Environment	Security Issues	Weaknesses
Wang et al.(2012)	Anonymity	Amazon EC2	data privacy, authorization, accountability	Unbalancing between the number of consumers and CSP efficiency
Itani et al.(2012)	Privacy as Services (PasS)	Hyper-V	data privacy, availability, data protection	Apt of tamper-resistance (device/memory), leakage of third trusted party
Stephen et al.(2013)	Obfuscation	Xen-Server	data privacy, key distribution, confidence	Inconvenient between the key revocation and re-distribution with no. of users
Emanuel et al.(2013)	Cryptographic Model	Hyper-V	CIA issues	Cryptographic algorithm hacked by DPA family attackers
Doelitzscher et al.(2011)	Abuse Identification	Own Cloud	Non-repudiation, integrity, digital signature	Don't offering a deeper quantitative compilation of security risks

Bethencourt et al. (2011) presented an Attribute-Based Encryption (ABE) model in the cloud environment and social networks. The model allows consumers to participate in two or more groups. These groups help to assign the encryption key for each registered consumer. In order to compute and distribute the encryption key for each consumer involved in the groups, the logical expression is used. The computational cost (time and space) and rekeying to members in the same group are central weakness in the ABE model.

Mather et al. (2012) discussed the encryption mechanisms, key management capabilities and expatriated multi-entity key management mechanism in cloud computing. Also, this study examined the status of cloud computing security depending on security management, data security, and identity management. This study explored the urge for more transparency to providing the security capability in the cloud environment, therefore, the need for standardization and the creation of legal agreements reflecting the operational SLAs. However, this study does not explain the role of SLA in the security of an open cloud environment.

Cutillo et al. (2009) presented the simple shared key - consumer side storage model. The encryption key is generated based on the consumer attributes and shared with all consumers in the group. This key is given by CSP using consumer public key. In case the CSP wants to change the encryption key to revoke a particular consumer, the CSP needs to change the deployed key with a newly inherited key. In addition, the new inherited key needs to be distributed to everyone again and the decryption key is stored on the consumer machines. Consequently, the key should be transferred only to group not to all the consumers connected to the network, this is a useful advantage of this model.

Rawal et al. (2012) described the perfect alliance between cloud computing and quantum computing trends, which guarantees data safety for hosted files on remote computers or datacenter. He encrypted heavy duty of data by using the highly processing servers as a quantum computer, which hides input, processing and output data from malicious and attacks based on the quantum computations mechanism. However, the performance examination of such hybrid technique on practical cloud environment is missing.

Miao Zhou (2012) presented the tree-based key management model in cloud computing. The vital idea of this study is to design a secure and flexible key management mechanism for the data in cloud computing. The cloud database remains private and secure while some selected data and key nodes are shared with other parties in the cloud. The flexibility of key management is achieved and the security is proved in such proposed model. Finally, Table 2 summarizes the key management studies in the cloud environment by describing the innovative model, advantages and disadvantages for each one.

BACKGROUND

Cloud computing technology is a result of the integration of current computing technologies. These computing technologies, which are deployed based on the cloud functionality, are virtualization, service-oriented architecture (SOA), utility computing, grid computing, parallel computing, and cluster computing. Virtualization and SOA are core technologies for cloud computing (Nelson, Charles, Fernando, Marco, Tereza, Mats and Makan, 2014). Virtualization abstracts the underlying physical infrastructure, which is the most equipped component, and makes it accessible and easy to be used and managed (Syam, Subramanian and Thamizh, 2010). Whereas, SOA offers an easier way for cloud framework understanding and management (Chadwick, Casanova, 2011).

Table 2. Characteristics of the cloud key management studies

Authors	Innovative Model	Advantages	Disadvantages
Bethencourt et al. (2011)	Attribute-Based Encryption(ABE)	Assign keys for each registered clients into involved group	Computational cost in ABE, key assigned
Mather et al.(2012)	multi-entity key management	Defeating a passive and a side channel attacks, enhancing of identity management	Conflicted with SLA led to apt to sniffing attack
Cutillo et al.(2009)	Simple Shared Key 1-Client-side	Defeating a distributed DoS attacks, almost active attacks	Key group storage vulnerable to authentication attacks
Rawal et al.(2012)	Quantum cloud computing	Guarantees data protection for hosted files on remote computers from malicious and attacks	High costly to implement, coverage distance limitation
Miao Zhou.(2012)	tree-based key management	Design a secure and flexible key management mechanism	Leakage for key generation and distribution

Despite most of the computing technologies trends suffered from the security issues, such as data security, cryptographic key distribution, key availability, identity, etc. Nevertheless, the major challenge in security issues addressed in data transmission, especially for cloud computing trend. Since the consumer's confidential data and business logics reside in the remote cloud servers, competitors and intruders are expected to attack such transmission process (Mandeep, Manish, 2012). This section presents in detail the cloud security precautions, classical cryptographic cloud algorithms, quantum technology features, and basic cloud encryption models.

Cloud Security Precautions

The improvement of cloud computing technology reinforced by the improvement of the security concerns. Thus, various cloud security management has been developed.

CSA security guidance (CSA, 2012, ENISA security assessment 2014, and IDC, 2014) highly focus on different security issues related to cloud computing. Such issues require further studies in order to appropriately handle and enhancing the technology acceptance and adoption. Accordingly, in order to concentrate and organize information related to cloud security next subsections shed light on the distinctive cloud security issues such as network security, cloud data security, and virtualization.

Network Security

Almost problems associated with network communications and configurations effect on cloud security infrastructures (Manpreet, Rajbir, 2013). Potential levels of cloud network security are (Nelson, Charles, Fernando, Marco, Tereza, Mats and Makan, 2014):

- **Connection Level:** distributed architectures, massive resource sharing and synchronization between cloud virtual machines require Virtual Private Network (VPN) and domain controller connection mechanisms. These mechanisms protected the cloud network environment against most types of attacks like spoofing, man-in-middle, and side channel attacks.

- **Firewalls Level:** firewalls protect the CSP (internal IaaS) against insiders and outsiders intruders (Jensen, Schwenk, Gruschka and Iacono, 2009). They also enable VM isolation, filtering the addressing mechanism, prevention of DoS, and detection external attacks by combination with sub-domain controller policy.
- **Configurations Level:** configurations help to provide a level of security and privacy without performance or efficiency compromised.

Cloud Data Security

In order to achieve a secure cloud data environment, Confidentiality, Availability, Integrity and Traceability (CAIT) requirements must be provided. So, the following mechanisms must be guarantee (William, 2012; Omer, Safia, El-Sayed and Abdel-Badeeh, 2014).

- **Cryptographic Mechanism:** a practice method to secure sensitive data by the transformation of a cloud consumer's data into ciphertext. In the cloud environment, a cryptographic data deploys as a service offered by CSP. So, the cloud consumers' must take the time to learn about the provider's policies and procedures for encryption and key management. Finally, the cloud encryption capabilities of the service provider need to match the level of sensitivity of the data being hosted.
- **Replications Mechanism:** it is essential to avoid data loss, it achieves based on many intelligent algorithms such as, Replica Location Services (RLS) (Doelitzscher, Reich, Kahl., Clarke, 2011), Quantum Evolutionary Algorithm (QEA) (Ammar,Khaled, Muneer, Eman, 2013) and others (Christain, Mario, 2011).
- **Disposal Mechanism:** elementary data disposal techniques are insufficient and commonly referred as deletion, and it is considered essential requirements for cloud datacenters. Finally, in the cloud environment the complete destruction of data including log references and hidden backup registers (Omer, Safia, El-Sayed and Abdel-Badeeh, 2014).

Cloud Computing Attacks

Despite cloud computing environments are getting more familiar, its main risk is the intrusion caused by the attackers. A most known communication attack mechanisms in a cloud computing environment which are discussed in (Omer, Safia, El-Sayed and Abdel-Badeeh, 2014).

Virtualization

According to (Syam, Subramanian and Thamizh, 2010) the main problem associated with virtualization technologies are VMs'- isolation, hypervisor vulnerabilities, data leakage, and VM identification.

- **Isolation:** Despite logically VM-isolated, all VMs share the same hardware and consequently the same resources. This act is vulnerable for allowing malicious entities to exploit data leaks and cross-VM attacks (Soren, Sven, and Hugo, 2013).

- **Hypervisor Vulnerabilities:** It is the central component of virtualization technology. However, it suffers from many security vulnerabilities like escape affords attackers, hyper-jacking (thin hypervisor) and others. The solutions of this problem are still scarce and often proprietary, demanding further studied to harden these security aspects.
- **Data Leakage:** exploit hyper vulnerabilities and lack of isolation controls in order to leak data from virtualized infrastructures, obtaining sensitive consumers data and affecting confidentiality and integrity (Omer, Safia, El-Sayed and Abdel-Badeeh, 2014).
- **VM Identification:** lack of controls for identifying VMs that are being used for executing a particular process or substantial files.

Consumer Identification

Consumer identification is an important aspect of cloud computing. Only authorized user has ability to write, access and the data contents (Omer, Safia, El-Sayed and Abdel-Badeeh, 2014). Therefore, the authorization manner with the encryption provision give a secure environment for data resident in the cloud. Without user "id" verification, the system will not allow any of the requests made to some transactions, which will ultimately help in data privacy and security.

Standard Cloud Cryptographic Models

This section illustrates the basic cryptographic mechanisms that deployed in the cloud computing environment through the last three years.

Cipher Cloud Model

Cipher cloud is a new emerging rend in encryption/decryption processes for cloud data files. It protected enterprise data using formatting and operations-preserving encryption and tokenized in any private or public cloud environment without affecting functionality, usability, or performance (Omer, Safia, El-Sayed and Abdel-Badeeh, 2014). In addition, Cipher cloud provides a unified cloud encryption gateway with award-winning technology to encrypt sensitive data in real-time before it is sent to the cloud

As shown in Figure 1, consumers probably have data stored in multiple clouds such as Google, Amazon, Azure, and many others. Cipher cloud work as a firewall security gateway that sits between users and cloud applications and it applies encryption to the data before sensitive data leave the enterprise. Furthermore, it offers multiple AES-compatible encryptions and tokenized options, including format and function-preserving encryption algorithms. Consumers see the real data when gaining access to an application through the Cipher Cloud security gateway, but the data stored in a cloud application is encrypted.

Moreover, by applying encryption in a cloud security gateway, cipher cloud eliminates the inherent security, privacy, and regulatory compliance risks of cloud computing. The cipher cloud security gateway uses flexible, configurable policies to identify sensitive data and automatically encrypt/decrypt data between users and the cloud using encryption keys that remain under the control at all times.

Finally, cipher cloud reverses the process when consumers access cloud applications over the algorithm decrypting data in real time so that users browse the actual data rather than the encrypted version that resides within the cloud datacenter.

Figure 1. Cipher cloud architecture

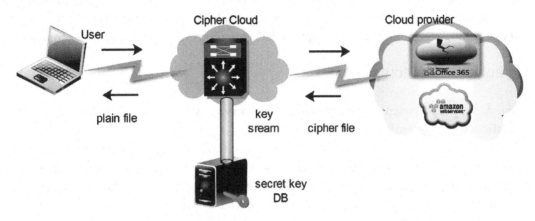

Cryptographic as-a-Service Model

Soren et al. present a security architecture that permits establishing secure consumer-controlled-cryptography-as-a-service (CaaS) in the cloud. CaaS provides consumers to be full control of their credentials and cryptographic primitives. All these operations provided based on Trusted Platform Module (TPM) known as sub inherited domain from Xen hypervisor. Figure 2 illustrates the CaaS architecture using Xen hypervisor.

All consumers' operations run in a protected and secure execution domain that achieved by modifying the Xen hypervisor and the leveraging standard Trusted Computing Technology (TCT). Moreover, this model is legacy-compatible by installing a transparent cryptographic layer for the storage and network I/O on the VM. Finally, this type of cryptographic data cloud protects consumers from any unauthorized

Figure 2. CaaS Architecture

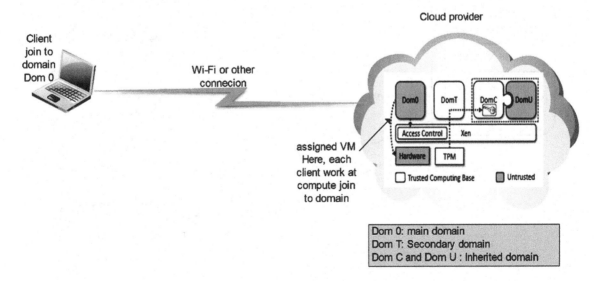

access that tries to extract cryptographic material from the VM – either from a privileged management domain or from outside the VM. However, this model vulnerable to authentication and side channel attacks due to all controlling mechanisms and encryption/decryption processes assigned to the consumer side.

Cryptographic Cloud Storage Model

Patil D. and Akshay R proposed a virtual private storage services that would satisfy the standard requirements (Confidentiality, Integrity, Authentication,.etc.).

Most of the desires are obtained by encrypting the files stored in the cloud environment, but encryption makes it very complex to search through such files or to collaborate in real time editing. This model introduced an architecture for a cryptographic storage service that would solve the security problems of "backups, archives, health record systems, secure data exchange, and e-discovery".

This architecture is based on three components see Figure 3:

- **Data Processor (DP):** Processes the data before sending it to the cloud.
- **Data Verifier (DV):** Validates the data's consistency and integrity.
- **Token Generator (TG):** Generates an indexing token allowing the service provider to retrieve files.

The consumer solution contains using a local application that has the three above mentioned components. Before uploading data to the cloud, consumers' uses the data processor to encrypt and encode the documents along with their meta-data (tags, time, size, etc.). Then, send them into the cloud environment. When consumers' wants to download some documents, he/she uses the TG to generate an index token

Figure 3. Cryptographic cloud storage architecture (Patil D. and Akshay R., 2012)

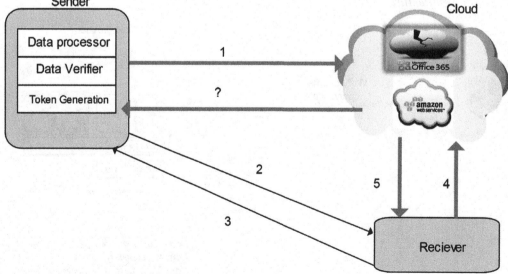

and a decryption key. Moreover, the token is sent to the cloud storage provider to select the encrypted files to be downloaded or browsed. After that, the DV is invoked to verify the integrity of the data using a master key. The document is decrypted using the decryption key.

In general, the encryption process strategy in cloud environments mainly depends on encrypting the data in two different phases;

1. The transmission process before sending the data to the cloud and
2. The storage process after the transmission and before the storing process.

Cloud Cryptographic Algorithms (CCA)

According to cloud cryptographic models mentioned above, all of them relied on modern classical encryption algorithms (symmetric and asymmetric). In most cases, cloud computing designer and programmer use the symmetric encryption algorithm due to efficiency, scalable and easy to implementation (Omer, Safia, El-Sayed and Abdel-Badeeh, 2013). Employing an appropriate strength encryption process is essential, so, many encryption algorithms have been developed and implemented in order to provide more secure data transmission in the cloud environment. Data Encryption Standard (DES), Advanced Encryption Standard (AES), Rivest Cipher-4 (RC4), Blowfish, and 3DES fare well-known of symmetric category, while, Rivest, Shanon, Adelman (RSA) and Deffi-Hillman(DH) for asymmetric type. Table 3 summarizes the characteristics of the encryption algorithms, both symmetric and asymmetric (Winkler, 2011; Omer, Safia, El-Sayed and Abdel-Badeeh, 2013; William, 2012).

Obviously from the above table, that the symmetric encryption techniques are more popularly used than asymmetric ones in cloud computing. In a cloud environment, a cryptographic key deploys to one type of encryption algorithms to provide the encryption/decryption processes. These algorithms assist in providing the data CIAT continuously (William, 2012)

Omer K. et al. (2013) implemented the mentioned symmetric and asymmetric algorithms in order to ensure the data security in a cloud environment. In addition, they examined the performance of such algorithms, considering the time of the encryption/ decryption process and the size of the output encrypted files. Accordingly, symmetric encryption techniques are faster than the asymmetric encryption

Table 3. Encryption Algorithms characteristics (S= symmetric, A= asymmetric)

Algorithm	Category	Key size (bits)	Input size (bits)	Attack apt	Initial vector size (bits)
AES	S	128; 192; 256	128	Non recognized yet	128
DES	S	56	64	Brute force attack	64
3-DES	A	112- 168	64	Brute force attack	64
RC4	S	256	256	Bit flipping attack	256
Blowfish	S	32-448	32	Dictionary attack	64
RSA	A	>1024	>1024	Timing attack	-
DH	A	n-Key Exchange	n	Ping attack	-

techniques, and AES algorithm guarantees more efficiency from others. Moreover, all algorithms in both categories (symmetric and asymmetric) archive the inverse proportion relation between the running time and the input file size, except the RSA algorithm. The RSA runs time changes slightly with the input file size increase (Omer, Safia, El-Sayed and Abdel-Badeeh, 2013).

Despite the encryption process uses complex techniques for random key generation based on mathematical models and computations, its encryption strategy considered vulnerable. So, if the intruder is good enough in mathematical computation field such quantum attack, he/she can easily decrypt the cipher and retrieve the original transmitted or stored documents. Furthermore, the key distribution problem ascends from the fact that communicating parties must somehow share a secret key before any secure communication can be initiated, and both parties must ensure that the key remains secret. Of course, direct key distribution is not always feasible due to risk, inconvenience, and cost factors (Winkler, 2011).In some situations, the direct key exchange is possible through a secure communication channel. However, this security can never guarantee. A fundamental problem remains because, in principle, any classical private channel can be monitored passively, without the sender or receiver knowing that the eavesdropper has taken place (Christain, Mario, 2010). Thus, in order to overcome this obstacle, key distribution, and mathematical computations, an unconditional secure concept must be provided. QKD system provides an unconditional security concept, because of, it ultimately depends on quantum mechanics in key generation and management (Christain, Mario, 2010; Bart De Decker, André Zúquete, 2014).

Quantum Technology

Recently, quantum technology (QT) flourished and spread rapidly in many disciplines, DNA, AI, and quantum communications are examples of such disciplines. The importance of QT is lying in its ability to solve the key challenges associated with distributed computing environments based on QKD (Ammar, Khaled, Muneer, Eman 2013; Christain, Mario, 2010). This section illustrates an unconditional QKD security scheme. As shown in Figure 4, QKD enables secret quantum keys exchanging between two different parties through two communication channels, classical and quantum channels (Omer, Safia, El-Sayed and Abdel-Badeeh, 2014). It is an alternative to the classical encryption algorithms (symmetric or asymmetric categories) and used to solve the common existing scheme problems such as key distribution, management, and defeating attacks (Omer, Safia, El-Sayed and Abdel-Badeeh, 2015).

Furthermore, in order to exchange the keys between communication parties, well-known protocols were developed such as Charles H. Bennett and Gilles Brassard-1984 (BB84) and Artur Ekert-1991 (E91). After then, these protocols are utilized by QKD for exchanging process. This chapter utilizes a BB84 protocol since it enjoys with many advantages with E91 protocol. Higher bit rate (up to 6 Mbps), secure up to 140 KM and resistance against Photon number splitting (PNS) and Man-in-the-middle attacks (Solange G., Mohammed A., 2014) are examples of these advantages. Finally, BB84 protocol utilizes four primary phases in order to generate a final secret quantum key. These phases illustrated as follows:

Raw Key Extraction (RKE)

The main purpose of RKE phase is to eliminate all possible errors occurred during the bits discussion (generation and transmission) over the quantum channel. Negotiated parties (i.e. Sender and receiver) compare their filter types used for each photon, unmatched polarization is eliminated otherwise, bits are considered (Omer, Safia, El-Sayed and Abdel-Badeeh, 2014).

Figure 4. QKD architecture

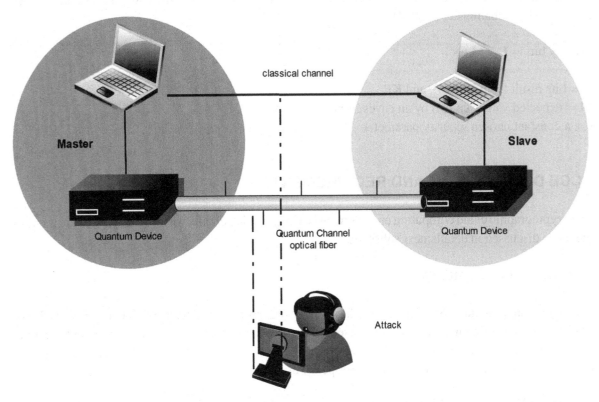

Error Estimation (EE)

The negotiation process might occur over a noisy quantum and unsecured (public) classical channel. Such channel can cause a partial key damage or physical noise of transmission medium (Solange G., Mohammed A., 2014). In order to avoid such problems, both parties determine an error threshold value "*Emax*" when they are sure that there is no eavesdropping on a transmission medium. So as to calculate the error percentage (*Er*), the raw bits are monitored and compared with the Emax, if *Er* > *Emax*, then it is probably either unexpected noise or eavesdroppers.

Key Reconciliation (KR)

Key reconciliation is implemented to minimize the mentioned errors associated with the key as much as possible. It divides the raw key into blocks of K bits; then parity bit calculations are done for each block (Solange G., Mohammed A., 2014). The creating blocks and parity calculations are performed for N-rounds depending on the length of the raw key.

Privacy Amplification (PA)

Privacy Amplification is the final step in the quantum key extraction. It is applied to minimize the number of bits based on equation one that a listener might know. Sending and receiving parties apply a shrinking method to their bit sequences in order to obscure the eavesdropper ability to capture bit sequence (Solange G., Mohammed A., 2014).

Privacy bits = **L – M – s** (1)

L = bits result from RK, EE, and KR
M = expected values known by an eavesdropper
s = a constant chosen security parameter

CCCE DEVELOPMENT AND REQUIREMENTS

The cryptographic cloud computing environment (CCCE), which entails software and hardware requirements, is discussed in details next subsections.

Software Requirements

In this section, a randomness property of the qubits generation based quantum cipher system and proposed encryption algorithm(QAES) be presented associated with a simulator of QAES and quantum cipher. In general, the environment has been implemented using Visual Studio Ultimate 2012 (VC#) based Windows Server 2012 Data Center as operating system.

Quantum Key Distribution Usage

Quantum key generation mainly relies on photons' exchanging between parties over limited distances (314-kilometer) (Solange, Mohammed, 2014; Eduared, 2014,). Such distance limitation is considered as an obstacle to the vast organization and evading usage of such quantum communications based world area network. Therefore, to overcome this obstacle, NIST and DIEHARD algorithms have been implemented for testing and evaluating the randomness rates for a quantum key generation. The computation of randomness rate in the NIST and DIEHARD algorithms completely depend on p-value (Omer, Safia, El-Sayed and Abdel-Badeeh, 2014; Matthew, Caleb, Lamas, Christian, 2013). In general, the calculation for randomness of binary digits can be summarized into the following steps:

Stating the null hypothesis (assume that the binary sequence is random).
Computing a sequence test static with different test suite (based on the bit level)
Calculating the *p*-value (always P-value).
Compare the *p*-value produced to α (usually α=0.01 for all randomness testers), if the *p*-value less than 0.01, then sequence digits generated are failing (S. Juan, 2012).

In a sense, NIST and DIEHARD implemented on the output of RKE, which obtained before PA phase. After then, these algorithms are run on the output of PA phase as well. Regarding (Omer, Safia, El-Sayed and Abdel-Badeeh, 2014), Figure 5 shows the average of the P-values for five QKD-rounds with equal length (100000-bits); the P-value obtained depending on 14 tests are mentioned in S. Juan, 2012.

As shown in Figure 5, the P-value indicates the true randomness of the qubits generation and periodically changed with the rounds' contents. The randomness characteristic helps to adopt the QKD as a source to generate a random number that used with various encryption algorithms (Omer, Safia, El-Sayed and Abdel-Badeeh, 2014).

Symmetric Quantum Encryption Algorithm

This subsection describes a new trend of the symmetric quantum standard encryption algorithm (QAES). This trend incorporates both the QKD and the enhanced version of the AES in order to provide an unconditional security level (Christain, Mario, 2010) for any cipher system built on symmetric encryption algorithms. Figure 6 illustrates that the QAES utilizes the dynamic quantum S-box (DQS-boxes) that is generated from the QKD and exploits the generated key in the encryption /decryption process, instead of the ordinary used static S-boxes.

The DQS-boxes enjoy the dynamic mechanism, which in turn, the contents of each S-Box changes consequently in each round with the change of the key generation. Such dynamic mechanism aids in solving the mechanical problems associated with the traditional S-Boxes such as avoiding an off-line analysis attack and resistant to the quantum attack. Figure 7 shows the pseudo-code of DQS-box has been developed.

Figure 7 shows the achieving process of the DQS-box and InvDQS-box generation by choosing the index d of the bytes *b* from the quantum cipher, which depends on variables *i*, m and *l*. The operation of DQS-box generation is terminated when m equals to 256, which represents the interval value of DQS-

Figure 5. Randomness tests for qubits generation based 5-QKD different rounds

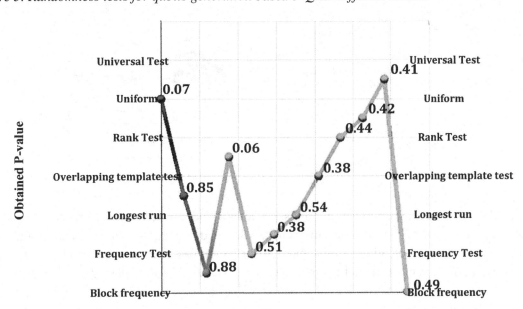

Figure 6. Single round for QAES

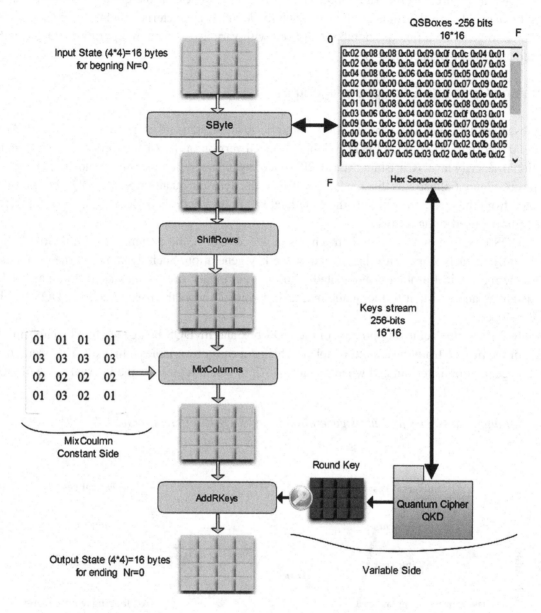

box [0-255]. Furthermore, the number of rounds, key length, and input plain text equivalent to classical AES algorithm. Accordingly, QAES development and design do not contradict the security of the AES algorithm and all the mathematical criteria and transformation functions remain unchanged. For more details about QAES architecture and nature of work see (Omer, Safia, El-Sayed and Abdel-Badeeh, 2014). Figure 8 shows the performance examination of QAES in the CCCE considering the time of the encryption/ decryption process and the size of the output encrypted files. This examination implemented using several input file sizes: 500kb, 1000kb, 1500kb, 2000kb, 3000kb, and 4000kb and the running time is calculated in milliseconds.

Figure 7. Pseudo code of DQS-box

Algorithm: Generation a DQS-box and Inverse DQS-box[1]

- **Input: stream of a quantum key q from QKD cipher**
- **Output: hexadecimal numbers which are arrange in 2-D matrix [16*16].**

// Encryption Process

1. *Initial value* $(i = 0, m = 1, and\ l = 1)$
2. *while* $(m < 256$
   {
        a. $i = i + 1;$
        b. $d = 1 + (m + 1 * l)\ mod\ 176$
        c. $S(i + 1) = S(i) + b(d) mod\ 256;$
        d. $l = 0;$
3. *for* $j = 1\ to\ m\ do$
   {
        a. *If* $(S(i + 1) = S(j)$ *//compare between* $S(i + 1)$ *and* $S(j)$ *and compute the elelmets*
        b. *Go to step* 4
        c. *else*
        d. *Go to step* 2
        e. $J + +;$
   }
4. *if* $l = j$
   {
        a. $DQSbox(m + 1) = DQSbox(i + 1);$
        b. $m = m + 1$
   }
   } *// end for while*

// Decryption process

5. *for* $m = 1\ to\ 256\ do$
   {
   $InvDQSbox(DQSbox(m) + 1) = m - 1;$
   }

Comparing the QAES with others encryption algorithms, theQAES reflects a higher security level. However, it takes longer time than others due to the time consumed in the quantum key generation process (time for quantum negotiation and time required for the encryption / decryption process).

Hardware Requirements

CCCE utilizes many operations such as the number of VMs, quality of services (QoS), storage capacity and other features depending on the IaaS layer. This layer helps consumers to rent virtual resources like network and VMs and configure them according their needs.

Accordingly, the bare-metal Hyper-V and the System Center 2012 SP1(SCSP1) components are explained and implemented (Aidan, Hans, Patrick, Damian, 2012). System Center Virtual Machine

Figure 8. An efficient of QAES on Quantum Cloud environment

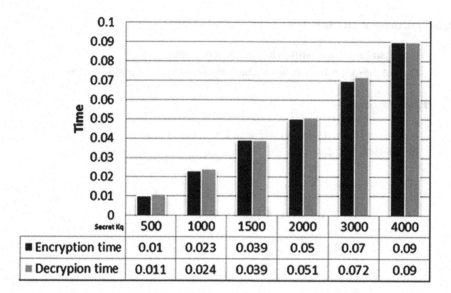

Secret Kq	500	1000	1500	2000	3000	4000
■ Encryption time	0.01	0.023	0.039	0.05	0.07	0.09
▦ Decrypion time	0.011	0.024	0.039	0.051	0.072	0.09

Manager (SCVMM), System Center Operation Manager (SCOM), Application Controller (AC), and Operation Services Manager (OSM) are basic components of SCSP1. The main host server utilizes the Core i5 (4.8GHz) with 16GB of RAM with 2TB-HDD as the central hardware. As shown in Figure 9, CCCE includes the following servers:

- **Domain controller "qcloud.net":** It is the central server that manages a single sign process and offers a response multiple cloud services. It deploys a credential account for each trusted consumer and provides a trust connection among consumers and cloud instances. Moreover, it helps to defeat bot the insider attack and denial of service attack (DoS). Finally, it holds the right to access hardware resources.
- **SQL Server:** Each SCSP1 site database can be installed on either the default instance or a named instance of an SQL Server installation. The SQL Server instance can be co-located with the site server, or on a remote computer. In the CEEE, a remote SQL Server is implemented and configured as a failover cluster in either a single instance or a multiple instance configuration. It is responsible for keeping the credential of *SCVMM* and *SCOM* services and creating the report viewer for all operations.
- **SCVMM Server:** it manages the virtualized data center, visualization host, and storage resources. It can integrate with other system center components (mentioned above), deploy a management console operations and cloud configuration wizards. Moreover, it creates VM templates, capability profiles (Aidan, Hans, Patrick, Damian, 2012), ISO images, private cloud objects, and self-service user roles.
- **AC server:** it mainly depends on *SCVMM* to manage applications and services, which in turn, are deployed in private or public cloud infrastructures. It provides a unified self-service portal that helps to configure, deploy, and manage VMs and services on predefined templates. Although some administrator tasks can be performed via the *APPC* console, the users for APPC cannot be considered as administrators.

Figure 9. CCCE servers architecture

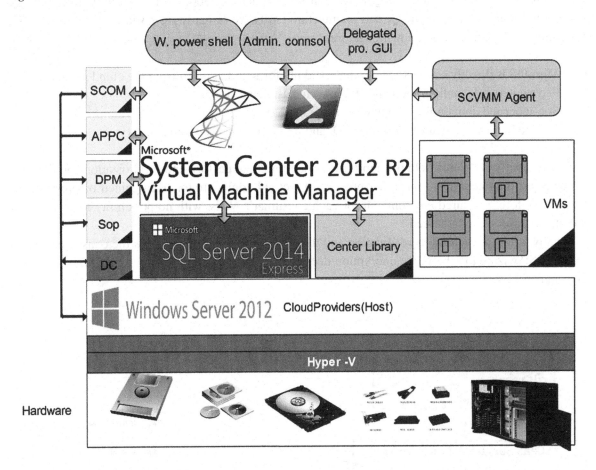

- **SCOM:** A robust, comprehensive monitoring tool which provides the infrastructure that is flexible and cost-effective, helps ensure the predictable performance and availability of vital applications and offers comprehensive monitoring for datacenter and cloud.
- **StarWind (v.8) server:** it replaces the expensive SAN and NAS physical shared storage. Since it is a software-based and hypervisor-centric virtual machine, which provides a fully fault-tolerant and high-performing storage for the virtualization platform (StarWind Software, 2014). It could seamlessly be integrated into the hypervisor platforms, such as Hyper-V, Xen Server, Linux and Unix environments. In the CCCE, the SCVMM libraries, VHD file, and cloud applications are assigned to *StarWind* server after the integration through the logical unit (LUN) at the fabric panel.

CRYPTOGRAPHIC SERVICE LAYER

This section describes a proposed cryptographic service in the CCCE. This layer provides (i) the secret key provisioning to VMs' consumers, (ii) separating both consumers' cryptographic primitive and (iii) credential accounts based on trusted domain. QCaaS applied to the multiple trusted consumers, which renting the VMs, concurrently. Integrating such service achieves both confidentiality and integrity protection. Figure 10 depicts the QCaaS architecture (software & hardware resources) for single VM. Accordingly, QCaaS has the following features:

- Mini-OS is directly connected with the cloud platform and isolated from the cloud instances.
- Private network configuration and IP for each trusted consumer.
- Sub-inherited domain for each new cryptographic service.
- Special hardware resources (CPU, HDD, and memory) assigned for each service.

Consequently, it assures both the appropriate load for cloud performance optimization and the consumer controlling activities (consumer prevents the cloud administrator from gained or preserve his data). Therefore, a secured environment for each consumer's VMs, with no possibility for insiders or external attackers, is guaranteed.

Finally, after the signing in verification and the VM renting, QCaaS deploys the consumer wizard and the CSP wizard to achieve the encryption/decryption processes and connect to the Quantum Cloud environment.

Figure 10. QCaaS architecture

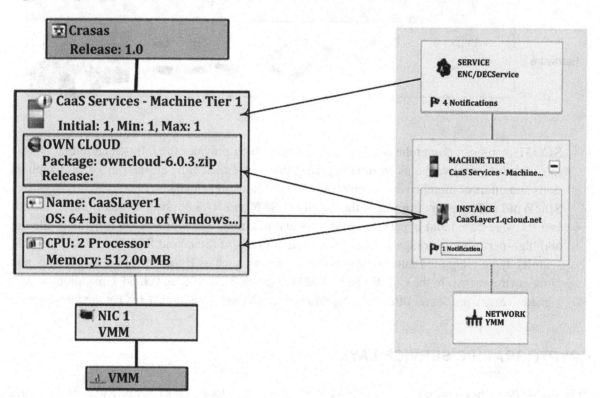

CCCE MAIN BUILDING BLOCKS

CCCE generates the encryption keys based on quantum mechanics instead of classical mathematic operations. Such quantum provide unbroken key and eavesdropper detection. Most definite criteria associated with CCCE came from the nature of the quantum mechanism. Substantially, CCCE encrypts cloud data based QAES using two implemented modes (online and offline).

- **Online Mode:** Consumers directly negotiate with QCaaS based on QKD-BB84 protocol, in order to get a final secret key, which used with QAES algorithm to encrypt files. However, a consumer and QCaaS-provider are not able to know the secret key until the negotiations of their bases are finished (PA phase).
- **Offline Mode:** According to subsection (*QKD Usage*) mentioned above, QCaaS deploys a selected random key for the particular consumer through the VPN-connection domain. Such key is exploited as a seed by QAES algorithm to provide a key session for cryptographic rounds and encrypted files. Furthermore, some classical concepts (randomness test and key session) and quantum techniques (encoding photons) are applied in order to improve the key distribution. However, BB84 cannot be used in such mode because no negotiation between connected partied are achieved.

Additionally, CCCE aims to:

- Improve the availability and the reliability of the cloud computing cryptographic mechanisms by deploying both key generation and key management techniques based on QCaaS layer.
- Manipulate massive computing processes that cannot be executed using the personal computer only.

As shown in Figure 11, CCCE consists of the cloud network that entails Windows Server 2012 Datacenter and Hyper-V installations and configurations with N- full-VMs. These VMs classified as, cloud infrastructure such SCVMM, SCOM, APPC, SQL, DC, cloud instances (VMs rented from the consumer), and VMs for cryptographic processes.

CCCE PHASES

Registration and verification, encryption/decryption, and uploading/downloading are primary phases of CCCE. It discussed based on two modes.

Registration and Verification Phase

Firstly, the end user registers as a consumer to the CSP. The CSP verifies the MAC address and assigns and generates a certificate authority (CA) to authorize the consumer via Kerberos authentication function. Secondly, the CSP checks the resources availability and picks up, depended on the Microsoft Load Balancing (MLB) (Aidan, Hans, Patrick, Damian, 2012), the lowest load VM among the others. Finally, the VM-IP address is assigned to the consumer. Accordingly, due to such assigned process, when the consumer needs to reconnect his/her VM is assigned directly after the authentication achieved.

Figure 11. CCCE main building blocks

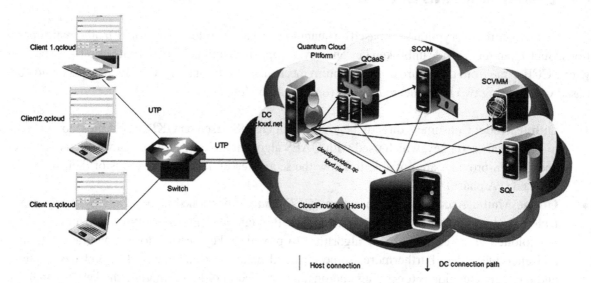

Encryption / Decryption Phase

The encryption/decryption phase entails online and offline modes. In the online mode, the final secret key is generated as a result of the negotiation between the consumer and the QCaaS. Whereas, in the offline mode, the qubits is directly sent by the QCaaS to the authenticated consumer. Finally, in order to gain a secured communication for file transmission, the QAES-256 is used in both modes during the encryption/decryption process.

- **Consumer: E_n (P, K_q) ←P'** // trusted client encrypts the file (P) on the own machine using QAES.
- **IQCaaS: D (P', K_q) ←P** // service decrypts an encrypted file (P') on CCCE using QAES.

Uploading / Downloading Phase

In this phase, necessary steps for uploading / downloading files in the CCCE are illustrated. The following is the uploading process in *the on-line* mode:

- The Consumer sends a request to CSP, (http://sharepoint2:8088/scvm_layout/request), for authentication.
- CSP sends the corresponding registered VM-IP successful authentication.
- CSP assigns a QCaaS layer and deploys a console wizard to the consumer.
- The Consumer starts the negotiation with QCaaS service.
- Consumer encrypts a file on the own machine by QAES-256-bits.
- The Consumer sends the file to the cloud environment via secure web-services.
- QCaaS decrypts the sending file and saves it.
- While, the uploading process steps in the *off-line mode* are:

- The Consumer sends a request to CSP, (http://sharepoint2:8088/scvm_layout/request), for authentication.
- CSP sends the corresponding registered VM-IP successful authentication.
- CSP assigns a QCaaS layer and deploys a console wizard to the consumer.
- QCaaS generate a pseudo-random number based quantum cipher and create a secret key.
- QCaaS deploys a secret key to the consumer.
- The Consumer encrypts a file on the own machine by QAES-256-bits.
- The Consumer sends the file to the cloud environment via secure web-services.
- QCaaS decrypts the sending file and saves it.

The steps for the downloading process are the inverse of uploading one.

DISCUSSIONS

In this section, CCCE is analyzed based on the security management, QCaaS functions, and DoS defeating.

Security Management

The rapid growth of cloud computing usage leads to more complications in the security management task that is mainly responsible for providing a secure environment to both consumer and CSP. Confidentiality is one of the security management complications that can be assured by encrypting data. However, the primary barrier of the encryption techniques is still the key management issues. CSA and NIST classify the key management as the most complex part of any security system (Juan, 2012).

Accordingly, CCCE has overcome the key availability problem by deploying a new cloud service layer (QCaaS) that combines the developed AES algorithm and the QKD technique (Omer, Safia, El-Sayed and Abdel-Badeeh, 2014). This hybrid technique:

- Supports scalability in dynamic key distribution via two implemented modes.
- Defeats the most types of attack such as (man-in-the-middle-attack, side-channel attack)
- Provides independent and trusted communication for each user.

QCaaS Main Roles

QCaaS protects the consumer's cryptographic key and file through the communication. Moreover, due to the isolation criteria for the resources, QCaaS prevents an attacker or malicious from information extraction through the cloud.

- **Securing the Consumer:** QCaaS provides the encryption/decryption process by cooperating both consumer's machine and cloud servers, this corporation defeats two types of attacks (man-in –the middle attack and authentication attack).

- **Consumer Encryption Permissions:** QCaaS helps the consumer for encrypting the flying data, which in turn, provides a higher level of security.
- **Key Protection:** Key generation and key distribution processes are critical in any cloud storage environment; therefore, keys must be carefully generated and protected. QCaaS achieves these processes by dynamic key generation based QKD (Omer, Safia, El-Sayed and Abdel-Badeeh, 2014; Rawal V., Dhamija A., Sharma, 2012). After then, keys are expired as soon as the sending or receiving files process completed.

DoS Attack Defeating

DoS attack is considered as the most critical threat to VMs environment. The threat lays in its ability to overcome the hypervisors misconfiguration. It allows a single VM to consume all available resources and causes starving for others on the same physical device. However, Quantum Cloud hypervisor prevents any VM from exploiting 100% of the shared hardware resources, including CPU, network bandwidth, and RAM. This feature provided by creating a standard Quota (see Figure 12) and controlling centralization of "qcloud.net" domain. Such quota deploys standard resources for each new VM creation. Domain controller name, number of processors and hardware resources are examples of such resources. If any VM exceeds this prevailing quote, the CSP sends alerts and destroys the connections.

Figure 12. VMs quota

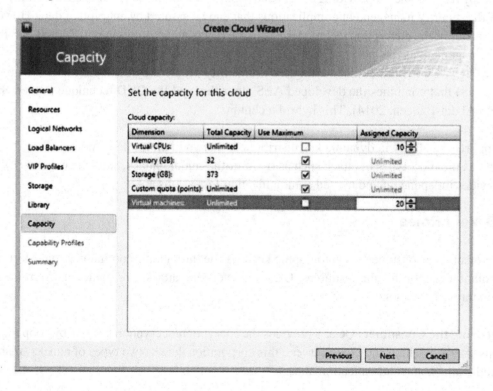

CONCLUSION AND FUTURE WORKS

Cloud computing allows consumers to use applications without installing or accessing their personal files on their personal machine via the internet. In cloud computing technology, there is a set of critical security issues, such as privacy, anonymity, telecommunications capacity, and reliability. However, the most significant problem in these issues is to provide a secure environment and assure it.

This chapter presented a CCCE, which entails both QCaaS and QAES (developed AES-based QKD) aiming to provide more flexibility and secure communication environment, improve the performance of the encryption/decryption process, and support more secure data transmission process using less computational time.

CCCE enjoys certain advantages when compared with the others, especially with respect to the secret key generation used in the encryption/ decryption process. It can be considered as the first cloud environment that integrates both the CSP principles and the QKD mechanisms. CCCE shows that the availability and the reliability of the secret key generation can be easily achieved based on two modes, On-line and off-line. CCCE poses more secure data transmission by provisioning secret keys among cloud's instances based on innovative cryptographic service QCaaS.

The QCaaS solves the key generation, key distribution and key management problems that emerged through the two implemented modes, since it is assigned to the two communication parties (consumer and CSP). Furthermore, QCaaS enjoys many advantages such as:

- Serving the consumer secure communication and protecting their sensitive data,
- Verifying and monitoring the identity of the original user depending on "qcloud.net" and Kerberos authentication function,
- deploying an encryption service with each VM,
- Achieving the encryption/decryption processes using QAES.

Generally, any privileged operations that traditionally could be done by "qcloud.net "administrators, such as building a new sub domain or forest, increasing the validity of the consumer, domain migration, and the cloud instances.

Finally, Cloud data encryption based quantum technology platform dispels all security fears through the cloud data transmission. This technology offers, a simple low-cost for the data protection, security tools for services integration, and an efficient disaster recovery.

In the future work, third trusted party (TTP) should be added to a cloud environment and consumer enterprise. This TTP works as a quantum cipher cloud and responsible for key generation and key deployment. Moreover, a secure cloud computing system that mainly depends on randomness ratio associated with the quantum system is going to be build.

REFERENCES

Aidan, F., Hans, V., Patrick, L., & Damian, F. (2012). *Microsoft Private Cloud Computing*. John Wiley publisher.

Andrew T., Juan K., James L., Miles Z., Elaine R., & Stefan S. (2013). A statistical test suite for random and pseudorandom number generators for cryptographic applications. NIST Special Publication 800-22 Revision.

Bethencourt, J., Sahai, A., & Waters, B. (2011). Ciphertext-policy attribute-based encryption, *Proceedings of the IEEE Symposium on Security and Privacy (SP '07)* (pp. 321–334).

Center for Quantum Technology. (n. d.). Retrieved from http://www.quantumlah.org/research/topic/qcrypto,1/9/2014

Chadwick, D., & Casanova, M. (2011). *Security API for private cloud. Proceedings of the 3rd IEEE International on cloud computing technology and sciences, CloudCom* (pp. 792–798). CPS.

Chander, K., & Yogesh, S. (2013). Enhanced security architecture for cloud data security. International journal of advanced research in computer science and software engineering, 3(5).

Christain, K., & Mario, P. (2010). *Applied Quantum cryptography*. Lect. Notes Phys.: Vol. 797. Berlin, Heidelberg: Springer. Doi:10.1007/978-3-642-04831-9

CSA, (2012). *Security a-a-services guidance for critical areas in cloud computing, Category 8.*

Cutillo, A., Molva, R., & Strufe, T. (2009). Safe book: A privacy-preserving online social network is leveraging on real-life trust. *IEEE Communications Magazine, 47*(12), 94–101. doi:10.1109/MCOM.2009.5350374

De Decker, B., & Zúquete, A. (Eds.), (2014). *Communications and Multimedia Security*. Springer.

Doelitzscher, F., Reich, C., Knahl, M., & Clarke, N. (2011). *An autonomous agent-based incident detection system for cloud computing, 3rd IEEE International on cloud computing technology and sciences, CloudCom* (pp. 197–204). CPS.

Eduared, G. (2014). An Experimental Implementation of Oblivious Transfer in the Noisy Storage Model. Nature Communications Journal, 5.

Emmanuel S., Navdeep A., Parshant T., Bhanu P. (2013). Cloud Computing: Data Storage Security Analysis and its Challenges. *International Journal of Computer Applications*, 70(24).

ENISA security. (2014). Retrieved from http://www.enisa.europa.eu/

Faiza, F. (2012). Management of symmetric cryptographic keys in a cloud-based environment. *Proceedings of the 2nd IEEE international conference on cloud computing technology and science.*

Farhad, A., Seyed, S., & Athula, G. (2013). Cloud computing: security and reliability issues. Communication of the IBIMA (Vol. 1).

IDC. (2014). IDC Ranking of issues of Cloud Computing model. Retrieved from http://www.idc.com/

Itani, W., Kayassi, A., & Chehab, A. (2012). Energy-efficient incremental integrity for securing storage in mobile cloud computing. *Proceedings of the International Conference on Energy Aware Computing (ICEAC10)*. Cairo, Egypt.

Jensen, M., Schwenk, J., Gruschka, N., & Iacono, L. (2009). On Technical Security Issues in Cloud Computing. IEEE ICCC, Bangalore (pp. 109-116).

Juan, S. (2012). *Statistical testing of random number generators*. National Institute Standards Technology.

Juan, S. (2012). *Statistical testing of random number generators ", National Institute Standards Technology*. NIST.

Mandeep U., & Manish T. (2012). Implementing Various Encryption Algorithm to Enhance the Data Security of Cloud in Cloud Computing. *International Journal of Computer Science and Information Technology*, 2(10).

Manpreet, W., & Rajbir, N. (2013). Implementing Encryption Algorithms to EnhanceData Security of Cloud in Cloud Computing. *International Journal of Computers and Applications*, 70(18).

Mather, T., & Kumaraswamy, S. (2012). *Cloud security and privacy; An enterprise perspective on risks and compliance* (1st ed.). O'Reilly Media.

Matthew, G. (2013). Statistical tests of randomness on QKD through a free-space channel coupled to daylight noise. *Journal of Lightwave Technology*, 3(23).

Matthew, P., Caleb, H., Lamas, L., & Christian, K. (2008). *Daylight operation of a free space, entanglement-based quantum key distribution system*. Centre for Quantum Technologies, National University of Singapore.

Mohammad, G., John, M., & Ingo, K. (2010). An analysis of the Cloud Computing Security Problem. *Proceedings of APSE 2010 Cloud Workshop*, Sydney, Australia.

Mohammad, O.K.J., Abbas, S., El-Horbaty, E.-S.M., & Salem, A.-B.M. (2013). A Comparative Study of Modern Encryption Algorithms based On Cloud Computing Environment. *Proceedings of the 8th International Conference for Internet Technology and Secured Transactions (ICITST-2013)* (pp. 536-541).

Mohammad, O.K.J., Abbas, S., El-Horbaty, E.-S.M., & Salem, A.-B.M., (2014). Cryptographic Cloud Computing Environment as a More Trusted Communication Environment. *International Journal of Grid and High Performance Computing, 6*.

Mohammad, O.K.J., Abbas, S., El-Horbaty, E.-S.M., & Salem, A.-B.M. (2014). Statistical Analysis for Random Bits Generation on Quantum Key Distribution. *Proceedings of the 3rd IEEE- Conference on Cyber Security, Cyber Warfare, and Digital Forensic (CyberSec2014)* (pp. 45-52).

Mohammad, O.K.J., Abbas, S., El-Horbaty, E.-S.M., & Salem, A.-B.M. (2014). Advanced Encryption Standard Development Based Quantum Key Distribution, the 9th International Conference for Internet Technology and Secured Transactions (ICITST-2014), pp.446-456.

Mohammad, O.K.J., Abbas, S., El-Horbaty, E.-S.M., & Salem, A.-B.M. (2015). Quantum Key Distribution: Simulation and Characterizations. *International Conference on Communication, Management and Information Technology (ICCMIT 2015)*, Prague (pp. 78-88).

Nelson, G., Charles, M., Fernando, R., Marco, S., Tereza, C., Mats, N., & Makan, P. (2014). A quantitative analysis of current security concerns and solutions for cloud computing, Journal of cloud computing: advanced, systems and applications, 1(11).

Odeh, A., Elleithy, K., Alshowkan, M., & Abdelfattah, E. (2013). Quantum key distribution by using RSA. *Proceeding of 3rd International Conference on Innovative Computing Technology (INTECH).*

Padmapriya, A., & Subhasri, P. (2013). Cloud Computing: Security Challenges and Encryption Practices. *International Journal of Advance Research in Computer Science and Software Engineering, 3*(3).

Patil D., & Akshay R. (2012). Data Security over Cloud Emerging Trends in Computer Science and Information Technology. International Journal of Computer Applications, pp. 123-147.

Patil D., Akshay R. (2012), "Data Security over Cloud Emerging Trends in Computer Science and Information Technology", proceeding published in International Journal of Computer Applications, pp. 123-147.

Rawal V., Dhamija A., Sharma S. (2012). Revealing New Concepts in Photography & Clouds. *International Journal of Scientific & Technology Research, 1*(7).

Solange, G., & Mohammed, A. (2014). Applying QKD to reach unconditional security in communications. European research project SECOQC. Retrieved from www.secoqc.net

Soren, B., Sven, B., & Hugo, I. (2013). Consumer –controlled cryptography-as-a-service in the cloud. *Proceedings of 11th International Conference, ACNS 2013.*

StarWind Virtual SAN- Quick Start Guide. (2014). *StarWind Software.* USA.

Sunita, M., & Seema, S. (2013). *Distributed Computing* (2nd ed.). USA: Oxford University Press.

Syam, P., Subramanian, R., & Thamizh, D. (2010). Ensuring data security in cloud computing using sobol sequence. *Proceedings of the 1st international conference on parallel, distributed and grid computing (PDGC).*

Wang Q., Cong X., Min S. (2012). Protecting Privacy by Multi-dimensional K-anonymity. *Journal of Software, 7*(8).

William, S. (2012). Cryptography and network security (5th ed.). Prentice Hall.

Winkler, J. (2011). Securing the cloud: cloud computer security techniques and tactics.

Yau, S. S., & An, H. G. (2010). Confidentiality Protection in Cloud Computing Systems. *Int J Software Informatics, 4*(4), 351.

Zhou, M., Mu, Y., Susilo, W., Yan, J., & Dong, L. (2012). Privacy enhanced data outsourcing in the cloud. *Journal of Network and Computer Applications, 35*(4), 1367–1373. doi:10.1016/j.jnca.2012.01.022

KEY TERMS AND DEFINITIONS

Advanced Encryption Standard (AES): A symmetric block cipher used 128-bit block data encryption technique developed by Belgian cryptographers Joan Daemen and Vincent Rijmen. The U.S government adopted the algorithm as its encryption technique in October 2000. AES works at multiple network layers simultaneously. In addition, such algorithm take 128; 192 or 256 bits of key size.

Cloud Computing: A type of computing that relies on sharing computing resources rather than having local servers or personal devices to handle applications and it is a general term for anything that involves delivering hosted services over the Internet. These services are broadly divided into three categories: Infrastructure-as-a-Service (IaaS), Platform-as-a-Service (PaaS) and Software-as-a-Service (SaaS).

Cloud Computing Cryptographic Algorithm: A mathematical algorithm, used in conjunction with a secret key, that transforms original input into a form that is unintelligible without special knowledge of the secret information and the algorithm. Such algorithms are also the basis for digital signatures and key exchange.

Hyper-V: A native hypervisor; it can create virtual machines on x86-64 systems and starting with Windows 8. Hyper-V supersedes Windows Virtual PC as the hardware virtualization component of the client editions of Windows NT. A server computer running Hyper-V can be configured to expose individual virtual machines to one or more networks. Hyper-V was first released along Windows Server 2008 and became a staple of the Windows Server family ever since.

Quantum Key Distribution: A new mechanisms that uses quantum mechanics to guarantee secure communication. It enables two communication parties to produce a shared random secret key known only to them, which can then be used to encrypt and decrypt messages. It is often incorrectly called quantum cryptography, as it is the most well-known example of the group of quantum cryptographic tasks. The important and unique property of quantum distribution is the ability of the two communicating users to detect the presence of any third party trying to gain knowledge of the key.

Quantum Technology: A new field of physics and engineering, which transitions some of the stranger features of quantum mechanics, especially quantum entanglement and most recently quantum tunneling, into practical applications such as quantum computing, quantum cryptography, quantum simulation, quantum metrology, quantum sensing, quantum communication, intelligent quantum system, and quantum imaging.

System Center Configuration Manager (SCCM): A Windows product that enables administrators to manage the deployment and security of devices and applications across an enterprise. SCCM is part of the Microsoft System Center 2012 systems management suite. The SCCM integrated console enables management of Microsoft Application Virtualization (App-V), Microsoft Enterprise Desktop Virtualization (Med-V), Citrix XenApp, Microsoft Forefront and Windows Phone applications from a single location.

Chapter 5
Handling Critical Issues of Big Data on Cloud

Madhavi Vaidya
VES College, India

ABSTRACT

Big Data is driving radical changes in traditional data analysis platforms. To perform any kind of analysis on such voluminous and complex data, scaling up the hardware platforms becomes impending. With the entire buzz surrounding Big Data; it is being collected at an unprecedented scale. Big Data has potential to revolutionize much more than just research. Loading large data-sets is often a challenge. Another shift of this Big Data processing is the move towards cloud computing. As many communities begin to rely on cloud based data management, large shared data goes up extensively. Analysis of such large data on distributed processing system or cloud is a bit difficult task to handle. The aim of this chapter is to provide a better understanding of the design challenges of cloud computing and analytics of big data on it. The challenge is related to how a large extent of data is being harnessed, and the opportunity is related to how effectively it is used for analyzing the information from it.

INTRODUCTION

Data is the information that has been translated into a form that is more convenient to move or process; this is the definition given on whatis.com. Wikipedia says it is a set of values of qualitative and quantitative variables; pieces of data are individual pieces of information. Generally, data is said as distinct pieces of information, usually formatted in a special way. The value of Big Data can only be extracted by data analytics. Although many different data analytics algorithms and techniques including statistical analysis, data mining, and machine learning can be on Big Data, they all rely on extremely intensive computations. Big data is a phenomenon that is characterized by the rapid expansion of raw data. The challenge is related to how a large extent of data is being exploited, and the opportunity is related to how effectively it is used for analyzing the information from it on cloud. The most useful approaches and categories of data tools which are to be chosen have been discussed in this chapter.

DOI: 10.4018/978-1-4666-9834-5.ch005

The Need of Data Processing

Firstly, we have to study why the data has to be processed. There are certain reasons for which the data is being processed. The data can be:

- **Incomplete:** Lacking attribute values, containing attribute data.
- **Noisy:** Containing errors or outliers.
- **Inconsistent:** Containing discrepancies in code or names.
- The quality data should be available.

To obtain the required information from huge, incomplete, noisy and inconsistent set of data is the need of data processing.

The steps of Data Processing:

- Data Cleaning
- Data Integration
- Data Transformation
- Data Reduction
- Data Summarization

Let's study the above steps of Data Processing one by one which are depicted in Figure 1.

- **Data Cleaning:** Data cleaning is especially required when integrating heterogeneous data sources. Data cleaning, also called data cleansing or scrubbing, deals with detecting and removing errors and inconsistencies from data in order to improve the quality of data. Data quality problems are present in single data collections, such as files and databases, e.g., due to misspellings during data entry, missing information or other invalid data.
- **Data Integration:** It combines data from multiple sources into a coherent data store, as in data warehousing. In short it is an integration of multiple databases, data cubes, or files.

Figure 1. Data Processing Flowchart

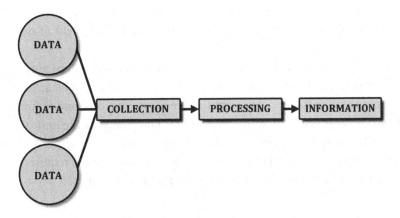

- **Data Transformation:** Data Transformation operations, such as normalization and aggregation, are additional data preprocessing procedures that would contribute towards the success of mining process.
- **Data Reduction:** Data reduction obtains a reduced representation of the data set that is much smaller in volume, yet produces the same analytical results.
- **Data Summarization:** It is the process of representing the collected data in an accurate and compact way without losing any information, it also involves getting information from collected data referred (Son,2012).

BACKGROUND WORK

Achieving business success in today's global economy requires the ability to make the right data available in the right form to the right people at the right time. In many organizations, this is difficult because each division collects and processes its own data differently. Various types of distributed systems and applications have been developed and are being used extensively in the real world to generate the data. Achieving better system performance is using a distributed system. In a distributed system, several computers are connected together usually by LAN. Now, we can characterize distributed system with a simple definition: A distributed system is a collection of independent computers (nodes) that appears to its users as a single coherent system and viewpoints on what distributed systems are, Coulouris defines a distributed system as "a system in which hardware or software components located at networked computers communicate and coordinate their actions only by message passing" ; and Tanenbaum defines it as "A collection of independent computers that appear to the users of the system as a single computer".

The main features of a distributed system include:

- **Functional Separation:** Based on the functionality/services provided, capability and purpose of each entity in the system.
- **Inherent Distribution:** Entities such as information, people, and systems are inherently distributed. For example, different information is created and maintained by different people. This information could be generated, stored, analyzed and used by different systems or applications which may or may not be aware of the existence of the other entities in the system.
- **Reliability:** Long term data preservation and backup (replication) at different locations.
- **Scalability:** Addition of more resources to increase performance or availability.
- **Economy:** Sharing of resources by many entities to help reduce the cost of ownership.

As a consequence of these features, the various entities in a distributed system can operate concurrently and possibly autonomously. Tasks are carried out independently and actions are coordinated at well-defined stages by exchanging messages. Also, entities are heterogeneous, and failures are independent. Generally, there is no single process, or entity, that has the knowledge of the entire state of the system. Various kinds of distributed systems operate today, each aimed at solving different kinds of problems. The challenges faced in building a distributed system vary depending on the requirements of the system. In general, however, most systems will need to handle the following issues:

- **Heterogeneity:** Various entities in the system must be able to interoperate with one another, despite differences in hardware architectures, operating systems, communication protocols, programming languages, software interfaces, security models, and data formats.
- **Transparency:** The entire system should appear as a single unit and the complexity and interactions between the components should be typically hidden from the end user.
- **Fault tolerance and failure management:** Failure of one or more components should not bring down the entire system, and should be isolated. If one or more nodes fail, other nodes are able to provide all functionality. This property is also known as availability or reliability.
- **Scalability:** The system should work efficiently with increasing number of users and addition of a resource should enhance the performance of the system.
- **Concurrency:** Shared access to resources should be made possible.
- **Openness and Extensibility:** Interfaces should be cleanly separated and publicly available to enable easy extensions to existing components and add new components.
- **Migration and load balancing:** Allow the movement of tasks within a system without affecting the operation of users or applications, and distribute load among available resources for improving performance.
- **Security:** Access to resources should be secured to ensure only known users are able to perform allowed operations.
- **Availability and Reliability:** Availability means that the system can serve client a request at a moment when the client connects to the system. Reliability means that the system is available all the time when the client is connected to it. Files can also be moved among nodes.

This makes it a challenge to know exactly what information is available, from where to get it, how to share it and how to store it. The new operations model that brings together a set of existing technologies to run business in altogether different manner was required. This model was named as "cloud" used after Google's CEO Eric Schmidt used the word to describe the business model of providing services across Internet in 2006. Certainly, the lack of a standard definition of cloud computing has generated not only market hypes, but also a fair amount of skepticism and there is a doubt for handling the data safely from it. The main reason for the existence of various perspectives of cloud computing is to run the business in a different manner. The issues and challenges have been discussed in this chapter for using the Big Data on cloud. How this Big Data can be processed and analyzed has been elucidated.

What Is Big Data?

In today's world, volumes of data grow exponentially in all realms from personal data to enterprise and global data. Thus it is becoming extremely important to be able to understand data sets and organize them.

The concept of big data has been widespread within computer science since the earliest days of computing. "Big Data" originally meant the volume of data that could not be processed (efficiently) by traditional database methods and tools. The most useful approaches and categories of data tools which are to be chosen have been discussed here. Each time a new storage medium was invented, the amount of data accessible explode because it could be easily accessed. The focus will be mainly on "big data" problems. The applications generate hundreds or thousands of requests in a second. Sites where sales is done like Amazon or Flipcart. Real-time calculations done for determining Twitter's trending tweets.

This refers to the quantification of the information and points related to data like:

- Information
- Volume
- Forms of Data
- Rapid Data arrival- Scale up and Scale down

- **Information:** Processed data is nothing but information.
- **Volume:** Volume describes the amount of data generated by organizations or individuals. Such data is generated from the sensor devices, mobile platforms, social and geographical data and the data can be in the form of structured and unstructured format.
- **Rapid Data Arrival:** The data retrieval is possible in the following ways:
  - ○ **Horizontal Scaling:** Horizontal scaling involves distributing the workload across many servers which may be even commodity machines. It is also known as "scale out", where multiple independent machines are added together in order to improve the processing capability. Typically, multiple instances of the operating system are running on separate machines.
  - ○ **Vertical Scaling:** Vertical Scaling involves installing more processors, more memory and faster hardware, typically, within a single server. It is also known as "scale up" and it usually involves a single instance of an operating system.

Big Data Characteristics

Today it is mostly focused on handling the data which is reviewed here in terms of the most useful approaches and categories of data tools to choose from. Each time a new storage medium was invented, the amount of data accessible explode because it could be easily accessed. They have been found in applications that generate hundreds or thousands of requests in a second. Sites where sales is done like Amazon or Flipcart; and the software that process terabytes or even petabytes of data. Real-time calculations done for determining Twitter's trending tweets.

Big data is a phenomenon that is characterized by the rapid expansion of raw data. The challenge is related to how a large extent of data is being harnessed, and the opportunity is related to how effectively it is used for analyzing the information from it. It is now common place to distinguish big data solutions from conventional IT solutions by considering the following four dimensions.

- **Volume:** Volume describes the amount of data generated by organizations or individuals. Big data solutions must manage and process larger amounts of data.
- **Velocity:** Velocity describes the frequency at which data is generated, captured and shared. Big data solutions must process more rapidly arriving data. By Velocity, they mean both the rate at which data arrive and the time in which it must be acted upon
- **Variety:** Big data solutions must deal with more kinds of data, both structured and unstructured in nature. By Variety, they usually mean heterogeneity of data types, representation, and semantic interpretation
- **Veracity:** Big data solutions must validate the correctness of the large amount of rapidly arriving data.

Today it is mostly focused on handling this Big Data. The most useful approaches and categories of data tools are reviewed to choose from data warehouse to Business Intelligence (BI) now, we all are experiencing unexpected growth in structured and unstructured data is very huge. The unstructured data can be from word, excel, PowerPoint documents or PDF, HTML document, telecom data, satellite data etc. Actually, after reading the material on it, there is one more dimension one can think about, that is Complexity. The four V's can be referred through the Figure 2.

Complexity

Organizations capture a variety of data formats and comb through massive data sources in real-time to analyze and identify patterns within the data. There are some examples, identifying fraud for credit card customers, financial trends for investment organizations, predicting power consumption for energy companies.

Here, are few examples of big data to get the idea:

- Twitter produces over 90 million tweets per day
- Walmart is logging one million transaction per hour
- Facebook creates over 30 billion pieces of content ranging from web links, news, blogs and photos etc. The volume of the business data worldwide, across all companies, doubles every 1.2 years, according to estimates is elaborated in white paper by Ajay Chandramouly and Kelly Stinson (2013).

Use of Big Data

Big Data allows corporate and research organizations to do things not previously possible economically. It is used for:

- Analysis
- Business Trends

Figure 2. 4 V's of big data

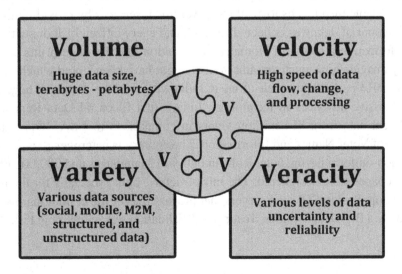

- Prevent Diseases
- Combat Crime
- Centralization of the data etc.

Potential of Big Data

The use of big data offers tremendous unexploited potential for creating value. Organizations in many industry sectors and business functions can leverage big data to improve their allocation and coordination of human and physical resources, increase transparency, accountability and facilitate the discovery of new ideas and insights. Sectors with greatest potential for big data:

- Healthcare
- Public Sector
- Retail
- Manufacturing
- Telecommunication

Cases of Big Data

- **Case 1:** According to a trial calculation, the amount of event data generated in the U.S. is estimated to be 7 million pieces per second, which adds up to a few tens to hundreds of PBs per month if accumulated as they are without compression. This value is not equal to the amount of data actually transferred to data centers and processed.
- **Case 2:** Massive amount of sensor data is also a big challenge for Big data. All the industries at present dealing with this large amount of data make use of small portion of it for analysis because of the lack of the storage infrastructure and the analysis techniques. Moreover sensor data is characterized by both data in motion and data at rest. Thus safety, profit and efficiency all require large amount of data to be analyzed for better business insights.
- **Case 3:** Recently the Aadhar Identity card or UID was introduced by the Government of India which would enable the citizens to avail the government services by providing them a unique ID. Here large amount of data was collected for each and every citizen of India which included storing basic information along with biometric information like the fingerprints and picture of iris. We can only imagine how much amount of data might have been stored which is in varied forms.
- **Case 4:** The 2014 parliamentary elections in India witnessed two trends: a huge increase in new voters and massive advances in technology. India's first Electoral Data Repository project involved different data from 814 million voters in comparison to USA, Indonesia and UK with diverse range of Voter Names and Information. The country is heterogeneous and diverse, as well as vast and non-uniform having voter Rolls in PDF in 12 languages and 900,000 PDFs, amounting to 25 million pages were deciphered. The infrastructure, built especially for the project, included 64 node Hadoop, PostgreSQL and servers that process master file containing over 8 Terabytes of data, it is really a Big Data. Besides, Testing and Validation was another big task. 'First of a Kind'

Heuristic (machine learning) algorithms were developed for people classification based on Name, Geography etc., which help in identification of Religion, Caste and even Ethnicity elaborated in an article on Big Data issue (Data Economy,2014).

CHALLENGES IN HANDLING BIG DATA

Actually, there are two types of fundamentals in databases, Row-oriented databases and Column-oriented databases. Row-oriented databases work tremendously well for online transaction processing with high update speeds, but they fall short on query performance as the data volumes raise and as data become more unstructured. Column-oriented databases store data with a focus on columns, and not on rows, allowing for huge data compression and very fast query times. They allow batch updates, having a much slower update time than traditional models.

- **Inconsistency and incompleteness:** Big Data includes the information generated from various sources, of varying reliability. Even after data cleaning and error correction, some incompleteness and some errors in data are likely to remain. This incompleteness and these errors are managed during data analysis.
- **Scale:** Scaling is the ability of the system to adapt to increased demands in terms of data processing. To support big data processing, different platforms incorporate scaling in different forms. Horizontal scaling increases performance in small steps as needed. It is possible to scale up the system using horizontal scaling. There is a type of vertical scaling also where it is easy to manage and install hardware within a single machine. Managing large and rapidly increasing volumes of data has been a challenging issue for many decades.
- **Privacy and Data Ownership:** Security concerns about data protection is a major obstacle preventing companies from taking full advantage of their data. However, there is great public apprehension regarding the inappropriate use of personal data, particularly through linking of data from multiple sources. Managing privacy is effectively both a technical and a sociological problem, which must be addressed jointly from both perspectives to realize the promise of big data. Many online services today require us to share private information on number of social networking sites but beyond record-level access control we do not understand what it means to share data, how the shared data can be linked, and how to give users fine-grained control over this sharing.
- **Timeliness:** The larger the data set to be processed, the longer it will take to analyze. The design of a system that effectively deals with size is likely also to result in a system that can process a given size of data set faster. For example, consider a traffic management system with information regarding thousands of vehicles and local hot spots on roadways. The system may need to predict potential congestion points along a route chosen by a user, and suggest alternatives.
- **Heterogeneous Data:** Unstructured data represents almost every kind of data being produced like social media interactions, to recorded meetings, to handling of PDF documents, fax transfers, to emails and more. When humans consume information, a great deal of heterogeneity is comfortably tolerated. Machine analysis algorithms expect homogenous data and are poor at understanding nuances. Actually for this, the data has to be structured in first step of data analysis. Structured

data is always organized into highly mechanized and manageable way. It shows well integration with database but unstructured data is completely raw and unorganized. Working with unstructured data is cumbersome and of course costly too. Converting all this unstructured data into structured one is also not feasible. Structured data is the one which is organized in a way so that it can be managed easily. Digging through unstructured data is costly and unmanageable process.

- **Inconsistency and Incompleteness:** Big Data increasingly includes information provided by increasingly diverse sources, of varying reliability. Uncertainty, errors, and missing values are endemic, and must be managed. On the bright side, the volume and redundancy of Big Data can often be exploited to compensate for missing data, to crosscheck conflicting cases, to validate trustworthy relationships, to disclose inherent clusters, and to uncover hidden relationships and models.

While most such errors will be detected and corrected by others in the crowd, we need technologies to facilitate this. As humans, we can look at reviews of a product, some of which are gushing and others negative, and come up with a summary assessment based on which we can decide whether to buy the product. We need computers to be able to do the equivalent. The issues of uncertainty and error become even more pronounced in a specific type of crowdsourcing called participatory- sensing. In this case, every person with a mobile phone can act as a multi-modal sensor collecting various types of data instantaneously (for example, picture, video, audio, location, time, speed, direction, acceleration). The extra challenge here is the inherent uncertainty of the data collection devices. The fact that collected data is probably spatially and temporally correlated can be exploited to better assess their correctness. Even after error correction has been applied, some incompleteness and some errors in data are likely to remain. This incompleteness and these errors must be managed during data analysis. Doing this correctly is a challenge. Recent work on managing and querying probabilistic and conflicting data suggests one way to make progress.

TYPES OF DATA

There are several database types that fit into this category, such as key-value stores and document stores, which focus on the storage and retrieval of large volumes of unstructured, semi-structured, or even structured data. They achieve performance gains by doing away with some (or all) of the restrictions traditionally associated with conventional databases, such as read-write consistency, in exchange for scalability and distributed processing.

After visiting above cases, the role of the variety has been observed here. It can be studied that volume and velocity of data streaming through enterprise systems is on the rise, and so is the amount of discussion about the best way to handle it. But while the big data phenomenon is giving organizations a broad range of new options for data analysis, it also compounds the business challenges associated with collecting and collating, managing, organizing and protecting data which can be realized from the data life cycle management.. Successfully leveraging big data for analytics demands that companies develop strategies to reduce the cost of managing data and reduce the risk involved in organizing and protecting that data.

Data Life Cycle Management

To efficiently manage data throughout its entire lifecycle, IT leaders must keep three objectives in mind:

1. The trustworthiness of data is critical for both analytics and regulatory compliance.
2. Both structured and unstructured data must be managed efficiently. Actually, there is always an unstructured data in vast manner.
3. Data privacy and security must be protected when the data is gathered and used for analysis.

The data lifecycle stretches through multiple phases as it is created, used, shared, updated, stored and eventually archived or defensively disposed. The phases of technical support required for Big Data Processing are as below:

*   **Creating Data:** the data is to be needed by an organization is to be studied and decided. The management of data is gathered from various sources.
*   **Processing Data:** Collected data is grouped properly; it has to be ensured that it is ethically sourced and valid. How to make the analysis and what type of analysis is to be done for the grouped data is to be determined
*   **Analyze Data:** The data analysis is done by creating hypothetical situations explained by Han and Kamber (2006) and Sharpio-Parker (2006) in the books authored by them on Data Mining, by preparing data for the preservation
*   **Preserving Data:** Back up of the data is taken from time to time. The data is migrated from the external devices like RFIDs, Sensors or mobile platform systems. The data may be unstructured in nature. For example, data may be collected or generated from the RFID devices, the mobile platforms, sensor alarming systems or some other data generated from web links, news, blogs and photos etc. frequently.
*   **Giving Access to Data:** The data is distributed and shared from distributed systems or mobile platform systems. Later it is made available for all the users to find out the results from the same.
*   **Re-Using Data:** the reusability of information for undertaking new projects and new research is done

Three elements of data lifecycle management play an especially important role in several phases of existence of data:

1. Test Data Management

During the process of developing new data sources, whether on databases or data warehouses, testers make the automation of the creation of realistic, right sized data sources that mirror the behaviors of existing production databases. To ensure that queries can be run easily and accurately, the testers must create a subset of actual production data and reproduce actual conditions to help identify defects or problems as early as possible in the testing cycle.

The organizations must mask sensitive information in for compliance and privacy. Applying data masking techniques to the test data means testers use fictional data; no actual sensitive data is revealed.

2. Data Masking and Privacy

Whether information is stored in Hadoop or a data warehouse, certain part of the data should be masked which has been gathered from unauthorized users, for that the data masking is done to maintain the privacy. The aggregate data has to be collected and studied. For example, social security numbers and dates of birth are to be masked by a pharmaceutical company that is submitting drug-testing results to the U.S. Food and Drug Administration may mask but masking patients' ages and other demographic information is of no use. Masking certain data this way satisfies corporate and industry regulations by removing identifiable information, while still maintaining business context.

3. Archiving

Effective data lifecycle management includes the intelligence to archive data. Such archives are based on specific parameters such as the age of the data. It can also help storage administrators to archive dormant data in a data warehouse, thereby improving overall warehouse performance. In addition, effective data lifecycle management enables IT to query archived data in Hadoop-based systems, providing flexible access to that data. The effect is to reduce the total cost of ownership of data sources by intelligently archiving and compressing historical data, while ensuring that data is available for applicable analytical purposes is elucidated in the article published (IBM, 2013, pp. 6-8).

As organizations look to big data environments to analyze and manage critical business decisions, they face significant challenges related to data lifecycle management:

- Archive data into Hadoop
  - To make an analytics to make informed decisions across structured data including archived data, and unstructured data
  - Optimize storage, maintenance and licensing costs by migrating rarely used data to Hadoop
- Growing amounts of data is creating the capability of the data warehouse and other big data systems
- Creating realistic test data for testing data warehouse environments
- Preventing the exposure of confidential data in both production and non-production environments

Big Data plays role in the following domains. The domains can be Healthcare, Financial Services, Telecommunications, Transportation, Insurance, Energy and Utilities and Supply Chain Management. Big Data is set to revolutionize Integrated Business Planning, a core element in business operations that extends the process of balancing supply and demand to all aspects of the supply chain, financial processes and strategic planning. Following is the case which can be studied to check the role of the Big Data which is used to improve the visibility of Supply Chain Management.

Supply chain management also makes use of large data; it is a suitable model to convert this huge diverse raw data into actionable information so that businesses can make critical business decisions for efficient supply chain planning. The role of Big Data in supply chain planning process has following stages:

- **Acquire Data:** The biggest driver of supply chain planning is data. Acquiring all the relevant data for supply chain planning is the first step. It involves below given steps:
  - **Data Sourcing:** Data is available in different forms across multiple sources, systems and geographies. It contains extensive details of the data in demand which may be historical in nature and other relevant information. The data can be the data about the data i.e. metadata, about the items, customer's data in terms of the purchase history or social media data, the transportation data is in terms of GPS and logistics data.
  - **Data Curation:** Firstly analysis of the raw data is performed, which application of models are suitable and standards to reduce data heterogeneity, acquire further information and adapt formats.
    - Metadata Production
    - Standardization
    - Selection of data models and structures.
  - **Data Extraction and Cleansing:** The data is in different format may be structured or unstructured in nature. The structured data is originated from the various transactions. But the unstructured data can be generated from social media, images, sensor data etc. as said previously. The large volume of data gets generated from the heterogeneous platforms. Choice of Big Data tools for data cleansing and enhancement plays a crucial role in supply chain planning.
  - **Data Representation:** When such huge volume of data gets generated from the heterogeneous platform then designing it is really a herculean task and may create some serious performance issues. Selection of appropriate database design and executing according to business objectives is an important task.
- **Analyze Data:** Analyzing the above cleansed data and forecasting the values gained from it are required for supply chain planning. There are various tools available in the market for forecasting and supply chain planning.
  - **Optimization in Big Data Analysis:** Adoption of optimizing technique in Big Data analysis creates a new perspective and it helps in improving the accuracy of demand forecasting and supply chain planning. It is used for analyzing and drawing insights for highly complex system with huge data volume coming from various systems. Optimization model comprises of four components – input, goals, constraints and output.
    - **Input:** Real time quality data which is taken from sources is cleansed and integrated is an input
    - **Goals:** All the goals should be pertaining to the forecasting and supply chain planning like minimization cost and maximizing profit are decided
    - **Constraints:** All the conditions should be taken into considerations
    - **Output:** Results based on input, goals and constraints are used for strategy executions. The result can be production plan or logistics plan.
  - **Achieve Business Objective:** The final stage in this model is achieving business objectives through demand forecasting and supply chain planning has been explored in the article published on Big Data Challenges and Opportunities by Infosys (2013).

METHODS TO HANDLE BIG DATA

Handling the velocity of Big Data is not an easy task. First, the system should be able to collect the data generated by real time events streams coming at a rate of millions of events per second. Second, it needs to handle the parallel processing of this data as and when it is being collected. Third, it should perform event correlation using a Complex Event Processing engine to extract the meaningful information from this moving stream. These three steps should happen in a fault tolerant and distributed way. Even the data has to be secured as privacy and security of data is of huge concern. There are certain tools which are useful to handle the big data. This big data is processed by some of the following tools. Although their functionality is different from each other, all of them handle the large data. Some of them are as below –

Hadoop is an open source project hosted by Apache Software Foundation. It consists of many small sub projects which belong to the category of infrastructure for distributed computing. Apache Hadoop, a software framework implemented based on Java, executes distributed computing of massive data in a cluster composed of a huge number of computers. Hadoop enables an application program to support more than one thousand nodes and PB-level data. Hadoop is a general project name. Hadoop(2004) includes distributed storage (HDFS) and distributed computing (MapReduce) which can be referred from Figure 3.Hadoop mainly consists of:

- File System (The Hadoop File System)
- Programming Paradigm (Map Reduce)

Figure 3. Hadoop architecture

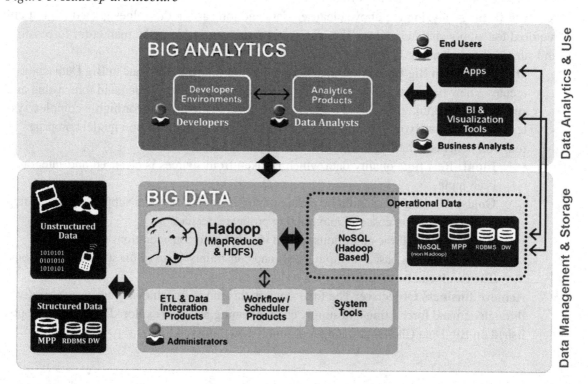

Hadoop is the most popular implementation of MapReduce, being an entirely open source platform for handling Big Data. It is flexible enough to be able to work with multiple data sources, either aggregating multiple sources of data in order to do large scale processing or even reading data from a database in order to run processor-intensive machine learning jobs. It enables the applications to work with thousands of computational independent computers and petabytes of data. It has several different applications, but one of the top use cases is for large volumes of constantly changing data, such as location-based data from weather or traffic sensors (Lopez, 2014), web-based or social media data, or machine-to-machine transactional data.

The other subprojects provide complementary services or they are building on the core to add higher-level abstractions. Both Google's and Hadoop's MapReduce systems have taken initial steps to ensure fault-tolerance for hardware, system software, and to some extent, for the algorithms in user application software. There exist many problems in dealing with storage of large amount of data.

MapReduce Framework

This is a programming paradigm that allows for massive job execution scalability against thousands of servers or clusters of servers. It also includes a distributed computational feature, MapReduce, which coordinates each of the servers in the cluster to operate on a part of the overall processing task in parallel. The key point of parallel processing is Divide and Conquer. That is, data is divided in an independent type and process it in parallel. The most widely known technology that helps to handle large-data would be a distribution data process framework of the MapReduce method.

Hadoop acts as a distributed computing operating system that provides a distributed file system across all nodes in the Hadoop cluster, as well as the ability to use other file systems. Numerous commercial and open source applications, toolkits, and data layers are available to operate on top of this core, providing job and task tracking, integration with other data processing solutions, scripting, and querying capabilities in SQL, as well as database functionality and content management for images, documents, and other types of data.

As we discussed earlier it's a top-level Apache project being built and used by a global community of contributors, written in the Java programming language. Yahoo! has been the largest contributor for the project. The Hadoop is used extensively across business in Yahoo!

Other tools that are used for data analytics are Storm and Kafka. Storm and Kafka are the future of stream processing, and they are already in use at a number of high-profile companies including Groupon, Alibaba, The Weather Channel, and many more. Spark is a next generation paradigm for big data processing developed by researchers at the University of California at Berkeley. It is an alternative to Hadoop which is designed to overcome the disk I/O limitations and improve the performance of earlier systems. The major feature of Spark that makes it unique is its ability to perform in-memory computations. Spark is a general engine for large-scale data processing that supports Java, Scala and Python and for certain tasks it is tested to be up to 100 times faster than Hadoop MapReduce when the data can fit in the memory. It can run on Hadoop Yarn manager and can read data from HDFS. This makes it extremely versatile to run on different systems.

WHAT IS CLOUD?

Cloud computing is computing in which large groups of remote servers are networked to allow centralized data storage and online access to computer services or resources. Cloud computing is a way to increase the capacity or add capabilities dynamically without investing in new infrastructure, training new personnel, or licensing new software. Actually, the main idea behind cloud computing is quite old. John McCarthy in 1960s had predicted that computing facilities will be provided to the general public like a utility. The term "cloud" has also been used in various contexts such as describing ATM networks(1990) and (S Tsuchiya, 2012). The definition used here given by (National Institute of Standard Technology), the idea of it is depicted in Figure 4.

Cloud Computing is a model for enabling convenient, on-demand network access to a shared pool of configurable computing resources(e.g. networks, servers, storage, applications and services) that can be rapidly provisioned and released with minimal management effort or service provider interaction.

Cloud computing requires three components: thin clients, grid computing, and utility computing. Thin clients are applications that make use of the virtualized computing interface. Users are commonly exposed to cloud computing systems through web interfaces to use services such as web-based email, search engines, and online stores. Grid computing harnesses the resources of a network of machines so that they can be used as one infrastructure. Utility computing provides computing resources on demand, where users "pay as they use". This is exemplified by Amazon EC2, which allows users to allocate virtual servers on demand, paying an hourly fee for each allocated server (Z.Xiao, 2014).

In the emerging computing model, the gadgets are mobile, devices with sensors (M. Vaidya & Deshpande, 2013, pp. 38-40) are connected, applications are interactive, development is collaborative, and service delivery needs to be immediate. Cloud computing can enable all these capabilities for businesses while optimizing costs and resource usage, since infrastructure (IaaS), platforms (PaaS) and software applications (SaaS) can be delivered on a usage-based service model. Users can get access to what they want as and when they need, instead of having to pay for any idle computing resources.

Big Data and cloud computing go hand-in-hand. Cloud computing enables to get more values from the great data sized from the companies. The analytics is enabled (D.Singh, 2014) in the journal of Big Data

Figure 4. Architecture of cloud computing

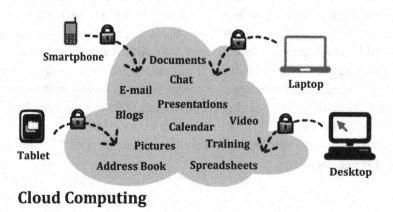

on data at a fraction of previous costs. This, in turn drives companies to acquire and store even more data, creating more need for processing power and driving a virtuous circle explored by (Parkhill D, 1966).

In the cloud deployment model, networking, platform, storage, and software infrastructure are provided as services that scale up or down depending on the demand as required.

Cloud Computing Model

1. Private Cloud

Private cloud is a new term that some vendors have recently used to describe offerings that emulate cloud computing on private networks. It is set up within an organization's internal enterprise datacenter. In the private cloud, scalable resources and virtual applications provided by the cloud vendor are pooled together and available for cloud users to share and use. There is a difference in private and public cloud is that, in the public cloud all the cloud resources and applications are managed by the organization itself, similar to Intranet functionality. Security is maintained in the utilization of data on the private cloud for its specified internal exposure. Only the organization and designated stakeholders may have access to operate on a specific Private cloud.

2. Public Cloud

Public cloud describes cloud computing in the traditional mainstream sense, whereby resources are dynamically provisioned by an off-site third-party provider on self-service basis over the Internet, via web applications/web services. It is typically based on a pay-per-use model. It is similar to a prepaid electricity metering system used on demand for cloud optimization. Public clouds are less secure than the other cloud models because it places an additional burden of ensuring all applications and data accessed on the public cloud are not subjected to malicious attacks.

3. Hybrid Cloud

Hybrid cloud is a private cloud linked to one or more external cloud services, centrally managed, provisioned as a single unit, and circumscribed by a secure network. It provides virtual IT solutions through a mix of both public and private clouds. In a hybrid cloud, part of the service infrastructure runs in private clouds while the remaining part runs in public clouds. Hybrid clouds offer more flexibility than both private and public clouds. Specifically they provide the tighter control and security over applications data as compared to public clouds, still facilitates on-demand service expansion and contraction.

There are some Cloud computing Delivery models defined, they are Infrastructure-as-a-Service (IaaS), Platform-as-a-Service (PaaS) and Software-as-a-Service(SaaS) which are elaborated in Table 1.

Infrastructure as a Serivce (IaaS) – It is a single tenant cloud layer where the Cloud computing vendor has dedicated resources are only shared with contracted clients at a pay-per-use fee. The computing hardware such as servers, networking devices and processing power can be used by the clients as per their need. IaaS completely abstracts the hardware beneath it and allows users to consume infrastructure as a service without bothering anything about the underlying complexities.

Table 1. Handling big data in cloud computing service models

Sr No	Task Done	Cloud Service Model
1	Data Collection	PaaS/SaaS
2	Data Curation	PaaS/SaaS
3	Data Integration and Aggregation	PaaS/SaaS
4	Data Storage	IaaS
5	Data Analysis	SaaS/PaaS

Platform as a service (PaaS) - It is a set of software and development tools hosted on the provider's servers. It is one layer above IaaS and abstracts everything up to Operating System, middleware etc. It offered PaaS works like IaaS but it provides an additional level of rented functionality. The use of virtual machines acts as a catalyst in the PaaS layer in cloud computing. The Virtual machines must be protected against the malicious attacks such as cloud malware. Therefore maintaining the integrity of applications and well enforcing accurate authentication checks during the transfer of data across the entire networking channels is fundamental.

Software as a Service(SaaS) – It is a software distribution model in which applications are hosted by a vendor or service provider and made available to the customers over an internet. SaaS is often associated with a pay-as-you-go subscription licensing model. Broadband service has become increasingly available, elaborated by (S. Arnold, 2009) to support user access from more areas around the world.

CLOUD COMPUTING CHARACTERISTICS

Measured Service

Cloud computing resource usage can be measured, controlled, and reported providing transparency for both the provider and consumer of the utilized service. Cloud computing services use a metering capability which enables to control and optimize resource use. This implies that just like air time, electricity or municipality water IT services are charged per usage metrics – pay per use. The more, the service of cloud is utilized, the higher the bill. This service is same as the utility companies sell power to subscribers, and telephone companies sell voice services, IT services such as network security management, data center hosting or even departmental billing can now be easily delivered as a contractual service.

Geo-Distribution and Ubiquitous Network Access

Clouds are generally accessible through the Internet hence the Internet is must and acts as service delivery network. Hence any device with Internet connectivity, be it a mobile phone, a PDA or a laptop, is able to access cloud services. Additionally, to achieve high network performance and localization, many of today's clouds consist of data centers located at many locations around the globe. A service provider can easily leverage geo-diversity to achieve maximum service utility.

Service Oriented

As mentioned previously, cloud computing adopts a service-driven operating model which provides service to the customers. Hence it places a strong emphasis on service management. In a cloud, each IaaS, PaaS and SaaS provider offers its service according to the Service Level Agreement (SLA) negotiated with its customers which assurances the critical objective to every provider.

Broad Network Access

Cloud Capabilities are available over the network and accessed through standard mechanisms that promote use by heterogeneous thin or thick client platforms such as mobile phones, laptops and PDAs.

Multi Tenacity

It is the one of the important characteristic of cloud computing advocated by the Cloud Security Alliance. It refers to the need for policy-driven enforcement, segmentation, isolation, governance, service levels, and chargeback/billing models for different consumer constituencies. Consumers might utilize a public cloud provider's service offerings or actually be from the same organization, such as different business units rather than distinct organizational entities, but would still share infrastructure.

Resource Pooling

The provider's computing resources are pooled together to serve multiple consumers using multiple-tenant model, with different physical and virtual resources dynamically assigned and reassigned according to consumer demand. The resources include among others storage, processing, memory, network bandwidth, virtual machines and email services. The pooling together of the resource builds economies of scale.

On-Demand Capabilities

A business will secure cloud-hosting services through a cloud host provider which could be your usual software vendor. The customer has access to the services and he has the power to change cloud services through an online control panel or directly with the provider. The users can be added/ deleted through storage networks and the same for the software as needed. Typically, there is monthly billing type of scenario for monthly subscription or a pay-for-what-you-use scenario. Generally, the terms of subscriptions and payments vary with each software provider explained in the white paper published by (D. Reeves, 2009).

ANALYSIS OF EXISTING CLOUD-BASED BIG DATA SOLUTIONS

Amazon Web Services

Amazon Web Services (AWS) is a set of cloud services, providing cloud based computation, storage and other functionality that enable organizations and individuals to deploy applications and services on an on-demand basis and at commodity prices. Amazon Elastic Compute Cloud (Amazon EC2) enables cloud users to launch and manage server instances in data centers. EC2 provides the ability to place instances in multiple locations. EC2 machines images are stored in and retrieved from Amazon Simple Storage Service. For cloud users, Amazon CloudWatch is a useful management tool which collects raw data from partnered AWS services such as Amazon EC2 and then processes the information into readable, near real time metrics. The metrics about EC2 include, for example, CPU utilization, network in/out bytes, disk read/write operations, etc.

Cloud users to launch and manage server instances in data centers using APIs or available tools and utilities. EC2 instances are virtual machines running on top of the Xen virtualization engine. After creating and starting an instance, users can upload software and make changes to it. When changes are finished, they can be bundled as a new machine image. An identical copy can then be launched at any time. Users have nearly full control of the entire software stack on the EC2 instances that look like hardware to them. On the other hand, this feature makes it inherently difficult for Amazon to offer automatic scaling of resources. EC2 provides the ability to place instances in multiple locations. Amazon Virtual Private Cloud (VPC) is a secure and seamless bridge between a company's existing IT infrastructure and the AWS cloud. Amazon VPC enables enterprises to connect their existing infrastructure to a set of isolated AWS compute resources via a Virtual Private Network (VPN) connection, and to extend their existing management capabilities such as security services, firewalls, and intrusion detection systems to include their AWS resources. For cloud users, Amazon CloudWatch is a useful management tool which collects raw data from partnered AWS services such as Amazon EC2 and then processes the information into readable, near real-time metrics. The metrics about EC2 include, for example, CPU utilization, network in/out bytes, disk read/write operations, etc.

Microsoft Windows Azure Platform

Microsoft's Windows Azure platform provides a specific set of services to cloud users. Windows Azure provides a Windows-based environment for running applications and it also stores data on servers in data centers. SQL Azure provides a Windows based environment for running applications and storing data on servers in data servers. Windows Azure platform can be used both by applications running in the cloud and by applications running on local systems. Windows Azure also supports applications built on the .NET Framework and other ordinary languages supported in Windows systems, like C#, Visual Basic, C++, and others. Windows Azure supports general-purpose programs, rather than a single class of computing. Developers can create web applications using technologies such as ASP.NET and Windows Communication Foundation (WCF), applications that run as independent background processes, or applications that combine the two. Windows Azure allows storing data in blobs, tables, and queues, all accessed in a RESTful style via HTTP or HTTPS. SQL Azure components are SQL Azure Database and "Huron" Data Sync. SQL Azure Database is built on Microsoft SQL Server, providing a database management system (DBMS) in the cloud. The data can be accessed using ADO.NET and other Windows data access interfaces. Users can also use on premises software to work with this cloud-based information. "Huron" Data Sync synchronizes relational data across various on-premises DBMSs is elaborated (Microsoft Azure, 2010).

Google App Engine

Google App Engine is a platform for traditional web applications in Google-managed data centers. Currently, the supported programming languages are Python and Java. Web frameworks that run on the Google App Engine include Django, CherryPy, Pylons, and web2py, as well as a custom Google-written web application framework similar to JSP or ASP.NET. Google handles deploying code to a cluster, monitoring, failover, and launching application instances as necessary. Current APIs support features such as storing and retrieving data from a BigTable which is a non-relational database, making HTTP requests and caching. Developers have read-only access to the filesystem (App Engine, 2014).

Google Big Query

Google Big Query is a web service allows interactive analysis of massive datasets. It is considered an IaaS, accessible through APIs, browsers or command line tools. Data can be loaded into a flat or nested table, stored as a columnar database, directly from the Google Cloud Storage or after being formatted according to JSON or CVS. Queries have to be written in the Big Query Sql dialect. It does not support Hadoop or MapReduce.

Opani

Opani, labelled as IaaS, is a big data service which just offers analytic capabilities like capturing; organization and storage of data are handled by the user who, in turn, can leverage existing or proprietary software like Ruby, Python or The R Project for Statistical Computing scripts to analyze them. Data can be stored on and accessed from various databases (like HBase and MySQL), Google Drive or Amazon Simple Storage Service (making it also possible to exploit Amazon's Map Reduce support). Opani also leverages Google Big Query to analyze unstructured data.

Pentaho Big Aata Analytics

Pentaho Big Data Analytics is a comprehensive, unified solution that supports the entire big data lifecycle, from data capturing to analysis and visualization of the results. The platform relies on Hadoop for data organization and storage, supporting different distributions (Intel, Hortonworks, Cloudera), but it also offers a series of embedded plugins and connectors to communicate with Nosql databases (MongoDB and Cassandra), all part of Embedded Pentaho Data Integration elaborated by (Qi. Zhang, 2010). To study the Big Data Storage on Cloud some case studies have been given below.

CASE 1: BIG DATA STORAGE ON CLOUD

Los Angeles Metropolitan Transportation Authority (LAMetro), Integrated Media Systems Center (IMSC) have been given access to high-resolution spatiotemporal transportation data from the LA County road network. This data arrives at 46 megabytes per minute and over 15 terabytes have been collected so far.

IMSC researchers have developed an end-to-end system called TransDec (for Transportation Decision-making) to acquire, store, analyze and visualize these datasets. Various components of TransDec corresponding to the Big Data flow are discussed here, depicted in Figure 5 which depicts the case of cloud.

- **Acquisition:** The current system acquires the following datasets in real-time.
- **Traffic Loop Detectors:** About 8,900 sensors located on the highways and arterial streets collect traffic parameters such as occupancy, volume, and speed at the rate of one reading/sensor/min.
- **Bus and Rail:** Includes information from about 2,036 busses and 35 trains operating in 145 different routes in Los Angeles County. The sensor data contain geospatial location of each bus every two minutes, next-stop information relative to current location, and delay information relative to predefined timetables.
- **Ramp Meters and CMS:** 1851 ramp meters regulate the flow of traffic entering into highways according to current traffic conditions, and 160 Changeable Message Signs (CMS) to give travelers information about road conditions such as delays, accidents, and roadwork zones. The update rate of each ramp meter and CMS sensor is 75 seconds.
- **Event:** Detailed free-text format information (for example, number of casualties, ambulance arrival time) about special events such as collisions, traffic hazards, and so on acquired from three different agencies.
- **Cleaning:** Data-cleaning algorithms remove redundant XML headers, detect and remove redundant sensor readings, and so on in real time using Microsoft's StreamInsight, resulting in minimizing the 46MB/minute input data to 25MB/minute. The result is then stored as simple tables into then Microsoft Azure cloud platform.
- **Aggregation/Representation:** Data are aggregated and indexed into a set of tables in Oracle 11g (indexed in space and time with an R-tree and B-tree). For example, the data are aggregated to create sketches for supporting a predefined set of spatial and temporal queries (for example, average hourly speed of a segment of north-bond I-110).
- **Analysis:** Several machine-learning techniques are applied, to generate accurate traffic patterns/models for various road segments of LA County at different times of the day may be at rush-hours, on weekends and in different seasons. Historical accident data is used to classify new accidents to predict clearance time and the length of induced traffic backlog.

Figure 5. Case of cloud computing

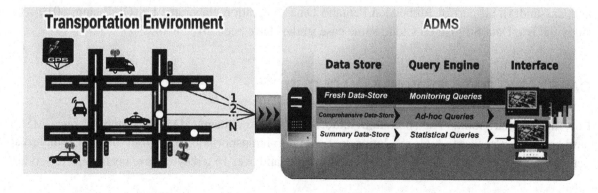

- **Interpretation:** Many things can go wrong in a complex system, giving rise to bogus results. For example, the failures of various (independent) system components can go unnoticed, resulting in loss of data. Similarly, the data format was sometimes changed by one organization without informing a downstream organization, resulting in erroneous parsing. To address such problems, several monitoring scripts have been developed, along with mechanisms to obtain user confirmation and correction. This whole case study is elaborated here (Jagdish, 2014, p.6).

CASE 2: GOOGLE APP ENGINE

Google App Engine is a platform for traditional web applications in Google-managed data centers. Currently, the supported programming languages are Python and Java. Web frameworks that run on the Google App Engine include Django, CherryPy, Pylons, and web2py, as well as a custom Google-written web application framework similar to JSP or ASP.NET. Google handles deploying code to a cluster, monitoring, failover, and launching application instances as necessary. Current APIs support features such as storing and retrieving data from a BigTable non-relational database, making HTTP requests and caching. Developers have read only access to the file system on App Engine.

The present Cloud computing design has some issues yet to be solved:

- Basic DBMS has not been tailored for cloud Computing
- Data acts as a serious issue so it would be ideal to have Data Centers closer the user than the provider
- Data Replication must be carefully done else it affects data integrity and gives an error prone analysis
- Deployment models should be set up
- Ability to run in a heterogeneous environment
- Data is encrypted before uploaded on the cloud. This is the biggest concern on cloud storage.

CASE 3: CISCO'S S-CLOUD ARCHITECTURE

Cisco IT initially developed S-Cloud for Cisco's private cloud, later adding more nodes on an enterprise public cloud platform. The private S-Cloud currently consists of two nodes, in Cisco's Allen, Texas and Mountain View, California data centers. Together these nodes provide 960 TB of raw capacity, of which 830 TB is usable. The S-Cloud infrastructure in the public cloud currently consists of four nodes, in North America, Europe, and Asia Pacific. Cisco InfoSec approved the security infrastructure for the S-Cloud public cloud, which includes authentication and authorization; encryption at rest and during transfer; and encryption key services. S-Cloud represents a new approach to managing big data that incorporates not only storage, but also servers and switches. It is object-based and uses HTTP as its primary interface, although teams that need to use Common Internet File Sharing (CIFS) or Network File Sharing (NFS) can do so using third-party software, referred from by (A. Katal, 2013).

CLOUD COMPUTING CHALLENGES

The traditional serial algorithm is inefficient for the big data. If there is enough data parallelism in the application, users can take advantage of the cloud's reduced cost model to use hundreds of computers for a short time costs. The scalability issue of Big data has lead towards cloud computing, which now aggregates multiple disparate workloads with varying performance goals into very large clusters. This requires a high level of sharing of resources which is expensive and also brings with it various challenges like how to run and execute various jobs so that we can meet the goal of each workload cost effectively

- **Data Location:** Cloud computing technology allows cloud servers to reside anywhere, thus the enterprise may not know the physical location of the server used to store and process their data and applications. Although from the technology point of view, location is least relevant, this has become a critical issue for data governance requirements. It is essential to understand that many Cloud Service Providers (CSPs) can also specifically define where data is to be located.
- **Blending Data:** The data which has been created by sharing various applications and multi-tenancy is one of the characteristics associated with cloud computing. Although many Cloud Service Providers have multi-tenant applications that are secure, scalable and customizable. Security and privacy issues are still often concerns among enterprises. Data encryption is another control that can assist data confidentiality.
- **Disaster Recovery:** It is a concern of enterprises about the resiliency of cloud computing, since data may be scattered around and collected from multiple servers and geographical areas. It may be possible that the data for a specific point of time cannot be identified. Unlike traditional hosting, the enterprise knows exactly where the location is of their data, to be rapidly retrieved in the event of disaster recovery. In the cloud computing model, the primary Cloud Service Provider (CSP) may outsource capabilities to third parties, who may also outsource the recovery process elaborated by (S. Kaisler et. al., 2013). This will become more complex when the primary CSP does not ultimately hold the data

CLOUD COMPUTING IMPLEMENTATIONS

Amazon's Elastic Computing Cloud (EC2) service manages the compute-resources just like a traditional OS has. A traditional OS provides a set of process interfaces, such as the POSIX interface, for applications to call to instantiate new processes or terminate existing ones. When processes are running, the OS manages the fair allocation of CPU cycles among the various processes. Similarly, EC2 provides a set of web services API for applications to call to instantiate new or terminate existing virtual machines. When virtual machines are running, EC2 manages the fair allocation of compute resources among virtual machines. A traditional OS provides a file interface, where an application could call the interface functions to open, read, write and close a file. Similarly, S3 exposes a set of web services API which applications could call to put and get objects. Like EC2, the web services API is designed to be scalable. In addition to the API, object storage is also implemented in a scalable fashion, i.e., objects are distributed among many servers and each object is replicated several times. As of July 2008, S3 stores 22 billion objects – a clear demonstration of its scalability. Amazon's Simple Queue Service (SQS) is similar to a UNIX pipe. In a UNIX pipe, a process can write messages at one end and another process could consume the messages at the other end. Unlike a UNIX pipe which is limited to processes running on the same hardware, anyone on the Internet could write to or read from a SQS queue. Amazon's SimpleDB service is most similar to the registry service in a Windows OS. As its name suggests, it could also be thought of as a simplified database. An application could write some data into SimpleDB, which will be persistently stored. SimpleDB also offers the ability to run simple queries against the stored data. Similar to EC2 and S3, both SQS and SimpleDB are designed to be highly scalable. Since all Amazon services are exposed as web services APIs, standard techniques to design scalable web applications, such as DNS load balancing and IP load balancing using hardware load balancers, could help make these services scalable. The Microsoft cloud OS also offers similar services. Microsoft Azure workers provide compute services. It differs from Amazon EC2 in that it provides computation capacity inside a .NET container instead of an x86 virtual machine. Similar to S3, Microsoft Azure blob provides storage service. Similar to SQS and Unix pipe, Microsoft Azure queue provides messaging service. Lastly, similar to SimpleDB and Windows registry, Microsoft Azure table provides persistent state storage service.

TECHNICAL CHALLENGES

Fault Tolerance

With the incoming of new technologies like Cloud computing and Big data it is always intended that whenever the failure occurs the damage done should be within reach rather than beginning the whole task from the scratch. Fault-tolerant computing is extremely hard, involving intricate algorithms. It is simply not possible to devise absolutely foolproof, 100% reliable fault tolerant machines or software. Thus the main task is to reduce the probability of failure to an "acceptable" level. Cloud computing provides a compelling platform for hosting large scale data intensive applications. Such applications are controlled by MapReduce frameworks such as Hadoop for scalable and fault tolerant data processing. Hadoop tasks such as sort, is I/O intensive, whether grep requires significant CPU resources. Furthermore, the VM is allocated to each Hadoop node may have heterogeneous characteristics. For example, the bandwidth available to a VM is dependent on other VMs collected on the same server. Hence, it is possible to optimize the performance and cost of a MapReduce application by carefully selecting its configuration parameter values and designing more efficient scheduling algorithms. By moderating the bottleneck resources, execution time of applications can be significantly improved for big data analysis on cloud computing environment.

Distributed file systems are key building blocks for cloud computing applications based on the MapReduce programming paradigm. In such file systems, nodes simultaneously serve computing and storage functions; a file is partitioned into a number of chunks allocated in distinct nodes so that MapReduce tasks can be performed in parallel over the nodes. For example, consider a word count application that counts the number of distinct words and the frequency of each unique word in a large file. In such an application, a cloud partitions the file into a large number of disjointed and fixed-size pieces (or file chunks) and assigns them to different cloud storage nodes (i.e., chunkservers). Each storage node (or node for short) then calculates the frequency of each unique word by scanning and parsing its local file chunks. In such a distributed file system, the load of a node is typically proportional to the number of file chunks the node possesses. Because the files in a cloud can be arbitrarily created, deleted, and appended, and nodes can be upgraded, replaced and added in the file system, the file chunks are not distributed as uniformly as possible among the nodes. Load balance among storage nodes is a critical function in clouds. In a load-balanced cloud, the resources can be well utilized and provisioned, maximizing the performance of MapReduce-based applications. State-of-the-art distributed file systems (e.g., Google GFS and Hadoop HDFS in clouds rely on central nodes to manage the metadata information of the file systems and to balance the loads of storage nodes based on that metadata. The centralized approach simplifies the design and implementation of a distributed file system.

Handling Fault Tolerance

There occur many problems also with using many pieces of hardware as it increases the chances of failure. The problem of failure is handled by the Hadoop Distributed File System and problem of combining data is handled by MapReduce programming Paradigm. They are the techniques which are used for big data processing. Even, it can be used on Cloud. MapReduce basically reduces the problem of disk reads and writes by providing a programming model dealing in computation with keys and values. Hadoop thus provides a reliable shared storage and analysis system. The storage is provided by HDFS and computations by MapReduce.

Security

The privacy of data is another huge concern, and one that increases in the context of Big Data. Managing privacy effectively is both a technical and a sociological problem, which should be addressed from the said perspective to realize the promise of using Big Data. An online services today require us to share private information may be shared now a days on social networking sites or applications, but a normal person doesn't come to know, how this data is shared, how this shared data can be linked, and how to give users fine-grained control over this sharing in an intuitive, but effective way. Privacy plays a vital role here but other aspect of data is ownership. The various security issues are data loss, phishing, botnet (running remotely on a collection of machines) pose serious threats to organization's data and software. Since service providers do not have access to the physical security of systems of data centers, they have to rely on the infrastructure providers to achieve full data security. The infrastructure provides must achieve following objectives:

1. **Confidentiality:** For sure data access and transfer. It is usually achieved using cryptographic protocols.
2. **Auditability:** Confirming from time to time whether security settings of applications has been tampered or not. It is generally achieved by remote confirmation services. Remote confirmation typically requires a trusted platform module (TPM) to generate non-forgeable system summary as a proof of system security. This system state is encrypted using TPM's private key.

Accountability and auditing are security issues that present a problem for both MapReduce and Big Data. Accountability is the ability to know when someone performs an action and holding them responsible for that action and inspected through auditing. A chain of accountability allows the members of a cloud ecosystem to ensure that obligations to protect data are observed by all who process the data, irrespective of where that processing occurs. But, it has been stated that the MapReduce accountability is only provided when the mappers and reducers are held responsible for the tasks they have completed. One solution to this issue that has been proposed is the creation of an Accountable MapReduce. This solution utilizes a set of auditors to inconspicuously perform accountability tests on the mappers and reducers in real-time. Through the monitoring of the results of these tests, malicious mappers or reducers can be detected and accountability can be provided.

Cloud service providers distribute datacenters globally to ensure reliability, provide locality of services and leverage incentives provided by local governments. A number of applications within the Smart Grid use the integrated information that is available. The information processing, analysis may be provided by third party vendors for use by consumers, utilities and other third party vendors. These applications include mobile apps, consumer usage analysis sites, information and aggregation and sharing services. Such applications may be deployed across cloud and non-cloud platforms. Data shared between such type of applications need to be secured and privacy preserved. Such smart grid applications explained by (Y. Simmhan et.al., 2011) will have to be designed with security and privacy.

HANDLING CRITICAL ISSUES OF BIG DATA ON CLOUD

The MapReduce paradigm has been widely used for large scale data-intensive computing within data centers. Compared with traditional methods for large-scale data analysis, such as parallel DBMS and data-intensive workflows, the MapReduce paradigm has several advantages including low cost for setup, deploy, and development, massively data parallelism, as well as fault tolerant processing. The most popular implementation of the MapReduce model is the Apache Hadoop on Demand, which allows applications to run on large clusters built with commodity hardware. The Hadoop framework transparently provides both reliability and data transfer. Other MapReduce implementations are available for various architectures, such as CUDA, Hyrax by (E.Merinelli, 2009, p.24) as a part of the research explains the mobile computing environment.

The Apache Hadoop on Demand (HOD) provides virtual Hadoop clusters over a large physical cluster. It uses the Torque resource manager to perform node allocation. myHadoop is a system for provisioning on-demand Hadoop instances via traditional schedulers on HPC resources. There are a number of projects that are MapReduce-like or based on Hadoop implementation. Examples include Twister, Sector/Sphere, and all-pairs. There are certain limitations for using MapReduce and Hadoop for large scale and multi datacenter environments. MapReduce and Hadoop for data processing are limited to compute infrastructures within a local area network, e.g., a single cluster within a data centre. The advantages of Hadoop and MapReduce tool have been elaborated but still there are some limitations, which are discussed below:

- It has been reported that large-scale big data applications in scientific domain will suffer performance degradation using the MapReduce and Hadoop solution due to the absence of high performance parallel file system (currently Hadoop is using HDFS) and runtime execution system optimization.

- The Hadoop MapReduce uses 'gfork'h to start multiple processes to execute Map and Reduce tasks. Therefore, this MapReduce cannot be deployed in traditional compute centres with Torque and Globus Toolkit as task execution manager. Furthermore the Hadoop MapReduce implementation does not include security models, thus it is not suitable for large-scale compute infrastructures.
- Large-scale scientific computing applications are typically expressed with diverse parallel patterns, which are not easily presented by the limited semantics of MapReduce.
- MapReduce and Hadoop currently do not efficiently support data-intensive workflow systems although there are some preliminary efforts.

There are some new fundamentals have come up and they have been detailed as below.

Mobile Cloud Computing

Hyrax, a MCC client that allows mobile devices to use Cloud Computing platforms. Hyrax allows applications to conveniently use data and execute computing jobs on smartphone networks and heterogeneous networks of phones and servers. Research has been focused primarily on the implementation and evaluation of MCC infrastructure based on MapReduce. The MCC platform is explained in SLL (Siyakhula Living Lab) using one or a combination of the following emerging cloud software environments and existing platforms: ownCloud, Eucalyptus, OpenNebula, OpenStack, OpenMobster, Twilio API, Open Cloud Computing Interface (OCCI), and Cloud Data Management Interface (CDMI). When evaluating the system we will take into consideration various important aspects of Mobile Cloud Computing systems. These include computational and communication requirements, mobile network impact, energy considerations, information security, system reliability and application usability explained by (J. Fan et.al., 2014).

Storage Services on Cloud

Currently, private and public cloud data centre providers support three storage service abstractions that differ the way they store, index, and execute queries over the stored data. The cloud service providers like Binary large object (BLOB) for binary files, for example Amazon S3, Azure Blob Storage. They can store anything from audio, video, photos to email messages as unstructured data when the Table-like storage is taken into consideration based on key-value store, for example, Amazon SimpleDB, HBase, BigTable and HyperTable. These types of storage services do not require fixed data schemas and support horizontal scalability. However, unlike relational database management system (RDBMS) they do not support ACID transaction principles, rather odder weaker consistency properties. RDBMS, such as Oracle and MySQL are suitable for managing relational or structured data, especially in the application scenario where ACID properties is a requirement. However, they can only support shared everything cloud application architecture elaborated by (Chang F & Dean et.al, 2006), which can be clustered, replicated, and scaled on demand.

Novel Cloud Architecture: Cloud MapReduce

Cloud MapReduce was initially developed at Accenture Technology Labs. It is a MapReduce implementation on top of the Amazon Cloud OS. Cloud MapReduce has minimal risk w.r.t. the MapReduce patent, compared to other open source implementations, as it is implemented in a completely different architecture than described in the Google paper. By exploiting a cloud OS's scalability, Cloud MapReduce achieves three primary advantages over other MapReduce implementations built on a traditional OS:

- It is faster than other implementations (e.g., 60 times faster than Hadoop in one case. Speedup depends on the application and data.).
- It is more scalable and more failure resistant because it has no single point of bottleneck.
- It is dramatically simpler with only 3,000 lines of code (e.g., two orders of magnitude simpler than Hadoop).

Following are the reasons which are discussed that makes Cloud MapReduce as fundamentally faster.

- **No Sorting:** As described above, the infinite size abstraction presented by SQS (both in terms of the number of queues and the size of each queue) allows us to bypass sorting.

Since sorting takes $O(n \log (n))$, Cloud MapReduce can perform even better when the data set is large.

- **Parallelize Processing and Copying:** Cloud MapReduce starts uploading reduce results as soon as they are produced in the map phase even before a map task finishes. This parallelizes the network transfer with the CPU intensive processing.
- **No Disk Paging:** Since the number of key-value pairs in a reduce task is unbounded, Hadoop may have to spill partial sorting results to disk multiple times in order to fit within the main memory.
- **No Staging:** Hadoop always stores the intermediate results on disks and then copies over the results to the hard disks on the destination node when instructed by the master. As a result, the data not only transits through the network once, but it also transits twice through the local disk. In comparison, Cloud MapReduce uses SQS as a staging area so that it can do everything in memory; therefore, the data only transits once through the network.
- **Finer Grain Job Assignment:** Because a task can be small, job assignments happen at a much finer granularity. Nodes of different capacity are automatically assigned work proportional to their capacity. A straggler is unlikely to drag on the overall computation for too long.

Implementation of MapReduce on top of the Amazon cloud OS has three primary advantages. First, it is simpler. It has 3,000 lines of Java code, two orders of magnitude simpler than a traditional implementation. Second, the implementation is more scalable because there is no single point of scalability bottleneck, and which has been proved by research. Last, cloud MapReduce implementation is faster. In one case, it is 60 times faster than the Hadoop implementation. R is the language by which data is analyzed (Revolution Analytics, 2011). Currently, most of the commercial clouds are implemented in large data centers and operated in a centralized fashion. Although this design achieves economy-of-scale and high manageability, it also comes with its limitations such high energy expense and high initial investment for constructing data centers. Recent work suggests that small sized data centers can be more advantageous than big data centers in many case; a small data center does not consume so much power, hence it does not require a powerful and yet expensive cooling system; small data centers are cheaper to build and better geographically distributed than large data centers.

FUTURE RESEARCH DIRECTIONS

Two methods which seem to increase the fault tolerance in Big Data in cloud computing environment are as below: First is to divide the whole computation being done into tasks and second is to assign these tasks to different nodes for computation. Restarting the whole computation becomes cumbersome process. Here, the role of applying Checkpoints plays a role. It keeps the state of the system at certain intervals of the time. In case of any failure, the computation can restart from last checkpoint maintained.

The problem of privacy of the data having huge importance that must be addressed to overcome the disbelief of end-users towards big data applications implemented in cloud. Data confidentiality problems are aggravated when the data to be analyzed come from different sources that use different security mechanisms and that are often associated with location information.

For maintaining the security and privacy of data on Cloud platforms, there is a technique which offers a secure sandbox, which safely executes and analyzes files for malicious behavior and other indicators of compromise for the file formats which include: executables, PDFs and other files. It is third party applications that can access restricted information from the utility and provide services to consumers.

CONCLUSION

The world has entered in the era of Big Data. Cloud computing has recently emerged as a compelling paradigm for managing and delivering services over the Internet. Many sectors of our economy are now moving to a data-driven decision making model where the core business analyses the huge and diverse amount of data. For explaining this, case on supply chain management has also been discussed here. This chapter surveys some data processing platforms like Hadoop, Spark and their use on cloud. On one hand Cloud Computing being attractive not only for personal users but also for small and middle enterprises, appears as an ideal solution for the efficient management and analysis of big data streams. However, there are many limitations and barriers in such effectiveness, especially in the light of the remote and local data movement overhead (network messages, memory and storage accesses). After critically analyzing the several cloud-based big data solutions available on the market, positioning them in the different phases of a well established data value chain, it has highlighted the potential, the urgent challenges to be faced and the early results related to the development of data-intensive applications distributed across multiple cloud-based data centres.

The evolution of mobile applications by (Lim & Hurson, 2002) enabled via Cloud Computing technology for use in developing countries clearly unfolds a much greater opportunity for developing countries to participate in the global knowledge economy on an equal footing with developed nations. However, despite the significant benefits offered by cloud computing, the people are skeptical in using them. Many key challenges including security, fault tolerance on cloud have been receiving attention from the research community. There is a great opportunity in this field for bringing significant impact in the industry.

REFERENCES

Arnold, S. (2009, August 19). Cloud Computing and the Issues of Privacy. *KM World* (pp. 14-22).

Chakravorty, A. (2013, October). Privacy Preserving Data Analytics for Smart Homes. *Proceedings of the IEEE Security and Privacy Workshops* (pp. 23-27).

Chandramouly, A., & Stinson, A. (2013 January). Enabling Big Data Solutions with Centralized Data Management (White paper). IT Best Practices Enterprise Data Management.

Chang, F., & Dean, J. et al.. (2006). Bigtable: A Distributed Storage System for Structured Data. *Proceedings of OSDI.*

Data community White Paper developed by leading researchers: Challenges and Opportunities with Big Data. (2012). Purdue University. Retrieved from www.purdue.edu/discoverypark/cyber/assets/pdfs/

Diagram of Hadoop Architecture. (n. d.). Retrieved from http://hadoop.apache.org/docs/r1.2.1/hdfs_design.html

Eigene, E. M. (2009, September). Hyrax: Cloud Computing on Mobile Devices using MapReduce. [Dissertation]. Carnegie Mellon University Pittsburgh.

Fan, J., Han, F., & Liu, H. (2014, August). Challenges of Big Data Analysis, National. *Scientific Review (Singapore)*, *1*(2).

Google App Engine. (n. d.). Retrieved from http://code.google.com/appengine

Han & Kamber. (2006). *Data Mining: Concept and Techniques*. Maurgan Kaufmann Publishers.

Hsiao H.-C., Chung, H.-Y., Shen, H., Chao, Y.-C. (2013, May). Load Rebalancing for Distributed File Systems in Clouds. *IEEE Transactions on Parallel and Distributed Systems*, 24(5), 951-962.

IBM Corporation Software Group. (2013). Wrangling big data: Fundamentals of Data Lifecycle Management, 1-12

Infosys Labs Briefings. (2013). Big Data-Challenges-Opportunities, 11(1).

Jagadish, H. V., Gehrke, J., Labrinidis, A., Papakonstantinou, Y., Patel, J. M., Ramakrishnan, R., & Shahabi, C. (2014, July). Big Data and its Technical Challenges. *Communications of the ACM*, *57*(7), 86–94. doi:10.1145/2611567

Kaisler, S., Armour, F., Espinsoa, J. A., & Money, W. (2013). Big Data: Issues and Challenges Moving Forward. *Proceedings of the Hawaii International Conference on System Sciences* (pp. 995-1004). doi:10.1109/HICSS.2013.645

Katal, A., Wazid, M., & Goudar, R. H. (2013 August). Big Data: Issues, Challenges, Tools and Good Practices. *Proceedings of the International Conference on Contemporary Computing (pp. 404-409)*. doi:10.1109/IC3.2013.6612229

Lim, J., & Hurson, A. R. (2002, November). Transaction Processing in Mobile Heterogeneous Database Systems. *IEEE Transactions on Knowledge and Data Engineering*, *14*(6), 1330–1346. doi:10.1109/TKDE.2002.1047771

Lopez, V. (2014). *Big and Open data challenges for Smart City*. Researching Group at Madrid.

Parkhill, D. (1966). *Article on The challenge of the Computer Utility*. Addison-Wesley Publications.

Piatetsky-Shapiro, G., & Parker, G. (2006). Module on Data Mining. Retrieved from www.kdnuggets.com

Reeves, D. (2009). *Enterprise Cloud Computing: Transforming IT*. Whitepaper Platform Computing.

Revolution Analytics White Paper. (2011). Advanced 'Big Data' Analytics with R and Hadoop.

Simmhan, Y., Kumbhare, A. G., Cao, B., & Prasanna, V. (2011, July). Analysis of Security and Privacy Issues in Smart Grid Software Architectures on Clouds. *Proceedings of the IEEE Conference on Cloud Computing* (pp. 582-589). doi:10.1109/CLOUD.2011.107

Singh, D., & Reddy, C.K. (2014). A Survey on Platforms for Big Data Analytics. *Journal of Big Data*, 8.

Son, N. H. (2012). Module on Data Preprocessing Techniques for Data Mining on Data Cleaning and Data Preprocessing. Retrieved from http://elitepdf.com/

The Article from Dataconomy. (2014). Big Data Complexity and India's Election. Retrieved from http://dataconomy.com/big-data-complexity-and-indias-election/

The NIST Definition of Cloud Computing. (n. d.). *National Institute of Standards and Technology*.

Tsuchiya, S., Sakamoto, Y., Tsuchimoto, Y., & Lee, V. (2012, April). Big Data Processing in Cloud Environments, FUJITSU Sc. *Tech Journal*, *48*(2), 159–168.

Vaidya, M., & Deshpande, S. (2013). Study of Hadoop-based Traffic Management System, IJCA Proceedings of ICRTITCS (Vol. 3, pp. 38-42).

Windows Azure (software). (n. d.). Microsoft. Retrieved from www.microsoft.com/azure

Xiao, Z., & Xiao, Y. (2014). Achieving accountable MapReduce in Cloud Computing. *Future Generation Computer Systems*, *30*, 1–13. doi:10.1016/j.future.2013.07.001

Zhang, Q., Cheng, L., & Boothbay, R. (2010). Cloud Computing: State-of-the-Art and Research Challenges. *J Internet Serv Appl, The Brazilian Computers & Society*, 2010.

KEY TERMS AND DEFINITIONS

Cloud Computing: A model for enabling convenient, on-demand network access to a shared pool of configurable computing resources(e.g. networks, servers, storage, applications and services) that can be rapidly provisioned and released with minimal management effort or service provider interaction. Defined by NIST.

Grid: A distributed, high performance computing and data handling infrastructure that incorporates geographically and organizationally dispersed, heterogeneous resources (computing systems, storage systems, instruments and other real-time data sources, human collaborators, communication systems) and provides common interfaces for all these resources, using standard, open, general-purpose protocols and interfaces.

Hybrid Cloud: The cloud infrastructure is a composition of two or more distinct cloud infrastructures (private, community, or public) that remain unique entities, but are bound together by standardized or proprietary technology that enables data and application portability (e.g., cloud bursting for load balancing between clouds).

Infrastructure as a Service (IAAS): The capability provided to the consumer is to provision processing, storage, networks, and other fundamental computing resources where the consumer is able to deploy and run arbitrary software, which can include operating systems and applications. The consumer does not manage or control the underlying cloud infrastructure but has control over operating systems, storage, and deployed applications and possibly limited control of select networking components.

Platform as a Service (PAAS): The capability provided to the consumer is to deploy onto the cloud infrastructure consumer-created or acquired applications created using programming languages, libraries, services, and tools supported by the provider. The consumer does not manage or control the underlying cloud infrastructure including network, servers, operating systems, or storage, but has control over the deployed applications and possibly configuration settings for the application-hosting environment.

Private Cloud: The cloud infrastructure is provisioned for exclusive use by a single organization comprising multiple consumers (e.g. business units). It may be owned, managed, and operated by the organization, a third party, or some combination of them, and it may exist on or off premises.

Public Cloud: The cloud infrastructure is provisioned for open use by the general public. It may be owned, managed, and operated by a business, academic, or government organization, or some combination of them. It exists on the premises of the cloud provider.

Software as a Service (SAAS): The capability provided to the consumer is to provision processing, storage, networks, and other fundamental computing resources where the consumer is able to deploy and run arbitrary software, which can include operating systems and applications. The consumer does not manage or control the underlying cloud infrastructure but has control over operating systems, storage, and deployed applications; and possibly limited control of select networking components.

Section 2
Managing Big Data of Special Types in Cloud Computing Environments

Chapter 6
Modeling and Indexing Spatiotemporal Trajectory Data in Non-Relational Databases

Berkay Aydin
Georgia State University, USA

Vijay Akkineni
Georgia State University, USA

Rafal A Angryk
Georgia State University, USA

ABSTRACT

With the ever-growing nature of spatiotemporal data, it is inevitable to use non-relational and distributed database systems for storing massive spatiotemporal datasets. In this chapter, the important aspects of non-relational (NoSQL) databases for storing large-scale spatiotemporal trajectory data are investigated. Mainly, two data storage schemata are proposed for storing trajectories, which are called traditional and partitioned data models. Additionally spatiotemporal and non-spatiotemporal indexing structures are designed for efficiently retrieving data under different usage scenarios. The results of the experiments exhibit the advantages of utilizing data models and indexing structures for various query types.

INTRODUCTION

In recent years, the rapid advancements in satellite imagery technology, GPS enabled devices, location-based web services, and social networks caused a proliferation of massive spatiotemporal data sets (Nascimento, Pfoser, & Theodoridis, 2003). Many consumer-oriented applications from social networks (Facebook, Twitter, Swarm) to mobile services including routing (Google Maps, Apple Maps), taxi services (Uber) etc. consume and generate spatio-temporal location data (Quercia, Lathia, Calabrese, Lorenzo, & Crowcroft, 2010). Furthermore, there are many massive spatiotemporal data repositories generated

DOI: 10.4018/978-1-4666-9834-5.ch006

by scientific resources that are monitoring the moving objects. These include solar events (Schuh *et al.*, 2013), animal migrations (Buchin, Dodge, & Speckmann, 2014), and meteorological phenomena (J. J. Wang et al., 2014). Most traditional relational database management systems provide efficient storage and retrieval schema for almost all types of data. However, usually, they are optimized for datasets of gigabytes of size and centralized processing. On the other hand, NoSQL databases, also known as non-relational databases, refer to a set of database systems that emphasize schema-free models, and ad hoc data organization. Many people are increasingly using these databases where scalability, high volume and fault tolerance of *big spatiotemporal data* are key deciding factors. NoSQL databases being an umbrella for several types of data stores such as key-value store, column store, document store, graph database and several other storage formats, there is no *one-for-all* spatiotemporal model used in non-relational databases; and appropriateness of a particular solution depends on the problems to be solved.

Relational database management systems such as *PostgreSQL* (with *PostGIS*), *Oracle* (*Spatial and Graph*) are designed to store, index and query data that represents geometric objects with spatial characteristics. However, because of the computationally expensive (both processing and storage-wise) spatial and spatiotemporal joins, the scalability of the relational databases are restricted. Many modern applications, including real time object tracking and spatiotemporal data analyses require massive amounts of data ingestion, storage, and query streaming. These tasks require a demand for horizontal scalability.

For solving these problems in traditional RDBMS settings, vertical scaling (increase in processing power and memory of an individual processing unit) is needed. In non-relational databases, horizontal scaling (increasing the number of computers/nodes in a distributed system) can be used for addressing such problems. For our work, we have used Apache Accumulo (Sawyer, O'Gwynn, Tran, & Yu, 2013), which is one of the popular column-based non-relational databases with notable features such as load balancing, horizontal scalability, automatic table partitioning (which will be presented in detail in *Related Work* section). Accumulo also provides custom server-side iterators that can be efficiently utilized when performing spatiotemporal operations needed in queries involving spatiotemporal predicates.

Specifically, in this work, we have approached the problem of storing massive trajectory-based spatiotemporal data in the context of non-relational databases. One part of the problem is the representation of a spatiotemporal trajectory to fit the underlying storage system. Before all else, the design of data models for storing spatiotemporal trajectories in key-value stores is presented. For comparison purposes, our first class of data models (traditional data model) mimics the traditional object-relational database organization. On the other hand, our second class of data models (partitioned data model) exploits the sorted nature of row identifiers in Accumulo database, and stores data using the identifiers of spatiotemporal partitions. For increasing the query performance of proposed data models for different scenarios, in-memory indexing structures are also designed. Further discussion of the indexing structures can be found in *Types of Queries and Indexing Trajectories* section.

The rest of this chapter is organized as follows. In *Related Work* section, related work on storing and indexing spatiotemporal trajectories in traditional (single machine) and distributed storage systems is presented. In *Non-relational Databases* section, background information on distributed non-relational databases with a focus on Accumulo database will be provided. In *Modeling Trajectories in Non-relational Databases*, our data models for storing trajectories are demonstrated. Next, the different types of queries and the indexing strategies for increasing the query performances are shown. Lastly, we present our experimental evaluation; and point future directions; then, conclude the paper.

RELATED WORK

R-tree (Guttman, 1984) is the traditional data structure that handles the two dimensional (spatial) and three dimensional (spatiotemporal) data. R-trees can be seen as the spatial extension of B-trees, and indexes the spatial dimension of data using the nested bounding rectangles (or cubes for three dimensional data). For many spatiotemporal indexing structures, R-trees or some versions of R-trees are used for handling spatial (and sometimes temporal) dimensions in spatiotemporal data. In the literature, many spatiotemporal indexing structures are presented. These include multi-version structures such as HR-tree, STR-tree, MV3R-tree, or trajectory-oriented structures such as TB-tree, Polar-tree, Chebyshev Polynomial Indexing and SETI (Mokbel, Ghanem, & Aref, 2003) (Nguyen-Dinh, Aref, & Mokbel, 2010).

For indexing spatiotemporal trajectory data, initially, three dimensional R-trees have been used by considering time dimension as the third dimension and storing the whole trajectories or the segments of the trajectories into rectangular cuboids, which are reflected in the leaf nodes of R-tree. Trajectory-bundle trees (TB-tree) are optimized R-trees that preserves the trajectories by storing the segments of each in distinct leaf nodes (Pfoser, Jensen, & Theodoridis, 2000). Scalable and Efficient Trajectory Index (SETI), partitions the spatial dimension into fixed grid cells, and uses an R-tree for indexing the temporal dimension (Chakka, Everspaugh, & Patel, 2003). Start/End timestamp B-tree (SEB-tree) follows a fixed spatial partitioning strategy; and, each spatial partition is indexed using the start and the end times of the segments of the trajectory (Song & Roussopoulos, 2003). Conceptually similar (fixed spatial partitioning and data-driven temporal index) structures include Multiple Time-Split B-tree (MTSB-tree) (Zhou, Zhang, Salzberg, Cooperman, & Kollios, 2005) and Compressed Start-End Tree (CSE-tree) (Wang, Zheng, Xie, & Ma, 2008).

Aforementioned indexing strategies primarily focus on indexing the spatiotemporal data (in particular trajectories). On the other hand, storage systems, such as *TrajStore* (Cudre-Mauroux, Wu, & Madden, 2010), have been suggested for large-scale spatiotemporal data in traditional settings. Recently, several approaches were introduced for using distributed systems to store the spatiotemporal data. *Geopot*, introduced by Lee and Liang, discusses a cloud-based geo-location data management system with local in-memory spatial indexing structures (2011). Fox, Eichelberger, Hughes, and Lyon proposed a storage methodology for storing spatiotemporal data in Accumulo database (2013). Recently, Ke *et al.* proposed a practical spatiotemporal database schema based on MongoDB (MongoDB is classified as a NoSQL database) and a hybrid indexing approach spatiotemporal trajectories using HBSTR-tree, which combines hash table, B*-tree, and spatiotemporal R-tree (2014).

NON-RELATIONAL DATABASES

Non-relational databases (also referred as NoSQL databases) are storage systems that provide simple application programming interfaces for data retrieval without enforcing the constraints of the relational data model. CAP Theorem coined by Brewer (2000) states that any distributed system cannot guarantee consistency, availability and partition tolerance simultaneously. Relational Databases usually focus on the consistency and the availability. On the other hand, NoSQL databases (including Accumulo, database chosen for this work) are often optimized for the partition tolerance and availability aspects. Recently, NoSQL databases have become popular due to their capability of handling *big data*, as they are able to provide horizontal scaling schemata and simple data access mechanisms.

The proliferation of spatiotemporal data stems from following reasons (Shekhar & Chawla, 2003): (1) update operations on trajectory datasets are performed very commonly in real life datasets; (2) volume of the spatiotemporal trajectory datasets tends to be very big because of the stored geometric representations, and (3) data analytics performed on trajectory data requires massive data transfers.

Accumulo Database

In this work, for storing trajectories, we have opted using Accumulo database, which is a top-level Apache project among others like Cassandra and HBase (Fox, Eichelberger, Hughes, & Lyon, 2013). Accumulo is a column family oriented database, that is inspired by Google's *BigTable* database model, where stored are key-value pairs, lexicographically sorted based on their keys (Chang *et al.*, 2008). In BigTable design, keys are comprised of row identifier, column identifier, timestamp; while value fields contain byte arrays. Accumulo, built using BigTable's design, includes cell-level security, and more importantly, server-side iterators. Note that Accumulo is a sparse, distributed, sorted and multi-dimensional key-value storage system that depends on Apache Hadoop Distributed File System (HDFS) for data storage and Apache Zookeeper for configuration (Sen, Farris, & Guerra, 2013).

The key components of the Accumulo's architecture, shown in Figure 1, are master, tablet servers, garbage collector, logger, and monitor. The main function of the *master* is to monitor the cluster for the

Figure 1. The key components of Accumulo database

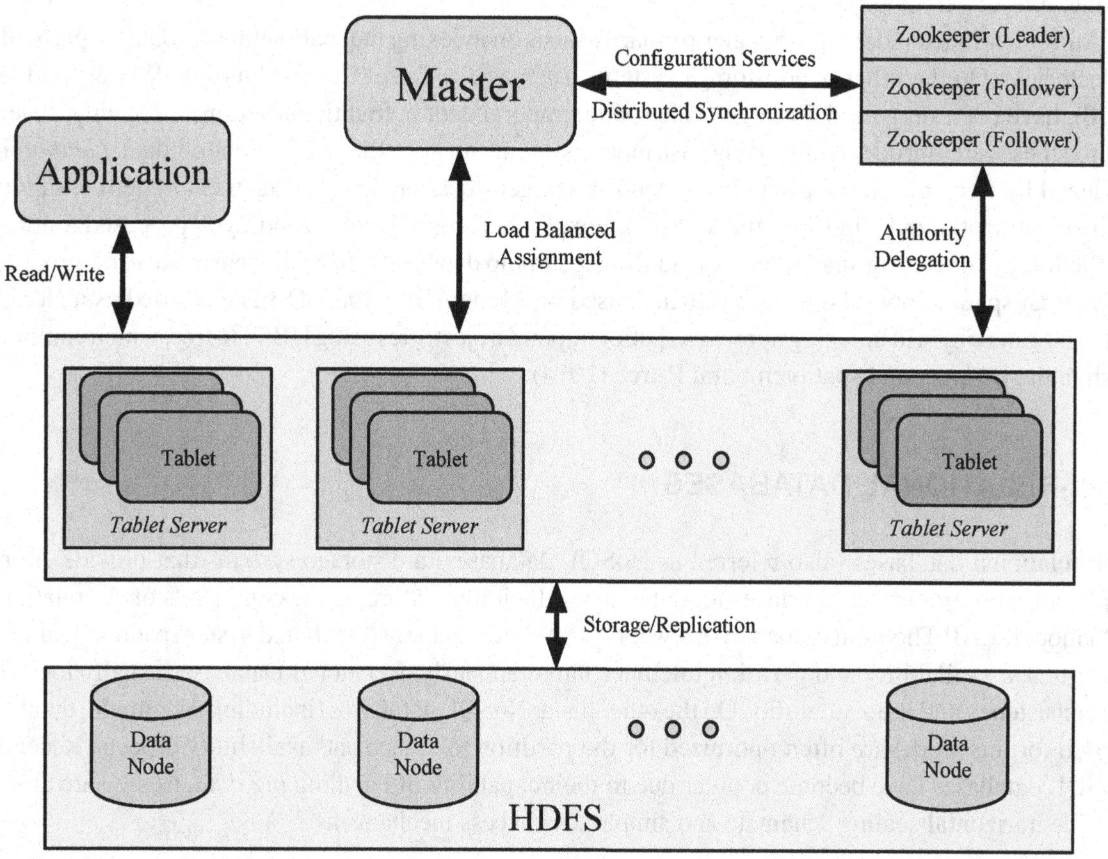

status of tablet servers, assign tablets (partition of tables) to tablet servers, and perform load balancing. The master also handles tablet server failures and recovery processes. *Tablet server* component is responsible for handling all the reads and writes for the tables. In a typical deployment, one tablet server is co-located with one HDFS datanode. Tablet server gets registered with Accumulo software by obtaining a lock from Zookeeper. Another task of tablet servers is handling of minor and major compactions. Minor compaction is the process of flushing the data stored in memory to sorted files stored on disk. Major compaction is merging these sorted files into a bigger file. Additional components (not shown in Figure 1) include: (1) garbage collector that deletes files, which are no longer used, from HDFS; (2) monitor that is used for monitoring key metrics of system resources used by Accumulo; (3) logger for tracing the system events.

Some features of Accumulo that cater well for spatiotemporal trajectory data are automatic table partitioning, load balancing, horizontal scalability, server side iterators, and failure recovery (Sen, Farris, & Guerra, 2013). One convenient feature of Accumulo key-value store is automatic table partitioning, where the tables are split after crossing a pre-configured threshold. Using this feature, tables can be stored across multiple tablet servers evenly, and the system can provide parallelized access to data. Load balancing provided by Accumulo spreads the workload of tablets to tablet servers evenly and ensures that no tablet server is overloaded. Load balancing is essential when implementing a distributed system for scalability purposes (e.g. avoiding hotspots in spatiotemporal data analysis by distributing the workload). Furthermore, horizontal scalability (also known as scaling out –adding more nodes to a system for increasing the workload capacity) can be achieved with Accumulo. In contrast to traditional object-relational databases used for spatiotemporal data in single machine settings, the scaling in Accumulo is cheaper because of the commodity hardware used by the distributed file system in the back end of Accumulo. Note that, traditional databases are usually scaled vertically (also known as scaling up –increasing the system resources such as memory or processing power). The main way of retrieving data from Accumulo is via the server-side iterators whose main function is to traverse over the data with optionally filtering or transforming data. Server side iterators, which can lead to big performance increases by offloading some of the computations to the tablet servers. The key strength of the functionality and data representations provided by Accumulo is the ability to store sparse multi-dimensional data. This makes it a good candidate for storing and manipulating large-scale spatiotemporal trajectory data.

It is important to note the generic key-value data model of Accumulo database. Accumulo does not only have simple keys for each value, but key fields are partitioned into smaller conceptual fields that are: Row ID, Column (Family, Qualifier, Visibility), Timestamp. Row ID is the main attribute of a key, and the rows in tables are sorted primarily using Row IDs. Each Row ID is unique for a particular row, therefore, provides faster accessing mechanisms. Column fields (Family, Qualifier, and Visibility) sorts the table after Row IDs. Column Family determines the locality groups while Column Qualifier provides uniqueness within a row. Column Visibility controls user access. Timestamp field controls the versioning.

While we selected using Accumulo, the models presented in this work can be applied to other NoSQL databases with minimal modifications. Some of the other popular NoSQL databases include HBase, Cassandra, MongoDB, CouchDB, Redis, Memcached. Redis and Memcached databases are in-memory databases; therefore, the storage space is limited to available memory. MongoDB and CouchDB, both classified as document stores (the records are structured as JSON documents), are less-commonly used for very large datasets. HBase and Cassandra, more similar to Accumulo, are considered as column-oriented databases, and are inspired by BigTable design. Cassandra is a highly available system while

HBase and Accumulo values consistency more (see CAP theorem – (Brewer, 2000)). Note that HBase and Accumulo are very similar systems built on top of HDFS, and our models can be mapped to HBase with minimal efforts.

MODELING TRAJECTORIES IN NON-RELATIONAL DATABASES

Formal Definition of Spatiotemporal Trajectory

Our definitions follow the conceptual spatiotemporal trajectory (with its geometric facet) modeling from Spaccapietra *et al.* (2008). We formally define the spatiotemporal trajectories and its building blocks used in our work as follows. Firstly, a time-geometry pair object, denoted as *tGeo*, is a composite object representing certain geometry at a particular timestamp. Each time-geometry pair consists a valid timestamp, meaning the timestamp value cannot be empty. On the other hand, the geometry object can take all types of geometries defined in OGC (OpenGIS Consortium) specification (Cox *et al.*, 2002), including points, polygons, etc. According to OGC, an empty geometry is also allowed.

$$tGeo_i := \langle t_i, Geometry_i \rangle$$

A trajectory, identified by a unique identifier (denoted as *trajId*) is an ordered list of timestamp-geometry pair objects. This list signifies the geometric representations of a trajectory in a particular time interval.

$$Trajectory := trajId, \left[tGeo_{start}, tGeo_{start+1}, ..., tGeo_{end} \right]$$

Note that we consider a continuous trajectory whose geometric representations are valid (alive) between start (birth) and end (death) times of the trajectory. Nevertheless, it is possible to have empty geometric representations. Each trajectory can only have one geometric representation for a particular timestamp. It is possible to use geometry collections (such as multipoint or multipolygon) to represent complex geometries.

The start and end times of a trajectory are the minimum and maximum time values, respectively, in the time-geometry pair list. They are denoted as t_{start} (start time) and t_{end} (end time). The start and end times are represented as a pair, and will be referred to as lifespan of trajectory hereafter. Lifespan of a trajectory is denoted as $lifespan_{Traj}$.

$$lifespan_{Traj} := \left(t_{start}, t_{end} \right)$$

Minimum bounding rectangle of a trajectory (represented as MBR_{Traj}) signifies the smallest enclosing rectangle (orthogonal to the coordinate system used) representing maximum extent of all geometries included in the entire time-geometry pair list of a trajectory. The minimum bounding rectangle of a trajectory can be found by finding the minimum bounding rectangle of the union of all geometries belonging to that trajectory.

$$MBR_{traj} = MBR\left(Geometry_{start} \cup Geometry_{start+1} \cup ... \cup Geometry_{end}\right)$$

The lifespan and minimum bounding rectangle of trajectory show the temporal and spatial extensions of trajectories. Note that these attributes are derived from original time-geometry pairs list, and they will be called *metadata attributes* hereafter. They will be stored for the purpose of efficient spatial and temporal filtering mechanisms.

Additionally, for many applications, a trajectory can be associated with many non-spatiotemporal attributes. In this work, the only non-spatiotemporal attribute considered is the unique identifier of trajectory.

Traditional Data Models

In traditional data models, the spatiotemporal trajectories are treated as regular objects in object-relational database settings. By regular objects, we mean the objects that are stored without their spatial or temporal properties. Within these models, we have designed two alternatives for placing the data in the non-relational databases. The first one will be called *column-fragmented traditional model*, in which the trajectories are fragmented into their time-geometry pairs, where each geometry is stored using a different column identifier.

In the second alternative, which will be called *whole-trajectory traditional model*, all of the time-geometry pairs of each trajectory are serialized (into byte arrays) and stored as a whole using the same key (as a row identifier). In addition to those for extending the spatiotemporal search capabilities of traditional data models, we propose to use metadata attributes for storing spatial and temporal characteristics of trajectories that are: minimum bounding rectangle and lifespan of trajectory.

Column-Fragmented Traditional Data Model (CTDM)

In the column-fragmented traditional model, the individual time-geometry pairs, which the trajectories are composed of, are separately stored using different key values. Figure 2 demonstrates the hierarchical decomposition of keys and values to be used. The unique trajectory identifier (*trajId*) is used as the row identifier (Row ID) field of the Accumulo key. On the other hand, the column identifiers are different for each geometry of a trajectory. As the time-geometry pairs are uniquely identified by their timestamp value, and the column qualifiers are used for uniqueness in Accumulo, it is preferable to set column qualifiers as timestamp values of time-geometry pair objects in a trajectory. Therefore, the column-fragmented model stores the each trajectory using same row identifier (which is trajectory identifier) along with different column qualifiers (which represents the unique timestamps in time-geometry pairs list). Note that, many fields (column family, column visibility, timestamp) are left empty ('*NULL*' is used in Figure 2 and Algorithm 1); and, they may be used for additional tasks such as security and data versioning. Essentially, in the column-fragmented traditional data model, each row in Accumulo stores a single trajectory; yet, each geometry in the list of time-geometry pairs is stored in a different column, where each geometry is identified by its corresponding timestamp value. Therefore, it is easier to access and modify a single time-geometry pair of a trajectory in this data model.

Figure 2. Hierarchical decomposition of key fields in column-fragmented traditional data model

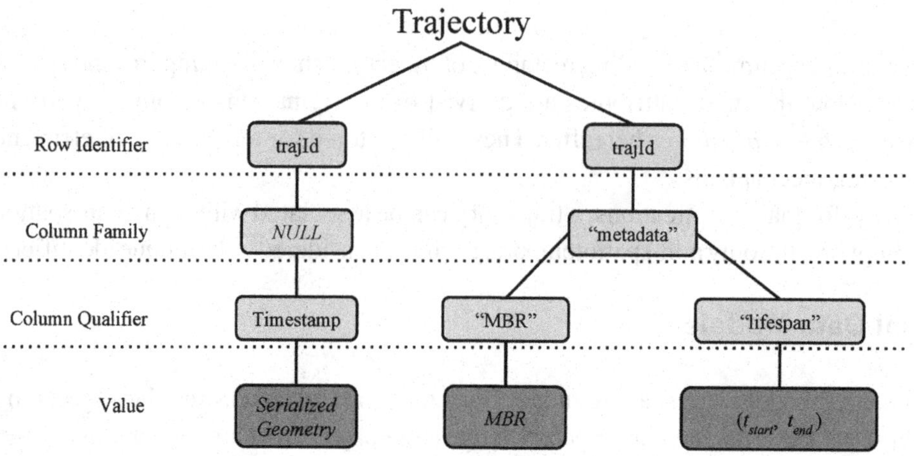

Algorithm 1: Insertion algorithm for column-fragmented traditional data model

Input:
Trajectory object: **traj**
Minimum bounding rectangle of traj: **mbr**
Lifespan of traj: **lifespan**
function *CTDM_Insert*

```
        rowIdentifier <- traj.trajId
        metaCF <- "metadata" //column family value for metadata attributes
        //column qualifier values are set to "MBR" and "lifespan"
        insert_meta(rowIdentifier, metaCF, "MBR", mbr)
        insert_meta(rowIdentifier, metaCF, "lifespan", lifespan)
        for each tGeo in traj.timeGeoList
                columnFamily <- NULL
                columnQualifier <- tGeo.t
                value <- serialize(tGeo.Geometry)
                insert(rowIdentifier, columnFamily, columnQualifier, value)
        endfor
end function
```

Furthermore, we project and recommend metadata attributes of each trajectory be stored in separate tables from the actual trajectory tables for faster access. However, the metadata attributes can also be stored using a separate column family value as in the insertion algorithm shown in Algorithm 1 –the string, "metadata", is used for the column family field (as a name of the column) for MBR and lifespan of trajectories.

Whole-Trajectory Traditional Data Model (WTDM)

In the whole-trajectory traditional model, the time-geometry pairs of a trajectory are stored as a whole, within a serialized binary object. The Figure 3 demonstrates the hierarchical decomposition of keys and values. Similar to column-fragmented alternative, row identifiers are set to be the trajectory identifiers. However, the entire list of time-geometry pairs of a trajectory is stored as a serialized byte array. The column identifiers (column family, column qualifier, column visibility) are left empty ('*NULL*' is used in Figure 3 and Algorithm 2) in this model. Similar to column-fragmented model, the metadata fields for minimum bounding rectangle and lifespan of the trajectory are also stored for efficient access.

This model provides faster access to the whole trajectory compared to column-fragmented traditional data model. Note that in the column-fragmented alternative, the geometries are fragmented into columns, whereas in the whole-trajectory traditional data model, all of the time-geometry pairs are stored together in a single serialized byte array. In the whole-trajectory traditional data model, it can be more difficult to modify the individual geometry objects.

Insertion and Search Algorithms

Algorithm 2: Insertion algorithm for whole-trajectory traditional data model

```
Input:
Trajectory object: traj
Minimum bounding rectangle of traj: mbr
Lifespan of traj: lifespan
function WTDM_Insert
        rowIdentifier <- traj.trajId
        metaCF <- "metadata" //column family value for metadata attributes
        //column qualifier values are set to "MBR" and "lifespan"
        insert_meta(rowIdentifier, metaCF, "MBR", mbr)
```

Figure 3. Hierarchical decomposition of key fields in whole-trajectory traditional data model

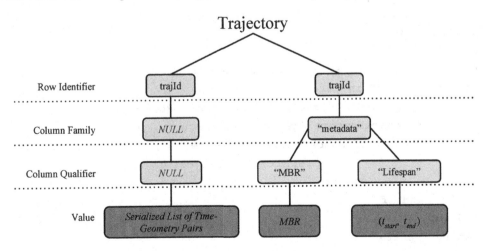

```
insert_meta(rowIdentifier, metaCF, "lifespan", lifespan)
value <- serialize(traj.timeGeoList)
columnFamily <- NULL
columnQualifier <- NULL
insert(rowIdentifier, columnFamily, columnQualifier, value)
end function
```

The *insertion* and generic *spatiotemporal search* (spatiotemporal range or window query) algorithms for the column-fragmented and whole-trajectory traditional data model are presented in Algorithms 1 through 3. The insertion Algorithms 1 and 2, insert the metadata attributes (note column family field is set to "metadata" –as a string); and, store the well-known binary (WKB) formatted geometric representation of geometry fields of time-geometry pairs in trajectory as demonstrated in the respective algorithms. The generic spatiotemporal search algorithm (Algorithm 3) initially applies a filter-and-refine step using above-mentioned metadata attributes with spatial and temporal predicates (See *metadata_search* function in Algorithm 3). For example, suppose the given are a spatiotemporal window defined over a spatial rectangle and a temporal interval; as well as *ends-before* temporal predicate and *overlaps* spatial predicate. Metadata search (*metadata_search*) procedure initially filters the trajectories using temporal predicate ends-before by selecting trajectories whose end times are less than the interval's end time. Later, the filtered trajectories' minimum bounding rectangles are examined whether they intersect with queried spatial rectangle for correctness and completeness of spatial overlap predicate. Lastly, the resulting trajectory identifiers are returned to spatiotemporal search for further inspection (by firstly checking temporal, then spatial predicates with the given query) of the given spatiotemporal window (spatial rectangle and time interval), as the overlap of minimum bounding rectangles does not guarantee the true spatiotemporal overlap.

Algorithm 3: Generic spatiotemporal search algorithm for traditional data models

Input:
A query predicate which consists of spatial and temporal bounds: **qp**
Spatial predicate showing condition: **sp**
Temporal predicate showing condition: **tp**

```
function search_TDM
    results <- []
    refinedTrajectoryIds <- metadata_search(qp, sp, tp)
    for each trajId in refinedTrajectoryIds
        trajectory <- getTrajectoryFromDatabase(trajId)
        if(checkTemporalPredicate(trajectory, qp, tp))
            if(checkSpatialPredicate(trajectory, qp, sp))
                results.add(trajectory)
            end if
        end if
    end for
    return results
end function
```

Updates on Traditional Data Models

The updates on spatiotemporal trajectories for traditional data models can be inspected in two parts: (1) updates on non-spatiotemporal attributes, and (2) updates on spatiotemporal attributes, namely the time-geometry pairs list. For both of the traditional data models, updates on non-spatiotemporal fields (we only consider the unique trajectory identifier as a non-spatiotemporal attribute) can be performed by finding the Row ID (which stores trajectory identifier) and simply updating it to desired value.

The updates on spatiotemporal attributes, on the other hand, are more complicated. For column-fragmented traditional data model, a particular update on the time-geometry pairs of a trajectory requires either addition, deletion, or modification of geometries and timestamps. While handling timestamps is intrinsically easier, updates on geometries require overriding the entire geometry or multiple geometries. Another challenge of updating spatiotemporal attributes is manipulating of metadata attributes. The updates on the lifespans of trajectories are easy and straightforward, while the updates on geometries are more difficult. When updating geometries, it is necessary to fetch the geometries of entire trajectory and re-calculate the MBR, in the event of an update that includes either modification or deletion of geometries, as it can reduce the size of MBR. When geometry updates only include addition of a geometry (or a list of geometries), it is only necessary to fetch the MBR and re-calculate the MBR using the MBR of the added geometry (or geometries). For whole-trajectory data model, it is necessary to fetch entire geometry for any update and re-write it back, as the time-geometry pairs of trajectory are stored as a serialized object. Therefore, we can argue that whole-trajectory data model may not be well-suited for frequently updated spatiotemporal trajectory data.

Algorithm 4: Trajectory cell partitioning algorithm for traditional data models

```
Input:
Trajectory object: traj
Coordinates of MBR of traj: (minX, maxX, minY, maxY)
Start and end times of traj: (ts, te)
Partitioning thresholds of space and time dimensions: ΔX, ΔY, ΔT
function partition
        cells <- []
        for timeStep from ts/ΔT to te/ΔT
                for xStep from minX/ΔX to maxX/ΔX
                        for yStep from minY/ΔY to maxY/ΔY
                                cell_i <- create3D_cell(timestep, xStep, yStep)
                                if(traj.intersects(cell_i)
                                        cells.add(cell_i)
                                end if
                        end for
                end for
        end for
        return cells
end function
```

Partitioned Data Models

While traditional data models use trajectory identifiers as the row identifiers in key fields, partitioned data models follow an approach in which the spatiotemporal characteristics of the trajectories are taken into account. A space-driven partitioning strategy is followed for the partitioned data models. While dynamic trajectory splitting/partitioning techniques are present (Rasetic, Sander, Elding, & Nascimento, 2005), a fixed spatiotemporal partitioning strategy has been used for our models. Note that, we are aiming to make use of the ordered nature of row identifiers in Accumulo by creating an artificial and fixed row identifier carrying the implicit spatiotemporal semantics extracted from the time-geometry pairs of trajectories.

The pseudo code for partitioning algorithm can be seen in Algorithm 4. Partitioning algorithm takes user-defined partitioning thresholds of ΔX, ΔY, and ΔT, which are utilized for creating the three-dimensional spatiotemporal cells (or voxels). Cells are uniquely identified with a partition identifier, composed from the three spatiotemporal dimensions. Temporal dimension is used as the leading dimension for the partition identifier, as it offers a natural ordering (unlike spatial dimensions that might need space-filling curves to create artificial ordering). Partitioning algorithm computes the set of three-dimensional cells that the time-geometry pairs of trajectory span through.

Next, we suggest two partitioned data models: (1) Whole-trajectory partitioned model, and (2) Segmented-trajectory partitioned model. These models will be explained in the following sections.

Whole-Trajectory Partitioned Data Model (WPDM)

Similar to whole trajectory traditional data model, the time-geometry pairs list of a trajectory is stored as a whole after serializing it into a byte array (namely, a binary object). However, the row identifier is the partition cell identifier, and the column qualifier is the trajectory identifier. For trajectories spanning through multiple partitioning cells, the same data (serialized list of time-geometry pairs) is duplicated for each cell. The decomposition of keys and values is shown in Figure 4. In Algorithm 5, the pseudocode for inserting a trajectory to database using whole-trajectory partitioned data model is demonstrated. Insertion algorithm initially determines the partitions of the trajectory; then, inserts the serialized time-geometry pairs list into the database using partition identifiers as the Row IDs.

The whole-trajectory partitioned model offers a crude but efficient accessing mechanism especially for spatiotemporal range queries, using the partition cell identifiers as row identifiers. However, it is important to note that because of the fixed partitioning schema, a trajectory can intersect with many partition cells, and the data may be replicated many times, causing the space overhead. Therefore, it should be expected that the whole-trajectory partitioned data model requires more space than other models presented in this chapter. (See the Experiments section for more detailed results.)

Segmented-Trajectory Partitioned Data Model (SPDM)

Algorithm 5: Insertion algorithm for whole-trajectory partitioned data model

```
Input:
Trajectory object: traj
Coordinates of MBR of traj: (minX,maxX,minY,maxY)
Start and end times of traj: (ts, te)
Partitioning thresholds of space and time dimensions: ΔX, ΔY, ΔT
```

Figure 4. Hierarchical decomposition of key fields in whole-trajectory partitioned data model

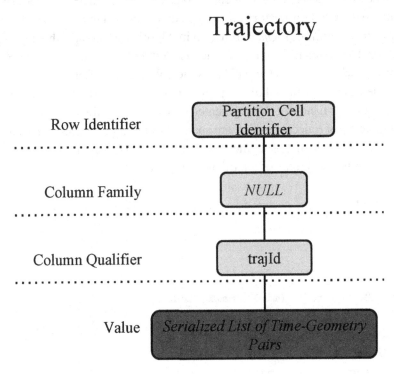

```
function WTPM_Insert
        rowIds <- partition(traj, (minX,maxX,minY,maxY), (ts, te), ΔX,  ΔY,
ΔT)
        columnFamily <- NULL
        for each cellId in rowIds
                columnQualifier <- traj.trajId
                value <- serialize(traj.timeGeoList)
                insert(cellId, columnFamily, columnQualifier, value)
        endfor
end function
```

In the segmented-trajectory partitioned data model, to decrease the amount of data duplications, the trajectory is firstly separated into trajectory segments if it spans through multiple spatiotemporal cells. Each trajectory segment has an associated trajectory identifier as well as a segment identifier. Segment identifier is essentially the same with the partition cell identifier (See Algorithm 4 for the determination of partition cell identifiers). A trajectory segment is defined as follows – "A trajectory segment contains a sublist of time-geometry pairs of its associated trajectory, where each of the time-geometry pairs belongs to one and only one partition cell". Given these, a trajectory segment has a trajectory identifier and a segment identifier representing the partition cell it belongs to. Each trajectory may only have one and only one trajectory segment for one partition cell. However, a time-geometry pair may belong to one or more partition cells.

The hierarchical decomposition of the segmented-trajectory partitioned data model is shown in Figure 5, and is very similar to the whole-trajectory partitioned data model. The insertion algorithm can be seen in Algorithm 6. Note that *partition_segment* function in Algorithm 6 creates the trajectory segments for a particular trajectory. The segment identifier (which is identical with the partition cell identifier) is set to be the row identifier, while trajectory identifier is the column identifier. The difference between two models is in the value fields. For the whole-trajectory partitioned model the entire trajectory is serialized and stored, on the other hand, for the segmented-trajectory partitioned model, stored are the parts (which is called segments) of trajectories that are spanning in that particular cell identified by segment (cell) identifier. Additionally, the list of segments (partition cells) of a particular trajectory is also stored to enable access to the other segments of a particular trajectory.

```
Algorithm 6: Insertion algorithm for segmented-trajectory partitioned data
model


Input:
Trajectory object: traj
Coordinates of MBR of traj: (minX, maxX, minY, maxY)
Start and end times of traj: (ts, te)
Partitioning thresholds of space and time dimensions: ΔX, ΔY, ΔT
function STPM_Insert
        <rowIds, segments> <- partition_segment(traj,
                        (minX, maxX, minY, maxY), (ts, te), ΔX,   ΔY,   ΔT)
        //partition_segment partitions the trajectory into trajectory segments
        //and returns the cellIds and trajectory segments as a map
        columnFamily <- NULL
        for each (cellId, segment) in <rowIds, segments>
                columnQualifier <- traj.trajId
```

Figure 5. Hierarchical decomposition of key fields in segmented-trajectory partitioned data model

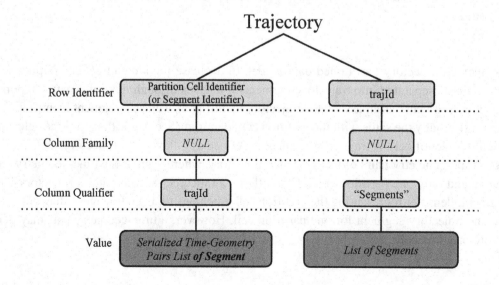

```
                        value <- serialize(segment.timeGeoList)
                        insert(cellId, columnFamily, columnQualifier, value)
            endfor
            insert_segments(traj.trajId, NULL, NULL, rowIds)
end function
```

The segmented-trajectory partitioned data model requires the extra storage of partition cell identifiers (or segment identifiers). However, in a particular row, identified by the partition cell identifier, the stored are the time-geometry pairs of the trajectory segments spanning in that particular cell. Therefore, it requires less space than whole-trajectory partitioned data model (see *Experiments* section), while providing faster access mechanisms compared to traditional data models for spatiotemporal queries.

Insertion, Spatiotemporal Search and Updates on Partitioned Data Models

Insertion algorithms for partitioned data models are shown in Algorithm 5 and 6. For both of the partitioned data models, insertion starts with the identification of partition cells. For each partition cell, either all of the time-geometry pairs (whole-trajectory partitioned data model), or the segments of time-geometry pairs (segmented-trajectory partitioned data model) are inserted as serialized binary objects. Note that for the segmented-trajectory partitioned data model, an extra step for segment partitioning is necessary.

The spatiotemporal search for partitioned data models (similar to the one described in Algorithm 3 for traditional data models) is intuitive. The generic spatiotemporal search initially requires the identification of partition cells the spatial and temporal predicates span through. Next, for all the identified partition cells, either whole trajectories or the segments of trajectories are returned. Later, those trajectories are further refined by checking the spatiotemporal predicates. Note that, duplicates should be eliminated when initially returning the results from database.

The updates for partitioned data models can be divided into two parts, the same as traditional data models. The updates on non-spatiotemporal attributes of a trajectory require brute-force search on unique trajectory identifiers, and later modification of the trajectory (or the segments of the trajectory).

The updates on spatiotemporal attributes are more complicated. For an update on a trajectory stored using whole-trajectory partitioned data model, the time-geometry pairs list of the trajectory is fetched from the database; and, the temporary update on the list is performed. Later, it is checked whether the partition cells of trajectory are changed. If they are not changed, the serialized time-geometry pairs list object of the trajectory is overwritten for all the partitions it spans through. If the updated partition cells are different from the previous version, the partition cells of trajectory that are valid for both versions are updated by overwriting the time-geometry pairs list. If applicable, the serialized time-geometry pairs list is inserted into new cells that trajectory spans through; or, the trajectory is deleted from the partition cells that it does not span through in the updated version.

For an update on a trajectory stored using segmented-trajectory partitioned data model, the updates are locally performed on each segment, when applicable. Similar to the whole-partitioned data model, the all of the trajectory segments are fetched, and updates are temporarily performed on the trajectory. Later, the new list of segments are created; and the database is updated accordingly by either modifying the segment in a particular cell, inserting a new segment in a different partition cell, or removing the segment of the trajectory from a partition cell.

TYPES OF QUERIES AND INDEXING TRAJECTORIES

In our system, we want to support the following query types:

- **Spatiotemporal Queries:** The primary goal of our work is to create data models that can answer queries with spatial or temporal or spatiotemporal predicates. By spatiotemporal queries, we mean queries that return entries in the database using the spatial or temporal aspects of our data. The specific use cases we have designed for our data models are following.

  - **Time range query:** Given a time range representing a time interval with two timestamps t_{start} and t_{end} ($t_{start} < t_{end}$), time range queries return trajectories having a temporal Boolean attribute in relation to the given timestamp. For example, for the query "Find trajectories that were alive in interval from 'September 10th, 2014 05:00:00' to 'September 11th, 2014 05:00:00'" returns trajectories whose lifetime overlaps with given interval from 'September 10th, 2014 5:00 AM' to 'September 11th, 2014 5:00 AM'. Considered temporal predicates for trajectories include starts-before, starts-after, ends-before, ends-after, overlaps, and disjoint.

  - **Timestamp query:** Given a timestamp representing a unique moment, timestamp queries search for trajectories having a temporal Boolean attribute in relation to the given timestamp. For instance, provided a timestamp query translated to natural language as "Find trajectories that ends-before 'September 10th, 2014 05:00:00'", trajectories whose end times are before the given timestamp 'September 10th, 2014 05:00:00' is included in query results. Considered temporal predicates for trajectories include starts-before, starts-after, ends-before, ends-after, overlaps, and disjoint.

  - **Purely spatial query:** Given a spatial object represented as a geometry (point, line, polygon etc.), purely spatial queries search for trajectories satisfying a spatial Boolean relation to union of all the geometries in the list of time-geometry pairs of trajectories. The considered spatial predicates include geometrical relations such as contains, covered-by, covers, equal, inside, overlaps, disjoint, touches, crosses. An example query could be searching for the trajectories that covers the given spatial point 'POINT (1.0, 2.0)'. Purely spatial queries could be separated into subclasses (e.g. spatial point, spatial polygon, spatial line, spatial multipoint etc.). However, for simplicity, they are investigated under the same kind of queries. Note that spatial predicates are not available for all types of geometries. For example, a spatial point type query cannot cover any trajectories, but may be covered-by a trajectory. On the other hand, a spatial polygon type query can cover and be covered-by trajectories.

  - **Spatiotemporal point query:** Given a spatial object represented as a geometry and a timestamp (as in timestamp queries), spatiotemporal point queries return the trajectories that are satisfying both temporal and spatial Boolean relationships. The spatiotemporal predicates include the ones in timestamp queries aggregated to purely spatial queries.

  - **Spatiotemporal window query:** Given a set of spatial objects represented as a list of geometries and a time range, spatiotemporal window queries return the trajectories that are satisfying Boolean temporal and spatial relationships listed in (time range and purely spatial queries). Spatiotemporal window queries are common for spatiotemporal join operations. For example, finding trajectories that are overlapping in both spatial and temporal dimensions can be done using spatiotemporal window queries.

- **Non-spatiotemporal Queries:** While spatiotemporal queries are our major part of the work, queries that are used for searching non-spatiotemporal attributes are also included. As the only non-spatiotemporal attribute of trajectories in our work is trajectory identifier, we only include search based on the trajectory identifier. The supported queries are as follows.
  - **Exact query:** Given a specific trajectory identifier, the exact queries search for the trajectory specified by this particular trajectory identifier.
  - **Range query:** Similar to exact queries, given a range of trajectory identifiers (specified by two trajectory identifiers), range queries search for trajectories whose trajectory identifiers fall in that particular range.

As mentioned earlier, the traditional models and the partitioned models have their weaknesses and strengths for particular types of queries. Traditional data models provide a better searching schema for non-spatiotemporal queries, while partitioned data models offer more promising searching structures for spatiotemporal queries. However, given the structure of our non-relational database, traditional data models does not suit well for spatiotemporal queries, while partitioned data models is not very appropriate for efficiently answering non-spatiotemporal queries. In order to eradicate these weaknesses, we suggest indexing methodologies for traditional and partitioned data models.

Spatiotemporal Indexing for Traditional Data Models

Scalable and Efficient Trajectory Index (SETI) was introduced by Chakka, Everspaugh, & Patel (2003). SETI is specifically designed for indexing trajectories and the intended use for this indexing structure is historical and persistent spatiotemporal data. For handling the spatial dimensions of trajectories, SETI uses a fixed grid. Each grid cell has an associated R-tree for handling temporal dimension.

For indexing trajectories in non-relational databases, we consider a version of SETI, which we will call Grid-mapped Interval Trees (G-IT) that uses interval trees for indexing temporal dimension and a fixed grid for indexing spatial dimensions. An illustration of the trajectory insertion to G-IT can be seen in Figure 6. The fixed grid file is formed using two parameters that are ΔX and ΔY, which would be used as the step sizes of spatial cells. The geometric representation of trajectories may span through more than one cells as the cells are fixed. For handling the trajectories that are spanning through more than one spatial cells, a duplication strategy is followed (Aydin *et al.*, 2014). Nevertheless, it is important to create the fixed spatial cells in such a way that there will be the minimal amount of duplications (in other words, the minimum amount of trajectories that are crossing more than one spatial cells). For minimizing the number of duplications, initial knowledge of movement and directional patterns of trajectories plays a remarkable role. Such knowledge can help determining the step sizes (ΔX and ΔY) of spatial cells, and reduce the number of duplications. For instance, in solar event based datasets (Schuh *et al.*, 2013), the movement is from left to right, selecting a larger horizontal step size and smaller vertical step size can decrease the amount of duplications.

Each cell in the fixed grid file is mapped to an interval tree handling the temporal dimension of the trajectories. Interval trees are essentially 1-dimensional R-trees that are usually preferred specifically for indexing interval-based time dimension (de Berg, van Krefeld, Overmars, & Schwarzkopf, 2000). Stored in the leaf cells of the interval trees are the trajectory identifiers. Note that, as we are designing the index to be an in-memory structure, we want to keep the leaf nodes as small as possible to eradicate the possible memory problems.

Figure 6. Insertion to Grid-mapped Interval Tree indexing structure

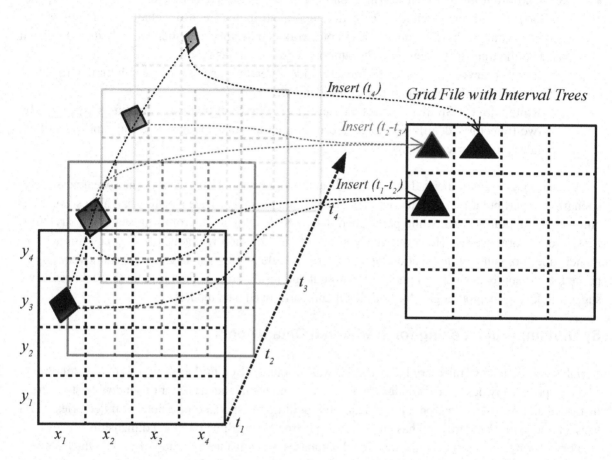

For the dynamic updates on the G-IT index, we followed a strategy similar to the update strategy presented for SETI (Chakka, Everspaugh, & Patel, 2003). The update procedure on G-IT starts with identifying the spatial cells that trajectory spans through which will be affected by a particular update. Note that the identification of the affected spatial cells requires fetching all the information about the trajectory stored in the index. In the case of an update that enhances the trajectory into new spatial cells, the trajectory identifiers are inserted to spatial cells on corresponding time intervals. For all other updates, the operation is performed by re-insertion of the trajectory to the index using modified time intervals.

G-IT index can be particularly well-suited for aforementioned spatiotemporal queries. For purely temporal query types (timestamp, time range queries) each interval tree in the index must be visited. The search in each interval tree requires logarithmic time (as the interval trees are R-tree based) with respect to the number of trajectories being stored in the respective interval tree. On the other hand, purely spatial queries require the search in the grid file, which requires constant time. The spatiotemporal queries in G-IT can be seen as a two-step filtering mechanism: spatial and temporal filtering. In a spatiotemporal query, firstly, the spatial predicate and the spatial portion of the query filters the cells that are not related to the query. Later, from the cells that are filtered, the temporal predicate and temporal portion of the query returns the actual results after eliminating the duplicates.

Inverted Index for Partitioned Data Models

Traditionally, the inverted index is used for text retrieval where each index entry (generally a word) points to the documents where the queried word occurs (Baeza-Yates & Ribeiro-Neto, 1999). The partitioned data models have better spatiotemporal querying characteristics as they encode the spatiotemporal semantics of trajectories in the keys. However, a direct non-spatiotemporal query to the non-relational database may result in unpredictable time requirements, simply because Accumulo is a column data store with no secondary indexes. For example, searching for a trajectory identifier that is not present in the database simply requires checking each entry in the database. In order to solve this unpredictable querying performance problem for partitioned data models, we suggest using a partition inverted index.

In partition inverted index, we treat a non-spatiotemporal attribute of a particular trajectory as the index entry (or a word in traditional text-retrieval oriented inverted index) and the partition cells as the documents. Figure 7 demonstrates an overview of partition inverted index to be used for partitioned data models. Simply, in the actual database, the indexed keys map the partition cells to the trajectories' trajectory identifiers and time-geometry pairs list; on the other hand, in the partition inverted index, the trajectory identifiers are mapped to the partition cell identifiers. A sorted multi-valued map structure is used for building the inverted index structure. Note that the map structure is based on a balanced tree implementation that have a logarithmic insertion and search time requirement. Therefore, each trajectory identifier that is mapped to one or more cells is stored in sorted fashion in the index.

The partition inverted index can be used for answering non-spatiotemporal queries listed earlier more efficiently. For exact queries, the partition index performs an exact value search on the index and returned values are later used for fetching the actual trajectories from the database. Specified by two trajectory identifiers, range queries return a set of trajectory identifiers. When performing range queries, the sorted nature of the partition inverted index is utilized. As balanced trees are used, the non-spatiotemporal range query requires logarithmic time.

Figure 7. Partition inverted index

Trajectories Stored in Database

Row	Values
Partition$_1$	→ Traj$_3$, Traj$_4$
Partition$_2$	→ Traj$_1$
Partition$_3$	→ Traj$_1$, Traj$_2$, Traj$_5$
Partition$_4$	→ Traj$_5$
Partition$_5$	→ Traj$_2$, Traj$_3$
Partition$_6$	→ Traj$_2$, Traj$_3$, Traj$_5$

Partition Inverted Index

Index Key	Index Entry
Traj$_1$.*trajId*	→ *Partition$_2$*, *Partition$_3$*
Traj$_2$.*trajId*	→ *Partition$_3$*, *Partition$_5$*, *Partition$_6$*
Traj$_3$.*trajId*	→ *Partition$_1$*, *Partition$_5$*, *Partition$_6$*
Traj$_4$.*trajId*	→ *Partition$_1$*
Traj$_5$.*trajId*	→ *Partition$_3$*, *Partition$_4$*, *Partition$_6$*

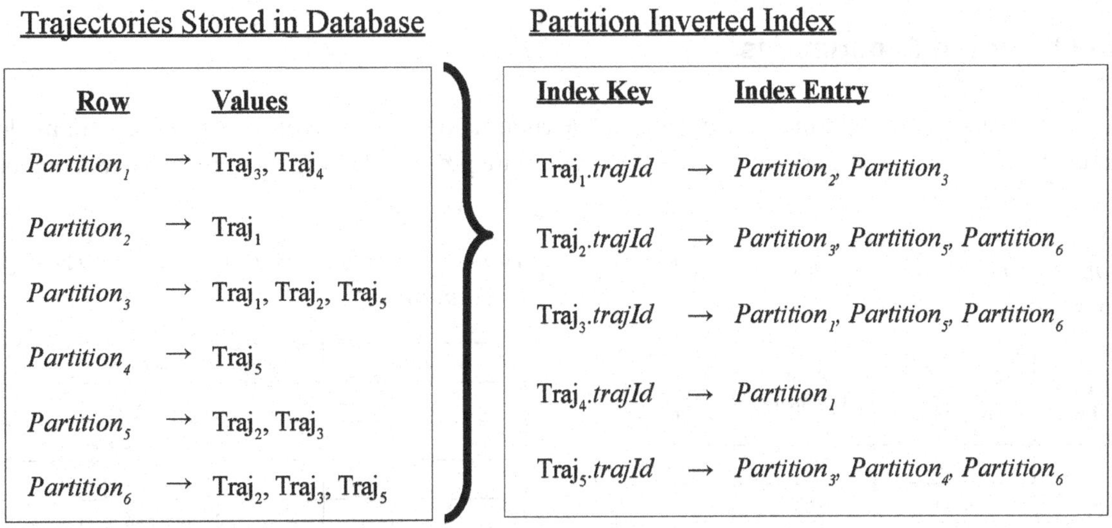

* *Traj$_i$* represents the trajectory objects stored in database.

* *Partition$_j$* denotes the partition cell identifier.

EXPERIMENTS

We have conducted a series of experiments to show the correctness and performance of the different data models and data access mechanisms. In this section, we will begin with demonstrating the datasets we have used and the experimental settings. Later, different aspects of the proposed data models and indexing strategies will be shown. The aspects include the space and time requirements of the data models as well as their performance when inserting and querying data.

Experimental Settings and Datasets

We have used three artificial datasets for testing our data models and indexing structures. The datasets are created using artificial dataset generator ERMO-DG (Aydin, Angryk, & Pillai, 2014) and include polygon-based trajectories with different spatiotemporal characteristics. For each dataset, the number of trajectories, the total number of time-geometry pairs, and the total number of points that polygon-based trajectories are comprised of are shown in Table 1.

The experiments are performed on cloud computing environment, Amazon Web Services. For all the experiments three data nodes are used for hosting tablet servers. The data node roles, as well as the other roles we have assigned nodes for our system in our experiments, are shown in Table 2. Nodes that are assigned with the role *NameNode* controls the distributed file system (HDFS). Zookeeper is used by Accumulo for determining the current state of processes, coordinating distributed tasks, ensuring fault tolerance, and storing configuration that can be modified on the fly without restarting Accumulo. *Secondary NameNode* role is an auditing system for Hadoop, performing periodical checkpoints. Accumulo *master* is responsible for load balancing, as well as error detection in tablet servers. The *tablet server* and *data node* roles are co-located for decreasing the network latency. Tablet servers are responsible for managing, in generic terms – reads and writes to, a subset of all tables. Data nodes simply store data in HDFS. The nodes used in AWS have all same system settings and are medium size computing instances (officially tagged as m3.xlarge) with 10-core 2.5 GHz Intel Xeon E5-2670 processors, 15 GB RAM, and 80 GB SSD storage.

Data Insertion Experiments

The first aspect of the experiments is related to the runtime performance of the proposed data models and indexing structures. The results of the experiments are presented in Figure 8. In Figure 8a, the total

Table 1. The attributes of datasets used in the experiments

Dataset Tag	# of Trajectories	# of Time-Geometry Pairs	# of Total Points
A	95997	1,200,120	7,336,090
B	209833	2,623,976	15,195,862
C	409421	5,117,811	33,430,017

Table 2. The systems settings applied in AWS for the experiments

Node Tags	Assigned Roles
Node 1	NameNode
Node 2	ZooKeeper Leader
Node 3	Secondary NameNode
Node 4	Accumulo Master
Node 5 – Node 6 – Node 7	Tablet Server & DataNode

Figure 8. Total database insertion time (a), index insertion time for traditional (b) and partitioned (c) data models

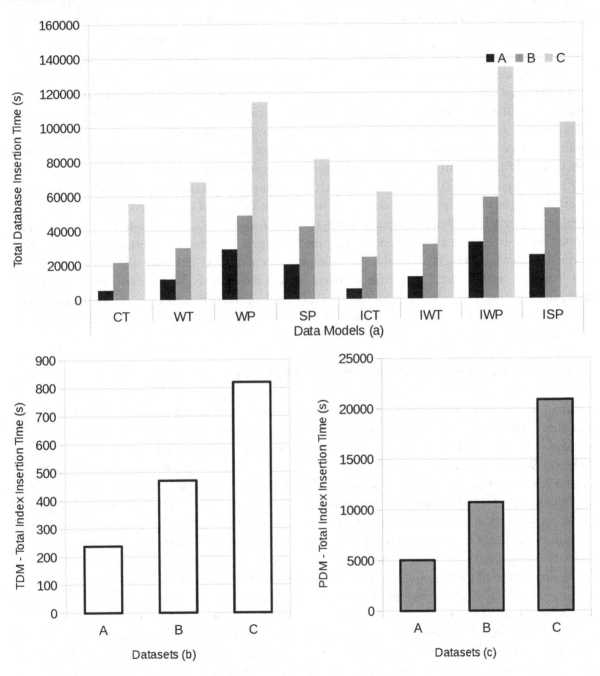

database insertion time (in seconds) for datasets A, B, and C are shown, for all data models along with their indexed versions. In Figure 8b, the total time spent for inserting the trajectories into G-IT index for traditional data models are demonstrated. Lastly, in Figure 8c, the total time spent for inserting the trajectories into partition inverted index for partitioned data models demonstrated.

In Figure 8a, a natural observation is that all datasets exhibit similar behaviors for each data model; namely, the size of the dataset reflects in the insertion time. For each dataset, column-fragmented traditional data model (*CT*) performed better than other data models. When compared to whole-trajectory data model (*WT*), column-fragmented data model inserts serialized polygon objects one by one, while whole-trajectory data model, serializes the entire time-geometry pairs list. We can assert that inserting bigger volumes of data takes more time. We can also see traditional data models performing better than partitioned data models during the insertion. The reason for that can be the extra time spent for preprocessing the trajectory data; namely, determining the cell partitions of trajectories or segmentation of trajectories. Additionally, the duplication strategy followed for partitioned data models is another factor that increases the amount of data to be inserted. We can also observe that the segmented-trajectory data model (*SP*) has a better insertion performance when compared to the whole-trajectory data model (*WP*). The preprocessing time spent before insertion for those two models are very similar; yet, we can assert that segmentation procedure decreased the amount of data to be inserted; as well as the time spent for the insertions. For all indexed models (*ICT, IWT, IWP, ISP*), their non-indexed versions performed better. It is much expected considering the time spent for creating, inserting, and maintaining the index structures. In Figure 8b and 8c, insertion time spent on G-IT index for traditional data models and "partition-inverted index" for partitioned data models, respectively. We can observe that both G-IT index and partition inverted index performs similarly for their respective data models. Note that, Figure 8b and 8c shows the total time spent on index insertions, and the number of trajectories in the datasets are approximately doubled every time.

Memory and Storage Requirements Experiments

This part of the experiments is related to memory and storage requirements of the different data models and their respective indexing structures. Our observations on storage requirements of data models in Accumulo database and the memory requirements of the indexing structures can be seen in Figure 9. In Figure 9a, database size for three database models under different data models is presented. Figure 9b and 9c demonstrate the memory requirements for traditional data models (Column-fragmented (*CT*) and Whole-trajectory (*WT*)) and partitioned data models (Whole-trajectory (*WP*), Segmented-trajectory (*SP*)), respectively. It is important to point out that the size of the database is measured using the total amount of data sent to Accumulo database during insertion phase, and the total amount of storage space being used can vary from system to system. Our database size measurements are significant due to the importance of the data volume being ingested in Accumulo. On the other hand, index sizes are measured by calculating the amount of memory space used by the internal data structures specific to Java programming language.

For all the datasets, the smallest database size is achieved using the column-fragmented traditional model for all datasets, while using whole-trajectory partitioned data model results in the largest database size. We can easily see the similarity between the insertion time requirements (shown in Figure 8a) and storage requirements (shown in Figure 9a). This is very natural, as the insertion of larger data requires more time. Our analysis for higher insertion time requirements using whole-trajectory traditional data model (*WT*) and partitioned data models (*WP, SP*) suggests that the higher volumes of data insertion (due to replications and serializations of internal data structures) causes the higher data insertion times. With our results shown in Figure 9a, it can be seen that insertion time to database and the amount of data inserted to database follows the same trend in our experiments.

Figure 9. Total database size in KBs (a) for different data models, memory (in KBs) used by G-IT index for traditional data models (b), and memory (in KBs) used by partition inverted index for partitioned data models (c)

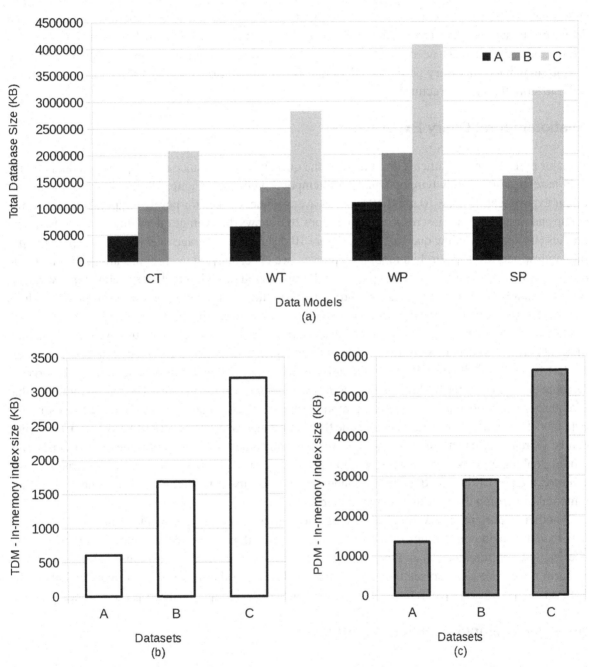

In Figure 9b, the memory requirements for in-memory G-IT index can be seen. Similarly, Figure 9c demonstrates the memory requirements for the partition inverted index. For our largest dataset (Dataset C), column-fragmented traditional data model (*CT*) creates a little more than 2GB of raw data while whole-trajectory traditional data model (*WT*) creates approximately 2.9 GB of raw data. The memory requirements for G-IT index for Dataset C (shown in Figure 9b), is approximately 3.1 KB. This result is very promising, because for over 400,000 trajectories (with only vector data that sums up to 2 to 2.9 GB), storage requirements for G-IT index are very low; therefore, it is suitable for in-memory storage. A similar situation also occurs for the partition inverted index. The amount of memory space required for partition inverted index (see Figure 9c) for Dataset C is approximately 57 MB. When compared to 4 GB database storage space needed for whole-trajectory partitioned data model and 3.1 GB space needed for the segmented-trajectory partitioned data model, it only requires 1.4% to 1.8% of actual storage in order to store the index structure.

Spatiotemporal Query Experiments

A major part of our experiments are related to the querying performance of our proposed data models with purely spatial, purely temporal and spatiotemporal predicates. Figure 10 demonstrates the results of our experiments. Figure 10.a and 10.b shows average query times for purely temporal queries (timestamp and time range queries, respectively). Figure 10.c shows the average query times for purely spatial queries (for spatial window query). Lastly, Figure 10.d shows the average query times for spatiotemporal window queries. For purely temporal predicates, we experimented using timestamp and time range queries with overlap (or intersection) predicate. Purely spatial querying includes spatial window query, with a rectangle geometry query window and overlaps predicate. Spatiotemporal window queries include a rectangle spatial window and a time range. Queries are tested with traditional and partitioned data models with no indexing, as well as the indexed traditional data models. Note that we did not include indexed partitioned data models as partition inverted index is designed for non-spatiotemporal queries.

As expected, for all types of queries included in our experiments, partitioned data models worked a lot more efficient than the traditional data models without indexing structures. The reason for that is that it requires a full scan to perform a spatiotemporal (or purely temporal and spatial) query for traditional data models. On the other hand, as we encode the spatiotemporal characteristics to row identifier (which can be searched efficiently in Accumulo) in the partitioned data models, partitioned data models only require looking up very few records stored in the database. The purely spatial query type requires more time for traditional data models without indexing because more trajectories are returned. Note that, temporal dimension is larger than spatial dimensions.

Another important observation for all types of queries in these experiments is indexed traditional data models provide very similar querying characteristics with partitioned data models. For many of the queries, indexed traditional data models (especially the column-fragmented traditional model (ICT)), perform better. We can also see that query times scale well in the means of time requirements. With different sized datasets (See Table 1), there is not much difference in the average query time.

Non-Spatiotemporal Query Experiments

Last part of the experiments is related to the performance of the partition inverted index for queries with no spatiotemporal characteristics. In this part, we have experimented whole-trajectory partitioned data model with the partition-inverted index. For the partitionn inverted index, a multi-map data structure is used. Figure 11 shows the results of our experiments. First two sets of columns show the average query time spent on performing an exact query. The last column shows total time spent on inserting data to database using indexed whole-trajectory partitioned data model.

Figure 10. Average time spent on temporal (timestamp in (a), time range in (b)), spatial (c), and spatiotemporal (d) queries

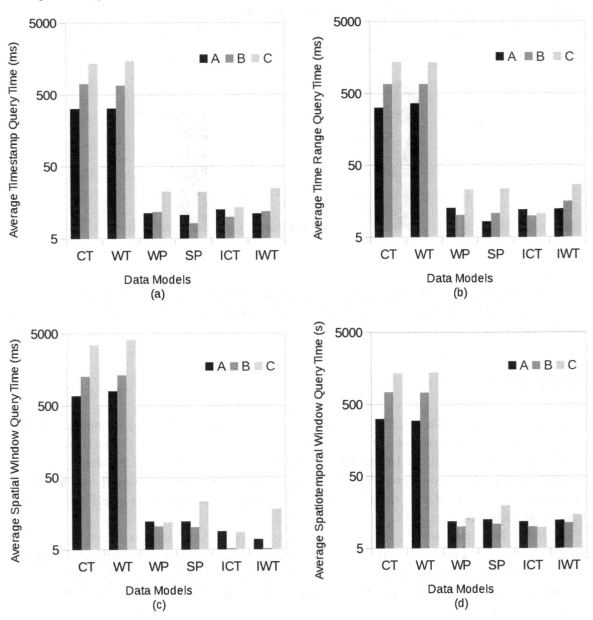

It is fair to state that partitioned data are not much appropriate models for non-spatiotemporal queries in the means of runtime performance. It can be seen that even the insertion time for indexed partitioned data models is much less than the average time spent on searching for a single record. Similar to traditional models' behavior on spatiotemporal queries, partitioned data models provide a poor schema for non-spatiotemporal queries. We can also argue that traditional data models answer the spatiotemporal queries faster than partitioned data models answer the non-spatiotemporal queries, because of the

Figure 11. Average time spent for exact (non-spatiotemporal) query with and without indexing structure (partition inverted index) in whole-trajectory partitioned data model. The last set of columns (IWP-Total Insertion) shows the total time spent on the insertion of datasets

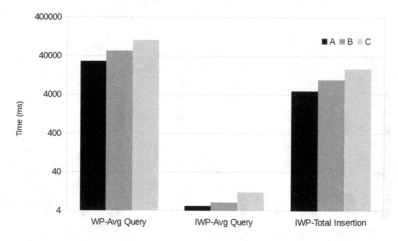

filter-and-refine strategy applied in the search algorithms of traditional data models (See Figure 10). Nevertheless, partitioned data models, using the partition-inverted index, can be tuned for better non-spatiotemporal query performance.

CONCLUSION

In this work, we addressed the problem of storing spatiotemporal trajectories in non-relational databases. For this problem, we have proposed two types of data models: (1) traditional data models, and (2) partitioned data models. Traditional data models mimic the classic relational database models by using the trajectory identifier as the row identifier in the database. On the other hand, partitioned data models use a partitioning algorithm, in order to find the spatial and temporal location of the trajectories; and, use it as the row identifier.

In addition to the data models, we have designed two in-memory indexing structures for providing efficient querying capabilities. For traditional data models, we have designed the G-IT spatiotemporal index, to strengthen the weak spatiotemporal querying performance of these models. For partitioned data models, we have designed the partition inverted index, which can be used for efficiently performing non-spatiotemporal queries.

Our experiments show that in the means of storage requirements, traditional data models are better. On the other hand, for spatiotemporal queries, partitioned data models are preferable if no index is to be used; yet, for non-spatiotemporal queries, partitioned data models perform poorly. Nevertheless, traditional data models with the G-IT indexing perform very similarly to partitioned data models. In a similar way, partitioned data models' non-spatiotemporal query performance can be increased using the partition-inverted index. In No SQL databases, data modeling is primarily driven by the nature of accessing the data and that is the reason they are called question-focused datasets.

For future work, our aim is to provide efficient join algorithms, especially for spatiotemporal predicates. Many relational database management system vendors provide this capability; however, non-relational databases provide better distributed computing model. In the era of big data, it is important to use non-relational databases for mining algorithms. The spatiotemporal join procedures are vital for many spatial/spatiotemporal data mining algorithms, as the performance of many spatiotemporal pattern-mining algorithms primarily rely on the efficient spatial and spatiotemporal join mechanisms.

REFERENCES

Aydin, B., Angryk, R. A., & Pillai, K. G. (2014, May 21-23). ERMO-DG: Evolving Region Moving Object Dataset Generator. *Proceedings of the Twenty-Seventh International Florida Artificial Intelligence Research Society Conference FLAIRS 2014*, Pensacola Beach, Florida.

Aydin, B., Kempton, D., Akkineni, V., Gopavaram, S. R., Pillai, K. G., & Angryk, R. A. (2014, October 27-30). Spatiotemporal indexing techniques for efficiently mining spatiotemporal co-occurrence patterns. *Proceedings of the 2014 IEEE International Conference on Big Data*, Washington, DC, USA (pp. 1–10). http://doi.org/ doi:10.1109/BigData.2014.7004398

Baeza-Yates, R. A., & Ribeiro-Neto, B. A. (1999). *Modern Information Retrieval*. ACM Press / Addison-Wesley.

Brewer, E. A. (2000, July 16-19). Towards robust distributed systems (abstract). *Proceedings of the Nineteenth Annual ACM Symposium on Principles of Distributed Computing*, Portland, Oregon, USA. (p. 7). http://doi.org/ doi:10.1145/343477.343502

Buchin, M., Dodge, S., & Speckmann, B. (2014). Similarity of trajectories taking into account geographic context. *J. Spatial Information Science*, *9*(1), 101–124. doi:10.5311/JOSIS.2014.9.179

Chakka, V. P., Everspaugh, A., & Patel, J. M. (2003). *Indexing Large Trajectory Data Sets With SETI*. CIDR.

Chang, F., Dean, J., Ghemawat, S., Hsieh, W. C., Wallach, D. A., Burrows, M., & Gruber, R. E. et al. (2008). Bigtable: A Distributed Storage System for Structured Data. *ACM Transactions on Computer Systems*, *26*(2), 1–26. doi:10.1145/1365815.1365816

Cox, S., Daisey, P., Lake, R., Portele, C., & Whiteside, A. (2005). *OpenGIS Geography Markup Language (GML) Implementation Specification (version 3.1.1)*. OGC Implementation Specification.

Cudré-Mauroux, P., Wu, E., & Madden, S. (2010, March 1-6). TrajStore: An adaptive storage system for very large trajectory data sets. *Proceedings of the 26th International Conference on Data Engineering, ICDE, Long Beach, California, USA* (pp. 109–120). http://doi.org/ doi:10.1109/ICDE.2010.5447829

De Berg, M., Cheong, O., van Kreveld, M., & Overmars, M. (2008). Computational Geometry: Algorithms and Applications (3rd ed.). Santa Clara, CA, USA: Springer-Verlag.

Fox, A., Eichelberger, C., Hughes, J., & Lyon, S. (2013, 6-9 October). Spatio-temporal indexing in non-relational distributed databases. *Proceedings of the 2013 IEEE International Conference on Big Data 2013*, Santa Clara, CA, USA (pp. 291–299). http://doi.org/ doi:10.1109/BigData.2013.6691586

Guttman, A. (1984). R-trees: A Dynamic Index Structure for Spatial Searching. *SIGMOD Record, 14*(2), 47–57. doi:10.1145/971697.602266

Ke, S., Gong, J., Li, S., Zhu, Q., Liu, X., & Zhang, Y. (2014). A Hybrid Spatio-Temporal Data Indexing Method for Trajectory Databases. *Sensors (Basel, Switzerland), 14*(7), 12990–13005. doi:10.3390/ s140712990 PMID:25051028

Lee, D., & Liang, S. H. L. (2011). Geopot: A Cloud-based geolocation data service for mobile applications. *International Journal of Geographical Information Science, 25*(8), 1283–1301. doi:10.1080/13 658816.2011.558017

Mokbel, M. F., Ghanem, T. M., & Aref, W. G. (2003). Spatio-Temporal Access Methods. *IEEE Data Eng. Bull., 26*(2), 40–49.

Nascimento, M. A., Pfoser, D., & Theodoridis, Y. (2003). Synthetic and Real Spatiotemporal Datasets. *IEEE Data Eng. Bull., 26*(2), 26–32.

Nguyen-Dinh, L.-V., Aref, W. G., & Mokbel, M. F. (2010). Spatio-Temporal Access Methods: Part 2 (2003 - 2010). *IEEE Data Eng. Bull., 33*(2), 46–55.

Pfoser, D., Jensen, C. S., & Theodoridis, Y. (2000, September 10-14). Novel Approaches in Query Processing for Moving Object Trajectories. *Proceedings of 26th International Conference on Very Large Data Bases VLDB 2000*, Cairo, Egypt (pp. 395–406).

Quercia, D., Lathia, N., Calabrese, F., Lorenzo, G. D., & Crowcroft, J. (2010, December 14-17). Recommending Social Events from Mobile Phone Location Data. *Proceedings of the 10th IEEE International Conference on Data Mining ICDM 2010, Sydney, Australia* (pp. 971–976). http://doi.org/ doi:10.1109/ ICDM.2010.152

Rasetic, S., Sander, J., Elding, J., & Nascimento, M. A. (2005, August 30 - September 2). A Trajectory Splitting Model for Efficient Spatio-Temporal Indexing. *Proceedings of the 31st International Conference on Very Large Data Bases*, Trondheim, Norway (pp. 934–945).

Sawyer, S. M., O'Gwynn, B. D., Tran, A., & Yu, T. (2013, September 10-12). Understanding query performance in Accumulo. *Proceedings of the IEEE High Performance Extreme Computing Conference HPEC 2013*, Waltham, MA, USA (pp. 1–6). http://doi.org/ doi:10.1109/HPEC.2013.6670330

Schuh, M. A., Angryk, R. A., Pillai, K. G., Banda, J. M., & Martens, P. C. (2013, *September 15-18*). A large-scale solar image dataset with labeled event regions. *Proceedings of the IEEE International Conference on Image Processing, ICIP 2013*, Melbourne, Australia (pp. 4349–4353). http://doi.org/ doi:10.1109/ICIP.2013.6738896

Sen, R., Farris, A., & Guerra, P. (2013, June 27-July 2). Benchmarking Apache Accumulo BigData Distributed Table Store Using Its Continuous Test Suite. *Proceedings of the IEEE International Congress on Big Data, BigData Congress 2013* (pp. 334–341). http://doi.org/ doi:10.1109/BigData.Congress.2013.51

Shekhar, S., & Chawla, S. (2003). *Spatial databases - a tour*. Prentice Hall.

Song, Z., & Roussopoulos, N. (2003, January 21-24). SEB-tree: An Approach to Index Continuously Moving Objects. *Proceedings of the 4th International Conference, MDM 2003*, Melbourne, Australia (pp. 340–344). http://doi.org/ doi:10.1007/3-540-36389-0_25

Spaccapietra, S., Parent, C., Damiani, M. L., de Macêdo, J. A. F., Porto, F., & Vangenot, C. (2008). A conceptual view on trajectories. *Data & Knowledge Engineering*, *65*(1), 126–146. doi:10.1016/j.datak.2007.10.008

Wang, J. (June), Young, K., Hock, T., Lauritsen, D., Behringer, D., Black, M., … Zhang, J. A. (2014). A Long-Term, High-quality, High Vertical Resolution GPS Dropsonde Dataset for Hurricane and Other Studies. *Bulletin of the American Meteorological Society*. doi:10.1175/BAMS-D-13-00203.1

Wang, L., Zheng, Y., Xie, X., & Ma, W.-Y. (2008, April 27-30). A Flexible Spatio-Temporal Indexing Scheme for Large-Scale GPS Track Retrieval. *Proceedings of the 9th International Conference on Mobile Data Management (MDM 2008)*, Beijing, China (pp. 1–8). http://doi.org/ doi:10.1109/MDM.2008.24

Zhou, P., Zhang, D., Salzberg, B., Cooperman, G., & Kollios, G. (2005, November 4-5). Close pair queries in moving object databases. *Proceedings of the 13th ACM International Workshop on Geographic Information Systems, ACM-GIS 2005,* Bremen, Germany (pp. 2–11). http://doi.org/ doi:10.1145/1097064.1097067

KEY TERM AND DEFINITIONS

Interval Tree: A tree-based ordered data structure used for the efficient retrieval of time intervals.

Inverted Index: A map-based indexing structure originally used for indexing words in a document. The structure provides a mapping from content to its location in the database.

Minimum Bounding Rectangle: Maximum extents of a 2-dimensional spatial object within a specific coordinate system.

Non-Relational Database: A class of database systems that does not follow the constraints and the rules of relational model, for providing simple storage and retrieval mechanisms for mostly large scale and real time web applications.

Partitioned Data Model: A class of data models for storing spatiotemporal trajectories in non-relational database systems that uses the spatiotemporal characteristics of trajectories by initially applying a fixed partitioning.

Time-Geometry Pair: An ordered pair of timestamp and geometry, representing a snapshot (geometric representation) of trajectory at a particular timestamp.

Traditional Data Model: A class of data models for storing spatiotemporal trajectories in non-relational databases systems that mainly uses non-spatiotemporal characteristics of trajectories.

Well-Known Binary: A portable representation of spatial geometries that are formed by contiguous stream of bytes.

Chapter 7
Parallel Queries of Cluster–Based k Nearest Neighbor in MapReduce

Wei Yan
Liaoning University, China

ABSTRACT

Parallel queries of k Nearest Neighbor for massive spatial data are an important issue. The k nearest neighbor queries (kNN queries), designed to find k nearest neighbors from a dataset S for every point in another dataset R, is a useful tool widely adopted by many applications including knowledge discovery, data mining, and spatial databases. In cloud computing environments, MapReduce programming model is a well-accepted framework for data-intensive application over clusters of computers. This chapter proposes a parallel method of kNN queries based on clusters in MapReduce programming model. Firstly, this chapter proposes a partitioning method of spatial data using Voronoi diagram. Then, this chapter clusters the data point after partition using k-means method. Furthermore, this chapter proposes an efficient algorithm for processing kNN queries based on k-means clusters using MapReduce programming model. Finally, extensive experiments evaluate the efficiency of the proposed approach.

INTRODUCTION

The *k* nearest neighbor query (*k*NN query) is a classical problem that has been extensively studied, due to its many important applications, such as knowledge discovery, data mining, and spatial databases. With the rapid growth of the spatial data, parallel *k*NN queries are a challenging task. MapReduce programming model processes large scale datasets by exploiting the parallel and distributed computing parallelism. The MapReduce programming model provides good scalability, flexibility and fault tolerance. Therefore, MapReduce programming model becomes an ideal framework of processing *k*NN queries over massive spatial datasets. This chapter proposes a method of parallel *k*NN queries based on k-means clusters using MapReduce programming model.

DOI: 10.4018/978-1-4666-9834-5.ch007

The k nearest neighbor query (kNN) is a special type of query that is k nearest neighbors from points in S for each query point r in dataset R. The kNN query typically serves as a primitive operation and is widely used in knowledge discovery, pattern recognition, and spatial databases. Now, lots of researches (Yao *et al.* 2010) have been devoted to improve the performance of kNN query algorithms. However, all these approaches are performed on a single, centralized server. In single machine, the computational capability and storage are limited, and its efficiency is low. How to perform the kNN query on parallel machines is an important issue in cloud computing environments.

ALL the existing work has concentrated on the spatial databases based on the centralized paradigm. Xia *et al.* (2004) proposed a novel kNN-join algorithm, called the Gorder kNN join method. Gorder is a block nested loop join method that exploits sorting, join scheduling and distance computation filtering and reduction to reduce both I/O and CPU costs. It is simple and yet efficient, and handles high-dimensional data efficiently. However, the system of centralized server will eventually suffer from performance deterioration as the size of the dataset increases. A solution is to consider the parallel query processing in distributed cloud computing environment.

Parallel spatial query processing has been studied in parallel database, cluster systems as well as cloud computing platform. In cloud computing environments, a large part of data-processing using MapReduce (Dean *et al.* 2004) programming model runs extensively on Hadoop. The MapReduce programming model provides a powerful parallel and distributed computing paradigm. Cui *et al.* (2014) addressed the problems of processing large-scale data using k-means clustering algorithm and proposed a novel processing model in MapReduce to eliminate the iteration dependence and obtain high performance. A data structure that is extremely efficient in exploring a local neighborhood in a geometric space is Voronoi diagram (Okabe *et al.* 2000). Given a set of points, a general Voronoi diagram uniquely partitions the space into disjoint regions. The region corresponding to a point p covers the points in space that are closer to p than to any other point.

This chapter presents a partitioning method using Voronoi diagram that is multi-dimensional spatial datasets partition into Voronoi cell. This chapter uses k-means clusters method to apply on the Voronoi cell. The k-means algorithm is a well-known method for partitioning n points that lie in the d-dimensional space into k clusters. Then, this chapter proposes a method of pivot for the Voronoi diagram-based data partitioning, which uses the k-means clusters algorithm to choose as pivot. Furthermore, this chapter proposes an efficient algorithm for processing kNN queries based on k-means clusters method using MapReduce programming model.

The objectives of the chapter are summarized as follows:

- This chapter proposes a partitioning method using Voronoi diagram that is multi-dimensional spatial datasets partition into Voronoi cell.
- This chapter proposes a k-means clusters method to apply on the Voronoi cell. The center point for each cluster is chosen as pivots of Voronoi diagram.
- This chapter proposes an efficient algorithm for processing kNN queries based on k-means clusters method using MapReduce programming model.

BACKGROUND

Related Works

Performing kNN queries in spatial databases has been extensively studied in the research of Xia *et al.* (2004). Yao *et al.* (2010) proposed both the kNN query and the kNN join in the relational database, used the user-defined-function that a query optimizer cannot optimize. The authors designed algorithms that could be implemented by SQL operators using a small constant number of random shifts for databases, and guaranteed to find the approximate kNN. However, these works focus on the centralized, single-thread method that is not directly applicable in MapReduce programming model. Zhang *et al.* (2009) proposed a parallel spatial join algorithm in MapReduce, dealing with only spatial distance joins, which does not solve kNN joins. Zhang *et al.* (2012) proposed novel algorithms in MapReduce to perform efficient parallel kNN joins on large data. The authors proposed the exact H-BRJ algorithms and approximate H-zkNNJ algorithms, and the H-zkNNJ algorithms deliver performance which is orders of magnitude better than baseline methods, as evidenced from experiments on massive real datasets. Jiang *et al.* (2010) proposed the performance study of MapReduce (Hadoop) on a 100-node cluster of Amazon EC2 with various levels of parallelism. The authors identify five design factors that affect the performance of Hadoop, and investigate alternative but known methods for each factor. Their works show that by carefully tuning these factors, the overall performance of Hadoop can be improved by a factor of 2.5 to 3.5 for the same benchmark, and is thus more comparable to that of parallel database systems.

Kim *et al.* (2012) investigated how the top-k similarity join algorithms can get benefits from the popular MapReduce framework. The authors first developed the divide-and-conquer and branch-and-bound algorithms. Next, the authors proposed the all pair partitioning and essential pair partitioning methods to minimized the amount of data transfers between map and reduce functions. Finally, the authors performed the experiments with not only synthetic but also real-life data sets. Okcan *et al.* (2011) proposed join model simplifies creation and reasoning about joins in MapReduce. Using this model, the authors derive a surprisingly simple randomized algorithm, called 1-Bucket-Theta, for implementing arbitrary joins (theta-joins) in a single MapReduce job.

Regarding the method of k-means clusters, Vattani (2011) presented how to construct a two-dimensional instance with k clusters for which the k-means algorithm requires $2^{\Omega(k)}$ iterations. Bahmani *et al.* (2012) proposed k-means++ initialization algorithm, which obtains an initial set of centers that is provably close to the optimum solution. About the work of parallel clustering algorithm, Ene *et al.* (2011) proposed clustering algorithms that can be used in MapReduce, which are the practical and popular clustering problems k-center and k-median. Ma *et al.* (2007) proposed a distributed k-median clustering algorithm for use in a distributed environment. Several approximate methods for computing the median in a distributed environment are proposed and analyzed in the context of the iterative k-median algorithm. Xu *et al.* (1999) presented PDBSCAN, a parallel version of the clustering algorithm. The authors uses the shared-nothing architecture with multiple computers interconnected through a network. A fundamental component of a shared-nothing system is its distributed data structure. The authors introduced a distributed spatial index structure in which the data is spread among multiple computers and the indexes of the data are replicated on every computer. Debatty *et al.* (2014). proposed a MapReduce implementation of G-means, a variant of *k*-means that is able to automatically determine k, the number of clusters. Other techniques that run a clustering algorithm with different values of *k* and choose the value of k that provides the best results have a computation cost that is proportional to nk^2. Zhao et al. (2009). proposed a fast parallel *k*-means clustering algorithm based on MapReduce, which has been widely embraced by both academia and industry. Akdogan *et al.* (2010) proposed the method of parallel geospatial query processing with the MapReduce programming model. The proposed approach creates a spatial index, Voronoi diagram, for given data points in two-dimensional space and enables efficient processing of a wide range of Geospatial queries. Vernica et al. (2010) proposed an efficient parallel set-similarity join in MapReduce. The authors propose a three-stage approach for end-to-end set-similarity joins, and take as input a set of records and output a set of joined records based on a set-similarity condition.

*k*NN Queries

In *n*-dimensional space *D*, given two points *r* and *s*, |*r*, *s*| represents the distance between point *r* and *s* in space *D*. In this chapter, the Euclidean distance is used as the distance.

$$| r,s |= (\sum_{i=1}^{n} (r[i] - s[i])^2)^{1/2} \tag{1}$$

where, *r*[*i*] (resp. *s*[*i*]) denotes the value of *r* (resp. *s*) along the ith dimension in space *D*.

Definition 1 [*k* nearest neighbors]: Given a point *r*, a dataset *S* in space *D* and an integer *k*, the *k* nearest neighbors of *r* from *S*, denoted as *k*NN(*r*, *s*), is a set of *k* point from *S* that $\forall p \in kNN(r, S)$, $\forall s \in S - kNN(r, S)$, |*p*, *r*|≤|*s*, *r*|.

Definition 2 [*k*NN queries]: Given two dataset *R* and *S* in space *D*, and an integer *k*. *k*NN queries of *R* and *S* (denoted as *knn*Q), combine each point *r* ∈ *R* with its *k* nearest neighbors from *S*.

$$knnQ(R, S) = \{(r, kNN(r, S)) \mid \text{for all } r \in R\} \tag{2}$$

Voronoi Diagram

The Voronoi diagram of a given set $P = \{p_1, p_2, ..., p_n\}$ of *n* points in R^d partitions the space of R^d into *n* regions. Each region includes all points in R^d with a common closest point in the given set *P* using the distance metric *Dist*(), which is proposed by the authors Okabe *et al.* (2000). The region corresponding to the point $p \in P$ contains all the points $q \in R^d$.

$$\forall p' \in P, p' \neq p, Dist(q, p) \leq Dist(q, p') \tag{3}$$

The equality holds for the points on the borders of *p*'s regions.

Figure 1 shows the Voronoi diagram of five points in two-dimensional space, where the distance metric is Euclidean. This chapter represents the region *V*(*p*) containing the point *p* as its Voronoi cell. Using Euclidean distance in two-dimensional space, *V*(*p*) is a convex polygon. Each edge of the convex

Figure 1. Voronoi diagram

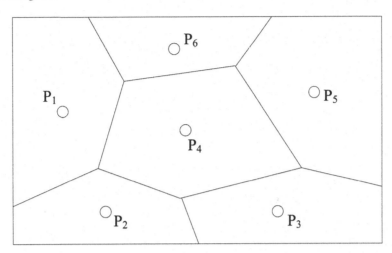

polygon is a segment of the perpendicular bisector of the line segment connecting *p* to another point of the set *P*. Each of these edges represents as Voronoi edge and each of its end-points as a Voronoi vertex of the point *p*. For each Voronoi edge of the point *p*, this chapter refers to the corresponding point in the set *P* as a Voronoi neighbor of *p*. This chapter uses *VN(p)* to denote the set of all Voronoi neighbors of *p*. The point *p* represents as the generator of Voronoi cell *V(p)*. Finally, the set given by $VD(P) = \{V(p_1), V(p_2), ..., V(p_n)\}$ is called the Voronoi diagram generated by *P* with respect to the distance function *Dist*().

Definition 3 [*Voronoi pivot*]: Given a Voronoi diagram *VD(P)*, select *n* objects as Voronoi pivots and then split the Voronoi diagram *VD(P)* into *n* disjoint Voronoi cells where each Voronoi cell is assigned to the partition with its closest pivot.

Throughout this chapter, the Euclidean distance function is used in two-dimensional space. Also, this chapter simply uses Voronoi diagram to denote ordinary Voronoi diagram of a set of points in two-dimensional space.

K-Means Algorithm

K-means algorithm is the well-known and commonly used clustering method. The algorithm takes the input parameter *k* and partitions a set *X* of *n* data points *D* in R^d into *k* clusters. Given the initial set of *k* cluster centers in R^d, every data point is assigned to the cluster whose center is closest to it. *K*-means wish to choose the collection of *k* centers *C*, so as to minimize the potential function:

$$\varphi = \sum_{x \in D} \min_{c \in C} \| x - c \|^2 \qquad (4)$$

The algorithm assigns each point to the cluster whose center is nearest. The center's coordinates are the arithmetic mean for each dimension separately over all the points in the cluster. Suppose *icb* is the convergent boundary, the *k*-means clustering algorithm as follows:

Algorithm 1: *K*-means (*D*, *k*)

Input: integer *k*, a set *X* of *n* data points *D*
Output: *k-means clustering*
1.   Let *i* = Float.MAXVALUE; *j* = 1
2.   Choose *k* centers from *D*, let $C^{(0)} = c_1^{(j)}, c_2^{(j)}, ..., c_k^{(j)}$
3.   for *i* > *icb* do
4.   from *k* clusters by assigning each points in *X* to its nearest
center
5.   find new centers of the *k* clusters $c_1^{(++j)}, c_2^{(++j)}, ..., c_k^{(++j)}$
6. $$i \leftarrow \sum_{m=0}^{k} \| c_m^j - c_m^{j-1} \|^2$$
7.   endfor
8.   output $C^{(j)}$

Firstly, the algorithm 1 randomly selects *k* objects from the whole points which represent initial cluster centers. Each remaining point is assigned to the cluster, which is most similar based on the distance between the points and the cluster center. The new mean of each cluster is then calculated. This process iterates until the criterion function converges.

MapReduce Programming Model

MapReduce is a popular programming framework to support data-intensive applications using shared-nothing clusters (Dean, 2004). A MapReduce program typically consists of a pair of user-defined map and reduce functions. The map function takes an input key-value pair and produces a set of intermediate key-value pairs. MapReduce runtime system then groups and sorts all the intermediate values associated with the same intermediate key, and sends them to the reduce function. The reduce function accepts an intermediate key and its corresponding values, applies the processing logic, and produces the final result which is typically a list of values.

map $(k_1, v_1) \rightarrow$ list (k_2, v_2)

reduce$(k_2,$ list$(v_2)) \rightarrow$ list (k_3, v_3) (5)

Figure 2 shows the framework of MapReduce programming model. Input data is loaded into HDFS (hoop distributed file system), where each file is partitioned into smaller data blocks, also called input splits. A file's splits are then distributed, and possibly replicated, to different machines in the cluster. A Map-Reduce computation begins with a Map phase where each input split is processed in parallel by as many map tasks as there are splits. Each input split is a list of key-value pairs. A map task applies the user-defined map function to each key-value pair to produce a list of output key-value pairs. To execute a MapReduce job, the users specify the input file, the number of desired map tasks *m* and reduce tasks *r*, and supply the map and reduce function.

The output key-value pairs from a map task are partitioned on the basis of their key k_2. Each partition is then sent across the cluster to a remote node in the shuffle phase. A shuffle and sort stage is com-

Figure 2. The framework of MapReduce programming model

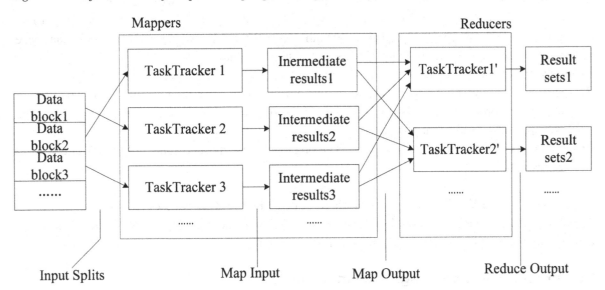

menced, during which the i'th reducer r_i copies records from $b_{i,j}$, the i'th bucket from each of the jth map task. Corresponding partitions from the map tasks are merged and sorted at their receiving nodes.

For each key, the associated values are grouped together to form a list. The key and the corresponding list are given to the user-specified reduce function. The reduce function is invoked once for each distinct k_2 and it processes a k_2's associated list of values $list(v_2)$, i.e. it is passed a $(k_2, list(v_2))$ pair per invocation. For every invocation, the reduce function emits 0 or more final key value pairs (k_3, v_3). The output of each reduce task $(list (k_3, v_3))$ is written into a separate distributed file residing in the DFS.

The resulting key-value pairs are written back to the DFS and form the final output. To reduce the network traffic caused by repetitions of the intermediate keys k_2 produced by each mapper, an optional combine function for merging output in map stage, combine $(k_2, list(v_2)) \rightarrow$ list (k_2, v_2), can be specified.

PARTITIONED METHOD BASED ON VORONOI DIAGRAM

This section partitions the two-dimensional data sets using Voronoi diagram.

Voronoi Diagram-Based Partitioned Method of Two-dimensional Space

The Voronoi diagram decomposes two-dimensional space into disjoint polygons. Given a set of point set S in two-dimensional space, the Voronoi diagram associates all point in the two-dimensional space to their closest point. Each point s has a Voronoi polygon consisting of all points closer to s than to any other point. Hence, the nearest neighbor of a query point q is closed Voronoi polygons. The set of Voronoi polygons associated with all the points is called the Voronoi diagram (VD). The polygons are mutually exclusive except for their boundaries.

Definition 4 [Voronoi Polygon]: Given set of points $P = \{p_1, p_2, ..., p_n\}$ where $2 < n < \infty$ and $p_i \neq p_j$ for $i \neq j$, i, j = 1, 2, ..., n, the Voronoi polygon of p_i is $VP(p_i) = \{p \mid d(p, p_i) \leq d(p, p_j)\}$ for $i \neq j$ and $p \in VP(p_i)$ where $d(p, p_i)$ specifies the minimum distance between p and p_i in Euclidean space.

Property 1: The Voronoi diagram for given set of points is unique.

Property 2: Let n and n_e be the number of points and Voronoi edges, respectively, then $n_e \leq 3n\text{-}6$.

Property 3: Every Voronoi edge is shared by two Voronoi polygons, the average number of Voronoi edges per Voronoi polygon is at most 6, i.e., $2*(3n\text{-}6)/n = 6n\text{-}12/n \leq 6$. This states that no average, each point has 6 adjacent points.

Property 4: The nearest points of p_i (e.g., p_j) is among the points whose Voronoi polygons share Voronoi edges with $VP(p_i)$.

Assume that the VD(P) is the Voronoi diagram of P. Figure 3 shows the Voronoi diagram of the space points. To bound the Voronoi polygons with infinite edges (e.g., $V(p_3)$), this section clips them using a large rectangle bounding the points in P (the dotted rectangle).

Constructing Voronoi Diagram with MapReduce

Construction of Voronoi diagram (VD) is suitable for MapReduce programming model, because Voronoi diagram can be obtained by merging multiple Voronoi polygons (VP). Specifically, each of Voronoi polygons (VP) can be created by the mappers using parallel method and the reducers using combining method in single Voronoi diagram (VD).

Figure 3. Voronoi diagram-based partition

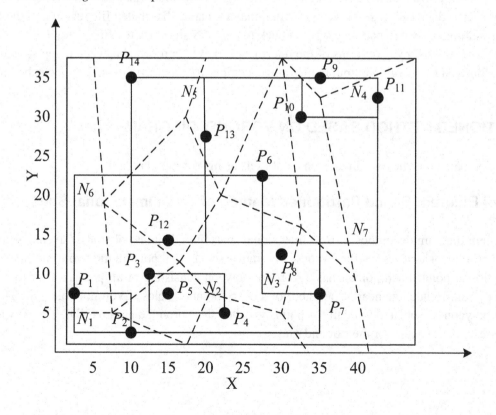

Given a set of data point $P = \{p_1, p_2, \ldots, p_n\}$ as input, firstly the point set is sorted in increasing order according to x coordinate. Secondly, the point set P is separated into several subsets of equal size. Finally, the Voronoi polygons (VP) are generated for the points of each subset, and then all of the Voronoi polygons (VP) are merged to obtain the final Voronoi diagram (VD) for the point set P.

Map phase of MapReduce programming model: Given a point set sorted by x coordinate, each mapper reads an input block using the format of <key, value>. Then each mapper generates a Voronoi polygons (VP) for the point set in its data block, marks the boundary polygons and emits the generated Voronoi polygons (VP) in the form of <key', value$_i$'> where i denotes the number of data block. The key' is common to all Voronoi polygons (VP), so that all Voronoi polygons (VP) can be grouped together and merged in the subsequent reduce phase.

Reduce phase of MapReduce programming model: The reducers aggregates all Voronoi polygons (VP) in the same group and combines them into a single Voronoi diagram (VD). In the reduce phase, the boundary polygons are detected with a sequential scan, and then new Voronoi edges and vertices are generated by delecting superfluous boundary portions from Voronoi polygons (VP). As the final output, the reducers emit each point and its Voronoi neighbors.

THE DISTANCE BETWEEN POINTS OF VORONOI DIAGRAM

In the Voronoi diagram, the most calculation of k-means algorithm is the calculation of the distances between points. The computation of the distance between one point with the clustering centers is irrelevant to the computation of the distance between other points with the corresponding centers. Let P is the set of pivots of the Voronoi diagram. $\forall\, p_i \in P$, P_i^Q represents the set of points from Q that takes p_i as their closest pivot. For a point q, let p_q and P_q^Q be its closest pivot and the corresponding partition in Voronoi diagram respectively.

Definition 5 [*Distance Threshold*]: Given a point set P and a point q, the distance threshold δ is all points (denoted as $\overline{P}$) of P, such that $\forall\, p' \in \overline{P}$, $|q, p'| \leq \delta$.

By splitting the dataset into a set of partitions, Hjaltason *et al.* (2003) proposed following theorem:

Theorem 1: Given two pivots p_i, p_j, let $HP\,(p_i, p_j)$ be the generalized hyperplane, where any point q lying on $HP\,(p_i, p_j)$ has the equal distance to p_i and p_j. $\forall\, q \in P_j^Q$, the distance of q to $HP\,(p_i, p_j)$, denoted as $dist\,(q, HP\,(p_i, p_j))$ is:

$$dist(q, HP(p_i, p_j)) = \frac{|q, p_i|^2 - |q, p_j|^2}{2 \times |p_i, p_j|} \tag{6}$$

Figure 4 shows the distance $dist\,(q, HP\,(p_i, p_j))$.
According to the triangle inequality,

$$|q, p_i|^2 = |q, q'|^2 + |q', p_i|^2$$

Figure 4. the distance dist (q, HP (p$_i$, p$_j$))

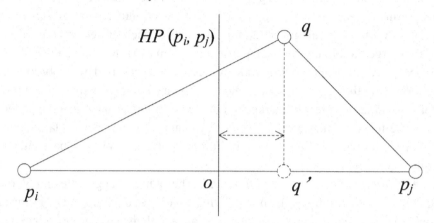

Similarly,

$$|q,p_j|^2 = |q,q'|^2 + |q',p_j|^2$$

Hence,

$$|q,p_i|^2 - |q,p_j|^2 = |q',p_i|^2 - |q',p_j|^2$$

$$|q,p_i|^2 - |q,p_j|^2 = (\frac{1}{2}|p_i,p_j| + dist(q,HP(p_i,p_j)))^2 - (\frac{1}{2}|p_i,p_j| - dist(q,HP(p_i,p_j)))^2$$

$$|q,p_i|^2 - |q,p_j|^2 = 2|p_i,p_j| \times dist(q,HP(p_i,p_j))$$

Clearly,

$$dist(q,HP(p_i,p_j)) = \frac{|q,p_i|^2 - |q,p_j|^2}{2 \times |p_i,p_j|}$$

Given point q, its belonging partition P_q^{ϱ}, and another partition P_i^{ϱ}, according to theorem 1, it is able to compute the distance from q to $HP(p_q, p_i)$. Hence, derive the following corollary.

Corollary 1: Given a partition P_i^{ϱ} and P_q^{ϱ}, if derive *dist* $(q, HP(p_q, p_i)) > \delta$, then $\forall q \in P_i^{\varrho}$, $|q, i| > \delta$.

PARALLEL k-MEANS ALGORITHM USING MAPREDUCE

The MapReduce programming model processes data according to (key, value) pairs and it expresses computation model in terms of two functions: map and reduce. The map function produces key-value pairs based on the input data and outputs a list of intermediate key-value pairs. All intermediate values corresponding to the same intermediate key are grouped together and passed to a reduce function. The reduce function performs a specific task on a group of pairs with same key and produces a list of key-value pairs that form the final output. This section introduces parallel kNN queries algorithm using MapReduce programming model.

First MapReduce Phase

The first MapReduce phase selects the pivots in point set R of two-dimensional space using k-means clustering algorithm for Voronoi diagram. Firstly, the master node assigns a key to each point $r \in R$, saves these keys to distributed file system (DFS), and adds the file to the distributed cache, which is communicated to all mappers during initialization.

Each mapper chooses k centers using k-means clustering method according to the algorithm1. Then, it assigns k centers in set R to k different groups.

Algorithm 2: Map logic algorithm

Input: the multi-dimensional point set R and S,
Output: key-value pairs
```
1.        assign a key to each point r ∈ R
2.        choose k centers using k-means clustering according to the algorithm
1
3.        assign k centers in set R to k different groups
4.        for m =1 to k do
5.              assign center of C_m to the nearest group
6.        endfor
7.        compute the center for each group
8.        for i=1 to k do
9.              i-th center as key k_i
10.       endfor
11.       for j=1 to k do
12.             j-th group as g_j
13.       endfor
14.       output key-value pairs (k_i, g_j)
```

From step 4 to step 6, the Map logic algorithm assigns center of each clusters C_m to the nearest group. Then, the algorithm 2 computes the center for each group. Furthermore, the algorithm 2 outputs key-value pairs. Meanwhile, the algorithm gets i-th center as key k_i. Then, the algorithm gets j-th group as g_j. Finally, the algorithm 2 outputs key-value pairs (k_i, g_j).

Algorithm 3: Reduce logic algorithm

Input: intermediate key-value pairs of Mappers
Output: key-value pairs of first MapReduce phase

```
1.          for each point r_i ∈ R do
2.                  choose k clustering centers using k-means algorithm
3.                  compute the distance between the point r_i and clustering cen-
ter according to formula (6)
4.                  assign input points to appropriate centers
5.          endfor
6.          let the clustering centers as the pivots
7.          for i=1 to k do
8.                  compute the central point p_i of the groups
9.          endfor
10.                 output key-value pairs  (p_i, G_i)
```

In the reduce stage, a reduce task is started to assign input point to appropriate clustering centers. The reduce function first chooses k clustering centers using k-means algorithm. From lines 1 to lines 6 of the algorithm 3, the reducer computes each point r_i, and computes the distance between the point r_i and clustering center according to formula (6). Then, the algorithm assigns input points to appropriate centers. From lines 7 to lines 9 of the algorithm 3, the reducer computes the central point p_i of the groups, and sets the clustering centers as the pivots. Finally, the algorithm outputs key-value pairs (p_i, G_i).

Second MapReduce Phase

The second MapReduce phase is to find the corresponding subset S_i for each R_i. Then, reducer performs the kNN join between a pair of S_i and R_i.

Algorithm 4: Second Map logic algorithm

Input: the outputted key-value pairs of first Reduce logic algorithm
Output: key-value pairs
```
1.          for each pivot p_i do
2.                  construct the Voronoi diagram to generate the Voronoi poly-
gons in point set P_i^R
3.                  the Voronoi polygons (VP_i) contains the partitions G_i
4.                  get the ID pid of the partitions G_i
5.          endfor
6.          for each point s_i ∈ S do
7.                  partition the point set S_i to P_j^S
8.          endfor
9.          for each P_i^R do
10.                 compute the distance dist (P_i^R, P_j^S) < δ
11.                 output key-value pairs (pid, (P_i^R, P_j^S))
12.         endfor
```

The second Map logic algorithm first constructs the Voronoi diagram to generate the Voronoi polygons in point set P_i^R. The pivots of the Voronoi diagram are the outputs of reducers in first MapReduce phase. Then, the master loads the file to the distributed cache, and starts mappers for each split of P_i^R and

P_j^S and written to distributed file system (DFS). From step 1 to step 5 of the algorithm 4, the algorithm gets the ID *pid* of the partitions G_i. The Voronoi polygons (VP$_j$) contains the partitions G_j. Moreover, for each points s_i the algoritm 4 partitions the point set S_i to P_j^S. Furthermore, the algorithm computes the distance *dist* (P_i^R, P_j^S) less than δ. Finally, the algorithm output key-value pairs $(pid, (P_i^R, P_j^S))$.

Algorithm 5: Second Reduce logic algorithm

Input: the outputted intermediate key-value pairs of second Map logic algorithm

Output: key-value pairs

```
1.        for each partition  P_i^R and  P_j^S do
2.                rank the  P_j1^S,  P_j2^S,  …,  P_jN^S according to the ascending order of
the distance |p_i,  p_j|
3.                if  |p_i,  p_j| < δ
4.                        output (r,  kNN(r,  S))
5.                else
6.                        updates kNN(r,  S) by s
7.                endif
8.        endfor
9.        output (r,  kNN(r,  S))
```

The algorithm 5 computes P_j^S for each $r_i \in P_i^R$. In this way, points in each partition of R and their potential k nearest neighbors will be sent to the same reducer. A reducer first ranks the $P_{j1}^S, P_{j2}^S, ..., P_{jN}^S$ according to the ascending order of the distance $|p_i, p_j|$. Each reduce task then calls the reduce function only once, passing in all points for its (P_j^S, P_i^R) partition. From line 1 to line 8 of the algorithm 5, the algorithm finds P_j^S for P_i^R. Moreover, the algorithm computes the distance between p_i and p_j. When the distance between p_i and p_j less than threshold δ. Finally, the algorithm outputs the key-value pairs(r, kNN(r, S)).

EXPERIMENTS

Experimental Setup

To evaluate the effectiveness of the method, this chapter used the OpenStreet dataset from the OpenStreetMap project for an empirical evaluation, and showed performance results of the parallel queries of k nearest neighbor based on k-means clustering in MapReduce (PKCM) method. The Openstreet dataset represents the road networks for a US state. The entire dataset has the road networks for 50 states, containing more than 160 million records in 8GB. All the experiments were implemented in JDK 6.0, and performed on a heterogeneous cluster consisting of 18 nodes with 2.9GHz Intel Pentium G2020 processor and 4GB of RAM. Each node is connected to a Gigabit Ethernet switch and runs hadoop 2.2.0.

This chapter generates a number of different datasets as R and S from the complete OpenStreet dataset. We extracted 40 million records from this dataset, where each record consists of 2 real values (longitude and latitude) and a description with variable length.

The experiment aims at evaluating the efficiency of different *k*NN queries methods: (1) The parallel queries of k nearest neighbor based on k-means clustering in MapReduce method, henceforth referred to as PKCM; (2) The Hadoop Block R-tree Join approach described in the work of Zhang *et al.* (2012), henceforth referred to as H-BRJ. The H-BRJ method is to build an index for the local S block in a bucket in the reducer, to help find *k*NNs of a record *r* from the local *R* block in the same bucket. For each block S_{bj} ($1 \leq j \leq n$), the H-BRJ method builds a reducer-local spatial index over S_{bj}, in particular the H-BRJ method used the R-tree, before proceeding to find the local *k*NNs for every record from the local *R* block in the same bucket with S_{bj}. Then, the chapter uses *k*NN functionality from R-tree to answer $kNN(r, S_{bj})$ in every bucket in the reducer. Bulk-loading a R-tree for S_{bj} is very efficient, and *k*NN search in R-tree is also efficient, hence this overhead is compensated by savings from not running a local nested loop in each bucket.

Query Performance Experiment

This section evaluates the execution time of PKCM and H-BRJ method with different dataset configurations. From the Figure 5, it can be seen that the overall execution time of the two approaches increases when we enlarge the data size. The PKCM method delivers much better running time performance than H-BRJ method. The trends in Figure 5 also indicate PKCM becomes increasingly more efficient than H-BRJ as the dataset sizes increase. In particular, when data size becomes larger, the running time of PKCM grows much slower than that of H-BRJ.

Figure 5. Execution times of PKCM and H-BRJ method

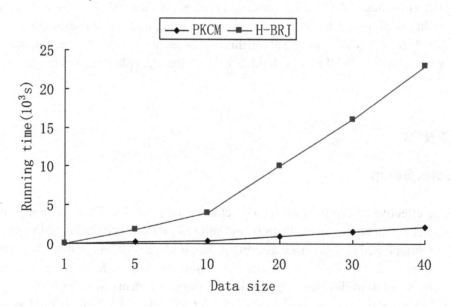

Precision and Recall of Different Queries Method

This section uses the formal precision and recall metrics to measure the retrieval quality. Precision is the ratio of the number of relevant query nodes retrieved to the total number of retrieved nodes:

$$Precision = \frac{|\ relevant \cap retrieved\ |}{|\ retrieved\ |} \tag{7}$$

Recall is the ratio of the number of relevant nodes retrieved to the total number of relevant nodes:

$$Recall = \frac{|\ relevant \cap retrieved\ |}{|\ relevant\ |} \tag{8}$$

This experiment measures the precision and recall of the results returned by PKCM and H-BRJ method. It can be seen that PKCM method outperforms H-BRJ method, and PKCM always achieves higher precision and recall than H-BRJ. The experiment uses the OpenStreet datasets and gradually increases datasets from 1 to 40. The average precision and recall of PKCM method are above 90% all the time. However, the average precision and recall of H-BRJ method are below 70%.

Figure 6. Precision of PKCM and H-BRJ method

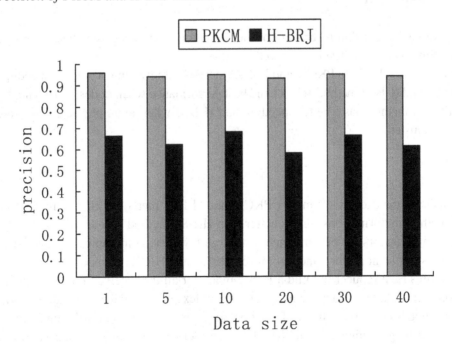

Figure 7. Recall of PKCM and H-BRJ method

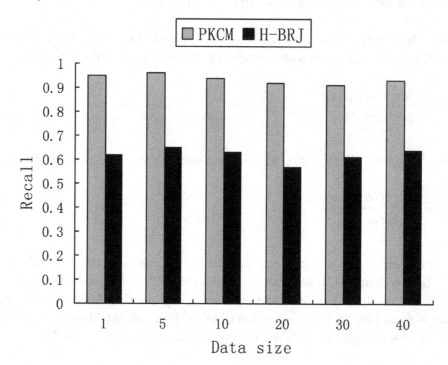

Speedup Experiment

The speedup for each algorithm is the ratio of the execution time on a given cluster configuration over the execution time on the smallest cluster configuration.

The Figure 8 shows that both PKCM and H-BRJ method achieve almost a linear speedup up to nodes 16. Both PKCM and H-BRJ method achieve the best performance when nodes n=16, and degrade when n>16. The PKCM method has a better speedup than H-BRJ when more physical slaves are becoming available in the cluster.

Effect of *k*

The Figure 9 shows the execution time for PKCM and H-BRJ method with different k. It can be seen that PKCM method performs consistently better than H-BRJ method. For small k values, kNN queries are the determining factors for performance. For large k values, communication overheads gradually become a more significant performance factor for PKCM and H-BRJ method.

H-BRJ requires each reducer to build a R-tree index for all the received points from S. To find the kNN for an point from R, the reducers will traverse the index and maintain candidate points as well as set of intermediate nodes in a priority queue. Both operations are costly for multi-dimensional space points, which result in the long running time. In PKCM, the parallel k-means method using MapReduce clusters

Figure 8. Speedup of PKCM and H-BRJ method

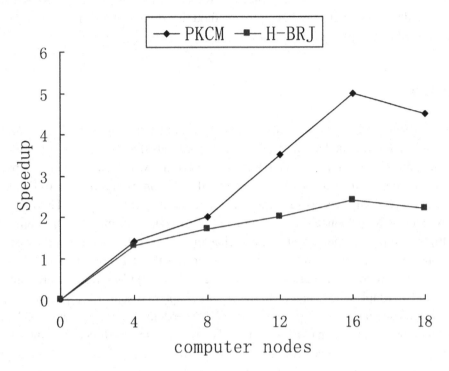

Figure 9. Execution time of PKCM and H-BRJ method with different k

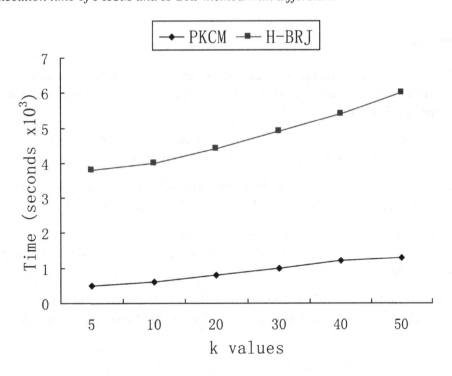

the space points into groups only if the distances between them are restricted by a distance threshold. The PKCM method designs an efficient mapping method that divides points into groups, each of which is processed by a reducer to perform the kNN query.

CONCLUSION

This chapter proposes a method of parallel kNN queries for big space data based on k-means algorithm in MapReduce programming model. Firstly, this chapter presents the kNN queries of multi-dimensional space data. Then, this chapter introduces the k-means algorithm, which can cluster the space data. Secondly, this chapter proposes the partitioned method based on Voronoi diagram in two-dimensional space. The Voronoi diagram decomposes two-dimensional space into disjoint polygons. This chapter constructs Voronoi diagram using MapReduce programming model, because Voronoi diagram can be obtained by merging multiple Voronoi polygons. Thirdly, this chapter proposes the method of the distance between points of Voronoi polygons. Moreover, this chapter proposes the definition of the distance threshold. Fourthly, this chapter proposes the parallel k-means algorithm using MapReduce programming model, which consists of two MapReduce phase. Moreover, this chapter presents the algorithm of parallel kNN query using MapReduce programming model. Finally, the extensive experimental results demonstrate that proposed method is better than existing works. The future research direction is the issue of parallel query for big data using MapReduce programming model which is a well-accepted framework for data-intensive applications over clusters of computers, and studies the problem of parallel geospatial query processing with MapReduce programming model further.

REFERENCES

Akdogan, A., Demiryurek, U., Banaei-Kashani, F., & Shahabi, C. (2010). Voronoi-based geospatial query processing with mapreduce. *Proceedings of the International Conference Cloud Computing*, Indianapolis, Indiana, USA (pp. 9-16). IEEE.

Bahmani, B., Moseley, B., Vattani, A., Kumar, R., & Vassilvitskii, S. (2012). Scalable k-means++. *Proceedings of the VLDB Endowment*, 5(7), 622–633. doi:10.14778/2180912.2180915

Cui, X., Zhu, P., Yang, X., Li, K., & Ji, C. (2014). Optimized big data k-means clustering using MapReduce. *The Journal of Supercomputing*, 70(3), 1249–1259. doi:10.1007/s11227-014-1225-7

Dean, J., & Ghemawat, S. (2004). MapReduce: simplified data processing on large clusters. *Proceedings of the Symposium on Operating System Design and Implementation*, San Francisco, California, USA (pp. 137-150). USENIX Association.

Debatty, T., Michiardi, P., Mees, W., & Thonnard, O. (2014). Determining the k in k-means with MapReduce. *Proceedings of the Workshops of the EDBT/ICDT 2014 Joint Conference*, Athens, Greece (pp. 19-28). CEUR-WS.org.

Ene, A., Im, S., & Moseley, B. (2011). Fast clustering using MapReduce. *Proceedings of the 17th ACM SIGKDD International Conference on Knowledge Discovery and Data Mining*, San Diego, CA, USA (pp. 681-689). ACM.

Hjaltason, G. R., & Samet, H. (2003). Index-driven similarity search in metric spaces. *ACM Transactions on Database Systems, 28*(4), 517–580. doi:10.1145/958942.958948

Jiang, D., Ooi, B. C., Shi, L., & Wu, S. (2010). The performance of MapReduce: An in-depth study. *Proceedings of the VLDB Endowment, 3*(1), 472–483. doi:10.14778/1920841.1920903

Kim, Y., & Shim, K. (2012). Parallel top-k similarity join algorithms using MapReduce. *Proceedings of the International Conference on Data Engineering*, Arlington, Virginia, USA (pp. 510-521). IEEE Computer Society. doi:10.1109/ICDE.2012.87

Ma, A., & Sethi, I. K. (2007). Distributed k-median clustering with application to image clustering. *Proceedings of the 7th International Workshop on Pattern Recognition in Information System*, Funchal, Madeira, Portugal (pp. 215-220). INSTICC.

Okabe, A., Boots, B., Sugihara, K., & Chiu, S. N. (2000). *Spatial tessellations, concepts and applications of Voronoi diagrams* (2nd ed.). John Wiley and Sons Ltd. doi:10.1002/9780470317013

Okcan, A., & Riedewald, M. (2011). Processing theta-joins using MapReduce. *Proceedings of the ACM SIGMOD International Conference on Management of Data*, Athens, Greece (pp. 949-960). ACM.

Vattani, A. (2011). K-means requires exponentially many iterations even in the plane. *Discrete & Computational Geometry, 45*(4), 596–616. doi:10.1007/s00454-011-9340-1

Vernica, R., Carey, M. J., & Li, C. (2010). Efficient parallel set-similarity joins using mapreduce. *Proceedings of the ACM SIGMOD International Conference on Management of Data*, Indianapolis, Indiana, USA (pp. 495-506). ACM.

Xia, C., Lu, H., Ooi, B. C., & Hu, J. (2004). Gorder: an efficient method for knn join processing. *Proceedings of the International Conference on Very Large Data Bases*, Toronto, Canada (pp. 756-767). Morgan Kaufmann. doi:10.1016/B978-012088469-8.50067-X

Xu, X., Jager, J., & Kriegel, H. (1999). A fast parallel clustering algorithm for large spatial databases. *Data Mining and Knowledge Discovery, 3*(3), 263–290. doi:10.1023/A:1009884809343

Yao, B., Li, F., & Kumar, P. (2010). K nearest neighbor queries and kNN-joins in large relational databases (almost) for free. *Proceedings of the International Conference on Data Engineering,* Long Beach, California, USA (pp. 4-15). IEEE. doi:10.1109/ICDE.2010.5447837

Zhang, C., Li, F., & Jestes, J. (2012). Efficient parallel kNN joins for large data in MapReduce. *Proceedings of the International Conference on Extending Database Technology*, Berlin, Germany (pp. 38-49). ACM. doi:10.1145/2247596.2247602

Zhang, S., Han, J., Liu, Z., Wang, K., & Xu, Z. (2009). SJMR: Parallelizing spacial join with MapReduce on clusters. *Proceedings of the IEEE International Conference on Cluster Computing*, New Orleans, Louisiana, USA (pp. 1-8). IEEE Computer Society. doi:10.1109/CLUSTR.2009.5289178

Zhao, W., Ma, H., & He, Q. (2009). Parallel k-means clustering based on MapReduce. *Proceedings of the First International Conference CloudCom*, Beijing, China (pp. 674-679). Springer.

KEY TERMS AND DEFINITIONS

Distance Between Points r and s: In n-dimensional space D, given two points r and s, $|r, s|$ represents the distance between point r and s in space D. In this chapter, the Euclidean distance is used as the distance. $|r, s| = (\sum_{i=1}^{n} (r[i] - s[i])^2)^{1/2}$ where, $r[i]$ (resp. $s[i]$) denotes the value of r (resp. s) along the ith dimension in space D.

k Nearest Neighbors: Given a point r, a dataset S in space D and an integer k, the k nearest neighbors of r from S, denoted as kNN(r, s), is a set of k point from S that $\forall p \in k$NN(r, S), $\forall s \in S - k$NN(r, S), $|p, r| \leq |s, r|$.

k-Means Algorithm: k-means algorithm is the well-known and commonly used clustering method. The algorithm takes the input parameter k and partitions a set X of n data points D in R^d into k clusters.

kNN Queries: Given two dataset R and S in space D, and an integer k. kNN queries of R and S (denoted as $knnQ$), combine each point $r \in R$ with its k nearest neighbors from S. $knnQ(R, S) = \{(r, k$NN$(r, S)) \mid$ for all $r \in R\}$

MapReduce Programming Model: MapReduce is a popular programming framework to support data-intensive applications using shared-nothing clusters.

Voronoi Diagram: The Voronoi diagram of a given set $P = \{p_1, p_2, ..., p_n\}$ of n points in R^d partitions the space of R^d into n regions. Each region includes all points in R^d with a common closest point in the given set P using the distance metric $Dist()$. The region corresponding to the point $p \in P$ contains all the points $q \in R^d$. $\forall p' \in P, p' \neq p, Dist(q, p) \leq Dist(q, p')$

Voronoi Polygon: Given set of points $P = \{p_1, p_2, ..., p_n\}$ where $2 < n < \infty$ and $p_i \neq p_j$ for $i \neq j$, i, j = 1, 2, ..., n, the Voronoi polygon of p_i is VP$(p_i) = \{p \mid d(p, p_i) \leq d(p, p_j)\}$ for $i \neq j$ and $p \in$ VP(p_i) where $d(p, p_i)$ specifies the minimum distance between p and p_i in Euclidean space.

Chapter 8

Knowledge as a Service Framework for Collaborative Data Management in Cloud Environments – Disaster Domain

Katarina Grolinger
Western University, Canada

Miriam A. M. Capretz
Western University, Canada

Emna Mezghani
Université de Toulouse, France

Ernesto Exposito
Université de Toulouse, France

ABSTRACT

Decision-making in disaster management requires information gathering, sharing, and integration by means of collaboration on a global scale and across governments, industries, and communities. Large volume of heterogeneous data is available; however, current data management solutions offer few or no integration capabilities and limited potential for collaboration. Moreover, recent advances in NoSQL, cloud computing, and Big Data open the door for new solutions in disaster data management. This chapter presents a Knowledge as a Service (KaaS) framework for disaster cloud data management (Disaster-CDM), with the objectives of facilitating information gathering and sharing; storing large amounts of disaster-related data; and facilitating search and supporting interoperability and integration. In the Disaster-CDM approach NoSQL data stores provide storage reliability and scalability while service-oriented architecture achieves flexibility and extensibility. The contribution of Disaster-CDM is demonstrated by integration capabilities, on examples of full-text search and querying services.

INTRODUCTION

Each year, a number of natural disasters strike across the globe, killing hundreds and causing billions of dollars in property and infrastructure damage. As the number of such events increases, minimizing the impact of disasters becomes imperative in today's society.

DOI: 10.4018/978-1-4666-9834-5.ch008

The role of information and communication technology in disaster management has been evolving. Large quantities of disaster-related data are being generated. Behavior of critical infrastructures is being explored through simulation, response plans are being created by government agencies and individual organizations, sensory systems are providing potentially relevant information, and social media (Twitter, Facebook) have been flooded with disaster information (Hristidis, Chen, Li, Luis, & Deng, 2010). Traditional storage and data processing systems are facing challenges in meeting the performance, scalability and availability needs of Big Data. Current disaster data storage systems are disparate and provide few or no integration capabilities and limited potential for collaboration. To meet the needs of Big Data and make the most of available information, a reliable and scalable storage system supported by information sharing, reuse, integration, and analysis is needed.

Another vital element of a successful disaster management is collaboration among a number of teams including firefighters, first aid, police, critical infrastructure personnel, and many others. Each team or recovery unit is responsible for performing a well-defined task, but their collaboration is essential for decision-making and execution of well-organized and successful recovery operations. Such diverse disaster participants generate large quantities of heterogeneous data, making information gathering, storage, and integration especially challenging.

The activities of various disaster participants can be observed through four disaster management phases, as illustrated in Figure 1: mitigation, preparedness, response, and recovery (Coppola, 2011). *Mitigation* includes all activities undertaken to reduce disaster effects by avoiding or decreasing the impact of a disaster. The *preparedness* phase is concerned with preparing for disaster occurrence and includes activities such as planning, establishing procedures and protocols, training, and exercises. The transition from the preparedness to the response phase is triggered by disaster occurrence. The *response* is focused on addressing the direct, short-term effects of a disaster and includes immediate actions to save lives, protect property, and fulfill basic human needs. The transition to the *recovery* phase starts

Figure 1. Disaster management phases

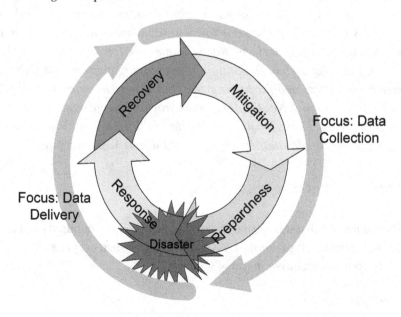

when the direct disaster threat subsides and includes activities focused on bringing society into a normal state. The approach presented in this chapter carries out both data collection and delivery through all four phases; however, the focus is on data collection during the mitigation and preparedness stages, while during the response and recovery phases, the focus is on data delivery. In other words, the main intent is not real-time collection of information during disaster response, but better use of the information collected in different phases.

Recent advances in NoSQL, cloud computing, and Big Data have been changing how data are captured, stored, and analyzed. NoSQL solutions have been especially popular in Web applications (Sakr, Liu, Batista, & Alomari, 2011), including Facebook, Twitter, and Google. However, the use of NoSQL solutions and cloud technologies in disaster management has been sparse. NoSQL data stores are suitable for use as cloud data management systems (Grolinger, Higashino, Tiwari, & Capretz, 2013) and therefore, many of the Database as a Service offerings, such as Amazon's SimpleDB and DynamoDB, are NoSQL data stores. Moreover, NoSQL data stores have a number of characteristics that can benefit disaster data management, including: simple and flexible data model, high availability, horizontal scalability, and low initial investment.

The research significance of this chapter is in providing a data management framework which effectively supports information needs of disaster management as well as other disaster-related activities. The proposed solution facilitates disaster preparedness, response, and recovery efforts by providing a flexible and expandable storage solution for diverse disaster data. Supporting global information sharing, reuse, and integration, the proposed solution provides improved and informed decision-making and therefore reduces the impact of disasters on human lives and property.

This chapter first introduces the motivating scenario and investigates related work. Next, a Knowledge as a Service (KaaS) framework for disaster cloud data management (Disaster-CDM) is presented. Disaster-CDM has the objectives of 1) facilitating information gathering and sharing through collaboration, 2) storing large amounts of disaster-related data from diverse sources, and 3) facilitating search and supporting interoperability and integration. This research aims to facilitate better decision-making in disaster situations by supporting better use of information through global information sharing, reuse, and integration. Moreover, by using NoSQL data stores, Disaster-CDM provides a flexible, highly scalable, and reliable storage for diverse disaster data. Adopting service-oriented architecture, Disaster-CDM achieves flexibility and extensibility while allowing for distributed deployments. Disaster-CDM was motivated by disaster scenarios and it was designed for the management of disaster-related data; however, it could potentially be applied for data management in other domains.

The case study presented at the end of this chapter illustrates the use of Disaster-CDM on the data collected during the Disaster Response Network Enabled Platform (DR-NEP) project. Disaster-CDM benefits are demonstrated by integration capabilities, on examples of full-text search and querying services.

MOTIVATING SCENARIO

This work was motivated by a CANARIE sponsored Disaster Response Network Enabled Platform (DR-NEP) project (The University of British Columbia, 2011). The project combined the expertise of a number of research groups, industry, government agencies, and response teams in multiple geographical locations with the aim of improving the capability to prepare for and respond to large disasters.

A crucial element of disaster management, and DR-NEP project in particular, is simulation because it provides a means of studying the behavior of critical infrastructures, as well as a way of exploring disaster response "what-if" scenarios. Therefore, disaster modeling and simulation played a major role in DR-NEP project, with a special focus on critical infrastructure (CI) interdependency simulation.

The participation of Western University in the DR-NEP project involved the investigation of critical infrastructure interdependencies in an incident that happened on its campus. As the event involved various infrastructures, it was simulated using several simulators including EPANET (United States Environmental Protection Agency, 2008) water distribution simulator and the I2Sim (Rahman, Armstrong, Mao, & Marti, 2008) interdependency simulator. Different disaster response strategies were explored and compared with decisions made during the event. Western University collected information directly related to the event such as the event reports and timelines, data pertaining to the involved infrastructures and a variety of other data that could help in better understanding and modeling the event.

As the DR-NEP project progressed, the quantity of available information was growing and it became difficult to manage it and even more difficult to find information relevant in a specific context or to locate correlated pieces of information. For example, finding information about a specific historic incident or locating all information about a stakeholder was largely a manual process and involved the user knowing the storage location of the information and/or searching for it using operating system search capabilities. This approach was very time consuming, unreliable and error prone.

Content management system (CMS) could alleviate this problem by providing a way to collect, organize, manage, and publish diverse content including documents, workflow information, and multimedia content. Commercial products such as HP's Autonomy (Hewlett-Packard, 2014) and IBM's Enterprise Content Management (ECM) (IBM, 2014) provide generic content management solutions for an enterprise. In contrast, Disaster-CDM focuses on providing knowledge as a service for the disaster management domain. High availability is essential as a system needs to remain operational even when a region is affected by a disaster; if a local data center fails, the system still needs to provide knowledge services to disaster responders. Disaster-CDM achieves high availability by taking advantage of NoSQL storage solutions.

Another requirement in the context of the DR-NEP project relates to simulation. As simulation models are often stored in binary files, the success of traditional CMS is limited. To include simulation models in text search or data analytics, simulation models need to be either extensively annotated or represented in another form more suitable for data integration and analysis. Disaster-CDM achieves this by transforming simulation models into an ontology-based representation.

Our previous work (Grolinger, Mezghani, Capretz, & Exposito, 2015) used Disaster-CDM in the context of Collaborative Knowledge as a Service (CKaaS) and demonstrated collaboration among distributed KaaS entities. This chapter complements the previous one by addressing knowledge acquisitions and storage aspects of the collaboration framework.

BACKGROUND

Research in disaster management involves many fields, including health science, environmental science, computer science, and a number of engineering disciplines. Crisis informatics (Palen *et al.*, 2010; Schram & Anderson, 2012), the area of research concerned with the role of information and technology in disaster management, has been attracting increased research attention recently.

Hristidis *et al.* (2010) surveyed data management and analysis in the disaster domain. The main focus of their survey was on data analysis techniques without the storage aspect. In contrast, in Disaster-CDM, storage and analysis are considered as integral parts. Hristidis *et al.* identified the following data analysis technologies as relevant in disaster data management: information extraction, information retrieval, information filtering, data mining, and decision support. Similarly, Disaster-CDM uses a number of technologies from information extraction and retrieval. Their survey reveals that the majority of research has focused on a very narrow area of disaster management, for example, a specific disaster event such as an earthquake or a flood, or specific disaster-related activities such as communication among actors, estimating disaster damage, and use of mobile devices. Hristidis *et al.* recognized the need for flexible and customizable disaster management solutions that could be applied in different disaster situations. Disaster-CDM aims to provide such a solution using NoSQL data stores.

Othman and Beydoun (2013) pointed out the importance of providing sharable disaster knowledge in facilitating better disaster decision-making. They proposed a Disaster Management Metamodel with the objective of improving knowledge sharing and supporting the integration and matching of different disaster management activities. Othman *et al.* (2014) analyzed the existing disaster models and created a unified view of disaster management in the form of metamodel across the four phases of disaster management. Although Othman *et al.* highlighted the large amount of information generated in the disaster domain, disaster data storage was not considered in their study. November and Leanza (2015) studied collecting and sharing information related to disasters, risks, and crisis; they described how information was gathered, processed, distributed, and used in different disaster and crisis situations. Their work highlighted the importance of information reformatting and reformulation in order to ensure that information reaches the stakeholders and that it is understood as intended. Similarly, Disaster-CDM is concerned with data collecting and sharing; but, the focus is on facilitating search and supporting interoperability and integration.

Silva *et al.* (2011) aimed to integrate diverse, distributed information sources by bringing them into a standardized and exchangeable common data format. Their approach focused on data available on public Web sites. Chou *et al.* (2011) proposed an ontology for developing Web sites for natural disaster management. Web elements contained in the ontology were identified using a ground theory approach with an inventory of disaster management Web sites. While Silva *et al.* (2011) and Chou *et al.* (2011) addressed disaster Web sites, Disaster-CDM is concerned with a variety of diverse data sources.

Palen *et al.* (2010) presented a vision of technology-supported public participation during disaster events. They focused on the role of the public in disasters and how information and communication technology can transform that role. Similarly to Hristidis *et al.* (2010), they recognized information integration as a core concern in crisis informatics.

Anderson and Schram (2011) also studied the role of public and social media in disaster events. They proposed a crisis informatics data analytic infrastructure for the collection, analysis, and storage of information from Twitter. In their initial study (Anderson & Schram, 2011), data were stored in a relational database, specifically MySQL. Later, after encountering scalability challenges, they transitioned to a hybrid architecture that incorporates relational database and NoSQL data store (Schram & Anderson, 2012). Similarly, Disaster-CDM also uses a combination of relational database and NoSQL data stores; however, a combination of several NoSQL data stores has been used to address the storage requirements of diverse data. The works of Choi and Bae (2015), Ilyas (2014), and de Albuquerque *et al.* (2015) also considered Twitter information in the context of disaster management. Choi and Bae (2015) presented a real-time system which monitors Tweeter feeds, analyzes disaster-related tweets, and displays disaster situations in a map. Ilyas (2014) focused on image data; the proposed system scrapes tweets for images and classifies the images using machine learning in order to assess the severity of damage. De Albuquerque *et al.* (2015) combine Twitter data with authoritative data including sensor and hydrological data to identify useful information for disaster management. In contrast to those works (Choi & Bae, 2015; de Albuquerque *et al.*, 2015; Ilyas, 2014), Disaster-CDM is a generic approach suitable for a variety of diverse data sources.

Disaster-CDM incorporates the KaaS approach to make disaster-related knowledge available as services and to enable the collaboration between consumers and providers. Within KaaS, a knowledge provider answers requests presented by knowledge consumers through knowledge services (Khoshnevis & Rabeifa, 2012). Generally, KaaS publishes knowledge models that represent a collection of learned lessons, best practices, and case studies as services that help consumers get knowledge from a distributed computing environment. This approach has been used in various domains: Lai *et al.* (2012) presented a KaaS model for business network collaboration in the medical context, and Qirui (2012) introduced the KaaS in the agricultural domain to provide farming recommendations. While those works store data in the relational database or do not address data management layer, the KaaS in Disaster-CDM accommodates both structured and unstructured data by taking advantage of relational databases and NoSQL data stores.

The collaboration aspect in the disaster management has been emphasized in the work of Waugh and Streib (2006) in which they discussed the importance of collaboration and argued why command and control approaches are problematic. The collaboration aspect in general has been extensively studied by Computer-Supported Cooperative Work (CSCW) (Association for Computing Machinery, 2014) and groupware researchers. Mittleman *et al.* (2008) classified collaboration technologies into four categories: jointly authored pages, streaming technologies, information access tools and aggregated systems. Disaster-CDM is somewhat similar to information access tools which provide ways to store, share and find related content; however, Disaster-CDM focuses on providing high availability in disaster management situations. Synchronous groupware such as chat systems, whiteboards, and video conferencing enables users to interact in real time, but requires simultaneous presence of participants. In contrast, Disaster-CDM entails an asynchronous approach in which participants contribute at different times. An asynchronous approach was chosen because the main objective of Disaster-CDM is not the online communication among disaster participants, but an approach that can make better use of data collected during the mitigation and preparedness stages.

A typical groupware system addresses various aspects of generic enterprise collaboration while Disaster-CDM focusses on the disaster management domain. Moreover, the Disaster-CDM framework is customizable as it can be easily expanded to include new data processing services capable of handling new data sources. The presented case study shows how the framework addresses simulation models and integrates them with other data sources which is not possible using general-purpose content management or CSCW tools.

DISASTER-CDM FRAMEWORK

A successful disaster management relies on the collaboration among participants; however, the diversity of the involved participants and their activities results in massive data heterogeneity. This heterogeneity of data, together with their volume, is one of the main challenges in providing a comprehensive solution that could be used by various stakeholders in diverse disaster situations. Disaster-CDM addresses those Big Data challenges by integrating NoSQL storage with the KaaS approach which provides disaster-related knowledge as a service.

The Disaster-CDM framework illustrated in Figure 2 is the adaptation of the framework proposed in our previous work (Grolinger, Mezghani, Capretz, & Exposito, 2013). It consists of two parts: knowledge acquisition and knowledge delivery services. *Knowledge acquisition* is responsible for acquiring knowledge from diverse sources, processing it to add structure to unstructured or semi-structured data, and storing it. Heterogeneous data from sources like documents, simulation models, social media, and

Figure 2. Disaster-CDM framework

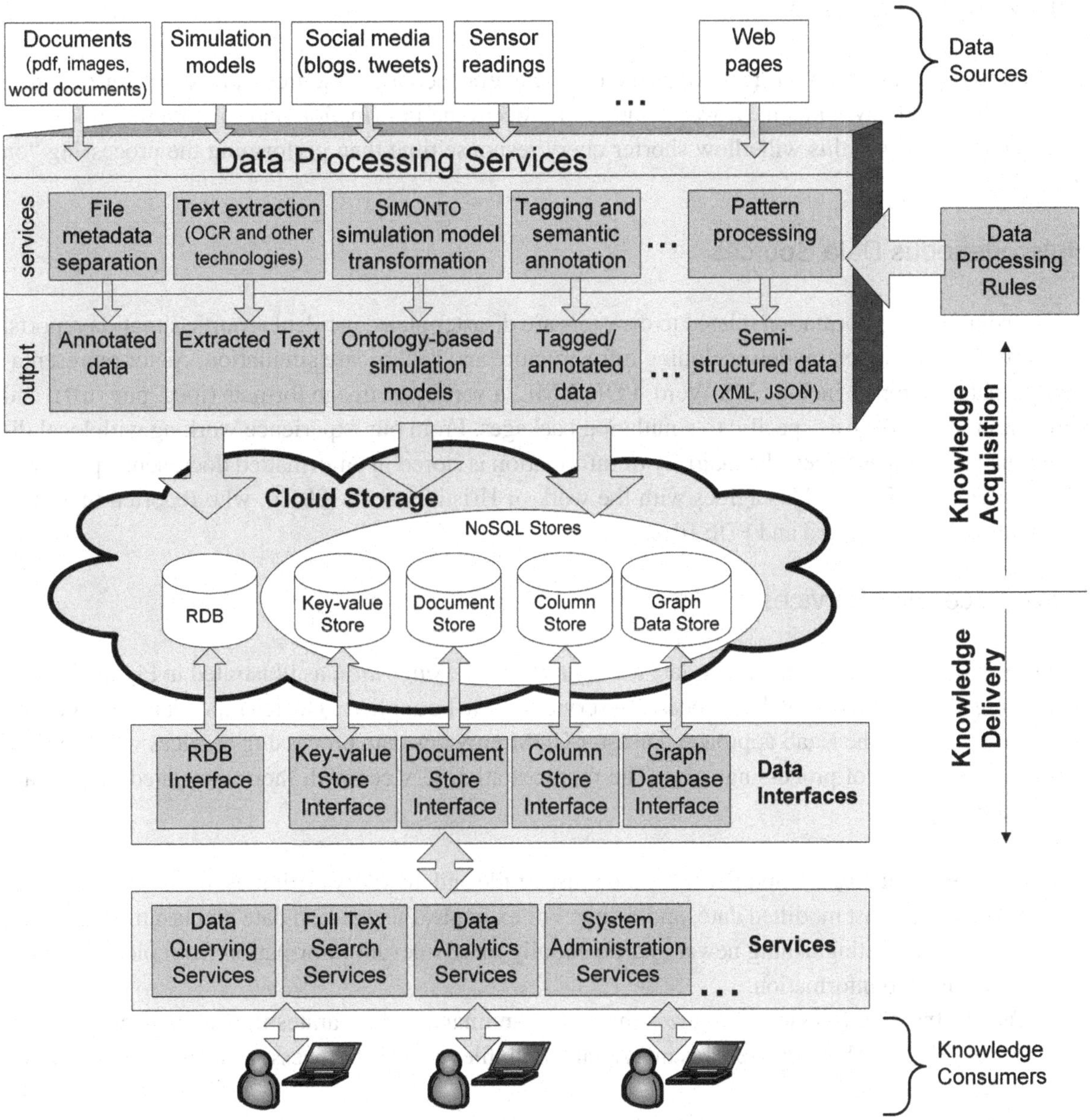

web pages, are handled by applying processes such as text extraction, file metadata separation, and simulation model transformation. This results in outputs including extracted text, annotated data, and ontology-based simulation models. Processed data are stored in a variety of relational databases and NoSQL data stores. *Knowledge delivery* services are responsible for integrating information from different data stores and delivering knowledge to consumers as a service. In contrast to the initial proposition (Grolinger, Mezghani, Capretz, & Exposito, 2013), the framework presented in Figure 2 has been extended to include the Key-value store as a NoSQL storage option and the full-text search as an additional knowledge service.

The following two subsections provide an overview of the two main parts of Disaster-CDM: knowledge acquisition and knowledge delivery.

Knowledge Acquisition

The knowledge acquisition services obtain data from heterogeneous data sources, process them, and store them in the cloud environment. It was decided to process the information and to store the processed, enriched data because this will allow shorter query response time than performing the processing "on the fly".

Heterogeneous Data Sources

A few examples of information related to disasters are disaster plans, incident reports, situation reports, social media, simulation models including infrastructure and health-care simulation. As for representation formats, examples include MS Word, PDF, XML, a variety of image formats (jpeg, png, tiff), and simulation model formats specific to simulation packages. From our experience working with local disaster management agencies, the majority of information is stored in unformatted documents, primarily MS Word and PDF files. This agrees with the work of Hristidis *et al.* (2010), who reported that most information is in MS Word and PDF files.

Data Processing Services

The processing is driven by the input data and by *data processing rules*, as illustrated in Figure 2. *Data processing rules* specify what data processing services are to be applied to which input data and in which order. According to the KaaS approach, Disaster-CDM provides data processing services which can be composed by means of processing rules. The representative services with their associated outputs are included in Figure 2:

- **File Metadata Separation Service** makes use of file and directory attributes, including file name, creation date, last modified date, and owner. For example, the creation date and last modified date can assist in distinguishing newer and potentially more relevant information from older and possibly outdated information.
- **Text Extraction Service** recognizes the text in an image and separates it. (Sumathi, Santhanam, & Devi, 2012). This step prepares images and PDF files for other processing steps such as tagging.

Text extraction is especially important in the case of diagrams such as flowcharts or event-driven process chains because these documents contain large amounts of text that can be used for tagging.

- **Pattern Processing Service** makes use of existing patterns within documents to extract the desired structure. Hristidis *et al.* (2010) observed that most of available disaster-related information is stored in unstructured documents, but that "typically the same organization follows a similar format for all its reports".

- **Simulation Model Service** is the process of converting simulation models into a representation which enables model queries and integration with other disaster-related data. To extract as much information as possible from simulation model files, an ontology-based representation of simulation models has been used (Grolinger, Capretz, Marti, & Srivastava, 2012).

- **Tagging and semantic annotation Services.** Tagging is the process of attaching keywords or terms to a piece of information with the objective of assisting in classification, identification, or search. Semantic annotations additionally specify how entities are related. In disaster management data tagging, both manual and automated tagging are needed.

The presented data processing services are common processes for addressing file-style data; nevertheless, Disaster-CDM can be easily expanded to include new data processing services.

Data Storage

Relational databases (RDBs) are traditional data storage systems designed for structured data. They have been used for decades due to their reliability, consistency, and query capabilities through SQL; however, RDBs are facing many challenges in meeting the requirements of Big Data. The new storage solutions, namely NoSQL data stores (Sakr *et al.*, 2011), have emerged in an attempt to address those challenges in cloud environments.

Disaster-CDM, as illustrated in Figure 2, accommodates both relational database and NoSQL data stores. The following discussion introduces the four NoSQL data store categories:

- **Key-value Data Stores** are used for fast and simple operations. They have the simplest data model: they provide a simple mapping from the key to the corresponding value. When using a key-value data store, relations between data are handled at the application level. This data model greatly restricts integration capabilities, and therefore it is avoided in Disaster-CDM.

- **Document Data Stores** offer a flexible data model with query possibilities. They focus on optimized storage and access for semi-structured documents as opposed to rows or records. Document data stores are considered an evolution of key-value data stores because they include all the benefits of the key-value data stores while adding query capabilities.

- **Column-family data stores** are on the surface similar to relational databases as they both have the notions of rows and columns. However, in the relational database columns are predefined and each row contains the same fixed set of columns, whereas in the column-family data store columns that form a row are determined by the client application and each row can have a different set of columns. Column-family data stores provide query capabilities.

- **Graph Data Stores** are specialized for efficient management of heavily linked data. Applications based on data with many relationships are well suited for graph data stores because the cost of intensive operations like recursive "join" operation can be replaced by efficient graph traversals.

Despite the advantages of NoSQL data stores, Disaster-CDM framework also accommodates relational databases. RDBs are still an appropriate solution for many applications because of their characteristics such as ACID (Atomicity, Consistency, Isolation, Durability) transactions, their status as an established technology, and their advanced query capabilities. Moreover, existing data in relational databases do not need to be migrated.

Knowledge Delivery

The Disaster-CDM knowledge delivery services will answer information requests submitted by service consumers by integrating data stored in the cloud environment. In this stage, the collaboration is achieved by providing the integrated knowledge as a service to collaboration participants. As presented in Figure 2, the data access is mainly composed of two parts:

- **Data interfaces:** Data interfaces enable translation of the generic query into a specific language that corresponds to the underlying data store system. Thus, the data stored in heterogeneous sources can be accessed, analyzed, and administered. An attempt to unify access to NoSQL systems is proposed in the work of Atzeni *et al.* (2013) where NoSQL models and their programming tactics are reconciled within a single framework.
- **Services:** This is the access layer for users. It provides services independently of how the data are stored. Thus, users are unaware of the storage architecture and are provided with a unified view of the data.

The application of the presented Disaster-CDM approach on data formats commonly presents in the disaster management domain, i.e. file-style data formats, is further detailed in the following section.

DATA MANAGEMENT FOR FILE-STYLE DATA

The Disaster-CDM framework is designed to accommodate heterogeneous data sources, including PDF files, MS Word documents, simulation models, Web pages, and social media data. The introduction of a new data source to the framework requires:

1. Adding a new processing block to existing data processing capabilities. For example, video processing would require a new process which would attach textual context to videos.
2. Defining data processing rules for the new data source. For instance, a video processing rule might specify that video files first undergo metadata extraction followed by a new video-specific process.
3. Determining the data storage appropriate for the new data source. Disaster-CDM does not define storage data structure or even the type of data store; in this step, the data store type suitable for the new data source is determined.

From the authors' experience working with local disaster data agencies, which agrees with the work of Hristidis *et al.* (2010), the majority of information is stored in unformatted documents, primarily MS Word and PDF files. Another crucial element of disaster management is simulation because it provides a means of studying the behavior of critical infrastructures. Consequently, this chapter focuses on processing information stored in files, including plain text, image and PDF files, MS Office documents including Word, PowerPoint, Excel, and Visio, and simulation model files. The common element among those information sources is that information is typically stored in self-contained and largely unrelated files.

Data Processing Services for File-Style Data

The main data processing services required to handle information stored in files are included in Figure 2. File metadata separation service is used in processing anything that is stored as a file. Tagging and semantic annotation services are applied on textual data; however, in the case of images or PDF files, text is first extracted from the image or PDF files and then passed on for tagging and semantic annotation. All files are tagged and semantically annotated unless other processes were unable to extract any text from the file. Some other data processing services are more format-specific, such as optical character recognition (OCR) or simulation model transformation.

Data Processing Rules

Data processing rules define how a category of data sources needs to be processed before being stored in a data store. They are influenced by the format of the data source and the available processing services.

For example, Algorithm 1 illustrates a data processing rule for all MS Office files. First, metadata are separated, and text is extracted. Next, if there are images in the file, they are extracted (line 4). For each image, text is extracted using OCR methods (lines 5 to 7). Finally, text extracted from the file and from the images is tagged (lines 8 and 9).

Algorithm 1. Data processing rule for MS Office files

```
1: if file = MSOfficeFile then
2:        processMetadata(file)
3:        fileText = extractText(file)
4:        images = extractImages(file) //extract all images
5:        for each image in images
6:               imageText += OCRProcess(image)
7:        end for
8:        tagText(fileText)
9:        tagText(imageText)
10: End
```

The presented algorithm represents generic processing for all MS Office files regardless of file type. However, some MS Office files, such as Excel files, possess additional formatting that can be exploited to add additional structure to data. For example, since Excel organizes data in tabular form, data processing can take advantage of this formatting and create table-like structures in a data store. In this case, a service needs to be added which can take advantage of this specific formatting, and the data processing rule needs to be refined to include Excel-specific processing.

Another category of files that is especially significant in disaster data management are simulation files. An example of a processing rule for simulation models is presented as Algorithm 2. Like the MS Office rule, it starts with metadata separation. Next, the simulation model is transformed to its corresponding ontology-based representation (line 5), which is described in an ontology representation language. Then *postProcessOntology* deals with specifics of the ontology representation language and prepares ontology-based representation for tagging; for example, it replaces special characters and separates compound words such as those in camel-case naming. Finally, as with MS Office files, the simulation model processing rule ends with text tagging.

Algorithm 2. Data processing rule for simulation models

```
1: if file = SimulationModel then
2:        processMetadata(file)
3:        //Transform simulation model to its corresponding
4:        //ontology-based representation
5:        ontModel = transformSimModelToOntology(file)
6:        fileText = postProcessOntology(ontModel)
7:        tagText(fileText)
8: end
```

Similarly to these rules for MS Office files and simulation model files, rules are defined for other file categories that need to be processed, including PDF files and a variety of image formats. Overall, generic file processing consists of separating metadata, extracting text from source files using file type-specific processing followed by tagging of extracted text. When a source file contains additional formatting, such as in Excel documents, data processing rules can use this formatting to add additional structure to processed data.

Data Storage

Flexibility of data storage is the core of the Disaster-CDM framework because it enables a choice of storage according to the characteristics of the data to be stored. For each data source category, two steps must be performed: determining the type of data store, and designing the data model.

Determining the type of data store consists of choosing among relational database, key-value, document, column-family, and graph data stores. The file-style data considered in this section are stored in self-contained, apparently unrelated files. Although the file contents might be related, this relation is not explicitly specified. Therefore, storage models focusing on relations, including relational database and graph data stores, are not the best suited for such data. The document data store model has been chosen here for the storage of file data because it is designed around the concept of a document, providing flexible storage while allowing structure specification within a document.

The data model design in the case of a document data store consists of defining a document structure. Document data store implementations differ in their internal representations of documents; however, they all encapsulate and encode data in some form of encoding. Therefore, the data model design is independent of the choice of data store implementation provided that the data store belongs to the document category.

Table 1 depicts the data model designed for storing file data in a document data store. It is a generic model for storing a variety of file-style data with flexibility that enables it to accommodate different file types and a variety of attributes. The presented data model is relatively standardized to support querying abilities. In contrast, allowing uncontrolled naming of fields within documents would negatively impact querying abilities. Several fields, such as *fileName* or *origFileLocation*, are mandatory because they are common for all file types and must exist in each document in the data store. On the other hand, other fields such as *docImageText* and *tag* are optional and exist only in documents that need to record those attributes. Two fields, *metaData* and *tag*, have a number of child fields for storing different attributes of the parent field. The number and names of the child fields are different among files of different types: for example, an image file might have *metaData* child fields such as *imageWidth* or *resolutionUnits*, but these child fields will not exist for other file types. With respect to *tag* fields, the number and names of the child fields depends on the tagging approach used.

To accommodate other types of data the data model from Table 1 can be extended by adding new fields. For example, to handle geolocation new fields would be added to the model to record geographical location. Consequently, this would allow for inclusion of geolocation is a search query.

Table 1. File storage data model: Document data store

Field Name	Child field name	Mandatory	Description
fileName		✓	Name of the original file
origFileLocation		✓	Full file path of the original file
origFileMachine		✓	Name of the computer from which the file originated
DBLoadDateTime		✓	Date and time that file was processed by Disaster-CDM
contentType		✓	Type of the content, such as PDF, MS Word, or MS PowerPoint
metaData	modified	✓	Metadata, including generic data such as creator and modified and created date and time. File-specific metadata such as number of slides or word count are also included here.
	created	✓	
	creator	✓	
	...	✗	
docText		✗	Text extracted from files, not including text from images.
docImageText		✗	Text extracted from images.
tag	[]	✗	Arrays of generic tags ([]), as well as arrays of dates, organizations, locations, and persons found in the file text.
	date []	✗	
	organization []	✗	
	location []	✗	
	person []	✗	
	...	✗	
_attachment		✓	File in its original form

CASE STUDY

The motivating scenario described at the beginning of this chapter was used for this case study. Specifically, Disaster-CDM was applied on data collected by Western University during the two-year period of the Disaster Response Network Enabled Platform (DR-NEP) project (The University of British Columbia, 2011). Public databases, such as Emergency Events database (http://www.emdat.be) and a number of databases from Global Risk Information Platform (http://www.gripweb.org/gripweb/?q=disaster-database) were considered; however, those databases contain only public information. In contrast, data set from DR-NEP project includes public data as well as sensitive data which are not accessible to the general public.

The collected data set is heterogeneous and includes data sources such as different institutions' disaster plans, reports of previous incidents, incident timelines, minutes of DR-NEP meetings as well as various other disaster response meetings, information about different critical infrastructures, risk analysis documents, and information about a number of disaster-related stakeholders. These data sources are owned by various participants who need to collaborate and share the owned information in order to achieve successful disaster management. Because simulation was of special interest in the DR-NEP project, the collected data include simulation models that were used to explore critical infrastructure interdependencies, specifically EPANET (United States Environmental Protection Agency, 2008) water-distribution models and the I2Sim (Rahman *et al.*, 2008) interdependency simulator models.

With respect to format, the data set includes text files, image files in a variety of formats, text and PDF files, and MS Office documents, including Word, Excel, PowerPoint, and Visio. Simulation model files are simulator-specific: I2Sim models are stored in a Simulink-style .mdl file format, while EPANET models are stored in .NET or .INP files.

Because this chapter focuses on knowledge acquisition and storage, the presented case study shows how knowledge from DR-NEP data set is acquired and stored. The benefits are demonstrated through the knowledge delivery services, specifically by full-text search and querying services.

Our previous work (Grolinger, Mezghani, Capretz, & Exposito, 2015) demonstrated simulation model processing and storage of the results in a graph data store, and illustrated simulation model querying for the purpose of model checking and validation. In contrast, this chapter is concerned with a variety of file-style sources.

Implementation

The Web application was implemented to provide access to the Disaster-CDM system using a Web browser. Specifically, this Web application provides access to KaaS including knowledge acquisition and knowledge delivery services from anywhere and from a variety of devices. Apache Wicket (Apache wicket, 2015), a component-based Web application framework for the Java programming language, was used for front end development. The following subsections describe the implementation of the two main Disaster-CDM components: data processing services, and data storage.

Data Processing Services

Disaster-CDM provides data processes as services: each data processing component is implemented as a separate Web service. This choice of architecture enabled flexible deployment of services in the cloud environment and the service composition for the provision of knowledge acquisition services. Specifically, the RESTful (Representational State Transfer) Web service architecture was used with the GlassFish application server (GlassFish, 2014). In this case study data processing services were deployed on the Windows machine with Intel Core i7 processor with 16GB RAM; however, they can be deployed on a cluster or a cloud.

This case study focuses on data stored in a variety of file formats, and therefore it implements the data processing required for such data sources. Implementations of most of the data processing approaches from Figure 2 are available either as open source or commercial products. This case study uses open source products, adopts them when needed, and wraps them as RESTful Web services. The following data processing entities have been implemented:

- File metadata separation uses the Apache Tika Toolkit (The Apache Foundation, 2013).
- Text extraction from MS Office documents was also performed by Apache Tika; however, Tika is incapable of extracting text from images. Therefore, text extraction from image files and from images embedded in MS Office files was performed using the Tesseract (Smith, 2007) Optical Character Recognition (OCR).
- Simulation model transformation applies the approach proposed by Grolinger *et al.* implemented in Java.
- Tagging was carried out using the General Architecture for Text Engineering (GATE) tool suite (Cunningham *et al.*, 2013). Specifically, an information extraction system called ANNIE (A Nearly-New IE system), which is distributed with GATE, was used.

Data Storage

This case study focused on data stored as files, and accordingly the storage model chosen was document data stores, as presented in Data Storage subsection. The data model portrayed in Table 1 is designed for NoSQL document data stores and can be realized in any document data store implementation. This case study used the Apache CouchDB document data store (Anderson, Lehnardt, & Slater, 2010).

CouchDB is designed for Web applications, it used HTTP for an API and JavaScript Object Notation (JSON) to represent documents. The primary reasons for choosing CouchDB were its scalability, high availability, and partition tolerance. Ability to scale over many commodity servers enables CouchDB to store large amounts of data, while its high availability ensures system operation even when a region is affected by a disaster and a local data centre fails. Partition tolerance refers to the ability of the system to remain operational in the presence of network partitions, which is especially relevant in disaster-related applications because it can be expected that parts of the network will fail. CouchDB achieves partition tolerance using an asynchronous replication approach; multiple replicas possibly placed on geographically distant locations have their own copies of data, and in case of network partition, each replica modifies its own copy. At a later time, when network connectivity is restored, the changes are synchronized.

The primary way of querying and reporting on CouchDB documents is through views which use the MapReduce model with JavaScript as a query language. In the MapReduce model, the Map function performs filtering and sorting while the Reduce function carries out grouping and aggregation operations.

The Apache Lucene library (McCandless, Hatcher, & Gospodnetic, 2010) provides full-text search of data stored in CouchDB. In general, Lucene is an open-source, high-performance text search engine library written in Java. It is suitable for almost any application which requires full-text search and has been recognized for its utility in Internet search engines. With respect to Disaster-CDM, Lucene enables ranked searches and field specific searches such as searching for a specific file name or an author. This case study takes advantage of CouchDB-Lucene project (CouchDB-lucene project, 2012) which integrates Lucene with CouchDB. For the purpose of the presented case study, CouchDB was deployed on a single machine with Intel Core i7 processor with 16GB RAM; however, this setup can be changed for a cluster or a cloud.

Knowledge Acquisition Services

Western University stored the data collected as part of the DR-NEP project on a server in a dedicated area. It was the responsibility of the individual participants to place data that needed to be shared among participants onto the server. Therefore, this case study uses data from this DR-NEP server as its data source. In the knowledge acquisition stage, these data were processed by data processing services and loaded into the Disaster-CDM system, specifically into the CouchDB. A total of 1129 files were successfully loaded into the Disaster-CDM system, resulting in the same number of documents in the data store. A number of files failed to load; however, further review revealed that they were in file formats which are outside the scope of this case study, including pub, zip, mat, dll, and exe. Nevertheless, the number of these files is small, and including them in the knowledge acquisition process would not have resulted in a major system improvement.

Table 2 shows a number of files of each type loaded into the system. As expected, there were many MS Word and PDF files. Furthermore, the number of PowerPoint presentation files (pptx) was large, which may be explained by the nature of the DR-NEP project, which was a multidisciplinary project involving a large number of stakeholders, in which presentations were often used to transfer knowledge

Table 2. Loaded file types

File Type	# of Files
pdf	247
m	149
pptx	104
h	73
jpg	64
docx	60
txt	54
png	51
.	.
.	.
.	.
net	20
mdl	12

or convey findings. In addition, a large number of .m and .h text files were found, but their significance in knowledge delivery is minor because they are MATLAB and C-language program files. With regard to simulation data, there were 20 EPANET model files (.net) and 12 MATLAB model files (.mdl).

Presently, the knowledge from each file is acquired once, and the system does not keep track of subsequent changes to the file. New files can be loaded into the system at any time.

Knowledge Delivery Services

Two knowledge delivery services are illustrated: full-text search and querying. The two are complementary approaches for accessing data stored in a NoSQL data store, with each one exhibiting strengths for specific data access tasks.

Full-Text Search

Storing data in a document data store enables variants of full-text search. Three variants of full-text search have been observed:

- **Searching attached documents:** This search relied solely on document attachments in the CouchDB data store. Because original files were attached to the CouchDB document in their initial form, this search was somewhat similar to using an indexing and search engine, Lucene in this case, directly on the original files. This strategy does not take advantage of any data processing performed during knowledge acquisition and is the baseline for comparison with other strategies.
- **Searching extracted text:** This strategy includes only the contents of *docText* fields. Because text extracted from images is in *docImageText* field, this strategy ignores text contained in images, including text in image files and text in images embedded in other documents. Note that ontology-based simulation models are stored in *docText* fields and therefore are included in this strategy.
- **Searching extracted text, including text from images:** This approach takes full advantage of Tika text extraction as well as OCR text extraction by including both fields, *docText* and *docImageText*, in the search. This strategy takes full advantage of the data processing performed in the knowledge acquisition stage.

A full-text search screen from the implemented Web application is displayed in Figure 3. This application enables users to choose among the three described search strategies; on the screen in Figure 3, the extracted text strategy is selected. The result of searching for the term "power house" are displayed in the table with two columns: document and last modified. It can be noted that the search result is made up of various file types, including pdf and text files, MS Word, PowerPoint, and simulation model files. Some of the files appear several times with different last modified date; this is caused by files residing in different folders, but having the same name. Disaster-CDM does not check whether files with the same name have identical content, but rather creates a new document in the data store for each loaded file.

Table 3 provides an overview of different strategies with respect to the main file categories addressed in this case study. For the three file categories, PDF, text and I2SIm model files, all three search strategies were virtually the same. Even though searching I2Sim models produced the same results set, the ranking of the documents was different because the searches were based on different text content. The

Figure 3. Full-text search

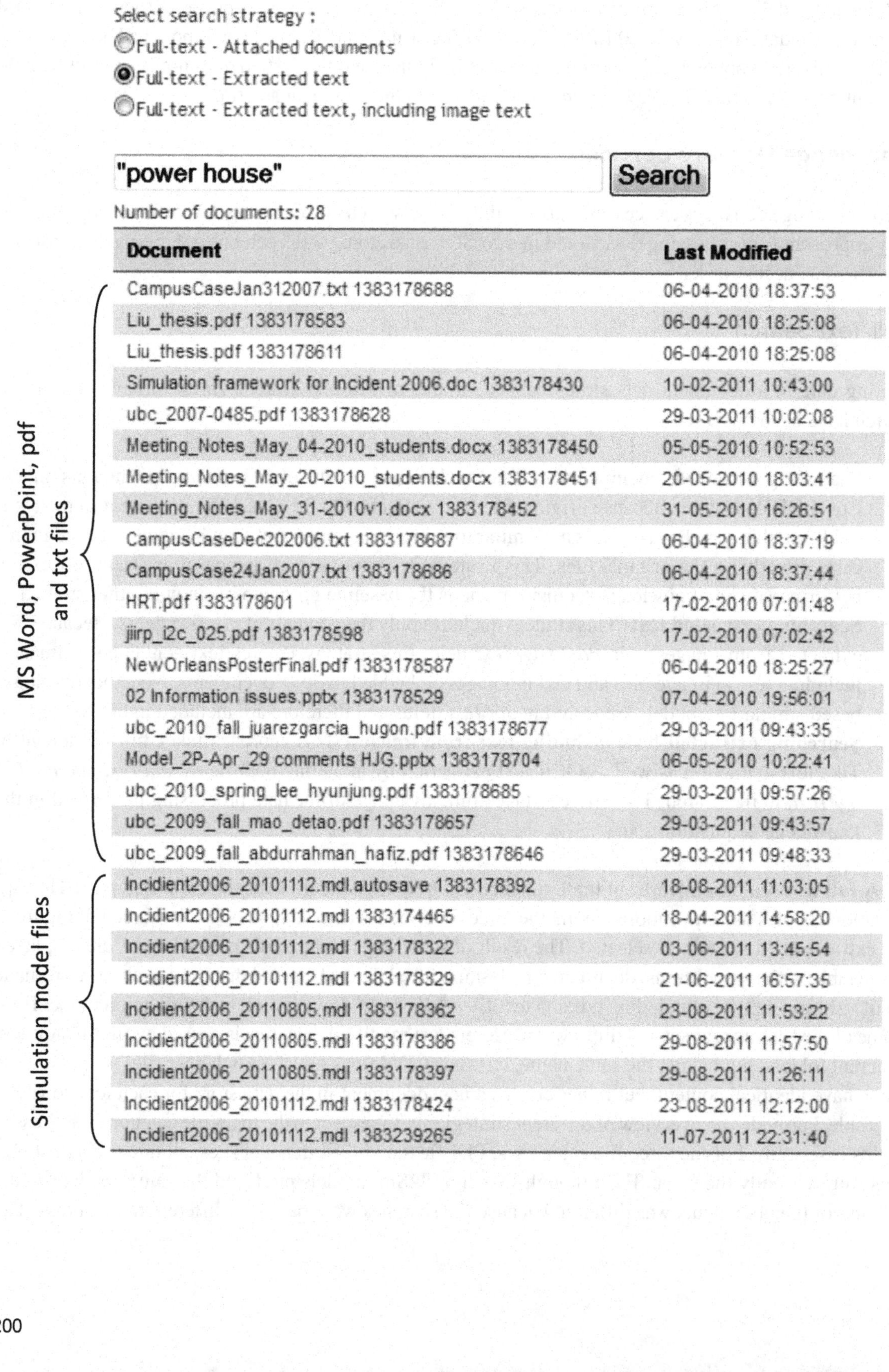

Select search strategy :

- ○ Full-text - Attached documents
- ◉ Full-text - Extracted text
- ○ Full-text - Extracted text, including image text

| "power house" | Search |

Number of documents: 28

Document	Last Modified
CampusCaseJan312007.txt 1383178688	06-04-2010 18:37:53
Liu_thesis.pdf 1383178583	06-04-2010 18:25:08
Liu_thesis.pdf 1383178611	06-04-2010 18:25:08
Simulation framework for Incident 2006.doc 1383178430	10-02-2011 10:43:00
ubc_2007-0485.pdf 1383178628	29-03-2011 10:02:08
Meeting_Notes_May_04-2010_students.docx 1383178450	05-05-2010 10:52:53
Meeting_Notes_May_20-2010_students.docx 1383178451	20-05-2010 18:03:41
Meeting_Notes_May_31-2010v1.docx 1383178452	31-05-2010 16:26:51
CampusCaseDec202006.txt 1383178687	06-04-2010 18:37:19
CampusCase24Jan2007.txt 1383178686	06-04-2010 18:37:44
HRT.pdf 1383178601	17-02-2010 07:01:48
jiirp_i2c_025.pdf 1383178598	17-02-2010 07:02:42
NewOrleansPosterFinal.pdf 1383178587	06-04-2010 18:25:27
02 Information issues.pptx 1383178529	07-04-2010 19:56:01
ubc_2010_fall_juarezgarcia_hugon.pdf 1383178677	29-03-2011 09:43:35
Model_2P-Apr_29 comments HJG.pptx 1383178704	06-05-2010 10:22:41
ubc_2010_spring_lee_hyunjung.pdf 1383178685	29-03-2011 09:57:26
ubc_2009_fall_mao_detao.pdf 1383178657	29-03-2011 09:43:57
ubc_2009_fall_abdurrahman_hafiz.pdf 1383178646	29-03-2011 09:48:33
Incidient2006_20101112.mdl.autosave 1383178392	18-08-2011 11:03:05
Incidient2006_20101112.mdl 1383174465	18-04-2011 14:58:20
Incidient2006_20101112.mdl 1383178322	03-06-2011 13:45:54
Incidient2006_20101112.mdl 1383178329	21-06-2011 16:57:35
Incidient2006_20110805.mdl 1383178362	23-08-2011 11:53:22
Incidient2006_20110805.mdl 1383178386	29-08-2011 11:57:50
Incidient2006_20110805.mdl 1383178397	29-08-2011 11:26:11
Incidient2006_20101112.mdl 1383178424	23-08-2011 12:12:00
Incidient2006_20101112.mdl 1383239265	11-07-2011 22:31:40

MS Word, PowerPoint, pdf and txt files (bracket grouping the first eighteen rows)

Simulation model files (bracket grouping the last nine rows)

attached document strategy searched mdl files, which are text files, directly, while the other two strategies searched the ontology-based simulation models. Consequently, the attached document strategy ranked simulation models lower than the other two strategies.

With regard to MS Office files, the difference among the various searches depended on whether or not they were using text extracted from images. The data set for this case study contained 82 MS Word files (doc and docx), of which only 8 contained images from which text was successfully extracted. In contrast, out of 140 PowerPoint files (ppt and pptx), only 6 did not benefit from the OCR process. Therefore, the OCR process had a higher impact on processing PowerPoint files than on processing Word files. With respect to image files, out of 116 images, text was successfully extracted from 75; however, some of the extracted text did not contain readable words and therefore was not beneficial for searching. Therefore, the OCR process had greater impact on PowerPoint files than on image files, which can be explained by the common use of diagram-style graphs in PowerPoint presentations.

Transforming simulation models into their corresponding ontology-based representations did not have a major impact with I2Sim models, but was essential for including EPANET models in the text search. The attached document strategy did not search EPANET models because they are represented in .net binary files; however, the extracted text strategies searched EPANET models by taking advantage of the ontology-based simulation models stored in *docText* fields.

Note that the attached document search strategy took advantage of the CouchDB-Lucene project (CouchDB-lucene project, 2012), which uses Apache Tika (The Apache Foundation, 2013) to search the attached documents. This case study also used Tika to extract text from files, and therefore the only major difference between the attached-document and the extracted text strategies was with respect to the EPANET model files. Only the extracted text strategy searched the EPANET model files.

Full-text search can also be achieved by applying text search engine such as Lucene directly on the file system containing disaster-related data; however, such search ignores text contained in images as well as text in images embedded in other documents. In contrast, full-text search in Disaster-CDM includes image text because OCR performed in the knowledge acquisition stage extracted text from

Table 3. Search strategies

	Search Strategy		
File type	**Attached document**	**Extracted text**	**Extracted text including text from images**
PDF files	✓	✓	✓
MS Office files	✓ Does not include text from images	✓ Does not include text from images	✓
Image files	✗	✗	✓
Text files	✓	✓	✓
Simulation model files			
Simulation files - I2Sim model files (.mdl)	✓ (mdl file are text files)	✓	✓
Simulation files - EPANET model files (.net)	✗	✓	✓

images. Moreover, direct full-text search on the file system does not include EPANET .net model file as they are binary file. Disaster-CDM transforms EPANET model files into ontology-based representation, and consequently includes them in full-text search. Additionally, storing data in NoSQL data store facilitates querying file-style data and allows Disaster-CDM to take advantage of scaling and replication capabilities provided by the NoSQL store.

Querying File-Style Data

The documents contained in the document store are semi-structured: the data within a document is encoded, but each document can have a different structure. The data model designed for storage of file-style data, as presented in Table 1, was flexible enough to enable storage of diverse data, but at the same time was relatively standardized to support querying abilities. In this case study, querying was used to obtain aggregate information about the contents of the data store, such as the number of documents of each type or the number of documents containing images. Aggregate querying is illustrated here on a simple example, that of counting the documents of each type. In CouchDB, this is achieved by views which make use of the MapReduce approach. The Map function extracts the value of the *fileExtension* field from within each document, while the Reduce function groups by *fileExtension* (which is in the *key* argument passed to the Reduce function), and counts the entries for each *fileExtension*.

```
Map function:
        function(doc) {
                emit(doc.fileExtension, 1);
        }
Reduce function:
        function (key, values) {
                return sum(values);
        }
```

The data presented in Table 2 were obtained by executing this query. As illustrated, obtaining such information from the Disaster-CDM system is very simple; however, doing this without the Disaster-CDM system would require extensive manual efforts or use of specialized (custom or off-the-shelf) software.

The full-text search described in the previous subsection did not take full advantage of the tagging performed during data acquisition. When text was extracted from documents, tagging was performed, and the results were stored within different *tag* fields. Because the tag fields are encoded within the document, they facilitate querying. For example, as part of the DR-NEP project, Western University explored an accident on the university campus which involved a local power plant. During data acquisition, the text extracted from documents was forwarded to the tagging processes. If a power plant was mentioned in a document, the ANNIE tagging process recognized 'power plant' as an organization and therefore tagged it as *organization='power plant'*. Consequently, the resulting document in the data store contained the following entry: tag: {organization: ["power plant"]}. This document structure can be used to find all documents referring to power plants and CouchDB view created for this purpose is displayed in Listing 1. The Map function outputs the *organization* tag as the first array element because this is a search criterion. In addition, this view includes *fileName* to identify the original file and *creationDate* to distinguish more recent documents. The Reduce function eliminates duplicates produced by the Map function. After this view is created, data can be queried by specifying values in HTTP calls. A few rows of the results of searching for the organization tag "power plant" are displayed in Table 4.

Listing 1. Querying for "Power Plant" - Map and Reduce functions for CouchDB view

```
Map function
function(doc) {
        if (doc.tag.Organization && Array.isArray(doc.tag.Organization)) {
        doc.tag.Organization.forEach(function (organizationTag) {
            var creationDate = doc.metaData["dcterms:modified"];
            if (creationDate == null) {
                creationDate = doc.metaData["dcterms:created"]
                }
                emit([organizationTag.toLowerCase(), doc.fileName, cre-
ationDate], null);
            });
        }
}
Reduce function
function (key, values) {
        return null;
}
```

In this case study, only automated tagging was used, and therefore tags typically reassembled phrases found in text extracted from documents. In this situation, querying as described in the example gave similar results to the full-text search described in the previous subsection. However, Disaster-CDM was designed to allow manual tagging by end users in addition to automated tagging. In a manual tagging scenario, the effectiveness of queries similar to the *organization* tag example would be increased.

Discussion

Two knowledge delivery services were explored: full-text search and querying. This section further discusses benefits, advantages and drawbacks of the two approaches.

Table 4. Query results for "Power Plant"

Organization tag	File Name	Creation Date
power plant	11_02_17_DR_NEP_Audit.pptx	2011-02-17T15:21:42Z
power plant	11_09_08_DR_NEP_Audit_Final.pptx	2011-09-08T20:36:29Z
power plant	DeltaV-Chillers-a.jpg	2010-07-19T10:49:52Z
power plant	Disaster_phase2_Aug9.xlsx	2011-08-11T20:14:06Z
power plant	DisasterTable_phase2_Aug11_v1.xlsx	2011-08-12T15:48:49Z

- Various full-text search were investigated which allowed for the analysis of the effects of data processing performed during knowledge acquisition on the full-text search results. Overall, the benefits of data processes vary according to the file format as well as the file content. For example, as expected, the OCR process had a major impact on the image file searching; however, experiments showed that the PowerPoint files also benefited greatly from this process. Full-text search does not take advantage of automated tagging, and therefore, if the knowledge delivery relies only on the full-text search, the tagging process can be omitted.
- Querying service proved advantages in obtaining various types of aggregate information about the stored contents. Some of the query tasks explored in this case study, such as searching for a word or a phrase, can also be achieved by full-text search. In those circumstances full-text search has the advantage over querying due to its simple call interface and the ability to rank documents according to their relevance. However, the querying approach is promising with respect to manual tagging as it allows easy and fast access to tagged data.

Consequently, the two knowledge delivery services explored in this case study, full-text search and querying, are complementary services suitable for different tasks. Knowledge delivery services, together with knowledge acquisition services, facilitate collaboration by providing a platform for sharing and integrating disaster-related information.

The main limitation of the proposed approach is related to the knowledge acquisition services; data need to be processed according to data processing rules before they are stored in the cloud storage and used. This means that data are loaded into Disaster-CDM and not used in their original form or from their original locations. Consequently, the proposed approach does not carry out real-time data collection during disaster response, but is focused on data collection in other disaster phases. However, it is important to highlight that this design choice achieves shorter query response time than preforming the processing "on the fly".

The challenges of implementing the proposed framework are twofold. Firstly, for diverse data sources, different data processing services need to be implemented. The quality of the services provided to the end users is highly dependent on the implemented data processing services. Secondly, it is challenging to provide knowledge delivery services with diverse storage systems due to the difficulty of integrating different data models. Future research directions aim to address those challenges.

FUTURE RESEARCH DIRECTIONS

The knowledge acquisition and data storage components of the Disaster-CDM framework were the focus of this chapter. Directions for future research related to this aspect include data acquisition from other sources such as Web sites and social media, dynamic data processing rule specification, changes to existing knowledge (knowledge evolution), knowledge conflicts, and NoSQL data store comparison in the context of the presented framework.

This chapter has presented the main design of the knowledge delivery component without addressing details; thus future work will involve various aspects of knowledge delivery. Since NoSQL data stores were designed for different purposes, they differ greatly in their data models and querying abilities, which presents an obstacle to integration. Integration of NoSQL stores will be explored in order to accommodate different data stores within the framework and provide integrated knowledge to consumers.

The case study presented in this chapter involved query and full-text services, but analytics services were not addressed. Various Big Data analytics approaches will be explored with the objective of providing a better insight into disaster-related data and therefore better disaster management.

To successfully support collaboration on a global scale and across governments, industries, and communities, privacy and security will be addressed. This is challenging for a number of reasons, including cloud storage on third-party premises and in a shared multi-tenant environment, diversity of the storage models involved, and the large number of collaboration participants.

The presented Disaster-CDM framework is designed for use with disaster-related data; however, it could potentially be applied in other domains. For example, Disaster-CDM for file-style data, could be applied to any file-type data and is not restricted to disaster-related data. Future work will explore the potential of using the same framework, possibly with some adaptations, in other domains.

CONCLUSION

In recent years, we have witnessed a number of extreme weather events and natural disasters. At the same time, changes in software and hardware have created opportunities for new solutions in disaster management.

This chapter has presented Disaster-CDM, a framework for disaster data management. Disaster-CDM stores large amounts of data while maintaining high availability by using NoSQL solutions. Collaboration among partners, knowledge sharing, and integration are facilitated through knowledge acquisition and knowledge delivery services. The knowledge acquisition service is responsible for acquiring knowledge from diverse sources and storing it in the cloud environment, while knowledge delivery services integrate diverse information and deliver knowledge to consumers.

Special attention has been paid to data management for file-style data such as MS Office documents, PDF files and images because these are the formats most commonly present in the disaster management domain. File processing, data processing rules, and data storage for file-style data have been described.

The case study presented in this chapter demonstrated the use of Disaster-CDM on data collected during the Disaster Response Network Enabled Platform (DR-NEP) project. Specifically, knowledge was acquired from the DR-NEP data set and stored in a NoSQL document data store. Knowledge delivery was illustrated by querying and full-text search examples.

REFERENCES

Anderson, J. C., Lehnardt, J., & Slater, N. (2010). *CouchDB: The definitive guide*. Sebastopol, CA, USA: O'Reilly Media.

Anderson, K. M., & Schram, A. (2011). Design and implementation of a data analytics infrastructure in support of crisis informatics research: NIER track. *Proceedings of the 33rd International Conference on Software Engineering,* Honolulu, Hawaii (pp. 844-847). doi:10.1145/1985793.1985920

Apache wicket. (2015). Retrieved from https://wicket.apache.org/)

Association for Computing Machinery. (2014). Conference on computer-supported cooperative work and social computing (CSCW). Retrieved from http://cscw.acm.org/2015/index.php

Atzeni, P., Bugiotti, F., & Rossi, L. (2013). Uniform access to NoSQL systems. *Information Systems, 43*, 117–133. doi:10.1016/j.is.2013.05.002

Choi, S., & Bae, B. (2015). The real-time monitoring system of social big data for disaster management. *Computer Science and its Applications, 330*, 809-815.

Chou, C., Zahedi, F., & Zhao, H. (2011). Ontology for developing web sites for natural disaster management: Methodology and implementation. *IEEE Transactions on Systems, Man, and Cybernetics. Part A, Systems and Humans, 41*(1), 50–62. doi:10.1109/TSMCA.2010.2055151

Coppola, D. P. (2011). *Introduction to international disaster management*. Amsterdam, Netherlands: Butterworth-Heinemann.

CouchDB-lucene project. (2012). Retrieved from https://github.com/rnewson/couchdb-lucene

Cunningham, H., Maynard, D., Bontcheva, K., Tablan, V., Aswani, N., Roberts, I., . . . Heitz, T. (2013). Developing language processing components with GATE. University of Sheffield department of computer science. Retrieved from http://gate.ac.uk/sale/tao/split.html

de Albuquerque, J. P., Herfort, B., Brenning, A., & Zipf, A. (2015). A geographic approach for combining social media and authoritative data towards identifying useful information for disaster management. *International Journal of Geographical Information Science, 29*(4), 667-689. doi:10.1080/13658816.2014.996567

GlassFish. (2014). Retrieved from https://glassfish.java.net/

Grolinger, K., Capretz, M. A. M., Marti, J. R., & Srivastava, K. D. (2012). Ontology–based representation of simulation models. *Proceedings of the 24the International Conference on Software Engineering and Knowledge Engineering,* San Francisco Bay, CA, USA (pp. 432-437).

Grolinger, K., Higashino, W. A., Tiwari, A., & Capretz, M. A. (2013). Data management in cloud environments: NoSQL and NewSQL data stores. *Journal of Cloud Computing: Advances. Systems and Application, 2.* doi:10.1186/2192-113X-2-22

Grolinger, K., Mezghani, E., Capretz, M. A. M., & Exposito, E. (2013). Knowledge as a service framework for disaster data management. *Proceedings of the 22nd WETICE Conference* (pp. 313-318). Hammamet, Tunisia. doi:10.1109/WETICE.2013.48

Grolinger, K., Mezghani, E., Capretz, M. A. M., & Exposito, E. (2015). Collaborative knowledge as a service applied to the disaster management domain. *International Journal of Cloud Computing, 4*(1), 5–27. doi:10.1504/IJCC.2015.067706

Hewlett-Packard. (2014). HP autonomy. Retrieved from http://www.autonomy.com/

Hristidis, V., Chen, S., Li, T., Luis, S., & Deng, Y. (2010). Survey of data management and analysis in disaster situations. *Journal of Systems and Software, 83*(10), 1701–1714. doi:10.1016/j.jss.2010.04.065

IBM. (2014). IBM enterprise content management. Retrieved from http://www-03.ibm.com/software/products/en/category/enterprise-content-management

Ilyas, A. (2014). MicroFilters: Harnessing twitter for disaster management. Paper presented at the *IEEE Global Humanitarian Technology Conference* (pp. 417-424). doi:10.1109/GHTC.2014.6970316

Khoshnevis, S., & Rabeifa, F. (2012). Toward knowledge management as a service in cloud-based environments. *International Journal of Mechatronics. Electrical and Computer Technology, 2*(4), 88–110.

Lai, I., Tam, S., & Chan, M. (2012). Knowledge cloud system for network collaboration: A case study in medical service industry in China. *Expert Systems with Applications, 39*(15), 12205–12212. doi:10.1016/j.eswa.2012.04.057

McCandless, M., Hatcher, E., & Gospodnetic, O. (2010). *Lucene in action.* Stamford, CT, USA: Manning Publications.

Mittleman, D. D., Briggs, R. O., Murphy, J., & Davis, A. (2008). Toward a taxonomy of groupware technologies. *Lecture Notes in Computer Science, 5411,* 305–317. doi:10.1007/978-3-540-92831-7_25

November, V., & Leanza, Y. (2015). *Risk, disaster and crisis reduction: Mobilizing, collecting and sharing information.* Springer International Publishing; doi:10.1007/978-3-319-08542-5

Othman, S. H., & Beydoun, G. (2013). Model-driven disaster management. *Information & Management, 50*(5), 218–228. doi:10.1016/j.im.2013.04.002

Othman, S. H., Beydoun, G., & Sugumaran, V. (2014). Development and validation of a disaster management metamodel (DMM). *Information Processing & Management, 50*(2), 235–271. doi:10.1016/j.ipm.2013.11.001

Palen, L., Anderson, K. M., Mark, G., Martin, J., Sicker, D., Palmer, M., & Grunwald, D. (2010). A vision for technology-mediated support for public participation & assistance in mass emergencies & disasters. *Proceedings of the ACM-BCS Visions of Computer Science Conference,* Edinburgh, UK (pp. 1-12).

Qirui, Y. (2012). Kaas-based intelligent service model in agricultural expert system. *Proceedings of the 2nd International Conference on Consumer Electronics, Communications and Networks,* Yichang, China (pp. 2678-2680). doi:10.1109/CECNet.2012.6201763

Rahman, H. A., Armstrong, M., Mao, D., & Marti, J. R. (2008). I2Sim: A matrix-partition based framework for critical infrastructure interdependencies simulation. *Proceedings of the Electrical Power and Energy Conference,* Vancouver, BC, Canada (pp. 1-8). doi:10.1109/EPC.2008.4763353

Sakr, S., Liu, A., Batista, D. M., & Alomari, M. (2011). A survey of large scale data management approaches in cloud environments. *IEEE Communications Surveys and Tutorials, 13*(3), 311–336. doi:10.1109/SURV.2011.032211.00087

Schram, A., & Anderson, K. M. (2012). MySQL to NoSQL: Data modeling challenges in supporting scalability. *Proceedings of the 3rd Annual Conference on Systems, Programming, Languages and Applications: Software for Humanity* Tucson, AZ, USA (pp. 191-202). doi:10.1145/2384716.2384773

Silva, T., Wuwongse, V., & Sharma, H. N. (2011). Linked data in disaster mitigation and preparedness. *Proceedings of the Third International Conference on Intelligent Networking and Collaborative Systems* Fukuoka, Japan (pp. 746-751). doi:10.1109/INCoS.2011.113

Smith, R. (2007). An overview of the Tesseract OCR engine. *Proceeding of the Ninth International Conference on Document Analysis and Recognition* Curitiba, Brazil. doi:10.1109/ICDAR.2007.4376991

Sumathi, C. P., Santhanam, T., & Gayathri Devi, G. (2012). A survey on various approaches of text extraction in images. *International Journal of Computer Science and Engineering Survey, 3*(4), 27–42. doi:10.5121/ijcses.2012.3403

The Apache Foundation. (2013). Apache Tika toolkit. Retrieved from http://tika.apache.org/

The University of British Columbia. (2011). DR-NEP (disaster response network enabled platform) project. Retrieved from http://drnep.ece.ubc.ca/index.html

United States Environmental Protection Agency. (2008). EPANET - water distribution modeling. Retrieved from http://www.epa.gov/nrmrl/wswrd/dw/epanet.html

Waugh, W. L., & Streib, G. (2006). Collaboration and leadership for effective emergency management. *Public Administration Review, 66*(1), 131–140. doi:10.1111/j.1540-6210.2006.00673.x

ADDITIONAL READING

Apache. (2014). Hadoop. Retrieved from http://hadoop.apache.org/

Brewer, E. (2012). CAP twelve years later: How the "rules" have changed. *Computer, 45*(2), 23–29. doi:10.1109/MC.2012.37

Chang, F., Dean, J., Ghemawat, S., Hsieh, W. C., Wallach, D. A., Burrows, M., & Gruber, R. E. et al. (2008). Bigtable: A distributed storage system for structured data. *ACM Transactions on Computer Systems, 26*(2), 1–26. doi:10.1145/1365815.1365816

Dean, J., & Ghemawat, S. (2008). *MapReduce: Simplified data processing on large clusters.* New York: ACM; doi:10.1145/1327452.1327492

Hwang, K., & Hwang, K. (2012). *Distributed and cloud computing: From parallel processing to the internet of things.* Waltham, MA, USA: Elsevier/Morgan Kaufmann.

Kannimuthu, S., Premalatha, K., & Shankar, S. (2012). Investigation of high utility itemset mining in service oriented computing: Deployment of knowledge as a service in E-commerce. *Proceedings of the Fourth International Conference on Advanced Computing,* Chennai, India (pp. 1-8). doi:10.1109/ICoAC.2012.6416812

Kapucu, N., & Garayev, V. (2011). Collaborative decision-making in emergency and disaster management. *International Journal of Public Administration, 34*(6), 366–375. doi:10.1080/01900692.2011.561477

Lakshman, A., & Malik, P. (2010). Cassandra: A decentralized structured storage system. *Operating Systems Review, 44*(2), 35–40. doi:10.1145/1773912.1773922

Sadalage, P. J., & Fowler, M. (2013). *NoSQL distilled: A brief guide to the emerging world of polyglot persistence*. Upper Saddle River, NJ, USA: Addison-Wesley.

Stonebraker, M., Madden, S., Badi, D. J., Harizopoulos, S., Hachem, N., & Helland, P. (2007). The end of an architectural era: (It's time for a complete rewrite). *Proceedings of the 33rd International Conference on very Large Data Bases*, Vienna, Austria (pp. 1150-1160).

Sumathi, C. P., Santhanam, T., & Gayathri Devi, G. (2012). A survey on various approaches of text extraction in images. *International Journal of Computer Science and Engineering Survey, 3*(4), 27–42. doi:10.5121/ijcses.2012.3403

Waugh, W. L., & Streib, G. (2006). Collaboration and leadership for effective emergency management. *Public Administration Review, 66*(1), 131–140. doi:10.1111/j.1540-6210.2006.00673.x

KEY TERMS AND DEFINITIONS

Big Data: Collection of massive data sets too big to be processed using traditional approaches. It is characterized by the 3Vs: volume, velocity and variety.

Cloud Computing: A computing paradigm in which large groups of computing resources are networked in order to provide on-demand access to a shared resource pool.

Data Management: The process of controlling and managing information throughout its lifecycle.

Disaster Management: The organization and management of responsibilities and resources for dealing with emergencies in order to reduce the impact of disasters.

Knowledge as a Service: An on-demand, self-service computing paradigm in which a knowledge service provides answers questions presented by knowledge consumers.

NoSQL Data Store: NoSQL is used as an acronym for "Not only SQL", which emphasizes that SQL-style querying is not the crucial objective of these data stores. The term is used as an umbrella classification that includes a large number of immensely diverse data stores.

Ontology: An explicit formal specification of a conceptualization. It describes concepts in the domain and relations among them.

Chapter 9
A Review of RDF Storage in NoSQL Databases

Zongmin Ma
Nanjing University of Aeronautics and Astronautics, China

Li Yan
Nanjing University of Aeronautics and Astronautics, China

ABSTRACT

The Resource Description Framework (RDF) is a model for representing information resources on the Web. With the widespread acceptance of RDF as the de-facto standard recommended by W3C (World Wide Web Consortium) for the representation and exchange of information on the Web, a huge amount of RDF data is being proliferated and becoming available. So RDF data management is of increasing importance, and has attracted attentions in the database community as well as the Semantic Web community. Currently much work has been devoted to propose different solutions to store large-scale RDF data efficiently. In order to manage massive RDF data, NoSQL ("not only SQL") databases have been used for scalable RDF data store. This chapter focuses on using various NoSQL databases to store massive RDF data. An up-to-date overview of the current state of the art in RDF data storage in NoSQL databases is provided. The chapter aims at suggestions for future research.

INTRODUCTION

The Resource Description Framework (RDF) is a framework for representing information resources on the Web, which is proposed by W3C (World Wide Web Consortium) as a recommendation (Manola and Miller, 2004). RDF can represent structured and unstructured data (Duan, Kementsietsidis, Srinivas and Udrea, 2011), and more important, metadata of resources on the Web represented by RDF can be shared and exchanged among application programming without semantic missing. Here metadata mean the data that specify semantic information about data. Currently RDF has been widely accepted and has rapidly gained popularity. And many organizations, companies and enterprises have started using RDF for representing and processing their data. We can find some application examples such as the United

DOI: 10.4018/978-1-4666-9834-5.ch009

States (Data.gov), the United Kingdom (New York Times), New York Times (New York Times), BBC (BBC), and Best Buy (Chief Martec, 2009). RDF is finding increasing use in a wide range of Web data-management scenarios.

With the widespread usage of RDF in diverse application domains, a huge amount of RDF data is being proliferated and becoming available. As a result, efficient and scalable management of large-scale RDF data is of increasing importance, and has attracted attentions in the database community as well as the Semantic Web community. Currently, much work is being done in RDF data management. Some RDF data-management systems have started to emerge such as *Sesame* (Broekstra, Kampman and van Harmelen, 2002), *Jena-TDB* (Wilkinson, Sayers, Kuno and Reynolds, 2003), *Virtuoso* (Erling and Mikhailov, 2007 & 2009), *4Store* (Harris, Lamb and Shadbolt, 2009)), *BigOWLIM* (Bishop *et al.*, 2011) and *Oracle Spatial and Graph with Oracle Database 12c (Oracle)*. Here BigOWLIM is renamed to OWLIM-SE and further to GraphDB. Also some research prototypes have been developed (e.g., RDF-3X (Neumann and Weikum, 2008 & 2010), SW-Store (Abadi, Marcus, Madden and Hollenbach, 2007 & 2009) and RDFox (CS Ox).

RDF data management mainly involves scalable storage and efficient queries of RDF data, in which RDF data storage provides the infrastructure for RDF data management and efficient querying of RDF data is enabled based on RDF storage. In addition, to serve a given query more effectively, it is necessary to index RDF data. Indexing of RDF data is enabled based on RDF storage also. Currently many efforts have been made to propose different solutions to store large-scale RDF data efficiently. Traditionally relational databases are applied to store RDF data and various storage structures based on relational databases have been developed. Based on the relational perspective, Sakr and Al-Naymat (2009) present an overview of relational techniques for storing and querying RDF data. It should be noted that the relational RDF stores are a kind of centralized RDF stores, which are a single-machine solution with limited scalability. The scalability of RDF data stores is essential for massive RDF data management. NoSQL (for "not only SQL") databases have recently emerged as a commonly used infrastructure for handling Big Data because of their high scalability and efficiency. Identifying that massive RDF data management merits the use of NoSQL databases, currently NoSQL databases are increasingly used in massive RDF data management (Cudre-Mauroux *et al.*, 2013).

This chapter provides an up-to-date overview of the current state of the art in massive RDF data stores in NoSQL databases. We presents the survey from three main perspectives, which are key value stores of RDF data in NoSQL databases, document stores of RDF data in NoSQL databases and RDF data stores in graph databases. Note that, due to the large number of RDF data-management solutions, this chapter does not include all of them. In addition to provide a generic overview of the approaches that have been proposed to store RDF data in NoSQL databases, this chapter presents some suggestions for future research in the area of massive RDF data management with NoSQL databases.

The rest of this chapter is organized as follows. The second section presents preliminaries of RDF data model. It also introduces the main approaches for storing RDF data. The third section introduces NoSQL databases and their database models. The fourth section provides the details of the different techniques in several NoSQL-based RDF data stores. The final section concludes the chapter and provides some suggestions for possible research directions on the subject.

RDF MODEL AND RDF DATA STORAGE

Being a W3C recommendation, RDF (Resource Description Framework) provides a means to represent and exchange semantic metadata. With RDF, metadata about information sources are represented and processed. Furthermore, RDF defines a model for describing relationships among resources in terms of uniquely identified attributes and values.

The RDF data model is applied to model resources. A resource is anything which has a universal resource identifier (URI) and is described using a set of RDF statements in the form of (*subject, predicate, object*) triples. Here *subject* is the resource being described, *predicate* is the property being described with respect to the resource, and *object* is the value for the property.

Formally an RDF triple is defined as (s, p, o) in which s is called the subject, p the predicate (or property), and o the object. Triple (s, p, o) means that the subject s has the property p whose value is the object o. The abstract syntax of RDF data model is a set of triples. Among these triples, it is possible that an object in one triple (e.g., o_i in (s_i, p_i, o_i)) can be a subject in other triple (e.g., (o_i, p_j, o_j)). Then RDF data model is a directed, labelled graph model for representing Web resources (Huang, Abadi and Ren, 2011). A key concept for RDF is that of URIs (Unique Resource Identifiers), which can be applied in either of the s, p and o positions to uniquely refer to entity, relationship or concept (Kaoudi and Manolescu, 2015). In addition, literals are allowed in the o position. Let I, B, and L denote infinite sets of IRIs, blank nodes, and literals, respectively. Then we have

$$(s, p, o) \in (I \cup B) \times I \times (I \cup B \cup L).$$

Concerning the syntaxes for RDF, we have RDF/XML, N-Triple and Turtle. Among them, N-Triple is the most basic one and it contains one triple per line.

In (Bornea *et al.*, 2013), a sample of DBpedia RDF data is presented and it contains 21 tuples and 13 predicates. Let us look at a fragment of the sample, which contains 6 triples {(Google, industry, Software), (Google, industry, Internet), (Google, employees, 54,604), (Android, developer, Google), (Android, version, 4.1), (Android, kernel, Linux)} and 5 predicates {industry, employees, developer, version, kernel}. For a triple, say (Google, industry, Internet), its resource is *Google*, this resource has the property *industry*, and the value for the property is *Internet*. With the set of triples, we have an RDF graph shown in Figure 1.

Figure 1. An RDF graph

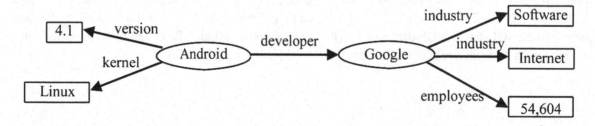

As we know, in the context of common data management, data are stored early in file systems and late in databases (such as relational databases and object-oriented databases). Similarly, RDF data management relies on RDF data storage also. It is especially true for managing large-scale RDF data in the real-world applications. Nowadays many approaches of RDF data storages have been developed. Given the large number of RDF data-management solutions, there is a richness of perspectives and approaches to RDF data storages. But few classifications of RDF data-storage approaches have been reported in the literature. Basically proposals for RDF data storage are classified into two major categories in (Sakr and Al-Naymat, 2009; Bornea *et al.*, 2013), which are *native stores* and *relational stores*, respectively. Here the native stores use customized binary RDF data representation and the relational stores distribute RDF data to appropriate relational databases. Viewed from three basic perspectives of the relational, entity and graph-based perspectives, proposals for RDF data storage are classified into three major categories in (Luo *et al.*, 2012), which are *relational stores*, *entity stores* and *graph-based stores*, respectively.

RDF data stores can be classified relying on the underlying infrastructure. First, for the native stores, we can identify *main-memory-based RDF native store* and *disk-based RDF native store*. The major difference between these two native stores is that the former works on RDF data stored completely in main memory and the latter works on RDF data stored in disk. The disk-based RDF native store is built directly on the file system. It is not difficult to see that the native stores can only deal with small-scale RDF data. At this point, traditional relational databases are hereby applied to store RDF data. In the relational stores of RDF data, different relational schemas can be designed, depending on how to distribute RDF triples to an appropriate relational schema. This has results in three major categories of RDF relational stores (Sakr and Al-Naymat, 2009; Bornea *et al.*, 2013; Luo *et al.*, 2012), which are *triple stores*, *vertical stores* and *property (type) stores*. In the tripe stores, all RDF triples are directly stored in a single relational table over relational schema (*subject, predicate, object*), and each RDF triple becomes a tuple of the relational database. In the vertical stores, a subject-object relation is directly represented for each predicate of RDF triples and a relational table contains only one predicate as a column name. As a result, we have a set of binary relational tables over relational schema (*subject, object*), each relational table corresponds to a different predicate, and this predicate can be the name of the corresponding relational table. In the type stores, one relational table is created for each RDF data type, in which an RDF data type generally corresponds to several predicates, and a relational table contains the properties as *n*-ary table columns for the same subject.

The reason why there are three major approaches for storing RDF data in relational databases is that each approach has its advantages and disadvantages simultaneously. First, the triple stores use a fixed relational schema and can hereby handle dynamic schema of RDF data, but the triple stores involve a number of self-join operations for querying. Second, the vertical stores using a set of relational tables generally involve many table join operations for querying and cannot handle dynamic schema of RDF data because new predicates of new inserted triples result in new relational tables. Finally the type stores involve fewer table join operations than the vertical stores using multiple relational tables and, compared with the triple stores using a single relational table, no self-join operations, but the type stores generally contain null values and multi-valued attributes, and cannot handle dynamic schema of RDF data because new predicates of new inserted triples result in changes to relational schema.

Several representative relational RDF data stores and their major features are summarized in Table 1.

It can be seen from Table 1 that any one of the approaches for relational RDF data stores presented above cannot deal with RDF data stores well. So some efforts have been made to store RDF data by

Table 1. Representative relational RDF data stores and their major features

	Typical store systems	Advantages	Disadvantages
Triple stores	*Sesame* (Broekstra, Kampman and van Harmelen, 2002); Hexastore (Weiss, Karras and Bernste, 2008)	*no null values; no multi-valued attributes; fixed relational schema*	*too many self-joins*
Vertical stores	*SW-Store* (Abadi, Marcus, Madden and Hollenbach, 2007 & 2009)	*no null values; no multi-valued attributes*	*too many table joins; dynamic relational schema*
Type stores	*Jena* (McBride, 2002); *FlexTable* (Wang, Du, Lu and Wang, 2010); *RDFBroker* (Sintek and Kiesel, 2006)	*few table joins*	*null values; multi-valued attributes; dynamic relational schema*

using two or more of three major store approaches together or revising three major store approaches (Kim, 2006; Sperka and Smrz, 2012; Bornea *et al.*, 2013). Such an approach is called *hybrid stores*, It should be noted that the hybrid stores cannot still satisfy the need of managing large-scale RDF data.

The native RDF stores and the relational RDF stores (including the triple stores, vertical stores, type stores and hybrid stores) are actually categorized as *centralized RDF stores*. Centralized RDF stores are single-machine solutions with limited scalability. To process large-scale RDF data, recent research has devoted considerable effort to the study of managing massive RDF data in distributed environments. *Distributed RDF stores* can hash partition triples across multiple machines and parallelize query processing. NoSQL databases have recently emerged as a commonly used infrastructure for handling Big Data (Pokorny, 2011). Massive RDF data management merits the use of NoSQL databases and currently NoSQL databases are increasingly used in RDF data management (Cudre-Mauroux *et al.*, 2013). Typically, NoSQL database stores of RDF data are distributed RDF stores. Depending on concrete data models adopted, the NoSQL database stores of RDF data are categorized into *key-value stores, column-family stores, document stores* and *graph databases stores*.

Summarily, we can classify current RDF data stores into the centralized RDF stores and the NoSQL database stores of RDF data (Papailiou *et al.*, 2013). The centralized RDF stores can be further classified into the native RDF stores and the relational RDF stores, in which the native RDF stores contain main-memory-based native RDF store and disk-based native RDF store, and the relational RDF stores include triple stores, vertical stores and type stores. The NoSQL database stores of RDF data are further classified into key-value stores, column-family stores, document stores and graph databases stores. Figure 2 illustrates this classification for RDF data stores.

The native RDF stores and the relational RDF stores have been reviewed in (Sakr and Al-Naymat, 2009). The focus of this chapter is to investigate NoSQL database stores of RDF data. Before that, we first sketch NoSQL databases in the following section.

NoSQL Databases for Big Data

Big Data is a term used to refer to massive and complex datasets made up of a variety of data structures. Big Data can be found in various application domains such as web clicks, social media, scientific experiments, and datacenter monitoring. Actually there is not a common definition of Big Data so far (Stuart and Barker, 2013). But Big Data are generally characterized by three basic *Vs*: *Volume, Variety* and *Velocity* (Laney, 2001).

Figure 2. Classification of RDF data stores

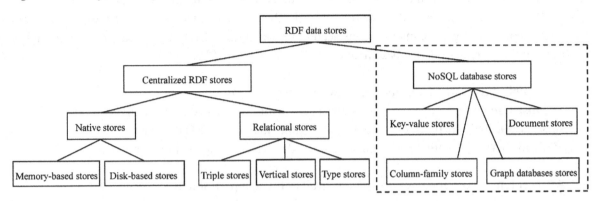

- **Volume:** Volume means that Big Data have big data scale in the range of TB to PB and even more.
- **Variety:** Variety means Big Data have rich data types with many formats such as structured data, unstructured data, semistructured data, text, multimedia, and so on.
- **Velocity:** Velocity means that Big Data must be processed speedily. Also Velocity means that Big Data are being produced speedily.

Then Big Data is high-volume, high-velocity and high-variety information assets that demand cost-effective, innovative forms of information processing for enhanced insight and decision making. In addition to the three *V*s above, a *V* associated with *Veracity* has been introduced to Big Data in (Snow, 2012) and a *V* associated with *Value* has been introduced to Big Data in (Gamble and Goble, 2011).

- **Veracity:** Veracity means that inherent imprecision and uncertainty in data should be explicitly considered so that the reliability and predictability of imprecise and uncertain Big Data can be managed.
- **Value:** Value means that Big Data must be worthwhile and has value for business.

The Veracity of data is a basis of Big Data processing because the data with volume and variety may contain errors, noises or imperfection. Actually the Veracity of data is a precondition and guarantee of Big Data management, which can increase the robustness and accuracy of Big Data processing. Regarding to the Value of data, Value sets a basic criterion in the choice and processing of Big Data, which is especially true in the context of the data with volume, variety and velocity.

Also there are several other *V*s which are applied to describe the properties of Big Data in literature (e.g., *Visualization*, *Visualization* and *Volatility*). Among them, Volatility means that Big Data that we are interested in are temporally valid. It is possible that, at one point, specific data are no longer relevant to the current processing and analysis of Big Data. It should be noted that the several *V*s mentioned above only characterize some properties of Big Data partially. So some other characteristics rather than the *V*s presented above are assigned to Big Data.

Being similar with common data (not Big Data) management, Big Data management needs database systems. As we know, the relational databases are very powerful and have been widely applied for structured, semi-structured and even unstructured data. However the relational databases are unable to manage Big Data. The reason is that the relational databases must meet ACID according to relational databases theory but Big Data management need CAP Theorem. ACID means the type of transaction processing done by relational database management system (RDBMS) as follows.

- **(A)tomcity:** if a part of operation fails, whole operation fails
- **(C)onsistency:** information is always consistent, avoid read/write errors at all costs
- **(I)solation:** multiple transactions at the same time do not impact each other
- **(D)urability:** information has to be stored into database, not queued in memory

CAP Theorem is described by consistency, availability and partition as follows.

- **(C)onsistency:** whenever data is written, everyone who reads the DB will see the latest version.
- **(A)vailability:** we can always expect each operation terminates in an intended response.
- **(P)artition:** tolerance: database can still be read from/written to when parts of it are offline; afterwards, when offline nodes are back online, they are updated accordingly.

It is clear that the relational databases are not solutions in Big Data management. A new type of databases called NoSQL is hereby proposed, which means "not only SQL" or "no SQL at all".

NoSQL database systems have emerged as a commonly used infrastructure for handling Big Data. Comparing to traditional relational databases, NoSQL solutions provide simpler scalability and improved performance (Hecht and Jablonski, 2011; Pokorny, 2011; Moniruzzaman and Hossain, 2013; Gudivada, Rao and Raghavan, 2014) and generally have some characteristics as follows (Tauro, Aravindh and Shreeharsha, 2012).

- Distributed processing
- High availability
- High scalability and reliability
- Scheme-less
- Replication support
- Handle structured and unstructured data
- Data access via API
- Less strict adherence to consistency
- Improvements in performance

It should be noted that NoSQL databases are very diverse and there are more than one hundred NoSQL databases. According to their data model, the various NoSQL databases are classified into four major categories as follows (Hecht and Jablonski, 2011; Grolinger *et al.*, 2013; Bach and Werner, 2014).

- Key-value stores
- Column-family stores
- Document stores
- Graph databases

Key-value stores have a simple data model based on key-value pairs, which contain a set of couples (key, value). A value is addressed by a single key. Here a value may be a string, a pointer (where the value is stored) or even a collection of couples (name, value) (e.g., in Redis (redis). Note that values are isolated and independent from others, in which the relationship is handled by the application logic.

Most column-family stores are derived from Google BigTable (Chang *et al.*, 2008), in which the data are stored in a column-oriented way. In BigTable, the dataset consists of several rows. Each row is addressed by a primary key and is composed of a set of column families. Note that different rows can have different column families. Representative column-family stores include Apache HBase, which directly implements the Google BigTable concepts. In addition, Cassandra (Lakshman and Malik, 2010) provides the additional functionality of super-columns, in which a column contains nested (sub)columns and super-columns are formed by grouping various columns together. According to (Grolinger *et al.*, 2013), there is one type of column-family store, say Amazon SimpleDB and DynamoDB (DeCandia *et al.*, 2007), in which only a set of column name-value pairs is contained in each row, without having column families. So SimpleDB and DynamoDB are generally categorized as key-value stores as well.

Document stores provide another derivative of the key-value store data model that uses keys to locate documents inside the data store. Most document stores represent documents using *JSON* (JavaScript Object Notation) or some format derived from it (e.g., *BSON* (Binary JSON)). JSON is a binary and typed data model which supports the data types list, map, date, Boolean as well as numbers of different precisions. Typically CouchDB and the Couchbase server use the JSON format for data storage, whereas MongoDB stores data in *BSON*.

Graph databases, a special category of NoSQL databases, use graphs as their data model. A graph is used to represent a set of objects, known as vertices or nodes, and the links (or edges) that interconnect these vertices. Representative graph databases include GraphDB (Güting, 1994) and Neo4j. Neo4j is an open-source, highly scalable, robust native graph database that stores data in a graph. Note that graph databases actually are developed originally for managing data with complex structures and relationships such as data with recursive structure and data with network structure rather than Big Data management. Generally graph databases run in single server (e.g., GraphDB and Neo4j). Recently few efforts have been made to develop distributed graph databases (Nicoara, Kamali, Daudjee and Chen, 2015). Typically Titan (thinkaurelius) is a scalable graph database optimized for storing and querying graphs containing hundreds of billions of vertices and edges distributed across a multi-machine cluster.

Illustrative representations of four kinds of NoSQL models are shown in Figure 3, which are presented by Grolinger *et al.* (2013).

Following the four major categories of NoSQL models, some NoSQL databases have been developed and applied. Table 2 lists several representative NoSQL databases.

In the NoSQL data models presented above, column-family store and document store can be regarded as a kind of extended key value stores, in which document store is regarded that the key values are set to be the documents, and column-family store is regarded that a key value is a combination of ID of row, column number and timestamp. So sometimes column-family stores of NoSQL databases such as HBase and Cassandra are generally called key value stores of NoSQL databases. The true key value store model is too simple for many application domains such RDF data management.

NoSQL databases are designed for storing and processing Big Data datasets. In the following, we investigate how massive RDF data management merits the use of NoSQL databases.

Figure 3. Different types of NoSQL data model

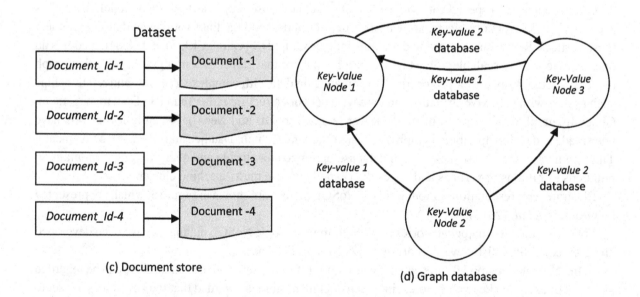

Key_1	Value_1
Key_2	Value_2
Key_3	Value_1
Key_4	Value_3
Key_5	Value_2
Key_6	Value_1
Key_7	Value_4
Key_8	Value_3

(a) Key value store

Dataset

	Column-Family-1		Column-Family-2
Row Key_1	Column Name-1	Column Name-2	Column Name-2
	Column Value-1	Column Value-2	Column Value-2

	Column-Family-1		
Row Key_2	Column Name-4	Column Name-5	Column Name-6
	Column Value-4	Column Value-5	Column Value-6

(b) Column-family store

Dataset

Document_Id-1	→	Document -1
Document_Id-2	→	Document -2
Document_Id-3	→	Document -3
Document_Id-4	→	Document -4

(c) Document store

(d) Graph database

RDF Data Storage in NoSQL Databases

NoSQL databases have emerged as a commonly used infrastructure for handling Big Data. NoSQL databases are not designed especially for RDF data management. But massive RDF data management merits the use of NoSQL databases for Big Data infrastructure because of the scalability and high performance of NoSQL databases for Big Data management. Depending on the concrete models of NoSQL databases,

Table 2. Representative NoSQL databases

	Representative NoSQL Databases	Remarks
Key value store	Redis; SimpleDB; DynamoDB	In SimpleDB and DynamoDB, a set of column name-value pairs is contained in each row.
Column-family store	BigTable; HBase; Cassandra; Hypertable[1]	Cassandra provides the additional functionality of super-columns.
Document store	CouchDB; Couchbase server; MongoDB	CouchDB and Couchbase server use the JSON format for data storage. MongoDB stores data in BSON (Binary JSON)
Graph database	GraphDB; Neo4j; Titan	GraphDB and Neo4j run in single server. Titan is a distributed graph databases

basically we have three kinds of RDF data stores in NoSQL databases, which are *storing RDF data in column-family stores of NoSQL databases*, *storing RDF data in document stores of NoSQL databases*, and *storing RDF data in graph databases*.

Storing RDF Data in Column-Family Stores of NoSQL Databases

Among the NoSQL systems available, HBase, which is *column-family stores of NoSQL databases*, has been the most widely applied. Apache HBase uses HDFS (Hadoop Distributed File System) as its storage back-end (Hua, Wu, Li and Ren, 2014), and supports MapReduce computing framework (Dean and Ghemawat, 2008). Being similar to relational databases, HBase uses data table named HTable, in which each row is uniquely identified by a row key. HBase generally creates indexing on the row keys. Like RDF triples storage in a relational database, RDF triples can be stored in HTable of HBase. We can identify several storage structures for HTable-based RDF store.

First, based on the idea of Hexastore schema developed by Weiss, Karras and Bernstein (2008), scalable RDF store based on HBase is proposed in (Sun and Jin, 2010). They store RDF triples into six HBase tables (S_PO, P_SO, O_SP, PS_O, SO_P and PO_S), which covers all combinations of RDF triple patterns. And they index RDF triples with HBase provided index structure on row key. Also based on HBase, two distributed triple stores H_2RDF and H_2RDF+ are developed in (Papailiou, Konstantinou, Tsoumakos and Koziris, 2012) and (Papailiou *et al.*, 2013), respectively. The main difference between H_2RDF and H_2RDF+ is the number of maintained indices (three versus six).

In addition, to manage distributed RDF data, HBase is sometimes applied by combining others together. HBase and MySQL Cluster, for example, are used in (Franke *et al.*, 2011). Combining the Jena framework with the storage provided by HBase, Khadilkar *et al.* (2012) developed several versions of a triple store. Figure 4 presents an overview of the architecture typically used by Jena-HBase (Khadilkar *et al.*, 2012).

Here six types layout are design, which are *simple layout, vertically partitioned (VP) layout, indexed layout, VP and indexed layout, hybrid layout*, and *hash layout*. In the simple layout, three HTable tables are created and each is indexed by subjects, predicates and objects (i.e., row key), and other two components are combined together as a column name. In the vertically partitioned (VP) layout, every unique predicate creates two HTable tables and each is indexed by subjects and objects. In the indexed layout, six HTable tables are created for representing the six possible combinations of a triple, namely, SPO,

Figure 4. Architectural overview of Jena-HBase

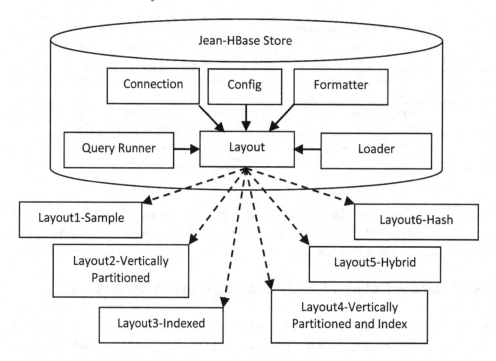

SOP, PSO, POS, OSP and OPS. In the VP and indexed layout, the vertically partitioned (VP) layout and the indexed layout are combined together. As a result, the VP and indexed layout contains the all HTable tables in the vertically partitioned layout as well as three additional HTable tables for SPO, OSP and OS. In the hybrid layout, the simple layout and the vertically partitioned layout are combined together. So the hybrid layout contains the three HTable tables in the simple layout as well as the all HTable tables in the vertically partitioned layout. The hash layout is a kind of hybrid layout with hash values for nodes and a separate table containing hash-to-node mappings. Khadilkar *et al.* (2012) compare with experiments these six layouts on features of data loading speed and querying efficiency and finally reveal that the hybrid layout has better performances. But the hybrid layout is complicated in design and implementation.

Storing RDF Data in Document Stores of NoSQL Databases

Document stores of NoSQL databases look like relational databases, in which each row is associated with a document instead of a tuple. It is clear that such a structure is suitable for storing semi-structure data. As mentioned above, documents in the document stores of NoSQL Databases are represented by using *JSON* (JavaScript Object Notation) or *BSON* (Binary JSON). Being a kind of data exchange format, JSON adopts text format and can be easily edited by persons and processed by machines simultaneously. As a result, it is convenient that JSON can be shared and exchanged among different systems.

In order to store massive RDF data in document stores of NoSQL databases, RDF data should be represented with JSON format. As we know, RDF triples contain three components, which are subjects, predicates and objects and meanwhile the structure of JSON only contains two components, which are keys and values. It is clear that they are not consistent. So it is necessary to establish a mapping to transform RDF to JSON. Basically we can identify several basic mappings from RDF to JSON as follows.

1. Triple-centered mapping
2. Subject-centered mapping
3. JSON-LD approach

In the triple-centered mapping, all triples in an RDF graph can be stored in a rooted document object. The value of this document object is an array, and each element of the array corresponds to a triple of RDF. In the subject-centered mapping, each subject of RDF data is treated as the *"Key"* of an JSON object, and the corresponding *"Value"* is some embedded objects (Alexander, 2008). The *"Key"* of these embedded objects is the predicate of the present subject. JSON-LD (Github), developed by W3C as a recommendation, is a data serialization and messaging format for Linked Data. It is primarily intended to be a way to use Linked Data in Web-based programming environments, to build interoperable Web services, and to store Linked Data in JSON-based storage engines. With JSON-LD, Linked Data which are represented by RDF can be easily stored in JSON-based document stores of NoSQL databases such as CouchDB. An JSON-LD document is an instance of RDF data model. JSON-LD can serialize a generic RDF data set after RDF data model is extended. Also a reverse serialization can be made with JSON-LD. API specifications in JSON-LD provide supports to obverse and reverse serializations between RDF and JSON-LD.

A simple example of JSON-LD from http://json-ld.org/ is shown in Figure 5. This fragment contains information about a person: his name is John Lennon, he was born on 1940-10-09, and his spouse is described in the website of http://dbpedia.org/resource/Cynthia_Lennon. For terms like "name", "born" and "spouse", their semantics are defined with IRIs (International Resource Identifiers). In addition, @ context is used to define the short-hand names that are used throughout a JSON-LD document, and @ id is used to uniquely identify things that are being described in the document with IRIs or blank node identifiers.

Figure 5. A simple example of JSON-LD

```
{

    "@context": "http://json-ld.org/contexts/person.jsonld",

    "@id": "http://dbpedia.org/resource/John_Lennon",

    "name": "John Lennon",

    "born": "1940-10-09",

    "spouse": "http://dbpedia.org/resource/Cynthia_Lennon"

}
```

Storing RDF Data in Graph Database

Compared to relational database model which uses flat relational table, graph databases adopt graph model with vertices, edges and property, and are hereby very suitable to handle the data with network structure (Angles and Gutierrez, 2008). Many techniques and algorithms proposed in the context of Graph Theory (GT) can be applied in graph databases. Neo4j is a popular graph database, in which the data model it uses to express its data is a graph, storing nodes and relationships that connect them, supporting user defined properties on both constructs. Basically Neo4j can traverse the vertices and edges of graph at the same speed and the traversing speed is not influenced by the amount of data constituting the graph. So Neo4j can support scalable store of big graph well.

RDF data model can be regarded as a kind of special graph model. It is advocated in (Angles and Gutiérrez, 2005) to store RDF data in graph databases. So it is a natural way to store massive RDF data in Neo4j. But the standard graph-database model is different from the triple-based RDF model. In order to manage massive RDF data with Neo4j, two basic approaches can be adopted. First, Neo4j can be extended and provided with an interface of processing RDF data, and RDF data are actually stored with native or relational stores. Second, massive RDF data can be directly stored in Neo4j. Following the second approach, DBpedia data are stored in Neo4j in the project of Dbpedia4neo (W3), and SPARQL (Simple Protocol and RDF Query Language) querying and some graph algorithms are then investigated.

As we know, SPARQL is a vendor-independent standard query language for the RDF triple data model (Prud'hommeaux and Seaborne, 2008), which is developed by W3C (World Wide Web Consortium). It should be noted that, although it is shown that graph databases can model RDF data in a natural way very well, some primary and useful querying operations for graph databases are not supported by current SPARQL query language. In this context, in order to manipulate RDF data, SPARQL query language should be extended to incorporate graph database query language primitives (Angles and Gutiérrez, 2005).

Summary and Future Work

With the increasing amount of RDF data which is becoming available, efficient and scalable management of massive RDF data is of increasing important. NoSQL databases are designed for storing and processing Big Data datasets, and massive RDF data management merits the use of Big Data infrastructure because of the scalability and high performance of cloud data management. In this chapter, we provide an up-to-date overview of the current state of the art in massive RDF data stores in NoSQL databases. RDF data management is a very active area of research, and there are a lot of research efforts in this area. The chapter presents the survey from three main perspectives, which are key value stores of RDF data in NoSQL databases, document stores of RDF data in NoSQL databases and RDF data stores in graph databases. Note that this chapter only concentrates on massive RDF data stores in NoSQL databases, and does not discuss issues of indexing and querying massive RDF data in NoSQL databases.

RDF data management typically involves the scalable storage and efficient queries of RDF data. In addition, to better serve a given query, it is needed to index RDF data, which is especially true for massive RDF data. RDF data stores in NoSQL databases provide an infrastructure for massive RDF data management. Currently some efforts are concentrating on massive RDF data querying based on cloud computing (e.g., Garcia and Wang, 2013; Husain *et al.*, 2010 & 2011; Kim, Ravindra and Anyanwu,

2013, Li *et al.*, 2013). It should be noted that RDF data management based on NoSQL databases has only recently been gaining momentum, and the research in this direction is in its infancy. There are many research challenges and many interesting research opportunities for both the data management community and the Semantic Web community. Here we emphasize several major directions for future research.

- First, following the success of NoSQL approaches for Big Data outside the RDF space in cloud environment, a major direction for research is the study and development of richer structural indexing techniques and related query processing strategies for RDF data in NoSQL databases.
- Second, in addition to SELECT type of querying in SPARQL (Simple Protocol and RDF Query Language), a standard RDF querying language, how NoSQL databases can well support other types SPARQL querying such as CONSTRUCT, ASK and DESCRIBE should be investigated.
- Finally, for massive RDF data management in the context of the diversity in RDF application domains (e.g., computing biology (Anguita *et al.*, 2013) and geological information systems (Garbis *et al.*, 2013)), novel RDF data store structures and querying strategies need to be developed on the basis of NoSQL databases.

ACKNOWLEDGMENT

The work was supported by the *National Natural Science Foundation of China* (61572118 and 61370075) and *the Program for New Century Excellent Talents in University* (NCET- 05-0288).

REFERENCES

Abadi, D. J., Marcus, A., Madden, S., & Hollenbach, K. (2007). Scalable semantic Web data management using vertical partitioning, *Proceedings of the 33th International Conference on Very Large Data Bases* (pp. 411-422).

Abadi, D. J., Marcus, A., Madden, S., & Hollenbach, K. (2009). SW-Store: A vertically partitioned DBMS for Semantic Web data management. *The VLDB Journal*, *18*(2), 385–406. doi:10.1007/s00778-008-0125-y

Alexander, K. (2008). RDF in JSON: A specification for serialising RDF in JSON. Retrieved from http://www.semanticscripting.org/SFSW2008

Angles, R., & Gutiérrez, C. 2005, Querying RDF data from a graph database perspective. *Proceedings of the 2005 European Semantic Web Conference* (pp. 346-360). doi:10.1007/11431053_24

Angles, R., & Gutierrez, C. (2008). Survey of graph database models. *ACM Computing Surveys*, 40: 1:1-1:39.

Anguita, A., Martin, L., Garcia-Remesal, M., & Maojo, V. (2013). RDFBuilder A tool to automatically build RDF-based interfaces for MAGE-OM microarray data sources. *Computer Methods and Programs in Biomedicine*, 111(1), 220-227.

Bach, M., & Werner, A. (2014). Standardization of NoSQL database languages: Beyond databases, architectures, and structure. *Proceedings 10th International Conference* (BDAS 2014). Ustron, Poland: Springer. doi:10.1007/978-3-319-06932-6_6

Bishop, B., Kiryakov, A., Ognyanoff, D., Peikov, I., Tashev, Z., & Velkov, R. (2011). Owlim: A family of scalable semantic repositories. *Semantic Web, 2*(1), 1–10.

Bornea, M. A., Dolby, J., Kementsietsidis, A., Srinivas, K., Dantressangle, P., Udrea, O., & Bhattacharjee, B. (2013). Building an efficient RDF store over a relational database. *Proceedings of the 2013 ACM International Conference on Management of Data* (pp. 121-132). doi:10.1145/2463676.2463718

Broekstra, J., Kampman, A., & van Harmelen, F. (2002). Sesame: A generic architecture for storing and querying RDF and RDF schema. *Proceedings of the 2002 International Semantic Web Conference* (pp. 54-68). doi:10.1007/3-540-48005-6_7

Chang, F., Dean, J., Ghemawat, S., Hsieh, W. C., Wallach, D. A., Burrows, M., Chandra, T., Fikes, A., & Gruber, R. E. (2008). BigTable: A distributed storage system for structured data, *ACM Transactions on Computer Systems, 26*(2), 4:1-4:26.

Cudre-Mauroux, P., Enchev, I., Fundatureanu, S., Groth, P., Haque, A., Harth, A., & Wylot, M. et al. (2013). NoSQL databases for RDF: An empirical evaluation. *Proceedings of the 12th International Semantic Web Conference* (pp. 310-325). doi:10.1007/978-3-642-41338-4_20

Dean, J., & Ghemawat, S. (2008). MapReduce: Simplified data processing on large clusters. *Communications of the ACM, 51*(1), 107–113. doi:10.1145/1327452.1327492

DeCandia, G., Hastorun, D., Jampani, M., Kakulapati, G., Lakshman, A., Pilchin, A., & Vogels, W. et al. (2007). Dynamo: Amazon's highly available key-value store. *Proceedings of the 21st ACM Symposium on Operating Systems Principles* (pp. 205-220). doi:10.1145/1294261.1294281

Duan, S., Kementsietsidis, A., Srinivas, K., & Udrea, O. (2011). Apples and oranges: a comparison of RDF benchmarks and real RDF datasets. *Proceedings of the 2011 ACM SIGMOD International Conference on Management of Data* (pp. 145-156). doi:10.1145/1989323.1989340

Erling, O., & Mikhailov, I. (2007). RDF support in the virtuoso DBMS. *Proceedings of the 1st Conference on Social Semantic Web* (pp. 59-68).

Erling, O., & Mikhailov, I. (2009). *Virtuoso: RDF support in a native RDBMS.* In R. De Virgilio et al. (Eds.), *Semantic Web Information Management* (Ch. 21, pp. 501–519). Springer-Verlag.

Franke, C., Morin, S., Chebotko, A., Abraham, J., & Brazier, P. (2011). Distributed semantic web data management in HBase and MySQL Cluster. *Proceedings of the 2011 IEEE International Conference on Cloud Computing* (pp. 105-112). doi:10.1109/CLOUD.2011.19

Gamble, M., & Goble, C. (2011). Quality, Trust and Utility of Scientific Data on the Web: Toward a Joint model. *Proceedings of the 2011 International Conference on Web Science,* Koblenz, Germany (pp. 15:1-15:8). doi:10.1145/2527031.2527048

Garbis, G., Kyzirakos, K., & Koubarakis, M. (2013). Geographica: A benchmark for geospatial RDF stores. *Proceedings of the 12th International Semantic Web Conference* (pp. 343-359).

Garcia, T., & Wang, T. (2013, September 16-18). Analysis of Big Data technologies and method - Query large Web public RDF datasets on Amazon cloud using Hadoop and Open Source Parsers. *Proceedings of the 2013 IEEE International Conference on Semantic Computing*, Irvine, USA (pp. 244-251). doi:10.1109/ICSC.2013.49

Grolinger, K., Higashino, W. A., Tiwari, A., & Capretz, M. A. M. (2013). Data management in cloud environments: NoSQL and NewSQL data stores. *Journal of Cloud Computing: Advances, Systems and Applications*, 2(22).

Gudivada, V. N., Rao, D., & Raghavan, V. V. (2014). NoSQL Systems for Big Data Management, *2014 IEEE World Congress on Services* (pp. 190-197). doi:10.1109/SERVICES.2014.42

Güting, R. H. (1994, September 12-15). GraphDB: Modeling and querying graphs in databases. *Proceedings of 20th International Conference on Very Large Data Bases*, Santiago de Chile, Chile (pp. 297-308).

Harris, S., Lamb, N., & Shadbolt, N. (2009). 4store: The design and implementation of a clustered RDF store. *Proceedings of the 5th International Workshop on Scalable Semantic Web Knowledge Base Systems* (pp. 94-109).

Hecht, R., & Jablonski, S. (2011). NoSQL evaluation: A use case oriented survey. *Proceedings of the 2011 International Conference on Cloud and Service Computing*, Hong Kong, China. IEEE. doi:10.1109/CSC.2011.6138544

Hua, X. Y., Wu, H., Li, Z., & Ren, S. P. (2014). Enhancing throughput of the Hadoop Distributed File System for interaction-intensive tasks. *Journal of Parallel and Distributed Computing*, 74(8), 2770–2779. doi:10.1016/j.jpdc.2014.03.010

Huang, J., Abadi, D. J., & Ren, K. (2011). Scalable SPARQL querying of large RDF graphs. *Proceedings of the VLDB Endowment*, 4(11), 1123–1134.

Husain, M. F., Khan, L., Kantarcioglu, M., & Thuraisingham, B. M. (2010, July 5-10). Data intensive query processing for large RDF graphs using cloud computing tools, *Proceedings of the 2010 IEEE International Conference on Cloud Computing*, Miami, USA (pp. 1-10). doi:10.1109/CLOUD.2010.36

Husain, M. F., McGlothlin, J. P., Masud, M. M., Khan, L. R., & Thuraisingham, B. M. (2011). Heuristics-based query processing for large RDF graphs using cloud computing. *IEEE Transactions on Knowledge and Data Engineering*, 23(9), 1312–1327. doi:10.1109/TKDE.2011.103

Kaoudi, Z., & Manolescu, I. (2015). RDF in the clouds: A survey. *The VLDB Journal*, 24(1), 67–91. doi:10.1007/s00778-014-0364-z

Khadilkar, V., Kantarcioglu, M., Thuraisingham, B. M., & Castagna, P. (2012). Jena-HBase: A distributed, scalable and efficient RDF triple store. *Proceedings of the 2012 International Semantic Web Conference*.

Kim, H. S., Ravindra, P., & Anyanwu, K. (2013, May 13-17). Optimizing RDF(S) queries on cloud platforms, *Proceedings of the 2013 International World Wide Web Conference*, Rio de Janeiro, Brazil (pp. 261-264).

Kim, S. W. (2006). Hybrid storage scheme for RDF data management in Semantic Web. *Journal of Digital Information Management*, 4(1), 32–36.

Lakshman, A., & Malik, P. (2010). Cassandra: A decentralized structured storage system. *ACM SIGOPS Operating System Review, 44*(2), 35–40. doi:10.1145/1773912.1773922

Laney, D. (2001). 3D data management: Controlling data volume, velocity and variety. Meta Group, Gartner. Retrieved from http://blogs.gartner.com/doug-laney/files/2012/01/ad949-3D-Data-Management-Controlling-Data-Volume-Velocity-and-Variety.pdf

Li, R., Yang, D., Hu, H. B., Xie, J., & Fu, L. (2013). Scalable RDF graph querying using cloud computing. *Journal of Web Engineering, 12*(1 & 2), 159–180.

Luo, Y., Picalausa, F., Fletcher, G. H. L., Hidders, J., & Vansummeren, S. (2012). In R. De Virgilio et al. (Eds.), *Storing and indexing massive RDF datasets, Semantic Search over the Web* (pp. 31–60). Springer-Verlag Berlin Heidelberg. doi:10.1007/978-3-642-25008-8_2

Manola, F., & Miller, E. 2004, RDF Primer, W3C Recommendation, http://www.w3.org/TR/2004/REC-rdf-primer-20040210/

McBride, B. (2002). Jena: A Semantic Web toolkit. *IEEE Internet Computing, 6*(6), 55–59. doi:10.1109/MIC.2002.1067737

Moniruzzaman, A. B. M., & Hossain, S. A. (2013). NoSQL Database: New Era of Databases for Big data Analytics - Classification, Characteristics and Comparison. *International Journal of Database Theory and Application, 6*(4), 1–14.

Neumann, T., & Weikum, G. (2008). RDF-3X: A RISC-style engine for RDF. *Proceedings of the VLDB Endowment, 1*(1), 647–659. doi:10.14778/1453856.1453927

Neumann, T., & Weikum, G. (2010). The RDF-3X engine for scalable management of RDF data. *The VLDB Journal, 19*(1), 91–113. doi:10.1007/s00778-009-0165-y

Nicoara, D., Kamali, S., Daudjee, K., & Chen, L. (2015). Hermes: Dynamic partitioning for distributed social network graph databases. *Proceedings of the 18th International Conference on Extending Database Technology* (pp. 25-36).

Papailiou, N., Konstantinou, I., Tsoumakos, D., Karras, P., & Koziris, N. (2013). H2RDF+: High-performance distributed joins over large-scale RDF graphs. *Proceedings of the 2013 IEEE International Conference on Big Data* (pp. 255-263). doi:10.1109/BigData.2013.6691582

Papailiou, N., Konstantinou, I., Tsoumakos, D., & Koziris, N. (2012). H2RDF: Adaptive query processing on RDF data in the cloud. *Proceedings of the 21st World Wide Web Conference*, 397-400. doi:10.1145/2187980.2188058

Pokorny, J. (2011). NoSQL databases: A step to database scalability in web environment. *Proceedings of the 2011 International Conference on Information Integration and Web-based Applications and Services* (pp. 278-283). doi:10.1145/2095536.2095583

Pokorny, J. (2011). NoSQL Databases: A step to database scalability in Web environment. *International Journal of Web Information Systems, 9*(1), 69–82. doi:10.1108/17440081311316398

Prud'hommeaux, E., & Seaborne, A. (2008). SPARQL Query Language for RDF, W3C Recommendation. Retrieved from http://www.w3.org/TR/2008/REC-rdf-sparql-query-20080115/

Sakr, S., & Al-Naymat, G. (2009). Relational processing of RDF queries: A survey. *SIGMOD Record, 38*(4), 23–28. doi:10.1145/1815948.1815953

Sintek, M., & Kiesel, M. (2006). RDFBroker: A signature-based high-performance RDF store, *Proceedings of the 3rd European Semantic Web Conference* (pp. 363-377).

Snow, D. (2012). Dwaine Snow's Thoughts on Databases and Data Management. Retrieved from http://dsnowondb2.blogspot.cz/2012/07/adding-4th-v-to-big-data-veracity.html

Sperka, S., & Smrz, P. (2012). Towards adaptive and semantic database model for RDF data stores. *Proceedings of the Sixth International Conference on Complex, Intelligent, and Software Intensive Systems* (pp. 810-815).

Stuart, J., & Barker, A. (2013). Undefined By Data: A Survey of Big Data Definitions.

Sun, J. L., & Jin, Q. (2010). Scalable RDF store based on HBase and MapReduce. *Proceedings of the 3rd International Conference Advanced Computer Theory and Engineering* (pp. V1-633-V1-636).

Tauro, C., Aravindh, S., & Shreeharsha, A. B. (2012). Comparative Study of the New Generation, Agile, Scalable, High Performance NOSQL Databases. *International Journal of Computer Applications*, 48(20).

Wang, Y., Du, X. Y., Lu, J. H., & Wang, X. F. (2010). FlexTable: Using a dynamic relation model to store RDF data. *Proceedings of the 15th International Conference on Database Systems for Advanced Applications* (pp. 580-594_. doi:10.1007/978-3-642-12026-8_44

Weiss, C., Karras, P., & Bernstein, A. (2008). Hexastore: Sextuple indexing for semantic web data management. *Proceedings of the VLDB Endowment, 1*(1), 1008–1019. doi:10.14778/1453856.1453965

Wilkinson, K., Sayers, C., Kuno, H. A., & Reynolds, D. (2003). Efficient RDF storage and retrieval in Jena2. *Proceedings of the Semantic Web and Databases Workshop* (pp. 131-150).

ADDITIONAL READING

Aluc, G., Özsu, M. T., & Daudjee, K. (2014). Workload matters: Why RDF databases need a new design. *Proceedings of the VLDB Endowment, 7*(10), 837–840. doi:10.14778/2732951.2732957

Cardoso, J. (2007). The Semantic Web vision: Where are We? *IEEE Intelligent Systems, 22*(5), 84–88. doi:10.1109/MIS.2007.4338499

Cattell, R. (2011). Scalable SQL and NoSQL data stores. *SIGMOD Record, 39*(4), 12–27. doi:10.1145/1978915.1978919

Cogswell, J. (n. d.). SQL vs. NoSQL: Which is better? Retrieved from http://slashdot.org/topic/bi/sql-vs-nosql-which-is-better/

Das, S., Srinivasan, J., Perry, M., Chong, E. I., & Banerjee, J. (2014, March 24-28). A tale of two graphs: Property graphs as RDF in Oracle. *Proceedings of the 2014 International Conference on Extending Database Technology*, Athens, Greece (pp. 762-773).

Decker, S., Melnik, S., van Harmelen, F., Fensel, D., Klein, M. C. A., Broekstra, J., & Horrocks, I. et al. (2000). The Semantic Web: The roles of XML and RDF. *IEEE Internet Computing, 4*(5), 63–74. doi:10.1109/4236.877487

Decker, S., Mitra, P., & Melnik, S. (2000). Framework for the Semantic Web: An RDF tutorial *IEEE Internet Computing, 4*(6), 68–73. doi:10.1109/4236.895018

Horrocks, I., Parsia, B., Patel-Schneider, P., & Hendler, J. (2005, September 11-16). Semantic Web architecture: Stack or two towers? *Proceedings of the 2005 International Workshop on Principles and Practice of Semantic Web Reasoning*, Dagstuhl Castle, Germany (pp. 37-41). doi:10.1007/11552222_4

Hunter, J., & Lagoze, C. (2001, May 1-5). Combining RDF and XML schemas to enhance interoperability between metadata application profiles, *Proceedings of the 2001 International World Wide Web Conference*, Hong Kong, China (pp. 457-466). doi:10.1145/371920.372100

Jing, H., Haihong, E., Guan, L., & Jian, D. (2011). Survey on NoSQL database. *Proceedings of the 2011 International Conference on Pervasive Computing and Applications* (pp. 363-366). doi:10.1109/ICPCA.2011.6106531

Kaoudi, Z., & Manolescu, I. (2014, June 22-27). Cloud-based RDF data management. *Proceedings of the 2014 ACM SIGMOD International Conference on Management of Data*, Snowbird, USA (pp. 725-729). doi:10.1145/2588555.2588891

Kelly, J. (2012). Accumulo: Why the world needs another NoSQL database. *Big Data*, Aug.

Kim, H. S., Ravindra, P., & Anyanwu, K. (2014). A semantics-oriented storage model for big heterogeneous RDF data. *Proceedings of the ISWC 2014 Posters & Demonstrations Track a track within the 13th International Semantic Web Conference*, Riva del Garda, Italy, October 21, 2014, 437-440.

Lane, A. (n. d.). A response to NoSQL security concerns. Retrieved from http://www.darkreading.com/blog/232600288/a-response-to-nosql-security-concerns.html

Moniruzzaman, A. B. M., & Hossain, S. A. (2013). NoSQL database: New era of databases for big data analytics - classification, characteristics and comparison.

Punnoose, R., Crainiceanu, A., & Rapp, D. (2012, August 31). Rya: A scalable RDF triple store for the clouds. *Proceedings of the 2012 International Workshop on Cloud Intelligence*, Istanbul, Turkey.

Schindler, J. (2012). I/O characteristics of NoSQL databases. *Proceedings of the VLDB Endowment, 5*(12), 2020–2021. doi:10.14778/2367502.2367565

Shadbolt, N., Berners-Lee, T., & Hall, W. (2006). The Semantic Web revisited. *IEEE Intelligent Systems, 21*(3), 96–101. doi:10.1109/MIS.2006.62

Shimel, A. (n. d.). Is security an afterthought for NoSQL? Retrieved from http://www.networkworld.com/community/blog/security-afterthought-nosql

Stonebraker, M. (2010). SQL databases v. NoSQL databases. *Communications of the ACM*, *53*(4), 10–11. doi:10.1145/1721654.1721659

Vidal, V. M. P., Casanova, M. A., Monteiro, J. M., Arruda, N. M. Jr, Cardoso, D. S., & Pequeno, V. M. (2014, October 21). A framework for incremental maintenance of RDF views of relational data. *Proceedings of the ISWC 2014 Posters & Demonstrations Track a track within the 13th International Semantic Web Conference*, Riva del Garda, Italy (pp. 321-324).

Wu, B. W., Zhou, Y. L., Yuan, P. P., Jin, H., & Liu, L. (2014, November 3-7). SemStore: A semantic-preserving distributed RDF triple store, *Proceedings of the 2014 ACM International Conference on Information and Knowledge Management*, Shanghai, China (pp. 509-518). doi:10.1145/2661829.2661876

KEY TERMS AND DEFINITIONS

ACID: ACID means four properties, which are (A)tomcity, (C)onsistency, (I)solation and (D)urability. ACID is the type of transaction processing done by relational database management system (RDBMS).

Big Data: Big Data is a broad term for data sets so large or complex that traditional data processing applications are inadequate. There is not a common definition of Big Data and Big Data are generally characterized by some properties such as volume, velocity, variety and so on.

CAP: CAP Theorem means three properties, which are Consistency, Availability and Partition Tolerance.

JSON: JSON (JavaScript Object Notation) is a binary and typed data model which is applied to represent data like list, map, date, Boolean as well as different precision numbers.

NoSQL Databases: NoSQL means "not only SQL" or "no SQL at all". Being a new type of non-relational databases, NoSQL databases are developed for efficient and scalable management of Big Data.

RDF: Resource Description Framework (RDF) is a W3C (World Wide Web Consortium) recommendation which provides a generic mechanism for representing information about resources on the Web.

SPARQL: SPARQL (Simple Protocol and RDF Query Language) is an RDF query language which is a W3C recommendation. SPARQL contains capabilities for querying required and optional graph patterns along with their conjunctions and disjunctions.

ENDNOTES

[1]   http://hypertable.org

Section 3
Two Application Scenarios of Big Data Management in Cloud Computing Environments

Chapter 10
The Attitudes of Chinese Organizations Towards Cloud Computing:
An Exploratory Study

Tomayess Issa
Curtin University, Australia

Theodora Issa
Curtin University, Australia

Yuchao Duan
Curtin University, Australia

Vanessa Chang
Curtin University, Australia

ABSTRACT

Cloud Computing become a significant factor in E-commerce and E-business processes and will reduce negative IT impacts on the environment without compromising the needs of future generations. This chapter aim to examine the attitudes of Chinese Organizations towards Cloud Computing adoption. This chapter provides an answer to the question: "What are the advantages and disadvantages of Cloud Computing adoption in Chinese organizations?" The answer was sought by means of an online survey of (N=121) respondents. The survey results revealed the Chinese position regarding the cloud movement, its strengths and weaknesses, the threats posed by Cloud Computing in China, and the specific advantages and disadvantages of this new technology that Chinese organizations and research communities should embrace for the realization of future cloud systems.

INTRODUCTION

Information Communication Technology products and services are used via several organizations and individuals to enhance their performance and productivity. However, this technology brings several negative impacts to the environment from e-waste, energy consumption and carbon emissions. To reduce this impact, organizations and various stakeholders should tackle this problem and impact by using a smart technology such as cloud computing. Cloud Computing is an Internet-based computing service that provides on-demand computing power, in addition to being cheaper, and requiring low maintenance

DOI: 10.4018/978-1-4666-9834-5.ch010

and fewer Information Technology (IT) staff. However, this technology can pose several risks in terms of security, privacy and legality. The study presented in this chapter was intended to assess, via an on-line survey, the strengths and weaknesses of Cloud Computing performance in Chinese organizations.

The preliminary analyses of collected data indicated that, for the majority of those surveyed, Cloud Computing technology is simply recognized and known, but 78% of the survey participants were unaware of whether or not their organizations are using cloud computing. From the responses to the final question in section one of the surveys it became evident that those who already know about 'cloud computing', albeit to a limited extent, regard such technology as being scalable, flexible, sustainable, green and decreases operating expenses, however, cloud computing adoption by Chinese organizations still is risky and vulnerable. A factor analysis tool was adopted to examine the survey outcomes, and the Cronbach's Alpha was .953, indicating excellent internal consistency of the scale items. Also, the survey outcomes confirmed that cloud computing usage in China increased various benefits, although some of the participants in the Chinese organizations voiced their concern regarding the level of risk and security associated with cloud computing

Finally, this chapter examines the level of awareness of Chinese organizations' – public and private – about cloud computing. This chapter is organized as follows: 1) Introduction; 2) Cloud Computing; 3) Advantages and Disadvantages of Cloud Computing; 4)Cloud Computing in Chinese Organizations; 5) Research Method and Question; 6) Participants 7) Results; 8) Discussion; 9) Limitation; 10) Conclusion.

CLOUD COMPUTING

Cloud Computing is reviewed from different aspects and this research focuses particularly on the attitude of Chinese organizations towards cloud computing. Thus, in the real world, cloud service providers can use the results to identify the requirements and concerns of potential Cloud Computing users in China in order to provide better cloud service. An actual example of the use of Cloud Computing is the cloud-based navigation service. Cloud Computing can be used to identify the state of traffic in urban road networks (Liu, Ma, Sun, & Dan, 2010). Traffic jams are now becoming a serious problem in China, according to China Daily (2012), with the number of registered cars in Beijing – the capital city of China – having passed five million in 2012. With the help of cloud computing, the dynamic traffic data can be received, analysed in the cloud-based server and sent to the GPS terminal or the end users. According to Ye (2011), the total output value of satellite navigation industry in China was 50 billion Yuan in 2010 (approximately equal to $7.7 billion Australian Dollar), and it will reach 265 billion Yuan (roughly $40.8 billion AUD) by the year of 2015; there will be 130 million satellite navigation terminals and 350 million end users at that time. The Cloud Computing industry will grow more quickly with the support of the theory; research articles like this one will help the service provider to have a better understanding of the cloud users' attitudes.

Cloud Computing is an Internet-based computing model whereby numerous servers and computers are connected to the Internet, resources, software or operating systems and can be shared by the users based on the requirements (Chi & Gao, 2011). As Armbrust et al. (2010) point out, Cloud Computing can be provided by the applications which are running as services via the Internet. Vouk (2008) holds the same opinion: Cloud Computing is about to move the software, hardware, data and other different devices from the local data centres to the cloud-based servers, in which case, end users can connect to those resources which are located in the cloud anywhere anytime via the client software. Minimizing the cost of computing and maximizing the profit are the main purposes of cloud computing.

There are different models of cloud services, namely SaaS (Software as a Service), PaaS (Platform as a Service) and IaaS (Infrastructure as a Service) (see Figure 1). Software as a service means that an application or software is running on a virtual server which can be accessed anywhere any time as long as there is an Internet connection (Cusumano, 2010). Google Calendar and Google Mail are based on the SaaS.

An advantage of SaaS is that it is timesaving. The implementation of the applications is quite time-consuming and is always accompanied by a failure rate. SaaS will make this process faster and the productivity can be improved (Liao & Tao, 2008). Moreover, software licenses are cheaper. Liao and Tao (2008) claim that as the software are offered by the cloud server provider and run in the cloud-based servers, it is not necessary for users to buy those software or to upgrade them; the provider will deal with those things. Several studies indicate (Cubitt, Hassan, & Volkmer, 2011; Marks, 2010 ; Schulz, 2009) by using the SaaS, there is no need for enterprises to install and maintain hardware, monitor devices, or maintain the software. High-level security can be provided by the SaaS as a result of the resource integration, and providers understand that the customers are concerned about the security of data. Providers of SaaS will regularly upgrade the software to the current version, which means that users are able to focus on their own work rather than have to pay much attention to the software compatibility.

The main disadvantage of SaaS (Liao and Tao 2008) is single point failure. The Internet connection is almost everything; the company can come to a standstill if the connection to the Internet has been

Figure 1. SaaS, PaaS, IaaS (Prepared by the authors)

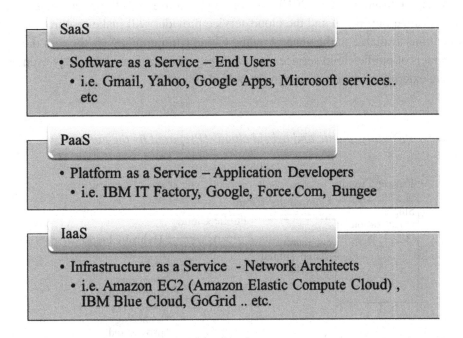

cut. The functionalities of the software, which is running in the cloud, might not be as good as the ones running on a local server. Response time cannot be controlled as it depends on the traffic of the Internet and the stability of cloud servers.

The PaaS is another cloud server model which can provide required resources to users in order to create applications and services in the cloud; in other words, users no longer need to download or install applications (Qayyum et al., 2011). For instance, the App Engine of Google is a type of PaaS.

IaaS is a storage space; hardware, servers and other devices can be offered by the IaaS platform provider; this equipment can be used directly and the platform provider is responsible for the maintenance tasks (Bhardwaj, Jain, & Jain, 2010). Amazon EC2 (Amazon Electric Cloud Computing) is a good example of IaaS. It was established 2006. Web interface and virtual machine instances are available for clients to manage the virtual machine which is provided by the Amazon EC2 (Juve et al., 2010). Amazon EC2 is a virtual computing environment from which users can launch instances via the interfaces of a web service. According to Juve et al. (2010), Amazon EC2 can be easily adopted using four steps: choose a pre-configured template image; configure the access level and security details of the network; choose the operating system and the type of instance; confirm whether the Amazon EC2 will run in different locations.

Just as cloud services have different models such as SaaS, PaaS and IaaS; there are different deployment models of Cloud Computing as well, namely: private, public, hybrid, and community (see Figure 2). According to Wyld (2010), in the private cloud method, the cloud infrastructure is owned solely by a company and it may be managed by the organization or a third party and may exist on the premises or off-premises. Schubert (2010) points out those private clouds are normally operated by the respective organization; the functionalities are not exposed to the customers directly and it is similar to Software as a Service from the customer's perspective. An example is eBay.

The cloud infrastructure can be accessed by the public cloud users or a large-scale industry group and is owned by the cloud provider (Wyld 2010). According to Rouse (2009), public cloud is based on the standard Cloud Computing model and the cloud service provider will make resources such as storage space or applications available to the general public Cloud Computing users through the Internet. The subscription models of public cloud services include a pay-per-usage model or may even be free while both internal and external providers maintain the hybrid cloud.

Figure 2. Private, community, public and hybrid clouds (Prepared by the authors)

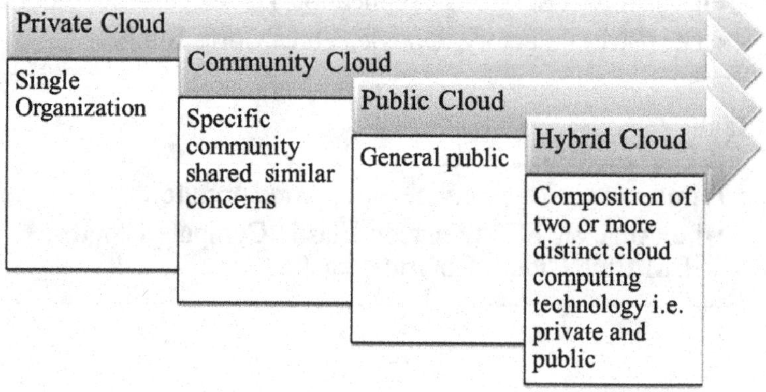

According to VMware (2010), hybrid cloud is a cloud infrastructure consisting of two or more clouds; private and public cloud can be combined under standardized technology and specific rules that enable application and data portability. The community cloud is shared by several organizations and supports a specific community that has shared concerns (e.g., mission, security requirements, policy, and compliance considerations); this cloud can be managed by the organizations or a third party and may exist on-premise or off-premise (Cisco, 2012). Schubert (2010) points out that, generally, cloud systems are restricted to the local infrastructure; for instance, public cloud service providers offer their own computing infrastructure to users. However, community clouds can either aggregate public clouds or be dedicated resource infrastructures. In other words, small or medium sized organizations can contribute their infrastructures and resources to build a community cloud from which all the organizations can benefit.

ADVANTAGES AND DISADVANTAGES OF CLOUD COMPUTING

Cloud Computing technology offers organizations many advantages in terms of cost, storage, access to information from, anywhere, anytime and any device. However, issues of security, technical glitches and privacy are major concerns for any organization (Avram, 2014; Berl et al., 2010; Issa, Chang, & Issa, 2010; Johnson, 2013; Lee & Zomaya, 2012; Marston, Li, Bandyopadhyay, Zhang, & Ghalsasi, 2011; Oliveira, Thomas, & Espadanal, 2014; Singh & Malhotra, 2012; Son, Lee, Lee, & Chang, 2014; Zissis & Lekkas, 2011; Zissis & Lekkas, 2012) (see Figure 3). Compared with traditional desktop software, Cloud Computing is considered as a cost-efficient method to use, maintain and upgrade. For instance, the licensing fees for traditional desktop software for different departments' terminals will require a lot in terms of investment (Viswanathan, 2012). On the other hand, several studies indicate (Cubitt et al., 2011; Marks, 2010 ; Singh & Malhotra, 2012; Velte, Velte, & Elsenpeter, 2010) that Cloud Computing provides cheaper IT services which can reduce the amount of investment that an organization makes in IT. What's more, there are different scalable options available such as pay-as-you-go and one-time-payment, which makes Cloud Computing a very reasonable choice for companies. All the data can be stored in the cloud, which provides companies with almost unlimited memory capacity. Therefore, companies do not need to be anxious about running out of memory space or increasing the current memory capacity.

Figure 3. Advantages and disadvantages of cloud computing (Prepared by the authors)

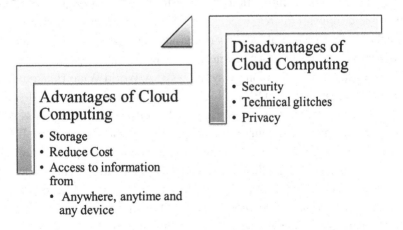

The process of backing up or restoring data and information from the cloud is much easier than doing these things on physical devices. Besides, majority of cloud service providers offer recovery services for customers in order to sharpen the competitive edge. Thus, it will be simpler for companies to back up or recover data compared with traditional methods of data storage.

By using Cloud Computing technology, the data stored in the cloud can be accessed anywhere any time as long as there is an Internet connection available. Users just need to register, and data can be reviewed or modified easily. Users will not be perplexed or inconvenienced by geographic locations and time zones because of this convenient feature of cloud computing.

Cloud Computing can also provide the advantage of speedy deployment. The entire cloud-based system can be fully functional in a short time after all the settings have been finalised. Companies need only to select the appropriate system configuration based on their requirements; the cloud service providers will handle other issues. In spite of the overwhelming benefits mentioned above, Cloud Computing also has several drawbacks. Organizations, especially small or medium sized ones, should be aware of the following disadvantages before moving to the cloud.

Several studies (Brender & Markov, 2013; Johnson, 2013; Zissis & Lekkas, 2011; Zissis & Lekkas, 2012) indicate that security is always a major issue of cloud computing. Before adopting cloud-computing technology, companies should be aware that all the data including sensitive information will be handed over to a third-party cloud service provider, and therefore there is a potential risk to the organization. Data may be stored anywhere as the cloud servers may be in different locations or even different countries. Hence, organizations need to make sure that the cloud service provider has the ability to keep all the data absolutely secure. Although it is true that data stored on the cloud servers can be obtained anytime from anywhere with an Internet connection, some unpredictable system dysfunctions can occur without timely warning. Companies have to face the fact that all technologies are always prone to outages and other technical issues. Moreover, a stable and reliable Internet connection is required in order to avoid network and connectivity problems as all the services are web-based. As a result of the data being stored in the cloud servers, organizations will face potential risks, which make them vulnerable to external hack attacks and threats.

CLOUD COMPUTING IN CHINESE ORGANIZATIONS

Recently, China has started to show more interest in the ICT (Information and Communications Technology) development and innovation area, especially the Cloud Computing technology. However, as a result of poor enforcement of intellectual property rights and the strict policy which discriminates against overseas-funded enterprises or foreign-owned enterprises in government procurement, the development of Cloud Computing in China still has a long way to go (BSA World Wide Headquarters, 2012).

According to the research report from BSA Global Cloud Computing Scorecard-A blueprint for Economic Opportunity (2012), strict laws on cybercrime and intellectual property laws have been promulgated by the Chinese government, although enforcement deficiencies are evident. If China can impose and implement effective and relevant Cloud Computing laws, then the digital economy, confidence and trust will be boosted (Zhang, 2010). On the other hand, there is an additional risk as a result of administration rules of Internet content in China including the mandatory rules of censorship and filtering of Internet content(BSA World Wide Headquarters, 2012). Overall, significant progress regarding Cloud Computing has been made and this new technology is quickly expanding in China.

Firstly, in the new period, national policy is promoting the development of cloud computing. There are seven emerging industries in China's current development strategy: energy saving, a new generation of information technology, biological sciences, alternative energy, advanced material and hybrid vehicle. Information technology, being in second position among all those sectors, indicates that the government attaches great importance to IT area. Cloud Computing is considered as a revolution of IT and it plays a significant role in communication and information technology and has therefore captured the government's attention. International Data Corporation (IDG) believes that by the end of 2012, the global market of Cloud Computing services will bring in an income of $420 billion U.S. (Chi & Gao, 2011). This great opportunity should not be ignored. Beijing, Shanghai, Wuxi and other major cities in China already have a Cloud Computing development plan. For instance, Shanghai is implementing a 3-year plan with 3.1 billion RMB invested; Beijing is trying to build a Cloud Computing base of world-class scale (Zhang, 2010).

Secondly, the industrial chain of Cloud Computing is taking shape: the ability to build Cloud-Computing infrastructure has improved and the overall strength of the software industry has increased equably. The network servers, storage and other relevant technologies or devices have vastly improved due to the great efforts made by the government (Chi & Gao, 2011). In addition, in recent years, the capacity to build Cloud Computing has continued to improve. Internet-based enterprises are growing rapidly in China. Meanwhile, large-scale network companies such as Tencent, Alibaba and Baidu have already accumulated rich experience and technology resources from cloud computing. Thus, Chinese corporations enrich the content of Cloud Computing constantly and the industrial chain of Cloud Computing in China is based on the contributions made by Chinese enterprises. The Cloud Computing industrial chain in China is gradually taking shape. The industrial chain is expected to provide benefits to all relevant sectors, and different corporations as shown below can represent each sector of the industrial chain: On-demand software, platform of hardware, automatic balance loading and virtualization. In this field, IBM, Cisco and the traditional leaders in the hardware and software manufacturing area play significant roles. Inspur, HuaSheng, ZTE and Lenovo are domestic enterprises also doing well in this area. Systems integrators are demanded for helping cloud users build the platform for software and hardware. Amazon and Google are international leaders in this area. The largest companies in this field in China include Inspur and Neusoft Group. Service providers are also included in the industry chain of Cloud Computing since they provide storage, personal and business computing or other resources. Tasks like computing or development of applications are based on these services. Pengboshi and SUJING Tech are doing well in the domestic service market.

The development of Cloud Computing provides good opportunities for Chinese industry and economy. For one thing, by using the cloud infrastructure services, small or medium size enterprises are able to redirect their resources easily to adopt a long-term strategy for their future development (Li, Tang, Guo, & Hu, 2010). In the traditional IT model, pre-investment is required in order to acquire the software and hardware. What is more, during the life cycle of a project, servers and software need to be maintained regularly which will require more investment. However, by shifting to the cloud, the new payment method, which is the pay-as-you-go model, will provide numerous benefits to companies. For instance, the Microsoft-hosted Exchange Online services allow customers to access their calendars or emails anywhere anytime at a cost of $10 U.S. monthly. For another, it is a good chance for domestic IT companies to catch up with the advanced international level of Cloud Computing field (Chen, Xu,

Wang, Li, & Jin, 2011). At present, Cloud Computing is still in the exploratory phase and technologies associated with this new concept are still immature; hence, if Chinese IT enterprises can seize this opportunity, a qualitative change may occur in the IT industry in China.

In addition, it is noted that Chinese IT companies have begun to change their strategy from simply adopting current technology from overseas top level corporations by creating their own new principles and technologies (Wei, Zhang, & Zeng, 2009). For instance, a company named 360 provides a free cloud-based antivirus program to the end users; the Baidu Company creates a frame computing system based on the cloud. It is a good signal for the domestic IT industry and it can be seen that these companies are becoming more creative and competitive than before (Li et al., 2010).

Besides the benefits that Cloud Computing can provide such as ease of development and management and scalability, several challenges of Cloud Computing should be taken into consideration as well, such as the ownership and control of data, privacy issues and trust (Erdogmus, 2009). Before implementing cloud computing, numerous aspects of security issues should be resolved by the service providers in order to increase the adoption of Cloud Computing (Christodorescu, Sailer, & Schales, 2009). On the other hand, some of the cloud service providers claim that the security processes and measures they provide are better than most of those offered by IT organizations; hence, their security status will be improved if their cloud solution can be adopted. Cellary and Strykowski (2009) claim that at the cloud service provider end, security of hardware and software can be ensured as a result of maintenance provided by professional security technicians. For the purpose of ensuring widespread adoption of cloud computing, relieving the security concerns of customers is a key issue which should be taken into consideration (Chebrolu, 2010). As the techniques of encryption become more mature, the security of Cloud Computing can be enhanced in the future. The complex integration of Cloud Computing presents significant challenges for Chinese organizations, including, malware detection and immediate intrusion response. In order to decrease the impact, problem analysis and solving should be done promptly (Li et al., 2010; Ye, 2011; Zaheer, 2012). During the entire life cycle of the service management in the cloud, incidence management should always be considered.

Chinese IT companies have discovered many potential advantages of cloud computing. They believe that by adopting this new technology, IT investment costs will be decreased and the capabilities of the corporations can be enhanced. Basically, Chinese IT companies prefer to use cloud servers offered by overseas providers. However, they may be concerned about the risks of sending sensitive data out of the country, so if the cloud service provider has a data centre located in China, the provider will be more popular (Zhou, Zhang, Xie, & Qian, 2010). Chinese Cloud Computing explorers prefer to adopt virtualization and outsource their IT infrastructure, as they do not really care about the ownership of IT infrastructure. In order to build cloud services internally, virtualization development attracts much attention nowadays (Wei et al., 2009). Overall, Chinese cloud explorers consider Cloud Computing to be a valuable technology with great potential which will play a significant role in improving China's economic competitiveness in the near future (Alter, Peng, Lin, & Harris, 2010).

RESEARCH METHOD AND QUESTION

The study presented in this chapter intended to answer: "What are the advantages and disadvantages of Cloud Computing adoption in Chinese organizations?" to answer this study, quantitative online survey is used by using the positivism research philosophy. In the beginning, a critical review of literature is organized to develop the research strategy and questions, and then an online survey is invented based on the findings of the literature review. Employing an online survey in any study will allow the researcher to answer the research questions; confirm and to endorse the findings of the literature review in line to develop new theoretical significance, and to answer the research questions. Using online survey can offer greater anonymity, less expensive and more accessibility (Gordon & McNew, 2008; Issa, 2013; Porter, 2004); on the other hand, online survey disadvantages are technical failure, computer viruses, internet crimes, hacking, and privacy, and these can lead to decrease in the response rate (Fan & Yan, 2010)

The online survey consisting of two sections namely the first section contains demographic questions, the responses to which will allow the generation of the profile of those surveyed. This first section concludes with an open question for respondents, inviting them to provide their opinion concerning the issue of 'cloud computing'. The second section contains fourteen statements seeking respondents' opinions using a seven-point Likert scale ranging from 'Strongly disagree' to 'Strongly agree' with an additional option 'Do not know'. The fourteen statements were intended to investigate and examine the attitudes in Chinese Organizations and their personnel towards this relatively new development in the ICT industry, i.e. 'Cloud computing'. The population of interest was managers in the Information Technology Organisations in China. This chapter derives from data gathered through this survey of 121 respondents, which was collected by using various techniques from social media i.e. Facebook, Linkedin, twitter and word of mouth. The survey data was collected within one month.

PARTICIPANTS

This study was conducted in China in order to examine the main concerns that Chinese organizations have with moving to the cloud. The survey was distributed to organizations in China and the survey response rate was 88.9%. Table 1 provides a summary of the respondents' details including gender, industry sector type and qualifications.

Table 2 shows the number of survey respondents in public and private organizations in China. It was noted that the majority of respondents work in small, medium and large organizations. Furthermore, the majority of respondents worked in communication services, education, and finance and insurance (24%, 21%, and 12% respectively) (see Table 3).

Finally, results presented in Table 4 confirm that 40% of personnel in Chinese organizations are still unaware of Cloud Computing applications, although 21% are currently using various applications such as Opera, Google Doc and MongoDB.

RESULTS

A total of 136 participants from China responded to the online survey. With 15 responses not accepted because of missing data, this resulted in 121 valid cases of responses for China for the following Factor Analysis. Based on the Mean and STD Deviation results, it was confirmed that the majority of the personnel in Chinese organizations have neutral agreement behind cloud-computing services; but in scalable services, efficient, green and sustainability factors the mean was higher compared to the other factors (see Table 5).

Table 1. Summary of the respondents' details: China

Number and Percentage of Questionnaires	
Questionnaires Distributed	136
Questionnaires Returned	121
Response Rate	88.9%
Gender	
Male Respondents	84
Female Respondents	53
Sector Type	
Public Sector Organization	70
Private Sector Organization	65
Qualifications	
Bachelor Degree	59
Master Degree	56
Doctorate (PhD)	10
Other, Please specify	13

Table 2. Number of employees in public and private organizations in China

0-50	**18**
51 to 200	10
201 to 500	10
501 to 2000	9
2001 to 8000	7
8001- 100000	9
Total	63

Table 3. Organization types in China

Organizations	Number	Percentage
Accommodation, Cafes and Restaurants	3	2%
Agriculture, Forestry and Fishing	2	1%
Communication Services	32	24%
Construction	5	4%
Cultural and Recreational Services	11	8%
Education	29	21%
Electricity, Gas and Water Supply	12	9%
Finance and Insurance	16	12%
Government Administration and Defence	8	6%
Health and Community Services	7	5%
Manufacturing	5	4%
Mining	4	3%
Personal and Other Services	13	10%
Property and Business Services	1	1%
Retail Trade	2	1%
Transport and Storage	2	1%
Wholesale Trade	2	1%

Table 4. Cloud computing usage in private and public organizations in China

Answer	Response
Don't Know	53
No	54
Yes If you answered 'yes' to this question, please provide details in the space below of applications you access via cloud computing.	29

Table 5. Descriptive statistics: Mean and STD deviation

	Mean	Std. Deviation
Cloud Computing is more flexible than traditional computing.	3.64	1.063
Cloud Computing is more efficient than traditional computing.	3.77	1.047
Cloud Computing helps organisations become 'greener'.	3.64	1.024
Cloud Computing helps provide scalable services.	3.81	1.075
Cloud Computing helps provides reliable services.	3.56	1.064
Cloud Computing helps provides ease of maintenance.	3.39	1.113
Cloud Computing makes staffing easier.	3.44	1.072
Cloud Computing decreases operating expenses.	3.50	1.111
Cloud Computing increases operating expenses.	3.03	1.110
Cloud Computing reduces capital costs.	3.40	1.029
Cloud Computing introduces security problems.	3.40	1.012
Cloud Computing is more risky than traditional computing.	3.31	1.017
Cloud Computing reduces organisations' carbon footprint.	3.55	1.017
Cloud Computing contributes to organisations' sustainability.	3.66	1.092

To assess the survey results, further research carried out by the researchers using SPSS version 21, adopted principal axis factoring for factor extraction, and oblique rotation was applied using the direct oblimin method to correlate the variables (Costello & Osborne, 2005; Hair, Black, Babin, & Anderson, 2009).

To measure the sampling adequacy, researchers carried out specific testing using Cronbach's Alpha, Kaiser-Meyer-Olkin and Bartlett's test. Firstly, the Cronbach's Alpha for all 14 variables was .953, indicating an excellent internal consistency of the items in the scale (Gliem & Gliem, 2003). Secondly, the Kaiser-Meyer-Olkin measure of sampling adequacy was .922 above the recommended value of .6, indicating that a good sample size has been obtained from the analysis (Hill, 2012). Thirdly, the Bartlett's test of sphericity is highly significant, $\chi^2 = 1474.258$, df $= 91$, p $< .000$, indicating that the items of the scale are sufficiently correlated to factors to be found (Burns & Burns, 2008). Finally, the communalities were all over .05 (see Table 6) except for statement 9, as Chinese organizations still have some concerns that Cloud Computing will increase operating expenses.

Furthermore, the researchers used principle components analysis to estimate the factor-loading matrix for the factor analysis model as well the standard correlation matrix. The Eigen values are assessed to determine the number of factors accounting for the correlations amongst the variables. As demonstrated

Table 6. Cloud computing – communalities

Communalities	Initial	Extraction
Cloud Computing is more flexible than traditional computing	.755	.751
Cloud Computing is more efficient than traditional computing	.796	.733
Cloud Computing helps organisations become 'greener'	.764	.733
Cloud Computing helps provide scalable services	.770	.747
Cloud Computing helps provide reliable services	.718	.703
Cloud Computing helps provide ease of maintenance	.712	.597
Cloud Computing makes staffing easier	.765	.700
Cloud Computing decreases operating expenses	.631	.561
Cloud Computing increases operating expenses	.489	.307
Cloud Computing reduces capital costs	.662	.602
Cloud Computing introduces security problems	.777	.726
Cloud Computing is more risky than traditional computing	.744	.977
Cloud Computing reduces organisations' carbon footprint	.698	.620
Cloud Computing contributes to organisations' sustainability	.691	.655

Extraction Method: Principal Axis Factoring.

in Table 7, this model of eight factors explains a total of 57.279% of the variation. The Eigen values and the amount of variances explained by each of these factors are presented in Table 7 (after rotation).

Furthermore, to measure the regression coefficients (i.e. slopes), the researchers carried out the factor loadings. The factor loadings are based on most of the items that have a high loading value and the one with the cleanest factor structure is considered as important; items Q8_13 and Q8_10 are shared factor loadings between the two factors (Costello & Osborne, 2005). The Q8_13 and Q8_10 under Factor 2 had a factor loading below .5 based on the rule of thumb of Stevens (1992) for a sample size above 100. Variables excluded are highlighted in light blue (see Table 8).

The Pattern Matrix revealed two factors: Factor 1: Operational benefits and Factor 2: Risk and security. The mean and standard deviation of the factor average is presented in Table 9.

Overall, it became evident that the organizations in China believed that using Cloud Computing tools is more efficient than traditional computing, scalable, easier, reliable, and flexible; moreover, the survey indicated that the use of Cloud Computing technology in China will assist organizations to become greener and more sustainable. However, the survey outcomes confirmed that although cloud-computing usage in China is believed to have various advantages, there is nevertheless some concern regarding the issue of risk and security.

DISCUSSION

The main aim of this chapter was to analyze the attitude of Chinese organizations towards Cloud Computing technology. Currently, the number of Internet users worldwide is increasing rapidly as a result of the development of the Internet infrastructure construction. Because of the increase in the number of

Table 7. Cloud computing: Total variance explained

Factor	Initial Eigenvalues			Extraction Sums of Squared Loadings			Rotation Sums of Squared Loadings[a]
	Total	% of Variance	Cumulative %	Total	% of Variance	Cumulative %	Total
1	8.473	65.177	65.177	8.168	62.831	62.831	8.028
2	1.092	8.401	73.578	.898	6.907	69.738	4.704
3	.670	5.157	78.735				
4	.565	4.345	83.079				
5	.449	3.453	86.532				
6	.342	2.632	89.164				
7	.308	2.366	91.531				
8	.274	2.108	93.638				
9	.212	1.628	95.266				
10	.198	1.523	96.788				
11	.158	1.219	98.007				
12	.141	1.083	99.090				
13	.118	.910	100.000				

Extraction Method: Principal Axis Factoring.

a. When factors are correlated, sums of squared loadings cannot be added to obtain a total variance.

Table 8. Cloud computing: Pattern matrix

	Factor	
	1	2
Cloud Computing is more efficient than traditional computing	.905	
Cloud Computing helps provide scalable services	.902	
Cloud Computing makes staffing easier	.875	
Cloud Computing helps provide reliable services	.871	
Cloud Computing is more flexible than traditional computing	.865	
Cloud Computing helps organisations become 'greener'	.821	
Cloud Computing contributes to organisations' sustainability	.794	
Cloud Computing decreases operating expenses	.758	
Cloud Computing helps provide ease of maintenance	.705	
Cloud Computing reduces organisations' carbon footprint	.638	.214
Cloud Computing reduces capital costs	.631	.216
Cloud Computing is more risky than traditional computing		.943
Cloud Computing introduces security problems	.107	.821

Extraction Method: Principal Axis Factoring.

Rotation Method: Oblimin with Kaiser Normalization.[a]

a. Rotation converged in 4 iterations.

Table 9. Cloud computing: Descriptive statistics (N=121)

	Mean	Std. Deviation
Factor 1: Operational benefits	3.60	1.073
Factor 2: Risk and Security	3.36	1.01

Internet users and companies' inability to efficiently handle the task load of network access, more and more corporations have started to adopt cloud technology in order to provide more flexible, efficient and reliable services to users. Cloud Computing is based on the Internet and all the data, software or even the operating system can be moved into the cloud, as long as there is an Internet connection. Data can be accessed anywhere at any time by the end users. Cloud Computing is becoming a significant factor in E-commerce and E-business processes. The literature review (Avram, 2014; Chang, Issa, & Issa, 2011; Marston et al., 2011; Oliveira et al., 2014; Son et al., 2014; Zissis & Lekkas, 2012) indicates that the most well-known Cloud Computing providers in China are Google, Microsoft and IBM. However, some companies with excellent reputations in the global Cloud Computing market like Amazon, Salesforce. com and EMC are not expanding in the Chinese cloud market.

Most organizations are aware that Cloud Computing can reduce capital costs, is easy to implement, and decreases operating expenses. Companies are greatly concerned about reducing capital costs, including reducing the initial IT equipment expenses and decreasing maintenance costs. However, a number of companies, especially small or medium-sized ones, doubt that Cloud Computing can really reduce costs. The most important advantage of Cloud Computing is that it decreases total capital costs; however, the lack of successful cases means that this has not been satisfactorily proven. The advantages of Cloud Computing includes cost efficiency, availability of almost unlimited storage, easy backup and recovery, easy access to information, and quick deployment, to name a few. Disadvantages of Cloud Computing include security in the cloud, technical issues, proneness to attack, etc. Organizations believe that the obstacles to the development of Cloud Computing in China include the following: lack of successful cases of cloud computing; lack of professional knowledge of cloud technology; network bandwidth and limited budget; security; lack of cloud industry standards and policies. The study confirmed the research question, as Chinese organizations still have some concerns about adopting Cloud Computing in their organizations; they perceive its weaknesses to be issues of security and risk. However, Cloud Computing does provide advantages in that it is scalable, efficient, easy to maintain, reliable, flexible, sustainable, green and reduce cost, nevertheless. Moreover, it was confirmed that the adoption of Cloud Computing in China would allow organizations to become more sustainable, especially in the Information Technology departments.

Figure 4 shows the new advantages and disadvantages factor (*New factors with red font color and italic*) by the Chinese organizations. This chapter added new theoretical significance about the attitudes of Chinese Organizations towards Cloud Computing, as the survey results confirmed that Cloud Computing adoption is scalable, efficient, easy to maintain, reliable, flexible, sustainable, green and decreases operating expenses, nevertheless, Cloud Computing adoption by the Chinese organizations is risky and vulnerable which confirmed the literature.

As security and risk are the most important concerns for organizations, future research could include an in-depth review of the security and privacy issues and possible solutions. Furthermore, it can be seen that security is the most important concern to Chinese organizations. For security purposes, both organi-

Figure 4. Advantages and disadvantages of cloud computing adoption in China (Prepared by the authors)

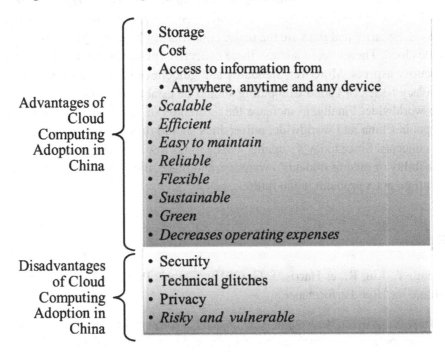

zations and cloud providers should have a backup solution; the business sensitive information should be encrypted. In addition, it is important to avoid cloud outages; the cloud provider should check the entire infrastructure regularly; main servers and backup servers should be in different locations in order to avoid power failure or any other unpredictable accident, so that if anything happens to the main servers, the backup servers will not be affected. For organizations, moving to the cloud is about balancing risks and benefits. They should not make the decision just because all other companies have the cloud plan; the cloud strategy should be based on the realities of each organization's circumstances and position.

LIMITATIONS

The study presented in this chapter was limited to a survey of 121 participants from both public and private organizations in China. The rationale for this study was to assess Chinese organizations' attitudes to Cloud Computing adoption. The online survey responses strongly indicated that Chinese organizations are aware of these concepts, although the level of awareness is low. Therefore, further research with larger and more diverse groups of organizations is required in the future to strengthen the research findings.

CONCLUSION

This chapter examined the strengths and weaknesses of Cloud Computing performance in Chinese organizations. As can be seen from the analysis, respondents from the public sector are more aware of cloud computing. Based on the survey result, the Chinese Organizations consider Cloud Computing is flexible and efficient than traditional computing. It can help Chinese Organizations to become greener and provides scalable, reliable services; it makes the maintenance and staffing easier, thereby decreasing operating expenses. Security and risks are the major concerns of Chinese organizations when considering a move to the cloud. Therefore, to address these concerns, further research should be carried out to examine the security aspects. Moreover, standards and guidelines tailored specifically to address the security and privacy issues of Cloud Computing should be established and implemented, not only in China, but also worldwide. Finally, to increase the awareness of cloud computing, sustainability and green IT concepts in China and worldwide, universities should develop and present courses and units related to these concepts. Since today's students will be tomorrow's leaders, universities and academics have the responsibility of raising students' awareness and make, their decisions part of the Information Technology solution, not a problem in the future.

REFERENCES

Alter, A. E., Peng, Y., Lin, R., & Harris, J. G. (2010). China's Pragmatic Path to Cloud Computing. Accenture Institute for High Performance.

Armbrust, M., Fox, A., Griffith, R., Joseph, A. D., Katz, R., Knowinski, A., & Zaharia, M. et al. (2010). A View of Cloud Computing. *Communications of the ACM, 53*(4), 50–58. doi:10.1145/1721654.1721672

Avram, M. G. (2014). Advantages and Challenges of Adopting Cloud Computing from an Enterprise Perspective. *Procedia Technology, 12*(0), 529-534.

Berl, A., Gelenbe, E., Di Girolamo, M., Giuliani, G., Meer, H., Dang, M., & Pentikousis, K. (2010). Energy-Efficient Cloud Computing. *The Computer Journal, 53*(7), 1046–1051. doi:10.1093/comjnl/bxp080

Bhardwaj, S., Jain, L., & Jain, S. (2010). Cloud Computing: A Study of Infrastructure as a Service (IAAS). *International Journal of Engineering and Information Technology, 2*(1), 60–63.

Brender, N., & Markov, I. (2013). Risk perception and risk management in cloud computing: Results from a case study of Swiss companies. *International Journal of Information Management, 33*(5), 726–733. doi:10.1016/j.ijinfomgt.2013.05.004

World Wide Headquarters, B. S. A. (2012). *BSA Global Cloud Computing Scorecard*. Washington, DC.

Burns, R. P., & Burns, R. (2008). *Business Research Methods and Statistics Using SPSS*. Atlanta, GA, USA: Sage.

Cellary, W., & Strykowski, S. (2009). e-government based on cloud computing and service-oriented architecture. *Proceedings of the 3rd International Conference on Theory and Practice of Electronic Governance* (pp. 5-10).

Chang, V., Issa, T., & Issa, T. (2011). Cloud computing and sustainability: an Australian public sector perspective. *Proceedings of the International Society for Professional Innovation Management (ISPIM) Conference*, Hamburg, Germany.

Chebrolu, S. B. (2010). Assessing the relationships among cloud adoption, strategic alignment and information technology effectiveness. *ProQuest Dissertations & Theses database,*

Chen, S., Xu, Y., Wang, P., Li, D., & Jin, D. (2011). The usage of cloud computing in China Regional Healthcare. *Proceedings of the 2011 IEEE International Conference on Cloud Computing and Intelligence Systems* (pp. 1-5).

Chi, C., & Gao, F. (2011). The Trend of Cloud Computing in China. *Journal of Software*, 6(7), 1230–1235. doi:10.4304/jsw.6.7.1230-1234

Beijing Car Ownership Exceeds 5 Million. (2012, September 19). China Daily. Retrieved from http://www.chinadaily.com.cn/china/2012-02/17/content_14628019.htm

Christodorescu, M., Sailer, R., & Schales, D. L. (2009). Cloud security is not (just) virtualization security: A short paper. *Proceedings of the 2009 ACM Workshop on Cloud Computing Security* (pp. 97-102).

Cisco. (2012, September 19). Cloud Computing in Higher Education: A Guide to Evaluation and Adoption. Retrieved from http://www.cisco.com/web/offer/email/43468/5/Cloud_Computing_in_Higher_Education.pdf

Costello, A., & Osborne, J. (2005). Best Practices in Exploratory Factor Analysis: Four Recommendations for Getting the Most from Your Analysis. *Practical Assessment, Research & Evaluation*, 10(7), 1–9.

Cubitt, S., Hassan, R., & Volkmer, I. (2011). Does Cloud Computing have a Silver Lining. *Media Culture & Society*, 33(1), 149–158. doi:10.1177/0163443710382974

Cusumano, M. (2010). Cloud computing and SaaS as new computing platforms. *Communications of the ACM*, 53(4), 27–29. doi:10.1145/1721654.1721667

Erdogmus, H. (2009). Cloud computing: Does Nirvana hide behind the Nebula. *IEEE Software*, 26(11), 4–6.

Fan, W., & Yan, Z. (2010). Factors affecting response rates of the web survey: A systematic review. *Computers in Human Behavior*, 26(2), 132–139. doi:10.1016/j.chb.2009.10.015

Gliem, J., & Gliem, R. (2003). Calculating, Interpreting, and Reporting Cronbach's Alpha Reliability Coefficient for Likert-Type Scales. Proceedings of the Midwest Research to Practice Conference in Adult, Continuing and Community Education (pp. 82 - 88).

Gordon, D., Wirz, M., Roggen, D., & Tröster, G., & Beigl, M. (2014). Group affiliation detection using model divergence for wearable devices. *Proceedings of the 2014 ACM International Symposium on Wearable Computers*, Seattle, Washington (pp. 19-26). ACM. doi:10.1145/2634317.2634319

Gordon, J., & McNew, R. (2008). Developing the Online Survey. *Nurs Clin N Am, 43*(4), 605 – 619..

Hair, J., Black, W., Babin, B., & Anderson, R. (2009). *Multivariate data analysis*. Upper Saddle River, NJ: Prentice Hall.

Hill, B. D. (2012). *The Sequential Kaiser-Meyer-Olkin Procedure As An Alternative For Determining The Number Of Factors In Common-Factor Analysis: A Monte Carlo Simulation* [Dissertation].

Issa, T. (2013). Online Survey: Best Practice. In P. Isaias, M.B. Nunes (Eds.), Information Systems Research and Exploring Social Artifacts: Approaches and Methodologies (pp. 1–19). Hershey, PA, USA: IGI Global. doi:10.4018/978-1-4666-2491-7.ch001

Issa, T., Chang, V., & Issa, T. (2010). The Impact of Cloud Computing and Organizational Sustainability. *Cloud Computing and Virtualization 2010*, Singapore.

Johnson, P. E. (2013). A Review of "Cloud Computing for Libraries". *Journal of Access Services, 10*(1), 71–73. doi:10.1080/15367967.2013.738572

Juve, G., Deelman, E., Vahi, K., Mehta, G., Berriman, B., Maechling, P., & Berman, B. P. (2010). Data Sharing Options for Scientific Workflows on Amazon EC2. *High Performance Computing, Networking, Storage and Analysis*, 1-9.

Lee, Y. C., & Zomaya, A. Y. (2012). Energy efficient utilization of resources in cloud computing systems. *The Journal of Supercomputing, 60*(2), 268–280. doi:10.1007/s11227-010-0421-3

Li, R., Tang, S., Guo, C., & Hu, X. (2010). Thinking the cloud computing in China. *Information Management and Engineering* (pp. 669-672).

Liao, H., & Tao, C. (2008). An Anatomy to SaaS Business Mode Based on Internet. *Paper presented at the 2008 International Conference on Management of e-Commerce and e-Government*. http://dx.doi.org:10.1109/ICMECG.2008.16

Liu, W. N., Ma, Q. L., Sun, D. H., & Dan, Y. F. (2010). Traffic State Identification Methods Based on Cloud computing Model. Retrieved from http://202.164.55.108/CSE/CSE/traffic%20state.pdf

Marks, E. A. (2010). *Executive's Guide to Cloud Computing*. USA: John Wiley and Sons.

Marston, S., Li, Z., Bandyopadhyay, S., Zhang, J., & Ghalsasi, A. (2011). Cloud computing — The business perspective. *Decision Support Systems, 51*(1), 176–189. doi:10.1016/j.dss.2010.12.006

Oliveira, T., Thomas, M., & Espadanal, M. (2014). Assessing the determinants of cloud computing adoption: An analysis of the manufacturing and services sectors. *Information & Management, 51*(5), 497–510. doi:10.1016/j.im.2014.03.006

Porter, S. (2004). Pros and Cons of Paper and Electronic Surveys. In *New Directions for Institutional Resaerch* (Vol. 2004, pp. 23–38). Wiley Periodicals, Inc. doi:10.1002/ir.103

Qayyum, J., Khan, F., Lal, M., Gul, F., Sohaib, M., & Masood, F. (2011). Implementing and Managing framework for PaaS in Cloud Computing. *International Journal of Computer Science Issues, 8*(5), 474–479.

Rouse, M. (2009). Traffic State Identification Methods Based on Cloud computing Model). Public Cloud. Retrieved from http://searchcloudcomputing.techtarget.com/definition/public-cloud

Schubert, L. (2010). Traffic State Identification Methods Based on Cloud computing Model). The Future of Cloud Computing-Opportunities for European Cloud Computing Beyond 2010. Retrieved from http://cordis.europa.eu/fp7/ict/ssai/docs/cloud-report-final.pdf

Schulz, W. (2009). What is SaaS, Cloud Computing, PaaS and IaaS? Retrieved from http://www.s-consult.com/2009/08/04/what-is-saas-cloud-computing-paas-and-iaas/

Singh, A., & Malhotra, M. (2012). Agent Based Framework for Scalability in Cloud Computing *International Journal of Computer Science & Engineering Technology*, April, 41-45.

Son, I., Lee, D., Lee, J.-N., & Chang, Y. B. (2014). Market perception on cloud computing initiatives in organizations: An extended resource-based view. *Information & Management, 51*(6), 653–669. doi:10.1016/j.im.2014.05.006

Stevens, J. (1992). *Applied multivariate statistics for the social sciences. NJ.* Hillsdale: Erlbaum.

Velte, A. T., Velte, T. J., & Elsenpeter, R. (2010). *Cloud Computing - A Practical Approach.* USA: McGraw Hill.

Viswanathan, P. (2012). Cloud Computing – Is It Really All That Beneficial? Retrieved from http://mobiledevices.about.com/od/additionalresources/a/Cloud-Computing-Is-It-Really-All-That-Beneficial.htm

VMware. (2010). Public Cloud Service Definition (Technical White Paper). Retrieved from http://www.vmware.com/files/pdf/VMware-Public-Cloud-Service-Definition.pdf

Vouk, M. A. (2008). Cloud Computing – Issues, Research and Implementations. *Journal of Computing and Information Technology, 16*(4), 235–246. doi:10.2498/cit.1001391

Wei, X., Zhang, J., & Zeng, S. (2009). Study of the Potential SaaS Platform Provider in China. *Proceedings of the 2009 WRI World Congress on Software Engineering, 4*, 78-80.

Wyld, D. (2010). The Cloudy Future of Government It: Cloud Computing and the Public Sector around the World. *International Journal of Web & Semantic Technology, 1*(1).

Ye, X. (2011). Cloud Computing Era Dawns for China's Navigation Industry Retrieved from http://english.peopledaily.com.cn/90882/7455078.html

Zaheer. (2012). China has the largest number of internet users with more than 500 million people. Retrieved from http://www.americanlivewire.com/china-has-the-largest-number-of-internet-users-with-more-than-500-million-people/

Zhang, Y. (2010). Cloud Computing Assisted Instructions in China. *Education and Information Technologies, 2*, 438–440.

Zhou, M., Zhang, R., Xie, W., & Qian, W. (2010). Security and Privacy in Cloud Computing: A Survey. *Proceedings of the 2010 Sixth International Conference on Semantics, Knowledge and Grids* (pp. 105-112).

Zissis, D., & Lekkas, D. (2011). Securing e-Government and e-Voting with an open cloud computing architecture. *Government Information Quarterly*, 2–13.

Zissis, D., & Lekkas, D. (2012). Addressing Cloud Computing Security Issues. *Future Generation Computer Systems, 28*(3), 583–592. doi:10.1016/j.future.2010.12.006

ADDITIONAL READING

Anderson, A., & Strecker, M. (2012). Sustainable Development: A Case for Education. *Environment: Science and Policy for Sustainable Development, 54*(6), 3-16.

Berl, A., Gelenbe, E., Di Girolamo, M., Giuliani, G., Meer, H., Dang, M., & Pentikousis, K. (2010). Energy-Efficient Cloud Computing. *The Computer Journal, 53*(7), 1046–1051. doi:10.1093/comjnl/bxp080

Buyya, R., Yeo, C. S., Venugopal, S., Broberg, J., & Brandic, I. (2009). Cloud Computing and emerging IT Platforms: Vision, hype, and reality for delivering computing as the 5th utility. *Future Generation Computer Systems, 25*(6), 599–616. doi:10.1016/j.future.2008.12.001

Goldsmith, S., & Samson, D. (2006). *Sustainable Development and Business Success*. Melbourne: Thomson.

Groot, M. (2008). *Metrics and Criteria for Success in Infrastructure Managing Financial Information in The Trade Lifecycle* (pp. 217–251). Burlington: Academic Press.

Grossman, R. L. (2009). The Case for Cloud Computing. Retrieved from Computer.org/ITPro

Hamm, S. (2008). Cloud Computing: Eyes on the Skies. Retrieved from http://www.businessweek.com/magazine/content/08_18/b4082059989191.htm

Hayward, B. (2012). Sustainable ICT. *Telecommunications Journal of Australia, 62*(5), 1–10. doi:10.7790/tja.v62i5.373

Issa, T., Chang, V., & Issa, T. (2010). The Impact of Cloud Computing and Organizational Sustainability. *Proceedings of the Cloud Computing and Virtualization 2010*, Singapore.

Issa, T., Chang, V., & Issa, T. (2010). Sustainable Business Strategies and PESTEL Framework. *GSTF International Journal on Computing, 1*(1), 73–80.

Issa, T., Issa, T., & Chang, V. (2011). Would teaching sustainable development business strategies shift students' mindsets? An Australian experience. *The International Journal of Environmental, Cultural. Economic & Social Sustainability, 7*(5), 257–272.

Jagers, N. (2009). Bringing Corporate Social Responsibility to the World Trade Organisation. In D. McBarnet, A. Voiculescu, & T. Campbell (Eds.), *The New Corporate Accountability - Corporate Social Responsibility and the Law* (pp. 177–206). Cambridge.

Lee, Y. C., & Zomaya, A. Y. (2012). Energy efficient utilization of resources in Cloud Computing systems. *The Journal of Supercomputing 60*(2), 268–280.

Mayo, R., & Perng, C. (2009). Cloud Computing Payback: An explanation of where the ROI comes from.

Mell, P., & Grance, T. (2011). *The NIST Definition of Cloud Computing*.

O'Neill, R. (2006). The advantages and disadvantages of qualitative and quantitative research methods. Retrieved from http://www.roboneill.co.uk/papers/research_methods.htm

O'Toole, W. (2011). *Event metrics and checklists Events Feasibility and Development* (pp. 231–250). Oxford: Butterworth-Heinemann. doi:10.1016/B978-0-7506-6640-4.10011-1

Poston, L. (2008). Computers Without Borders: Cloud Computing and Political Manipulation. Retrieved from http://profy.com/2008/05/25/cloudcomputingpolitics/

Prasad, A., Saha, S., Mishra, P., Hooli, B., & Murakami, M. (2010). Back to Green. *Journal of Green Engineering*, 1(1), 89-110.

Preston, R. (2008). Will Cloud Computing Rain On IT's Parade? *Information Week*, *1173*, 52.

Rainey, D. (2006). *Sustainable Business Development*. UK: Cambridge University Press. doi:10.1017/CBO9780511617607

Scott, J., Stahel, W., Lovins, H., & Grayson, D. (2010). *The Sustainable Business.*

Wakkary, R. (2009). *A Sustainable Identity: Creativity of Everyday Design.* Paper presented at the CHI2009. doi:10.1145/1518701.1518761

Weybrecht, G. (2010). *The Sustainable MBA - The Manager's Guide to Green Business.* UK: John Wiley & Sons.

Wirtenberg, J. (2009). *Beyond Green: Going Green and Sustainable Environments Transitioning to Green.* Retrieved from http://www.greenbaumlaw.com/Wirtenberg.ppt

KEY TERMS AND DEFINITIONS

Cloud Computing and Green IT: Smart Technology used to reduce energy and e-waste.

Cloud Computing Services: services made available to users via the Internet, i.e. SaaS (Software as a Service), PaaS (Platform as a Service) and IaaS (Infrastructure as a Service).

Cloud Computing Strategy: approach used by organizations to reduce energy, carbon emission and e-waste.

Cloud Computing Strengths: are flexible, efficient, scalable, reliable, reduce cost and maintenance.

Cloud Computing Weakness: are security, legal and law, privacy, physical location of data and unavailability of service due to crashes or bugs in the providers' storage.

Chapter 11
Green and Energy–Efficient Computing Architecture for E–Learning

K. Palanivel
Pondicherry University, India

S Kuppuswami
Kongu Engineering College, India

ABSTRACT

Information and Communication Technology (ICT) is one of the fast growing industries that facilitate many latest services to the users and therefore, the number of users is increasing rapidly. The usage of ICT and its life cycle produce hazardous substances that need to be addressed in efficient and green ways. The adoption of green computing involves many improvements and provide energy-efficiency services for data centers, power management and cloud computing. Cloud computing is a highly scalable and cost-effective infrastructure for running Web applications. However, the growing demand of Cloud infrastructure has drastically increased the energy consumption of data centers, which has become a critical issue. Hence, energy-efficient solutions are required to minimize the impact of Cloud environment. E-learning methodology is an example of Green computing. Thus, it is proposed a Green Cloud Computing Architecture for e-Learning Applications that can lower expenses and reduce energy consumption.

INTRODUCTION

Energy consumption is a bottleneck for Information computing and communication. Internet has provided an unlimited potential with access to eBooks, multimedia content, news, new ideas, and information access in general but, due to poor broadband infrastructure and available grid power to support the Internet and ICT growth the, developing regions have actually been left even further behind. The basic requirements in any developing region are a reliable electric power grid, network infrastructure, education, jobs, and a stable government and banking system.

DOI: 10.4018/978-1-4666-9834-5.ch011

With the growth of high speed networks over the last decades, there is an alarming rise in its usage comprised of thousands of concurrent e-commerce transactions and millions of Web queries a day. This ever-increasing demand is handled through large-scale datacenters, which consolidate hundreds and thousands of servers with other infrastructure such as cooling, storage and network systems. Many internet companies such as Google, Amazon, eBay, and Yahoo are operating such huge datacenters around the world. Traditionally, business organizations used to invest huge amount of capital and time in acquisition and maintenance of computational resources.

The emergence of Cloud computing is rapidly changing this *ownership-based* approach to *subscription-oriented* approach by providing access to scalable infrastructure and services on-demand. Moreover, Cloud computing also offers enormous amount of compute power to organizations which require processing of tremendous amount of data generated almost every day.

Cloud Computing provides an appropriate pool of computing resources with its dynamic scalability and usage of virtualized resources as a service through the Internet [Poonam, 2014]. The resources can be network servers, applications, platforms, infrastructure segments and services. It delivers services autonomously based on demand and provides sufficient network access, data resource environment and effectual flexibility. This technology is used for more efficient and cost effective computing by centralizing storage, memory, computing capacity of PC's and servers.

Cloud computing is a highly scalable and cost-effective infrastructure for running High Performance Computing (HPC), enterprise and Web applications [Ashish, 2013]. However, the growing demand of Cloud infrastructure has drastically increased the energy consumption of data centers, which has become a critical issue. The use of large shared virtualized datacenters, Cloud Computing can offer large energy savings. Also, the Cloud services can also further increase the internet traffic and its growing information database which could decrease such energy savings [Kamble 2013].

Cloud uses thousands of data-centers in order to process the user queries and to run these data-centers bulk amount of power is used for cooling and other processes. Every year this power consumption is gradually increasing and green cloud computing endeavors to reduce the same thus playing a helpful role to curb these issues. One area of research focuses on reduction in energy consumption and reduce the total power consumption by balancing load and effectively utilizing only a subset of the resources at hand. Some form of load balancing to save power during different load conditions. Many techniques are used to measure the power consumption in data-centers.

Many articles are been released on how Cloud Computing helps the developing world by just lowering ICT costs but, here it introduces Green computing aiming to reduce energy cost and CO_2 emissions as well as to effectively reuse and recycle power usage making the world *go-green*. Green computing is the environmentally responsible use of computers and related resources (Kaur 2014).

The approaches to Green Computing on Educational Institutions are power management, e-mail, on-line learning and energy/cost saving measures. Many institutions have chosen to include information on their websites about green computing efforts and how to reduce carbon footprints. Hence, energy efficient solutions are required to ensure the environmental sustainability of this new computing paradigm.

Green Cloud computing is envisioned to achieve not only efficient processing and utilization of computing infrastructure, but also minimize energy consumption [Gaganjot 2013]. Cloud computing with increasingly pervasive front-end client devices interacting with back-end data centers will cause an enormous escalation of energy usage. To address this problem, data center resources need to be managed in an energy-efficient manner to drive Green Cloud computing.

The energy efficiency of ICT has become a major issue with the growing demand of Cloud Computing. The educational cloud computing [Anjali 2013] can focus the power of thousands of computers on one problem, allowing researchers search and find models and make discoveries faster than ever. The Educational Institutions can also open their technology infrastructures to private, public sectors for research advancements. The role of cloud computing at Educational Institutions should not be underestimated as it can provide important gains in offering direct access to a wide range of different academic resources, research applications and educational tools. The architecture of an e-learning system [Palanivel 2014] developed as a distributed application, includes a client application, an application server and a database server, beside the hardware to support it.

Motivation

As new distributed computing technologies like Clouds become increasingly popular, the dependence on power also increases. One of the fundamental aspects of virtualization technologies employed in Cloud environments is resource consolidation and management. Using hypervisors within a cluster environment allows for a number of standalone physical machines to be consolidated to a virtualized environment, thereby requiring less physical resources than ever before. While this improves the situation, it often is inadequate. Large Cloud deployments require thousands of physical machines and megawatts of power. Therefore, there is a need to create an efficient Cloud computing system that utilizes the strengths of the Cloud while minimizing its energy and environmental footprint.

While the economic costs of operating the world's data centers can be extremely staggering as a whole, there is also another important consideration; the Environment. As current data center energy consumption is estimated at 2.4%, the overall CO_2 emissions due to the data centers represents sobering reality to the environmental impact the industry has created.

To properly address the sustainability of data centers, it would make sense to focus primarily on the sources of energy. In the meantime, it is imperative to focus on the data centers themselves to improve efficiency, not only for economic reasons, but also for the environment. Therefore, improving the energy efficiency within data centers does not look to revolutionize their sustainability, but instead to improve upon an already existing infrastructure. It is important to make what energy efficiency enhancements we can in order to minimize the global climate impact. With the tremendous advantages of Green Cloud computing, this technology is revolutionized the field of e-learning education.

Many supercomputers and large scale data centers are operated at a power envelope on the scale of Megawatts or even tens of Megawatts. Throughout the past, many of these resources were operated at an institutional level, where such power concerns were not dealt with directly by those that operate or administer such a data center. However recently these energy requirements have grown so large that institutions are starting to feel the economic burden.

Energy is an increasingly scarce and expensive resource. Now and in the future, green computing will be a key challenge for businesses and presents a leadership opportunity for all architects. When measuring the effectiveness of application architecture, there are several key criteria by which it can be measured. First and foremost, is the architecture's ability to fulfill the requirements. These requirements often include specific, measurable items relating to cost, scalability, testability, and so forth.

The key factors that have enabled the Cloud computing to lower energy usage and carbon emissions from ICT are *dynamic provisioning*, *multi-tenancy*, *server utilization* and *data center* efficiency

[Accenture 2010]. Due to these Cloud features, organizations can reduce carbon emissions by moving their applications to the Cloud. These savings are driven by the high efficiency of large scale Cloud data centers. Improving the resource utilization and reduce power consumption are key challenges to the success of operating a cloud computing environment. To address such challenges, it is proposed to design the Green - Cloud architecture for data center such e-Learning.

Objective

The aim of this chapter is to reduce the energy consumption by the data centers by performing optimal management of resources so as to keep some of the nodes in the data center groundless during low load conditions in the data centers. There is a possibility of migrating Virtual Machine (VM) in order to make some of the nodes groundless so that they can be shut down and the energy consumed by these nodes may be perpetuate.

Hence, it is proposed to design a Cloud-Oriented Green Computing Architecture for e-Learning Applications (COGALA). The COGALA Architecture for reducing the carbon footprint of Cloud Computing in a wholesome manner without sacrificing the Quality such as performance, responsiveness and availability offered by multiple Cloud providers. The COGALA consists of the client (e.g. can be a University or an Educational Institution), a client-oriented green cloud middleware and the green broker. The green cloud middleware provide the client a tool to better manage the distribution of tasks to cloud with the least carbon emission (i.e. least power consumption) and other relevant decision criteria. The middleware is composed of a user interface application and a windows service. This architecture is designed such that it provides incentives to both users and providers to utilize and deliver the most "Green" services respectively. Also, it addresses the environmental problem from the overall usage of Cloud Computing resources.

This chapter is organized as follows: Section 2 introduces about various technical details that required to write this chapter. Section 3 surveyed various architectures such as service-oriented, cloud-oriented and Green-Oriented. The proposed architecture is depicted in section 4 and finally section 5 concludes this chapter.

BACKGROUND

This section introduces Cloud Computing and its deployment/service models, Green Computing, impact of E-learning in Cloud Computing, Cloud Computing and energy usage, various energy efficiency models, etc.

e-Learning

e-Learning can be delivered and supported using a variety of electronic media, but is also the ideal complement to a traditional education or training program delivery. These technologies are used to create and deliver individualized, comprehensive, dynamic learning content that facilitates learning, anytime and anywhere. It is an innovative approach to communicating almost any type of instructional information.

e-Learning can be delivered and supported using a variety of electronic media but is also the ideal complement to a traditional education or training program. e- Learning is instruction that occurs when the instructor and the students are separated by time, distance, or both.

- **Synchronous Learning:** Synchronous e-Learning or training happens in real time with an instructor facilitating the training. Most commonly this type of learning may take place over the Internet using a variety of communication tools. The student logs in at a specific time and communicates directly with the instructor and/or other students. Synchronous e-Learning may also be accomplished through telephone, video conferencing, or two-way live television broadcasts between instructors and students in remote locations.
- **Asynchronous Learning:** Asynchronous e-Learning may be CD, DVD-ROM, Intranet, or Internet based. Students generally work on an interactive self-paced program of study. This may include access to instructors or experts through online bulletin boards, discussion groups, and e-mail. Programs may also be completely self-contained with links to various reference materials in place of an instructor. Asynchronous eLearning allows students to learn anywhere and usually at any time, as long as they have the proper equipment.

e-Learning has substantial benefits and offers unique opportunities for people who might otherwise have limited access to education and training. It incorporates innovative and creative approaches to instruction and provides unprecedented access to resources and information. e-learning methods have drastically changed the educational environment and also reduced the use of papers and ultimately reduce the production of carbon footprint. E-learning methodology is an example of Green computing.

Green Computing/Green IT

Green Computing is actually the study and practice of using and disposing of computers, servers and the associated subsystems such as monitors, printers, networking and systems of communications with minimal impact on nature.

The goals of Green Computing are:

1. To reduce the use of hazardous materials.
2. To maximize energy efficiency during the lifetime of the products.
3. To recycle the defunct products and factory wastage in order to enable biodegradability.

Green IT is not any application which can be incorporated into any existing systems or a product. It is actually an improvement over the existing systems and the way to move forward with the existing IT infrastructure. It is now high time we start working towards keeping the air clean, save our valuable resources like soil, water, fuel sources for our successors apart from saving finances as this is the biggest asset which we can pass it down to the future generations. Green IT also refers to the solutions of IT that saves energy.

Green ICT is referred from different stakeholders including IT analysts, vendors and providers that save energy at many levels like hardware, software and services within the business organizations. Green ICT also includes eco-friendly procurement, employee behavior, running data centers on sustainable generated energy, environmentally sound disposal of used electrical equipment, and as much recycling as possible. It is known that ICT is not basically green, because it itself consumes energy and resources during its production and lifetime. But ICT can be influenced to make business processes more energy-efficient, generating savings over and above the power input required for ICT itself. Green ICT allows a company with many facilities to reduce ongoing expenditure using energy-efficient hardware and intelligent utilizations of the infrastructures.

The adoption of green ICT is one of the important factors to achieve sustainable development in near future. It is a long term and continuous process from an individual to the top level organizational authorities where everyone needs to be concerned regarding this issue. All parties related to ICT industry like ICT manufacturers, vendors, service providers have to develop the green computing systems for the users and need to motivate them.

With the continuously increasing popularity and usage of cloud computing and the increasing awareness of the people across the globe towards the use of eco-friendly resources has forced the researchers to devise concepts towards an eco-friendly energy efficient flavor of cloud computing called *green cloud computing*. Green cloud computing facilitates the reduction of power consumption and CO_2 emission along with the reutilization of energy in an efficient way.

Cloud Computing

Cloud computing can be seen as a natural evolution of grid and utility computing. Grid computing delivers a high-performance computing system by combining and virtualizing a number of computing resources, distributed in multiple locations over the Internet, to solve very large computational problems. Utility computing involves the renting of computing resources on demand. The key concepts of cloud computing were adopted not only from grid and utility computing but also from existing IT technologies; for example, service-centered architecture (SOA), scalable and elastic IT resource delivery from virtualization models, and platform services from Web 2.0. More importantly, cloud computing can deploy many other additional features, such as scalability, flexibility, accessibility, reliability, and high performance, while reducing IT-related operating costs and implementing a green IT environment [Biswas, 2011].

Cloud computing is a model for enabling ubiquitous, convenient, on-demand network access to a shared pool of configurable computing resources (e.g., networks, servers, storage, applications, and services) that can be rapidly provisioned and released with minimal management effort or service provider interaction [Peter,2011]. The National Institute of Standards and Technology (NIST), in its definition of cloud computing, has identified five essential characteristics, four deployment models, and three service models of cloud computing. The five essential characteristics include on-demand self-service, rapid elasticity, measured service, broad network access, and resource pooling. The four deployment models are public, private, community, and hybrid cloud. Finally, the three service models include Infrastructure as a Service (IaaS), Platform as Service (PaaS), and Software as a Service (SaaS).

Cloud computing is offering on-demand services to end users. Clouds are deployed on physical infrastructure where Cloud middleware is implemented for delivering service to customers. Such an infrastructure and middleware differ in their services, administrative domain and access to users. Therefore, the Cloud deployments are classified mainly into three types: Public Cloud, Private Cloud and Hybrid Cloud.

- **Public Clouds:** Public Cloud is the most common deployment model where services are available to anyone on Internet. Some of the famous public Clouds are Amazon Web Services (AWS), Google AppEngine, and Microsoft Azure. Public Cloud offers very good solutions to the customers having small enterprise or with infrequent infrastructure usage, since these Clouds provide a very good option to handle peak loads on the local infrastructure and for an effective capacity planning.

- **Private Clouds:** The private Clouds are deployed within the premise of an organization to provide IT services to its internal users. The private Cloud services offer greater control over the infrastructure, improving security and service resilience because its access is restricted to one or few organizations. Such private deployment poses an inherent limitation to end user applications i.e. inability to scale elastically on demand as can be done using pubic Cloud services.

- **Hybrid Clouds:** Hybrid Clouds is the deployment which emerged due to diffusion of both public and private Clouds" advantages. In this model, organizations outsource non-critical information and processing to the public Cloud, while keeping critical services and data in their control.

- **Community Cloud:** In the community deployment model, the cloud infrastructure is shared by several organizations with the same policy and compliance considerations. This helps to further reduce costs as compared to a private cloud, as it is shared by larger group.

The available service models are classified as Software-as-a-Service (SaaS), Platform-as-a-Service (PaaS), and Infrastructure-as-a-Service (IaaS).

- **Infrastructure as a Service (IaaS)** is the supply of Hardware as a service (HaaS), that is, servers, net technology, storage or computation, as well as basic characteristics such as Operating Systems and virtualization of hardware resources [Hurwitz 2010]. Making an analogy with a mono computer system, the IaaS will correspond to the hardware of such a computer together with the Operating System that take care of the management of the hardware resources and ease the access to them.

- **Platform as a Service (PaaS)** At the PaaS level, the provider supplies more than just infrastructure, i.e. an integrated set of software with all the stuff that a developer needs to build applications, both for the developing and for the execution stages. In this manner, a PaaS provider does not provide the infrastructure directly, but making use of the services of an IaaS it presents the tools that a developer needs, having an indirect access to the IaaS services and, consequently, to the infrastructure [Hurwitz 2010].

- **Software as a Service (SaaS)** In the last level we may find the SaaS, i.e. to offer software as a service. It has its origins in the host operations carried out by the Application Service Provider.

Cloud computing has shown to be a very effective paradigm according to its features such as on-demand self-service since the customers are able to provision computing capabilities without requiring any human interaction; broad network access from heterogeneous client platforms; resource pooling to serve multiple consumers; rapid elasticity as the capabilities appear to be unlimited from the consumer's point of view; and a measured service allowing a pay-per-use business model. However, there are also some weak points that should be taken into account. Next, we present some of these issues:

- **Security, privacy and confidence:** Since the data can be distributed on different servers, and "out of the control" of the customer, there is a necessity of managing hardware for computation with encoding data by using robust and efficient methods. Also, in order to increase the confidence of the user, several audits and certifications of the security must be performed.
- **Availability, fault tolerance and recovery:** to guarantee a permanent service (24x7) with the use of redundant systems and to avoid net traffic overflow.
- **Scalability:** In order to adapt the necessary resources under changing demands of the user by providing an intelligent resource management, an effective monitorization can be used by identifying a priori the usage patterns and to predict the load in order to optimize the scheduling.
- **Energy efficiency:** It is also important to reduce the electric charge by using microprocessors with a lower energy consumption and adaptable to their use.

Energy Usage Model Using Cloud

The Cloud Computing model is for where the data is to be distributed, so that knowledge resources will be used by all sorts of user in the education streams. Clouds are essentially virtualized datacenters and applications offered as services on a subscription basis. They require high energy usage for its operation [Bianchini 2004]. For a datacenter, the energy cost is a significant component of its operating and up-front costs. Thus, energy consumption and carbon emission by Cloud infrastructures has become a key environmental concern.

The traditional data centers running Web applications are often provisioned to handle sporadic peak loads, which can result in low resource utilization and wastage of energy. Cloud datacenter, on the other hand, can reduce the energy consumed through server consolidation, whereby different workloads can share the same physical host using virtualization and unused servers can be switched off. Even the most efficiently built datacenter with the highest utilization rates will only mitigate, rather than eliminate, harmful CO_2 emissions. The reason given is that Cloud providers are more interested in electricity cost reduction rather than carbon emission. The Figure 1 shows that cloud and environmental sustainability.

Cloud computing, being an emerging technology also raises significant questions about its environmental sustainability. Through the use of large shared virtualized datacenters Cloud computing can offer large energy savings. However, Cloud services can also further increase the internet traffic and its growing information database which could decrease such energy savings. With energy shortages and global climate, the power consumption of data centers has become a key issue. Thus, there is a need of green cloud computing solutions that cannot only save energy, but also reduce operational costs.

According to Accenture Report [Accenture 2010], the dynamic provisioning, multi-tenancy, server utilization, data center efficiency, energy efficiency are four key factors that have enabled the Cloud computing to lower energy usage and carbon emissions from ICT. Due to these Cloud features, organizations can reduce carbon emissions by atleast 30% per user by moving their applications to the Cloud. These savings are driven by the high efficiency of large scale Cloud data centers.

e-Learning

e-learning is commonly referred to the intentional use of networked information and communications technology (ICT) in teaching and learning. Some other terms are also used to describe this mode of

Figure 1.

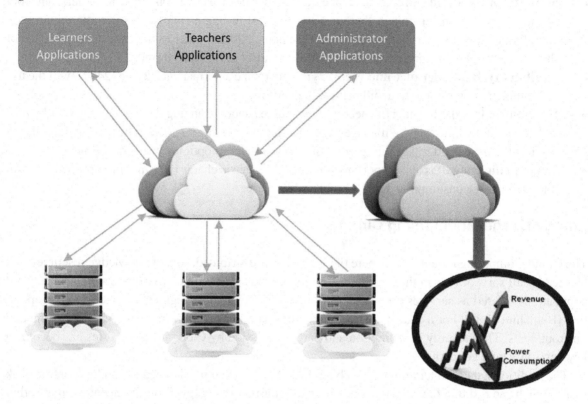

teaching and learning including online learning, virtual learning, distributed learning, network and web-based learning. The growth of e-learning is directly related to the increasing access to ICT, as well as its decreasing cost. The capacity of ICT to support multimedia resource-based learning and teaching is also relevant to the growing interest in e-learning. Usually, E-learning systems are developed as distributed applications, but not limited to. The architecture of an e-learning system, developed as a distributed application, includes a client application, an application server and a database server, beside the hardware to support it (client computer, communication infrastructure and servers). Among the learning technologies, web-based learning offers several benefits over conventional classroom-based learning. Its biggest advantages are the reduced costs since a physical environment is no longer required and therefore it can be used at any time and place for the convenience of the student.

Cloud computing applications provide flexibility for all educational universities, schools and institutions. The cloud platform in institutions' campuses provides effective infrastructure and deployment model for their dynamic demands. The benefits of cloud computing can support education institutions to resolve some of the common challenges such as cost reduction, quick and effective communication, security, privacy, flexibility and accessibility.

Cloud Computing for e-Learning

With the huge growth of the number of students, education contents, services that can be offered and resources made available, e-Learning system dimensions grow at an exponential rate. The challenges regarding this topic about optimizing resource computation, storage and communication requirements, and dealing with dynamic concurrency requests highlight the necessity of the use of a platform that meets scalable demands and cost control.

e-Learning in the Cloud can be viewed as Education Software-as-a-Service. Its deployment can be performed very quickly since the hardware requirements of the user are very low. Furthermore, as we stated previously, it lessens the burden of maintenance and support from the educational institution to the vendor, allowing them to focus on their core business, also obtaining the latest updates of the system without charges and sharing key resources using Web 2.0 technology.

Cloud Computing may promote a new era of learning taking the advantage of hosting the e-Learning applications on a cloud and following its virtualization features of the hardware, it reduces the construction and maintenance cost of the learning resources. At the present, the combination of cloud technologies and e-Learning has been scarcely explored. Some relevant efforts to use IaaS cloud technologies in education focuses on the reservation of Virtual Machines to students for a specific time frame.

One of the most interesting applications of cloud computing is educational cloud. The educational cloud computing can focus the power of thousands of computers on one problem, allowing researchers search and find models and make discoveries faster than ever. The Universities can also open their technology infrastructures to private, public sectors for research advancements. The efficiencies of cloud computing can help universities keep pace with ever-growing resource requirements and energy costs. The role of cloud computing at University education should not be underestimated as it can provide important gains in offering direct access to a wide range of different academic resources, research applications and educational tools.

e-Learning Data Center

e-learning providers such as Amazon, Google, IBM, Microsoft, and Sun Microsystems have begun to establish new data centers for hosting Cloud computing applications in various locations around the world to provide redundancy and ensure reliability in case of site failures. Since user requirements for cloud services are varied, service providers have to ensure that they can be flexible in their service delivery while keeping the users isolated from the underlying infrastructure.

Figure 2 shows an end user accessing Cloud services such as SaaS, PaaS, or IaaS over Internet. User data pass from his own device through an Internet service providers' router, which in turn connects to a Gateway router within a Cloud datacenter. Within datacenters, data goes through a local area network and are processed on virtual machines, hosting Cloud services, which may access storage servers. Each of these computing and network devices that are directly accessed to serve Cloud users contribute to energy consumption. In addition, within a Cloud datacenter, there are many other devices, such as cooling and electrical devices, that consume power. These devices even though do not directly help in providing Cloud service, are the major contributors to the power consumption of a Cloud datacenter.

- **User/Cloud Software Applications:** The Cloud computing can be used for running e-Learning applications owned by individual user or offered by the Cloud provider using SaaS. Here, eLearning applications are long running with high CPU and memory requirements then its execution will result in high energy consumption. Thus, energy consumption will be directly proportional to the e-Learning application's profile which will result in much higher energy consumption than actually required.

Figure 2.

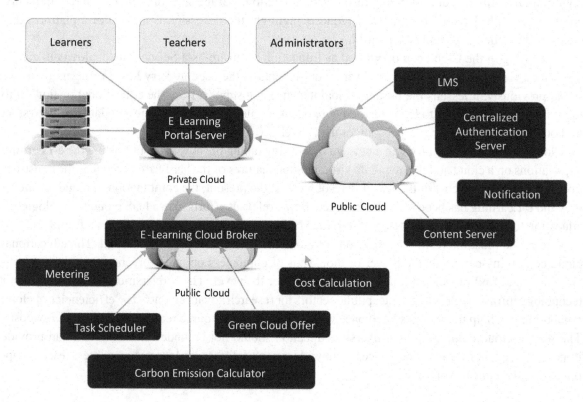

- **Cloud Software Stack:** The Cloud software stack leads to an extra overhead in execution of end user or learners applications. For instance, it is well known that a physical e-Learning applications server has higher performance efficiency than a virtual machine and IaaS providers offer generally access to a virtual machine to its end users [Cherkasova 2005].

- **Network Devices:** In Cloud computing, since resources are accessed through Internet, both applications and data are needed to be transferred to the compute node. In e-Learning applications, if data is really large, then it may turn out to be cheaper and more carbon emission efficient to send the data by mail than to transfer through Internet. The energy consumption of these devices remains almost the same during both peak time and idle state.

- **Datacenter:** A cloud datacenter could comprise of many hundreds or thousands of networked computers with their corresponding storage and networking subsystems, power distribution and conditioning equipment, and cooling infrastructures. These datacenters can consume massive energy consumption and emit large amount of carbon. Thus, to achieve the maximum efficiency in power consumption and CO_2 emissions, each of these devices need to be designed and used efficiently while ensuring that their carbon footprint is reduced. Power Usage Effectiveness (PUE) [Rawson, 2008] is a key factor in achieving the reduction in power consumption of a datacenter is to calculate how much energy is consumed in cooling and other overheads. PUE of datacenter can be useful in measuring power efficiency of datacenters and thus provide a motivation to improve its efficiency.

Green Computing for e-Learning

With the huge growth of the number of students, education contents, services that can be offered and resources made available, e-Learning system dimensions grow at an exponential rate. The challenges regarding this topic about optimizing resource computation, storage and communication requirements, energy efficiency and dealing with dynamic concurrency requests highlight the necessity of the use of a platform that meets scalable demands and cost control.

From the above study of current efforts in making Cloud computing energy efficient, it shows that even though researchers have made various components of Cloud efficient in terms of power and performance, still they lack a unified picture. Cloud providers, being profit oriented, are looking for solutions which can reduce the power consumption and thus, carbon emission without hurting their market. Therefore, it is provided provide a unified solution to enable e-Learning using Green Cloud Computing.

E-learning methods have drastically changed the educational environment and also reduced the use of papers and ultimately reduce the production of carbon footprint. e-Learning methodology is an example of Green computing. Green Computing or Green IT refers to the study and practice of using computing resources in an eco-friendly manner in order to tone down the environmental impacts of computing. It is the practice of using computing resources in an energy efficient and environmentally friendly manner. To reduce unnecessary energy consumption due to hazardous materials has become a major topic of concern today. The potential approaches to Green computing are power management, energy efficiency, working online, e-mail, virtualization, and cloud computing.

This section discussed about e-Learning, Green Computing, Cloud Computing, Cloud Computing and Energy Usage, features of clouds that enabling green computing, energy efficiency models, etc.

REVIEW OF EXISITNG WORKS

This section presents the existing works starting from ubiquitous computing, cloud computing, green computing, cloud green computing and various e-Learning architectures.

Cloud Computing and Data Centers

In [Jadeja 2012], the author presents that with the advent internet in the 1990s to the present day facilities of ubiquitous computing, the internet has changed the computing world in a drastic way. Cloud computing is a recent trends in IT that moves computing and data away from desktop and portable PCs into large data centers. There is a discussion on architectural design of cloud computing, its applications and issues that are security and privacy with its solutions.

In [Bhushan 2012], an author says that cloud computing is becoming an increasingly popular enterprise model in which computing resources are made available on-demand to the user as needed. It provide a comprehensive study on the motivation factors of adopting cloud computing, review the several cloud deployment and service models. There explore certain benefits of cloud computing over traditional IT service environment-including scalability, flexibility, reduced capital and higher resource utilization-are considered as adoption reasons for cloud computing environment. At last, it includes security, privacy, internet dependency and availability as avoidance issues.

In [Saroja 2011], the authors discussed on Cloud Computing that has become a scalable service consumption and delivery platform in the modern IT infrastructure. Cloud Computing is a style of computing which must cater to the following computing needs: Dynamism, Abstraction and Resource Sharing. The architecture, types of cloud, barriers to cloud, and creating an instance in Amazon has been discussed. Besides, the usage of Traditional Enterprise Datacenter Utilization, Virtualized Enterprise Datacenter Utilization and Cloud Enterprise Datacenter Utilization are compared.

In [Shengmei 2011], various authors discussed Virtualization as it is a term that refers to the abstraction of computer resources. The purpose of virtual computing environment is to improve resource utilization by providing a unified integrated platform for users and applications based on aggregation of heterogeneous and autonomous resources.

In [Pushtikant 2013], authors introduces a computer paradigm that is shifted to remote data centers from past few years and the software and hardware services available on the basis of pay for use. Data center management faces the problem of power consumption. This survey paper shows the requirement of green computing and techniques to save the energy by different approaches.

Green Computing or Green IT refers to the study and practice of using computing resources in an eco-friendly manner in order to tone down the environmental impacts of computing. It is the practice of using computing resources in an energy efficient and environmentally friendly manner.

In [Sharmila 2013], authors says Green computing, also called green technology, is the environmentally sustainable to use of computers and related resources like - monitors, printer, storage devices, networking and communication systems - efficiently and effectively with minimal or no impact on the environment.

In [Massoud 2012], author discussed about the pervasive use of cloud computing and the resulting rise in the number of data centers and hosting centers have brought forth many concerns including the electrical energy cost, peak power dissipation, cooling, carbon emission, etc. With power consumption becoming an increasingly important issue for the operation and maintenance of the hosting centers, corporate and business owners are becoming increasingly concerned.

In [Kyong 2011], authors says that survey shows that management techniques tailored to different types of servers and their associated workloads can provide substantial energy savings with little or no performance degradation.

In [Bianchini 2004], authors presented the today's environmental challenge is global warming, which caused by emission of carbon. The energy crisis brings green computing and green computing needs algorithm and mechanism to be redesigned for energy efficiency. This paper concluded that task consolidation particularly in clouds has become an important approach to streamline resources usage and in turn improve energy efficiency.

Authod [Shalabh 2013] discussed how Green Computing can be incorporated into different institutions, corporate/business sectors or may be in various IT companies.

In [Kaur 2014], the authors discussed about substituting to remote data centers on the basis of pay per use. Data Centre management faces the problem of power consumption. Green computing can give power to more energy efficient use of computing power. At last, Green computing is discussed.

In [Ankita 2013], the authors survey the key techniques to reduce the energy consumption and CO_2 emission that can cause severe health issues. We begin with a discussion on green matrices appropriate for data-centers and then throw light on green scheduling algorithms that facilitate reduction in energy consumption and CO_2 emission levels in the existing systems. At the same time the various existing architectures related to green cloud also discussed in this paper with their pros and cons.

In [Ujwala 2013], the authors released on how Cloud Computing helps the developing world by just lowering ICT costs but, here we introduce Green computing aiming to reduce energy cost and CO2 emissions as well as to effectively reuse and recycle power usage making the world go-green. This paper presents an approach for a low energy use data centers using cloud computing designed for developing regions, powered with renewable energy.

To reduce unnecessary energy consumption due to hazardous materials has become a major topic of concern today. The use of Green Cloud Computing has increased substantially in the recent past. A lot of research has been done to incorporate and enhance the applicability of Green Cloud in real life scenarios with these help of various parameters. Usage of energy is dramatically increases in data centers.

Authors [Cavdar 2012] and [Jain 2013] introduced for improving the energy efficiency of the running data centers, the Green grid is proposing some parameters like Power Usage Effectiveness (PUE) [White 2007] and Data Centre Efficiency (DCE) metrics [Rassmussen 2007].

PUE is the common parameter. According to Wikipedia "PUE is a measure of how efficiently a computer datacenter uses its power "The range of PUE is varies from 1.0 to infinity. If the value of PUE approaching 1.0 it means efficiency is 100% and full power is used by IT equipment's.

Author [Satoh 2013] also focus on reducing the usage of energy in data centers. But for the future energy management they develop an energy management System for cloud by the use of sensor management function with an optimized VM allocation tool. This system will help to reduce the energy consumption in multiple data centers and results shows that it will save 30% of energy. This system also used to reduce the energy in carbon emissions.

Cooling is other major issue that consumes huge amount of energy in data centers. Previously, the cooling is done by using mechanical refrigerator that supply chilled water for the IT equipment's. Now a day's pre cooling also called as free cooling is used. Free cooling minimizes the use of mechanical cooling. There are different hardware technologies like virtualization and software technologies like software efficient algorithm used to decrease the consumption of energy.

Author [Beik 2012] proposes an energy aware layer in software –architecture that calculate the energy consumption in data centers and provide services to the users which uses energy efficiently.

Author [Kaur 2013] performed the different challenges in the field of energy in cloud computing, a model is proposed by author to calculate the energy wasted by producing various gases in environment. The proposed model contains various fields Data, Analysis, Record, Put on guard, restrain along with the virtualization concept in green cloud to make it energy efficient and for healthy environment.

According to [Kliazovich 2010], expenses on cloud data centers maintenance and operation done in cloud are gradually increasing. In this paper author has focused on the work load distribution among the data centers so that energy consumption can be calculated in terms of packet level.

Author [Hosman 2013], gave a new challenge in the field of cloud computing, datacenters consumes a lot of energy and energy is available every time is not necessary, so the author is discussing in his paper about the solar energy. How the solar energy can play a vital role in data centers energy consumption is the hot topic of discussion. In this paper author proposed a small level cloud data center which is the combination of three technologies are "less power consumption platform, energy efficient cloud computing and DC power distribution".

Author [Owusu 2012] performed a survey to establish the current state of the art in the area of energy efficiency in cloud computing. They beautifully mention the field of energy efficiency as a controversial area to cloud computing. This paper discusses one area of controversy; the energy efficiency of cloud computing.

Author [Yamini 2012] introduced the key approaches like virtualization, Power Management, Recycling of material and telecommuting of green cloud computing very beautifully. The major focus of this paper is the consolidation or scheduling of task and resource utilization in green cloud computing to reduce the high consumption of energy. The decent results shown in the paper not for the direct drastic energy reduction but applies possible saving of electricity in huge cloud data centers.

According [Grg 2012], the demand of cloud is drastically increasing now a day and the consumption of energy and excretion of harmful gases is also extreme which is very harmful and a big issue in the field of health care and also a big reason of the increase in cost of operations in cloud. The author gave a presentable and evidential literature survey of the various different members of cloud which participate in the total energy consumption. Structure of cloud are discussed in this paper which turn on the use of green cloud computing.

In [Garg 2011], author contributes carbon green cloud architecture which points on the third party concept, consist of two types of directories named as green offer and carbon emission. These directories help us to provide and utilize the Green services from users and providers both. Green brokers access the services from green offers directory and scheduled services according to least CO2 emission.

In [Beloglazov 2010], author focuses on virtual machine for the reduction of the energy consumption. An author proposes the dynamic reallocation technique for VMs and toggles off the unused servers which results, considerable energy saving in the real Cloud Computing data centers.

In [Engin 2013], author presented some possible cloud solutions in e-learning environments by emphasizing its pros and cons. It is of paramount importance to choose the most suitable cloud model for an e-Learning application or an educational organization in terms of scalability, portability and security. We distinguish various deployment alternatives of cloud computing and discuss their benefits against typical e-learning requirements.

In [Tomm 2012] presented the real-time virtualized Cloud infrastructure that was developed in the context of the IRMOS European Project. The paper shows how different concepts, such as real-time scheduling, QoS-aware network protocols, and methodologies for stochastic modelling and run-time provisioning were practically combined to provide strong performance guarantees to soft real-time interactive applications in a Virtualized environment..

In [Anwar 2012] introduced the characteristics of the current E-Learning and then analyses the concept of cloud computing and describes the architecture of cloud computing platform by combining the features of E-Learning. The authors have tried to introduce cloud computing to e-Learning, build an e-learning cloud, and make an active research and exploration for it from the following aspects: architecture, construction method and external interface with the model.

Cloud computing has attracted a great deal of attention in the education sector as a way of delivering more economical, securable, and reliable education services. [Ji 2013] proposed and introduces a cloud-based smart education system for e-learning content services with a view to delivering and sharing various enhanced forms of educational content, including text, pictures, images, videos, 3-dimensional (3D) objects, and scenes of virtual reality (VR) and augmented reality (AR).

This section discussed about various existing works in the area from ubiquitous computing, cloud computing, green computing, cloud green computing and various e-Learning architectures.

COGALA ARCHITECTURE

In order to correctly and completely unify a Green aspect to the next generation of Distributed Systems, a green-oriented architecture is needed. Green architectural design requires careful consideration, at a level of detail greater than what generally takes place today, and it requires software architects and infrastructure architects to work together.

Challenges/Requirements

Designing data centers for high performance and extreme low energy usage requires a vertically and horizontally integrated effort to drive key energy-efficient technologies in computing (cloud computing), electronics (low power CPUs and systems), and building systems (spot rack cooling, higher ambient temperatures, and natural convention cooling). Collectively, these existing and cutting edge technologies address very significant near-term and long-term energy and computing challenges and environmental issues.

A cloud infrastructure generally encapsulates all those existing technologies in a web service based model to offer business agility, improved scalability and on demand availability. Cloud applications are deployed in data centers (DCs) where high capacity servers and storage systems are located. A fast growth of demand for cloud based services results into establishment of enormous data centers consuming high amount of electrical power. Energy efficient model is required for complete infrastructure to reduce functional costs while maintaining vital Quality of Service (QoS). Energy optimization can be achieved by combining resources as per the current utilization, efficient virtual network topologies and thermal status of computing hardwares and nodes.

Why Cloud Architecture?

Cloud computing saves energy by employing workload diversification, power-management flexibility and low power CPU.

1. **Workload diversification:** Because many different sorts of users will be availing themselves of diverse cloud resources – different applications, different feature set preferences and different usage volumes – this will improve hardware utilization and therefore make better use of power that is being used anyway to keep a server up and running.
2. **Power-management flexibility:** It is easier to manage virtual servers than physical servers from a power perspective. If hardware fails, the load can automatically be deployed elsewhere. Likewise, in theory, all virtual loads could be moved to certain servers when loads are light and power-down or idle those that are not being used.
3. Low power CPUs have recently come to market thanks to a design for developing regions. Today's low power CPUs offer compute abilities that greatly exceed servers of even five years ago. The trend today for data centers is no longer for more and more compute power, but rather for a balance between power and energy efficiency. For developing world markets, the trend toward energy efficiency is more important than any other single factor.

Cloud Computing Architecture

Cloud computing has a significant impact on teaching and learning environment [Fern, 2012]. It is highly practical in education for both students and teachers. The cloud based environment supports the creation of new generation of e-learning systems. In traditional web-based learning model, educational institutions invest a huge amount of money on hardware and software applications, infrastructure, maintenance and the appropriate training of staff to enable them to use technology effectively. However, in cloud oriented e-learning model, educational institutions without any infrastructure investments can get powerful software with lower or no up-front costs and fewer management headaches in the classroom. The development of e-Learning services within the cloud computing environment enables users to access diverse software applications, share data, collaborate more easily, and keep their data safely in the infrastructure.

Figure 3 shows architecture for e-learning system that the cloud-oriented architecture [Manop 2012] separate into three layers includes infrastructure, platform and application. On Infrastructure layer, the learning resources from the traditional system are transferred to the cloud database instead of the usual DBMS. Whereas on Platform layer, a new e-learning system that consists of the CMS, AMS, and other service components were developed. These components were developed to be the intermediary between cloud database and the applications. Finally on application layer, web application were developed for interacting with the student's client.

As the adoption of cloud computing increases, many academic institutions are introducing cloud computing technologies into their education systems, promising and delivering more scalable and reliable education services.

Green Computing Architecture

Green Cloud Computing points to a processing infrastructure that combines flexibility, service quality, and reduced use of energy. Energy crisis fuels green computing, and green computing needs algorithms and mechanisms to be redesigned for energy efficiency. There is a need to use computing resources

Figure 3.

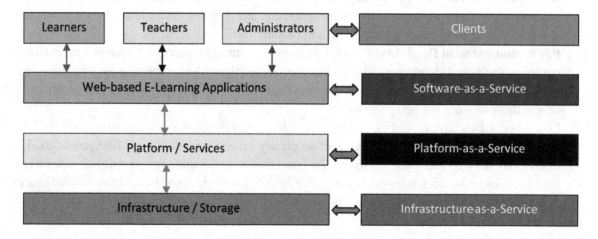

efficiently, effectively and economically. The various approaches to green information technology are *virtualization, power management, Materials Recycling* and *Telecommuting*. It is necessary to significantly reduce pollution and substantially lower power consumption.

The technology for energy efficient Clouds is "Virtualization," which allows significant improvement in energy efficiency of Cloud providers by leveraging the economies of scale associated with large number of organizations sharing the same infrastructure [Smith 2003]. By consolidation of underutilized servers in the form of multiple virtual machines sharing same physical server at higher utilization, companies can gain high savings in the form of space, management, and energy.

The Figure 4 shows the Cloud-Oriented Green Computing Architecture. In Green -Cloud computing infrastructure, there are four main entities involved and they are Consumers/Brokers, Green Resource Allocator, Virtual Machines (VMs) and Physical Machines. The *Cloud consumers* or their brokers submit service requests from anywhere in the world to the Cloud. It is important to notice that there can be a difference between Cloud consumers and users of deployed services.

The *Green Resource Allocator* acts as the interface between the Cloud infrastructure and consumers. It requires the interaction of the following components to support energy-efficient resource management. Multiple *Virtual Machines* (VMs) can be dynamically started and stopped on a single physical machine to meet accepted requests, hence providing maximum flexibility to configure various partitions of resources on the same physical machine to different specific requirements of service requests. Multiple VMs can also concurrently run applications based on different operating system environments on a single physical machine. The underlying *physical computing servers* provide hardware infrastructure for creating virtualized resources to meet service demands.

Green Cloud Architecture

Figure 5 shows architecture for e-learning system that the Green Cloud-oriented Architecture. The CO-GALA architecture can be divided into the following layers: *Infrastructure layer* as a dynamic and scalable physical host pool, *software resource layer* that offers a unified interface for e-learning developers,

Figure 4.

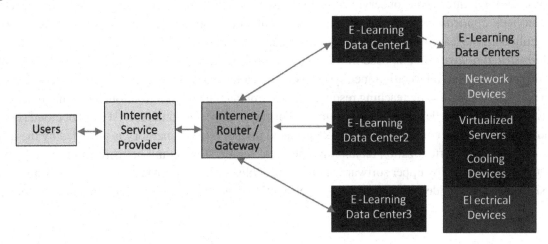

Figure 5.

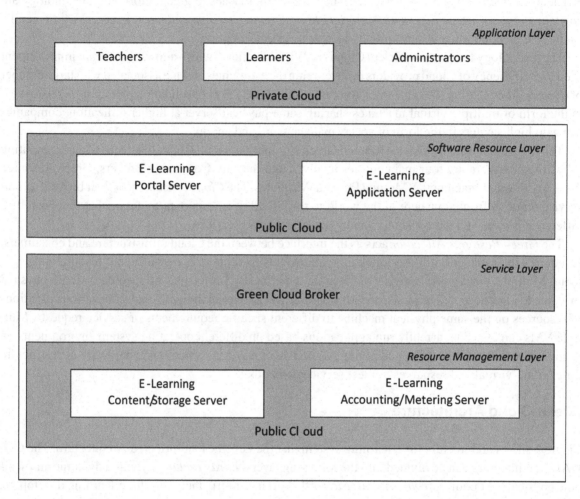

resource management layer that achieves loose coupling of software and hardware resources, *service layer*, containing three levels of services (software as a service, platform as a service and infrastructure as a service), *application layer* that provides with content production, content delivery, virtual laboratory, collaborative learning, assessment and management features.

Infrastructure layer is composed of information infrastructure and teaching resources. Information infrastructure contains Internet/Intranet, system software, information management system and some common software and hardware; teaching resources is accumulated mainly in traditional teaching model and distributed in different departments and domain. This layer is located in the lowest level of cloud service middleware, the basic computing power like physical memory, CPU, memory is provided by the layer. Through the use of virtualization technology, physical server, storage and network form virtualization group for being called by upper software platform. The physical host pool is dynamic and scalable, new physical host can be added in order to enhance physical computing power for cloud middleware services

The *Software Resource Layer* mainly is composed by operating system and middleware. Through middleware technology, a variety of software resources are integrated to provide a unified interface for software developers, so they can easily develop a lot of applications based on software resources and embed them in the cloud, making them available for cloud computing users.

The *Resource Management Layer* is the key to achieve loose coupling of software resources and hardware resources. Through integration of virtualization and cloud computing scheduling strategy, on-demand free flow and distribution of software over various hardware resources can be achieved.

The Service layer has three levels of services namely, SaaS (Software as a service), Paas (Platform as a service), and IaaS (Infrastructure as a service). In SaaS, cloud computing service is provided to customers. As is different from traditional software, users use software via the Internet, not to need a one-time purchase for software and hardware, and not to need to maintain and upgrade, simply paying a monthly fee.

The Application layer is the specific application of integration the teaching resources in the cloud computing model, including interactive courses and sharing the teaching resources. The interactive programs are mainly for the teachers, according to the learners and teaching needs, taken full advantage of the underlying information resources after finishing made, and the course content as well as the progress may at any time adjust according to the feedback, and can be more effectiveness than traditional teaching. Sharing of teaching resources include teaching material resources, teaching information resources (such as digital libraries, information centers), as well as the full sharing of human resources. This layer mainly consists of content production, educational objectives, content delivery technology, assessment and management component.

In the COGALA architecture, users submit their Cloud service requests through a new middleware. Green Broker that manages the selection of the greenest Cloud provider to serve the user's request. A user service request can be of three types i.e., software, platform or infrastructure. The Cloud providers can register their services in the form of green offers" to a public directory which is accessed by Green Broker. The green offers consist of green services, pricing and time when it should be accessed for least carbon emission. Green Broker gets the current status of energy parameters for using various Cloud services from Carbon Emission Directory. The Carbon Emission Directory maintains all the data related to energy efficiency of Cloud service. This data may include PUE and cooling efficiency of Cloud datacenter which is providing the service, the network cost and carbon emission rate of electricity, Green Broker calculates the carbon emission of all the Cloud providers who are offering the requested Cloud service. Then, it selects the set of services that will result in least carbon emission and buy these services on behalf users.

Energy Efficient Design

The COGALA architecture is designed such that it keeps track of overall energy usage of serving a user request. It relies on two main components, Carbon Emission and Green Cloud offers, which keep track of energy efficiency of each Cloud provider and also give incentive to Cloud providers to make their service "Green".

- **QoS requirements:** From user side, the Green Broker plays a crucial role in monitoring and selecting the Cloud services based on the user QoS requirements, and ensuring minimum carbon emission for serving a user. In general, a user can use Cloud to access any of these three types of services (SaaS, PaaS, and IaaS), and therefore process of serving them should also be energy efficient.

- **Green IT and cooling systems:** Cloud Computing use latest technologies for IT and cooling systems to have most energy efficient infrastructure. By using virtualization and consolidation, the energy consumption is further reduced by switching-off unutilized server. Various energy meters and sensors are installed and calculated the current energy efficiency of each service providers.

- **Green Grid:** To measure the unified efficiency of a datacenter and improve its' performance per-watt, the Green Grid has proposed two specific metrics known as the Power Usage Effectiveness (PUE) and Datacenter Infrastructure Efficiency (DciE).

PUE = Total Facility Power / IT Equipment Power

DCiE = 1 / PUE × 100

The Total Facility Power is defined as the power measured at the utility meter that is dedicated solely to the datacenter power. The IT Equipment Power is defined as the power consumed in the management, processing, and storage or routing of data within the datacenter.

- **Virtualization:** It is a term that refers to the abstraction of computer resources. Virtualization means "something which isn't real", but gives all the facilities of a real. It is the software implementation of a computer which will execute different programs like a real machine. At the very lowest layer is the actual hardware (Server). Above it is the virtualizing software Xen or VMware. The virtual machines capable of supporting a full operating system are known as system virtual machines. The hardware platform on which VM run is known as the host and the operating system running on the VM is known as the guest.

Pros and Cons

The expected benefits for which planned to implement COGALA are environment friendly, efficient and time saving. COGALA architecture has some constructive as well as destructive points. It gave the architecture for green cloud the major advantage of this architecture is Co2 emission directory, this directory measures the best suitable service which gives less carbon emission so straight away it indicates that energy will also decrease because Co2 emission and energy consumption both are directly proportionate to each other. Similarly the disadvantage is that only CO2 emission and energy is not the factor to be under consideration like Quality Provisioning, Security, etc. The major disadvantage which we observed here is that manager of the system is the central point of communication so if manager will crash then whole system will fall apart at the same time decision making done by manager is not intelligent and all work has been done manually.

FUTURE RESEARCH DIRECTIONS

The adoption of green ICT is one of the important factors to achieve sustainable development in near future. It is a long term and continuous process from an individual to the top level organizational authorities where everyone needs to be concerned regarding this issue. All parties related to ICT industry like ICT manufacturers, vendors, service providers have to develop the green computing systems for the users and need to motivate them. Individual awareness is one of the key features for green ICT adoption.

In this paper, it analyzed the benefits offered by Cloud computing by studying its fundamental definitions and benefits, the services it offers to end users, and its deployment model. E-learning system is facing challenges of optimizing large-scale resource management and provisioning, according to the huge growth of users, services, education contents and media resources. We have settle the goodness of a Cloud Computing solution. The features of the Cloud Computing platform are quite appropriate for the migration of this learning system, so that we can fully exploit the possibilities offered by the creation of an efficient learning environment that offers personalized contents and easy adaptation to the current education model. Then, it discussed the components of Clouds that contribute to carbon emission and the features of Clouds that make it "Green".

Even though the proposed Cloud-Oriented Green Computing Architecture embeds various features to make Cloud computing much more Green, there are still many technological solutions are required to make it a reality.

REFERENCES

Agarwal, S., Goswami, S., & Nath, A. (2013). Green Computing and Green Technology in e-Learning. *International Journal of Computers and Applications, 76*(7), 35–41. doi:10.5120/13262-0741

Al-Zoube, M., El-Seoud, S. A., & Wyne, M. F. (2010). Cloud Computing Based ELearning System. *International Journal of Distance Education Technologies, 8*(2), 58–71. doi:10.4018/jdet.2010040105

Ali, S.M. (2012). Challenges and Benefits of Implementing Tablets in Classroom for e-Learning in a K-12 Education Environment – Case Study of a School in United Arab Emirates. *International Journal of Engineering and Science, 3*(4), 39-42.

Atrey, A., Jain, N., & Ch, I. N. (2013). A Study on Green Cloud Computing, Intel. *Journal of Grid and Distributed Computing, 6*(6), 93–102. doi:10.14257/ijgdc.2013.6.6.08

Awate, A., Nikhale, S., & Chunarkar, P. (2013). A Path for Horizing your Innovative Work Environmental Sustainability and the Green Cloud Computing, Intel. *Journal of Pure and Applied Research in Engineering and Technology, 1*(8), 537–545.

Beik, R. (2012). Green Cloud Computing: An Energy-Aware Layer in Software Architecture. *Proceedings of the Spring Congress of the Engineering and Technology (S-CET)*, Xian. doi:10.1109/SCET.2012.6341950

Beloglazov, A., & Buyya, R. (2010). Energy Efficient Allocation of Virtual Machines in Cloud Data Centres. *Proceedings of the 10th IEEE/ACM International Symposium on Cluster Computing and the Grid (CCGrid)*, Melbourne, Australia.

Bianchini, R., & Rajamony, R. (2004). Power and energy management for server systems. *IEEE Computer*, *37*(11), 68–74. doi:10.1109/MC.2004.217

Bianchini, R., & Rajamony, R. (2004). Power and Energy Management for Server Systems. *Computer*, *37*(11), 68–74. doi:10.1109/MC.2004.217

Biswas, S. (2011). *Cloud computing vs Utility computing vs Grid computing: Sorting the Differences.* Cloud Tweaks.

Bora, U. J., & Ahmed, M. (2013). E-Learning using Cloud Computing. *International Journal of Science and Modern Engineering*, *1*(2), 9–12.

Cavdar, D., & Alagoz, F. (2012). A Survey of Research on Greening Data Centers. *Proceedings of the IEEE Global Communications Conference (GLOBECOM)*, Anaheim, CA. doi:10.1109/GLOCOM.2012.6503613

Charrington, S. (2010). Characteristics of Platform as a Service. *Cloud Pulse blog*. Retrieved from http://Cloudpulseblog.com/2010/02/the-essentialcharacteristics-of-paas

Cherkasova, L., & Gardner, R. (2005). Measuring CPU overhead for I/O processing in the Xen virtual machine monitor. *Proc. of Annual Technical Conference on USENIX, Anaheim*, USA.

Cucinotta, T., Checconi, F., Kousiouris, G., Konstaneteli, K., Gogouvitis, S., …, Stein, M. (2012). Virtualized e-Learning on the IRMOS real-time Cloud. *Service oriented computing and applications*, *6*(2), 151–166.

Fernandez, A., Peralta, D., Herrera, F., & Benítez, J. M. (2012). An Overview of E-Learning in Cloud Computing. *Proceedings of the Workshop on LTEC 2012* (pp. 35–46).

Garg, S. K., & Buyya, R. (2012). Green Cloud computing and Environmental Sustainability. In S. Murugesan, & G. R. Gangadharan (Eds.), Harnessing Green IT: Principles and Practices. Wiley-IEEE Press.

Garg, S. K., Yeo, C. S., & Buyya, R. (2011). Green Cloud Framework for Improving Carbon Efficiency of Clouds. *Proceedings of the 17th International European Conference on Parallel and Distributed Computing*, Bordeaux, France. doi:10.1007/978-3-642-23400-2_45

Hosman, L., & Baikie, B. (2013). Solar-Powered Cloud Computing datacenters. *IT Professional*, 15(2), 15-21.

Jadeja, Y., & Modi, K. (2012). Cloud computing - Concepts, Architecture and Challenges. In *Computing* (pp. 877–880). Electronics and Electrical Technologies.

Jain, A., & Pandey, U.S. (2013), Role of Cloud Computing in Higher Education. *Intl. Journal of Advanced Research in Computer Science and Software Engineering*, 3(7).

Jain, A., Mishra, M., Peddoju, S.K., & Jain, N. (2013). Energy Efficient Computing-Green Cloud Computing. *Proceedings of the International Conference of the Energy Efficient Technologies for Sustainability (ICEETS)*, Nagercoil (pp. 978-982).

Jeong, J.-S., Kim, M., & Yoo, K.-H. (2013). A Content-oriented Smart Education System based on Cloud Computing. *Intl. Journal of Multimedia and Ubiquitous Engineering*, 8(6), 313–328. doi:10.14257/ijmue.2013.8.6.31

Kamble, R.S., & Nikam, D.A. (2013). Green Cloud computing New Approach of Energy Consumption. *International Journal of Latest Trends in Engineering and Technology*, 3(2).

Karim, , F., & Goodwin, R. (2013). Using Cloud Computing in E-learning Systems. *Journal of Advanced Research in Computer Science & Technology*, 1(1), 65–69.

Kaur, G., & Kumar, P. (2013). Compositional Framework of Green Cloud. *Journal of Emerging Trends in Engineering and Development*, 3(1), 670-675.

Kaur, A. (2014). Green Computing: Emerging Trends in Information and Communication Technology. *Intl. Journal of Engineering Inventions*, 3(9), 42–46.

Kaur, M., & Singh, P. (2013). Energy Efficient Green Cloud: Underlying Structure. *Proceedings of the IEEE Conf. on the Energy Efficient Technologies for Sustainability (ICEETS)*, Nagercoil. doi:10.1109/ICEETS.2013.6533383

Kawade, U., & Kapse, S. (2013). Green Computing: An Integrated Approach to Cloud Computing Architecture. *Proceedings of National Conference on Emerging Trends: Innovations and Challenges in IT*.

Kim, K. H., Beloglazov, A., & Buyya, R. (2011). Power-Aware Provisioning of Virtual Machines for Real-Time Cloud Services. *Concurrency and Computation*, 23(13), 1491-1505.

Kliazovich, D., & Bouvry, P. (2010). Green Cloud: A Packet-level Simulator of Energy-aware Cloud Computing Data Centers. *Proceeding of the IEEE Global Telecommunications Conference (GLOBECOM)*, Miami, FL.

Lal Sahu, B., & Tiwari, R. (2012). A Comprehensive Study on Cloud Computing. *Intel. Journal of Advanced Research in Computer Science and Software Engineering*, Vol. 2(9).

Leloglu, E., Ayav, T., & Aslan, B. G. (2013). A Review of Cloud Deployment Models for e-Learning Systems. *Proceedings of the 43rd Annual IEEE/IFIP Intel. Conf. on Dependable Systems and Networks (DSN)* (pp. 1-2). doi:10.1109/DSN.2013.6575331

Li, S. L., Chen, X., Yang, Z., & Chen, J. (2011). Virtualization security for cloud computing service. *Proceedings of the International Conference on Cloud and Service Computing* (pp. 174-179).

Lohmosavi, V., Nejad, A. F., & Hosseini, E. M. (2013). E-learning ecosystem based on Service-Oriented Cloud Computing Architecture. *Proceedings of the 2013 5th conference on Information and Knowledge Technology*, Shiraz (pp. 24-29). doi:10.1109/IKT.2013.6620032

Malviya, P., & Singh, S. (2013). A Study about Green Computing. *International Journal of Advanced Research in Computer Science and Software Engineering*, 3(6).

Maskare, P.R., & Sulke, S.R. (2014). E-learning Using Cloud Computing. *International Journal of Computer Science and Mobile Computing*, 3(5), 1281 – 1287.

Masud, A.H., & Huang, X. (2012), An E-learning System Architecture based on Cloud Computing. *World Academy of Science, Engineering and Tech.*, 6, 736-740.

Masud, M. A. H., & Huang, X. (2012). An E-learning System Architecture based on Cloud Computing, World Academy of Science. *Engineering and Technology*, 62, 74–78.

Mell, P., & Grance, T. (2011). The NIST Definition of Cloud Computing. *NIST Special Publication 800-145*.

Mircea, M., & Andreescu, A. I. (2011). Using Cloud Computing in Higher Education: A Strategy to Improve Agility in the Current Financial Crisis. *Communications of the IBIMA*, 20(11), 1–15. doi:10.5171/2011.875547

Owusu, F., & Pattinson, C. (2012). The current state of understanding of the energy efficiency of cloud computing. *Proceedings of the IEEE 11th International Conf. of the Trust, Security, Privacy in Computing and Communications (TrustCom)*, Liverpool. doi:10.1109/TrustCom.2012.270

Massoud, P. (2012). Energy-Efficient Datacenters. *IEEE Trans. on Computer Aided Design*, 31(10).

Palanivel, K., & Kuppuswami, S. (2014). Towards Service-Oriented Reference Model and Architecture to e-Learning Systems. *Intel. Journal of Emerging Trends & Tech. Computer Science*, 3(4).

Paper, W. (2007). *Green Grid Metrics—Describing Data Centres Power Efficiency*. Technical Committee by the Green Grid Industry Consortium.

Phankokkruad, M. (2012). Implement of Cloud Computing for e-Learning System. *Proceedings of the International Conference on Computer & Information Science*. doi:10.1109/ICCISci.2012.6297204

Pocatilu, P. (2010). Cloud Computing Benefits for E-learning Solutions. *Economics of Knowledge*, 2(1), 9–14.

Pocatilu, P., Alecu, F., & Vetrici, M. (2009). Using Cloud Computing for E-learning Systems. *Proceedings of the 8th WSEAS Intel., Conference on Data networks, communications, computers*, Baltimore, USA (pp. 54-59).

Rawson, A., & Pfleuger, J. (2008). *Cader*. Green Grid Data Center Power Efficiency Metrics. Consortium Green Grid.

Report, A. M. (2010). Cloud computing and Sustainability: The Environmental Benefits of Moving to the Cloud. Retrieved from http://www.wspenvironmental.com/media /docs/newsroom/ Cloud_ computing_ and_ Sustainability_-_Whitepaper_-_Nov_2010.pdf

Sarojadevi, K., & Jeevitha, R. (2011). Uncloud the Cloud of Cloud Computing. Retrieved from http://www.caesjournals.org/spluploads/IJCAES-AISC- 2011-174.pdf

Satoh, F., Yanagisawa, H., Takahashi, H., & Kushida, T. (2013). Total Energy Management system for Cloud Computing. *Proceedings of the IEEE International Conference of the Cloud Engineering (IC2E)*, Redwood City, CA. doi:10.1109/IC2E.2013.46

Shinde, S., Nalawade, S., & Nalawade, A. (2013). Green Computing: Go Green and Save Energy. *International Journal of Advanced Research in Computer Science and Software Engineering*, 3(7).

Smith, J., & Nair, R. (2003). *Virtual Machines: Versatile Platforms for Systems and Processes*. Los Altos, CA: Morgan Kaufmann.

Yamini, R. (2012). Power Management in Cloud Computing Using Green Algorithm. *Proceedings of the IEEE-International Conference on Advances in Engineering, Science and Management ICAESM '12)*, Nagapattinam, Tamil Nadu.

Compilation of References

451 Research. (2011). *NoSQL, NewSQL and Beyond: The drivers and use cases for database alternatives.* Retrieved from http://451research.com/report-long?icid=1651

A Younis, Y., Kifayat, K., & Merabti, M. (2014). An access control model for cloud computing. *Journal of Information Security and Applications.*

Aazam, M., Khan, I., Alsaffar, A. A., & Eui-Nam, H. (2014, January 14-18). Cloud of Things: Integrating Internet of Things and cloud computing and the issues involved. *Paper presented at the 2014 11th International Bhurban Conference on Applied Sciences and Technology (IBCAST).*

Abadi, D. J. (2007). *Column Stores for Wide and Sparse Data.* Paper presented at the CIDR.

Abadi, D., Madden, S., & Ferreira, M. (2006). Integrating compression and execution in column-oriented database systems. *Paper presented at theProceedings of the 2006 ACM SIGMOD international conference on Management of data,* Chicago, IL, USA. doi:10.1145/1142473.1142548

Abadi, D. J., Marcus, A., Madden, S., & Hollenbach, K. (2007). Scalable semantic Web data management using vertical partitioning, *Proceedings of the 33th International Conference on Very Large Data Bases* (pp. 411-422).

Abadi, D. J., Marcus, A., Madden, S., & Hollenbach, K. (2009). SW-Store: A vertically partitioned DBMS for Semantic Web data management. *The VLDB Journal, 18*(2), 385–406. doi:10.1007/s00778-008-0125-y

Agarwal, S., Goswami, S., & Nath, A. (2013). Green Computing and Green Technology in e-Learning. *International Journal of Computers and Applications, 76*(7), 35–41. doi:10.5120/13262-0741

Aidan, F., Hans, V., Patrick, L., & Damian, F. (2012). *Microsoft Private Cloud Computing.* John Wiley publisher.

Akdogan, A., Demiryurek, U., Banaei-Kashani, F., & Shahabi, C. (2010). Voronoi-based geospatial query processing with mapreduce.*Proceedings of the International Conference Cloud Computing,* Indianapolis, Indiana, USA (pp. 9-16). IEEE.

Alexander, K. (2008). RDF in JSON: A specification for serialising RDF in JSON. Retrieved from http://www.semanticscripting.org/SFSW2008

Ali, S.M. (2012). Challenges and Benefits of Implementing Tablets in Classroom for e-Learning in a K-12 Education Environment – Case Study of a School in United Arab Emirates. *International Journal of Engineering and Science,* 3(4), 39-42.

Allcock, W., Bresnahan, J., Kettimuthu, R., Link, M., Dumitrescu, C., Raicu, I., & Foster, I. (2005). The Globus Striped GridFTP Framework and Server*Proceedings of the 2005 ACM/IEEE Conference on Supercomputing* (p. 54). Washington, DC, USA: IEEE Computer Society. doi:10.1109/SC.2005.72

Alohali, B., Merabti, M., & Kifayat, K. A New Key Management Scheme for Home Area Network (HAN) In Smart Grid.

Alter, A. E., Peng, Y., Lin, R., & Harris, J. G. (2010). China's Pragmatic Path to Cloud Computing. Accenture Institute for High Performance.

Al-Zoube, M., El-Seoud, S. A., & Wyne, M. F. (2010). Cloud Computing Based ELearning System. *International Journal of Distance Education Technologies, 8*(2), 58–71. doi:10.4018/jdet.2010040105

Amazon Web Services. (2014a). *Amazon SimpleDB*. Retrieved from http://aws.amazon.com/simpledb/

Amazon Web Services. (2014b). *Amazon DynamoDB*. Retrieved from http://aws.amazon.com/dynamodb/

AmazonS3. (2014). Retrieved from http://aws.amazon.com/documentation/s3/

Amies, A., Sluiman, H., Guo Tong, Q., & Ning Liu, G. (2012). Developing and Hosting Applications on the Cloud. IBM Press/Pearson.

Anderson, J. C., Lehnardt, J., & Slater, N. (2010). *CouchDB: the definitive guide*. O'Reilly Media, Inc.

Anderson, J. C., Lehnardt, J., & Slater, N. (2010). *CouchDB: The definitive guide*. Sebastopol, CA, USA: O'Reilly Media.

Anderson, K. M., & Schram, A. (2011). Design and implementation of a data analytics infrastructure in support of crisis informatics research: NIER track.*Proceedings of the 33rd International Conference on Software Engineering,*Honolulu, Hawaii (pp. 844-847). doi:10.1145/1985793.1985920

Andrew T., Juan K., James L., Miles Z., Elaine R., & Stefan S. (2013). A statistical test suite for random and pseudorandom number generators for cryptographic applications. NIST Special Publication 800-22 Revision.

Angles, R., & Gutierrez, C. (2008). Survey of graph database models. *ACM Computing Surveys*, 40: 1:1-1:39.

Angles, R., & Gutiérrez, C. 2005, Querying RDF data from a graph database perspective. *Proceedings of the 2005 European Semantic Web Conference* (pp. 346-360). doi:10.1007/11431053_24

Anguita, A., Martin, L., Garcia-Remesal, M., & Maojo, V. (2013). RDFBuilder A tool to automatically build RDF-based interfaces for MAGE-OM microarray data sources. *Computer Methods and Programs in Biomedicine*, 111(1), 220-227.

Apache wicket. (2015). Retrieved from https://wicket.apache.org/)

ApacheHBase. (2014). http://hbase.apache.org/

Armbrust, M., Fox, A., Griffith, R., Joseph, A. D., Katz, R., Knowinski, A., & Zaharia, M. et al. (2010). A View of Cloud Computing. *Communications of the ACM, 53*(4), 50–58. doi:10.1145/1721654.1721672

Arnold, S. (2009, August 19). Cloud Computing and the Issues of Privacy. *KM World* (pp. 14-22).

Association for Computing Machinery. (2014). Conference on computer-supported cooperative work and social computing (CSCW). Retrieved from http://cscw.acm.org/2015/index.php

Atrey, A., Jain, N., & Ch, I. N. (2013). A Study on Green Cloud Computing, Intel. *Journal of Grid and Distributed Computing, 6*(6), 93–102. doi:10.14257/ijgdc.2013.6.6.08

Atzeni, P., Bugiotti, F., & Rossi, L. (2013). Uniform access to NoSQL systems. *Information Systems, 43*, 117–133. doi:10.1016/j.is.2013.05.002

Avram, M. G. (2014). Advantages and Challenges of Adopting Cloud Computing from an Enterprise Perspective. *Procedia Technology, 12*(0), 529-534.

Awate, A., Nikhale, S., & Chunarkar, P. (2013). A Path for Horizing your Innovative Work Environmental Sustainability and the Green Cloud Computing, Intel. *Journal of Pure and Applied Research in Engineering and Technology*, *1*(8), 537–545.

Aydin, B., Kempton, D., Akkineni, V., Gopavaram, S. R., Pillai, K. G., & Angryk, R. A. (2014, October 27-30). Spatiotemporal indexing techniques for efficiently mining spatiotemporal co-occurrence patterns. *Proceedings of the 2014 IEEE International Conference on Big Data*, Washington, DC, USA (pp. 1–10). http://doi.org/ doi:10.1109/BigData.2014.7004398

Aydin, B., Angryk, R. A., & Pillai, K. G. (2014, May 21-23). ERMO-DG: Evolving Region Moving Object Dataset Generator.*Proceedings of the Twenty-Seventh International Florida Artificial Intelligence Research Society Conference FLAIRS 2014*, Pensacola Beach, Florida.

Bach, M., & Werner, A. (2014). Standardization of NoSQL database languages: Beyond databases, architectures, and structure. *Proceedings 10th International Conference* (BDAS 2014). Ustron, Poland: Springer. doi:10.1007/978-3-319-06932-6_6

Baeza-Yates, R. A., & Ribeiro-Neto, B. A. (1999). *Modern Information Retrieval*. ACM Press / Addison-Wesley.

Bahmani, B., Moseley, B., Vattani, A., Kumar, R., & Vassilvitskii, S. (2012). Scalable k-means++. *Proceedings of the VLDB Endowment*, *5*(7), 622–633. doi:10.14778/2180912.2180915

Bailis, P., Davidson, A., Fekete, A., Ghodsi, A., Hellerstein, J. M., & Stoica, I. (2013). Highly Available Transactions: Virtues and Limitations (Extended Version). *PVLDB*, *7*(3), 181–192.

Bandyopadhyay, D., & Sen, J. (2011). Internet of Things: Applications and Challenges in Technology and Standardization. *Wireless Personal Communications*, *58*(1), 49–69. doi:10.1007/s11277-011-0288-5

Beaver, D., Kumar, S., Li, H. C., Sobel, J., & Vajgel, P. (2010). Finding a Needle in Haystack: Facebook's Photo Storage*Proceedings of the 9th USENIX Conference on Operating Systems Design and Implementation* (pp. 1-8). Vancouver, BC, Canada: USENIX Association.

Behm, A., Borkar, V. R., Carey, R. M., Grover, J., Li, Ch., Onose, N., & Tsotras, V. J. et al. (2011). ASTERIX: Towards a Scalable, Semistructured Data Platform for Evolving-world Models. *Distributed and Parallel Databases*, *29*(3), 185–216. doi:10.1007/s10619-011-7082-y

Beijing Car Ownership Exceeds 5 Million. (2012, September 19). China Daily. Retrieved from http://www.chinadaily.com.cn/china/2012-02/17/content_14628019.htm

Beik, R. (2012). Green Cloud Computing: An Energy-Aware Layer in Software Architecture.*Proceedings of the Spring Congress of the Engineering and Technology (S-CET)*, Xian. doi:10.1109/SCET.2012.6341950

Beloglazov, A., & Buyya, R. (2010). Energy Efficient Allocation of Virtual Machines in Cloud Data Centres.*Proceedings of the 10th IEEE/ACM International Symposium on Cluster Computing and the Grid (CCGrid)*, Melbourne, Australia.

Berl, A., Gelenbe, E., Di Girolamo, M., Giuliani, G., Meer, H., Dang, M., & Pentikousis, K. (2010). Energy-Efficient Cloud Computing. *The Computer Journal*, *53*(7), 1046–1051. doi:10.1093/comjnl/bxp080

Bethencourt, J., Sahai, A., & Waters, B. (2011). Ciphertext-policy attribute-based encryption, *Proceedings of the IEEE Symposium on Security and Privacy (SP '07)* (pp. 321–334).

Beyer, K., Ercegovac, V., Gemulla, R., Balmin, A., Eltabakh, M., Kanne, C.-Ch., & Shekita, E. J. et al. (2011). Jaql: A scripting language for large scale semistructured data analysis. *PVLDB*, *4*(12), 1272–1283.

Bhardwaj, S., Jain, L., & Jain, S. (2010). Cloud Computing: A Study of Infrastructure as a Service (IAAS). *International Journal of Engineering and Information Technology*, 2(1), 60–63.

Bhattasali, T., Chaki, R., & Chaki, N. (2013, December 13-15). Secure and trusted cloud of things. *Paper presented at the 2013 Annual IEEE India Conference (INDICON)*.

Bianchini, R., & Rajamony, R. (2004). Power and energy management for server systems. *IEEE Computer*, 37(11), 68–74. doi:10.1109/MC.2004.217

Bishop, B., Kiryakov, A., Ognyanoff, D., Peikov, I., Tashev, Z., & Velkov, R. (2011). Owlim: A family of scalable semantic repositories. *Semantic Web*, 2(1), 1–10.

Biswas, S. (2011). *Cloud computing vs Utility computing vs Grid computing: Sorting the Differences*. Cloud Tweaks.

Bora, U. J., & Ahmed, M. (2013). E-Learning using Cloud Computing. *International Journal of Science and Modern Engineering*, 1(2), 9–12.

Borkar, V., Carey, M.-J., & Li, Ch. (2012). Inside "Big Data management": ogres, onions, or parfaits?*Proceedings of EDBT Conference*, Berlin, Germany (pp. 3-14).

Bornea, M. A., Dolby, J., Kementsietsidis, A., Srinivas, K., Dantressangle, P., Udrea, O., & Bhattacharjee, B. (2013). Building an efficient RDF store over a relational database. *Proceedings of the 2013 ACM International Conference on Management of Data* (pp. 121-132). doi:10.1145/2463676.2463718

Brender, N., & Markov, I. (2013). Risk perception and risk management in cloud computing: Results from a case study of Swiss companies. *International Journal of Information Management*, 33(5), 726–733. doi:10.1016/j.ijinfomgt.2013.05.004

Brewer, E. A. (2000). Towards robust distributed systems. *Paper presented at PODC 2000*, Portland, Oregon.

Brewer, E. A. (2000, July 16-19). Towards robust distributed systems (abstract). *Proceedings of the Nineteenth Annual ACM Symposium on Principles of Distributed Computing*, Portland, Oregon, USA. (p. 7). http://doi.org/ doi:10.1145/343477.343502

Brewer, E. A. (2012). CAP twelve years later: How the 'rules' have changed. *Computer*, 45(2), 22–29. doi:10.1109/ MC.2012.37 PMID:24976642

Broekstra, J., Kampman, A., & van Harmelen, F. (2002).Sesame: A generic architecture for storing and querying RDF and RDF schema. *Proceedings of the 2002 International Semantic Web Conference* (pp. 54-68). doi:10.1007/3-540-48005-6_7

Buchin, M., Dodge, S., & Speckmann, B. (2014). Similarity of trajectories taking into account geographic context. *J. Spatial Information Science*, 9(1), 101–124. doi:10.5311/JOSIS.2014.9.179

Burns, R. P., & Burns, R. (2008). *Business Research Methods and Statistics Using SPSS*. Atlanta, GA, USA: Sage.

Bu, Y., Howe, Y., Balazinska, M., & Ernstm, M. D. (2012). The HaLoop approach to large-scale iterative data analysis. *The VLDB Journal*, 21(2), 169–190. doi:10.1007/s00778-012-0269-7

Cattell, R. (2011). Scalable SQL and NoSQL data stores. *SIGMOD Record*, 39(4), 12–27. doi:10.1145/1978915.1978919

Cavdar, D., & Alagoz, F. (2012). A Survey of Research on Greening Data Centers. *Proceedings of the IEEE Global Communications Conference (GLOBECOM)*, Anaheim, CA. doi:10.1109/GLOCOM.2012.6503613

Cellary, W., & Strykowski, S. (2009). e-government based on cloud computing and service-oriented architecture. *Proceedings of the 3rd International Conference on Theory and Practice of Electronic Governance* (pp. 5-10).

Center for Quantum Technology. (n. d.). Retrieved from http://www.quantumlah.org/research/topic/qcrypto,1/9/2014

Chadwick, D., & Casanova, M. (2011). *Security API for private cloud. Proceedings of the 3rd IEEE International on cloud computing technology and sciences, CloudCom* (pp. 792–798). CPS.

Chakka, V. P., Everspaugh, A., & Patel, J. M. (2003). *Indexing Large Trajectory Data Sets With SETI.* CIDR.

Chakravorty, A. (2013, October). Privacy Preserving Data Analytics for Smart Homes. *Proceedings of the IEEE Security and Privacy Workshops* (pp. 23-27).

Chander, K., & Yogesh, S. (2013). Enhanced security architecture for cloud data security. International journal of advanced research in computer science and software engineering, 3(5).

Chandramouli, R., Iorga, M., & Chokhani, S. (2014). *Cryptographic Key Management Issues and Challenges in Cloud Services.* Springer. doi:10.1007/978-1-4614-9278-8_1

Chandramouly, A., & Stinson, A. (2013 January). Enabling Big Data Solutions with Centralized Data Management (White paper). IT Best Practices Enterprise Data Management.

Chang, F., Dean, J., Ghemavat, S., Hsieh, W.C., Wallach, D.A., Burrows, M.,... Gruber, R.E. (2008). Bigtable: A Distributed Storage System for Structured Data. *Journal ACM Transactions on Computer Systems, 26(2).*

Chang, F., Dean, J., Ghemawat, S., Hsieh, W. C., Wallach, D. A., Burrows, M., Chandra, T., Fikes, A., & Gruber, R. E. (2008). BigTable: A distributed storage system for structured data, *ACM Transactions on Computer Systems, 26(2),* 4:1-4:26.

Chang, V., Issa, T., & Issa, T. (2011). Cloud computing and sustainability: an Australian public sector perspective. *Proceedings of the International Society for Professional Innovation Management (ISPIM) Conference,* Hamburg, Germany.

Chang, F., & Dean, J. et al.. (2006). Bigtable: A Distributed Storage System for Structured Data.*Proceedings of OSDI.*

Chang, F., Dean, J., Ghemawat, S., Hsieh, W. C., Wallach, D. A., Burrows, M., & Gruber, R. E. et al. (2008). Bigtable: A Distributed Storage System for Structured Data. *ACM Transactions on Computer Systems, 26(2),* 1–26. doi:10.1145/1365815.1365816

Chao, L. (2012). *Cloud Computing for Teaching and Learning: Strategies for Design and Implementation.* Information Science Reference. doi:10.4018/978-1-4666-0957-0

Chaouchi, H. (2013). *The Internet of Things: Connecting Objects.* Wiley. doi:10.1002/9781118600146

Charrington, S. (2010). Characteristics of Platform as a Service. *Cloud Pulse blog.* Retrieved from http://Cloudpulseblog.com/2010/02/the-essentialcharacteristics-of-paas

Chebrolu, S. B. (2010). Assessing the relationships among cloud adoption, strategic alignment and information technology effectiveness. *ProQuest Dissertations & Theses database,*

Chen, L., & Gong, G. (2012). *Communication System Security.* Taylor & Francis.

Chen, S., Xu, Y., Wang, P., Li, D., & Jin, D. (2011). The usage of cloud computing in China Regional Healthcare.*Proceedings of the 2011 IEEE International Conference on Cloud Computing and Intelligence Systems* (pp. 1-5).

Cherkasova, L., & Gardner, R. (2005). Measuring CPU overhead for I/O processing in the Xen virtual machine monitor. *Proc. of Annual Technical Conference on USENIX, Anaheim,* USA.

Chi, C., & Gao, F. (2011). The Trend of Cloud Computing in China. *Journal of Software, 6(7),* 1230–1235. doi:10.4304/jsw.6.7.1230-1234

Chodorow, K. (2013). *MongoDB: the definitive guide*. O'Reilly Media, Inc.

Choi, S., & Bae, B. (2015). The real-time monitoring system of social big data for disaster management. *Computer Science and its Applications, 330*, 809-815.

Chou, C., Zahedi, F., & Zhao, H. (2011). Ontology for developing web sites for natural disaster management: Methodology and implementation. *IEEE Transactions on Systems, Man, and Cybernetics. Part A, Systems and Humans, 41*(1), 50–62. doi:10.1109/TSMCA.2010.2055151

Christain, K., & Mario, P. (2010). *Applied Quantum cryptography*. Lect. Notes Phys.: Vol. 797. Berlin, Heidelberg: Springer. Doi:10.1007/978-3-642-04831-9

Christodorescu, M., Sailer, R., & Schales, D. L. (2009). Cloud security is not (just) virtualization security: A short paper. *Proceedings of the 2009 ACM Workshop on Cloud Computing Security* (pp. 97-102).

Cisco. (2012, September 19). Cloud Computing in Higher Education: A Guide to Evaluation and Adoption. Retrieved from http://www.cisco.com/web/offer/email/43468/5/Cloud_Computing_in_Higher_Education.pdf

Clark, C., Fraser, K., Hand, S., Hansen, J. G., Jul, E., Limpach, C., . . . Warfield, A. (2005). Live Migration of Virtual Machines *Proceedings of the 2Nd Conference on Symposium on Networked Systems Design & Implementation* (Vol. 2, pp. 273-286). Berkeley, CA, USA: USENIX Association.

Clustrix. (2014). *Clustrix*. Retrieved from http://www.clustrix.com/

Cooper, B.F., Ramakrishnan, R., Srivastava, U., Silberstein, A., Bohannon, Ph., Jacobsen, H.A.,... Zemeni, R. (2008). PNUTS: Yahoo!'s hosted data serving platform. *Journal PVLDB* 1(2), 1277-1288.

Coppola, D. P. (2011). *Introduction to international disaster management*. Amsterdam, Netherlands: Butterworth-Heinemann.

Corbett, J. C., Dean, J. C., Epstein, M., Fikes, A., Frost, Ch., & Furman, J. J., ...Woodford, D. (2012). Spanner: Google's Globally-Distributed Database. *Proceedings of 10th USENIX Symposium on Operation Systems Design and Implementation (OSDI 2012)*, Hollywood.

Costello, A., & Osborne, J. (2005). Best Practices in Exploratory Factor Analysis: Four Recommendations for Getting the Most from Your Analysis. *Practical Assessment, Research & Evaluation, 10*(7), 1–9.

Couchbase. (2014). *Couchbase*. Retrieved from http://www.couchbase.com/

CouchDB-lucene project. (2012). Retrieved from https://github.com/rnewson/couchdb-lucene

Cox, S., Daisey, P., Lake, R., Portele, C., & Whiteside, A. (2005). *OpenGIS Geography Markup Language (GML) Implementation Specification (version 3.1.1)*. OGC Implementation Specification.

CSA, (2012). *Security a-a-services guidance for critical areas in cloud computing, Category 8*.

Cubitt, S., Hassan, R., & Volkmer, I. (2011). Does Cloud Computing have a Silver Lining. *Media Culture & Society, 33*(1), 149–158. doi:10.1177/0163443710382974

Cucinotta, T., Checconi, F., Kousiouris, G., Konstaneteli, K., Gogouvitis, S., ..., Stein, M. (2012). Virtualized e-Learning on the IRMOS real-time Cloud. *Service oriented computing and applications*, 6(2), 151–166.

Cucurull, J., & Guasch, S. (2014). *Virtual TPM for a secure cloud: fallacy or reality? daCosta, F. (2013). Rethinking the Internet of Things: A Scalable Approach to Connecting Everything*. Apress.

Cudré-Mauroux, P., Wu, E., & Madden, S. (2010, March 1-6). TrajStore: An adaptive storage system for very large trajectory data sets. *Proceedings of the 26th International Conference on Data Engineering, ICDE, Long Beach, California, USA* (pp. 109–120). http://doi.org/ doi:10.1109/ICDE.2010.5447829

Cudre-Mauroux, P., Enchev, I., Fundatureanu, S., Groth, P., Haque, A., Harth, A., & Wylot, M. et al. (2013).NoSQL databases for RDF: An empirical evaluation. *Proceedings of the 12th International Semantic Web Conference* (pp. 310-325). doi:10.1007/978-3-642-41338-4_20

Cui, X., Zhu, P., Yang, X., Li, K., & Ji, C. (2014). Optimized big data k-means clustering using MapReduce. *The Journal of Supercomputing, 70*(3), 1249–1259. doi:10.1007/s11227-014-1225-7

Cunningham, H., Maynard, D., Bontcheva, K., Tablan, V., Aswani, N., Roberts, I., . . . Heitz, T. (2013). Developing language processing components with GATE. University of Sheffield department of computer science. Retrieved from http://gate.ac.uk/sale/tao/split.html

Cusumano, M. (2010). Cloud computing and SaaS as new computing platforms. *Communications of the ACM, 53*(4), 27–29. doi:10.1145/1721654.1721667

Cutillo, A., Molva, R., & Strufe, T. (2009). Safe book: A privacy-preserving online social network is leveraging on real-life trust. *IEEE Communications Magazine, 47*(12), 94–101. doi:10.1109/MCOM.2009.5350374

Data community White Paper developed by leading researchers: Challenges and Opportunities with Big Data. (2012). Purdue University. Retrieved from www.purdue.edu/discoverypark/cyber/assets/pdfs/

de Albuquerque, J. P., Herfort, B., Brenning, A., & Zipf, A. (2015). A geographic approach for combining social media and authoritative data towards identifying useful information for disaster management. *International Journal of Geographical Information Science, 29*(4), 667-689. doi:10.1080/13658816.2014.996567

De Berg, M., Cheong, O., van Kreveld, M., & Overmars, M. (2008). Computational Geometry: Algorithms and Applications (3rd ed.). Santa Clara, CA, USA: Springer-Verlag.

De Decker, B., & Zúquete, A. (Eds.), (2014). *Communications and Multimedia Security.* Springer.

Dean, D., & Ghemawat, S. (2008). MapReduce: Simplified Data Processing on Large Clusters. *Communications of the ACM, 51*(1), 107–113. doi:10.1145/1327452.1327492

Dean, J., & Ghemawat, S. (2004). MapReduce: simplified data processing on large clusters.*Proceedings of the Symposium on Operating System Design and Implementation*, San Francisco, California, USA (pp. 137-150).USENIX Association.

Debatty, T., Michiardi, P., Mees, W., & Thonnard, O. (2014). Determining the k in k-means with MapReduce. *Proceedings of the Workshops of the EDBT/ICDT 2014 Joint Conference*, Athens, Greece (pp. 19-28). CEUR-WS.org.

DeCandia, G., Hastorun, D., Jampani, M., Kakulapati, G., Lakshman, A., Pilchin, A., & Vogels, W. et al. (2007). Dynamo: Amazon's highly available key-value store. *Proceedings of the 21st ACM Symposium on Operating Systems Principles* (pp. 205-220). doi:10.1145/1294261.1294281

Diagram of Hadoop Architecture. (n. d.). Retrieved from http://hadoop.apache.org/docs/r1.2.1/hdfs_design.html

Ding, L., Qiao, B., Wang, G., & Chen, C. (2011). An efficient quad-tree based index structure for cloud data management. In: Proceedings of WAIM 2011, LNCS, Vol. 6897, pp. 238–250.

Distefano, S., Merlino, G., & Puliafito, A. (2012, July 4-6). Enabling the Cloud of Things. *Paper presented at the 2012 Sixth International Conference on Innovative Mobile and Internet Services in Ubiquitous Computing (IMIS).*

Doelitzscher, F., Reich, C., Knahl, M., & Clarke, N. (2011). *An autonomous agent-based incident detection system for cloud computing, 3rd IEEE International on cloud computing technology and sciences, CloudCom* (pp. 197–204). CPS.

Dormando (2014). *Memcached*. Retrieved from http://memcached.org/

Drago, I., Mellia, M., Munafo, M. M., Sperotto, A., Sadre, R., & Pras, A. (2012). Inside dropbox: understanding personal cloud storage services. *Paper presented at theProceedings of the 2012 ACM conference on Internet measurement conference*, Boston, Massachusetts, USA. doi:10.1145/2398776.2398827

Duan, S., Kementsietsidis, A., Srinivas, K., & Udrea, O. (2011). Apples and oranges: a comparison of RDF benchmarks and real RDF datasets. *Proceedings of the 2011 ACM SIGMOD International Conference on Management of Data* (pp. 145-156). doi:10.1145/1989323.1989340

Edlich, S. (2012). *Choose the "Right" Database and NewSQL: NoSQL Under Attack Retrieved.* from http://www.infoq.com/presentations/Choosing-NoSQL-NewSQL

Edlich, S. (2014). *NoSQL*. Retrieved from http://nosql-database.org/

Eduared, G. (2014). An Experimental Implementation of Oblivious Transfer in the Noisy Storage Model. Nature Communications Journal, 5.

Eigene, E. M. (2009, September). Hyrax: Cloud Computing on Mobile Devices using MapReduce. [Dissertation]. Carnegie Mellon University Pittsburgh.

El-Sayed, H., Mellouk, A., George, L., & Zeadally, S. (2008). Quality of service models for heterogeneous networks: overview and challenges. *Annals of telecommunications, 63*(11-12), 639-668. doi: 10.1007/s12243-008-0064-z

Emary, I. M. M. E., & Ramakrishnan, S. (2013). *Wireless Sensor Networks: From Theory to Applications.* Taylor & Francis. doi:10.1201/b15425

Emmanuel S., Navdeep A., Parshant T., Bhanu P. (2013). Cloud Computing: Data Storage Security Analysis and its Challenges. *International Journal of Computer Applications*, 70(24).

Ene, A., Im, S., & Moseley, B. (2011). Fast clustering using MapReduce.*Proceedings of the 17th ACM SIGKDD International Conference on Knowledge Discovery and Data Mining*, San Diego, CA, USA (pp. 681-689). ACM.

ENISA security. (2014). Retrieved from http://www.enisa.europa.eu/

Enterprise, D. B. Corporation (2014). NoSQL for the Enterprise. Retrieved from http://www.enterprisedb.com/nosql-for-enterprise

Erdogmus, H. (2009). Cloud computing: Does Nirvana hide behind the Nebula. *IEEE Software*, *26*(11), 4–6.

Erling, O., & Mikhailov, I. (2007). RDF support in the virtuoso DBMS. *Proceedings of the 1st Conference on Social Semantic Web* (pp. 59-68).

Erling, O., & Mikhailov, I. (2009). *Virtuoso: RDF support in a native RDBMS.* In R. De Virgilio et al. (Eds.),*Semantic Web Information Management* (Ch. 21, pp. 501–519). Springer-Verlag.

Factor, M., Meth, K., Naor, D., Rodeh, O., & Satran, J. (2005). Object storage: the future building block for storage systems Local to Global Data Interoperability - Challenges and Technologies, 2005 (pp. 119-123).

Faiza, F. (2012). Management of symmetric cryptographic keys in a cloud-based environment. *Proceedings of the 2nd IEEE international conference on cloud computing technology and science.*

Fan, J., Han, F., & Liu, H. (2014, August). Challenges of Big Data Analysis, National. *Scientific Review (Singapore), 1*(2).

Fan, W., & Yan, Z. (2010). Factors affecting response rates of the web survey: A systematic review. *Computers in Human Behavior, 26*(2), 132–139. doi:10.1016/j.chb.2009.10.015

Farhad, A., Seyed, S., & Athula, G. (2013). Cloud computing: security and reliability issues. Communication of the IBIMA (Vol. 1).

Fernandez, A., Peralta, D., Herrera, F., & Benítez, J. M. (2012). An Overview of E-Learning in Cloud Computing. *Proceedings of the Workshop on LTEC 2012* (pp. 35–46).

Ferreira, L., Berstis, V., Armstrong, J., Kendzierski, M., Neukoetter, A., Takagi, M., & Hernandez, O. (2003). *Introduction to grid computing with globus.* IBM Corporation, International Technical Support Organization.

Foundation, D. B. (2014). *FoundationDB - Key-Value Store.* Retrieved from https://foundationdb.com/

Fox, A., Eichelberger, C., Hughes, J., & Lyon, S. (2013, 6-9 October). Spatio-temporal indexing in non-relational distributed databases. *Proceedings of the 2013 IEEE International Conference on Big Data2013*, Santa Clara, CA, USA (pp. 291–299). http://doi.org/ doi:10.1109/BigData.2013.6691586

Franke, C., Morin, S., Chebotko, A., Abraham, J., & Brazier, P. (2011). Distributed semantic web data management in HBase and MySQL Cluster. *Proceedings of the 2011 IEEE International Conference on Cloud Computing* (pp. 105-112). doi:10.1109/CLOUD.2011.19

Gál, Z., Almási, B., Dabóczi, T., Vida, R., Oniga, S., Baran, S., & Farkas, I. (2014). *Internet of Things: application areas and research results of the FIRST project.*

Gamble, M., & Goble, C. (2011). Quality, Trust and Utility of Scientific Data on the Web: Toward a Joint model.*Proceedings of WebSci'11 Conference*, Koblenz, Germany. doi:10.1145/2527031.2527048

Garbis, G., Kyzirakos, K., & Koubarakis, M. (2013). Geographica: A benchmark for geospatial RDF stores. *Proceedings of the 12th International Semantic Web Conference* (pp. 343-359).

Garcia, T., & Wang, T. (2013, September 16-18). Analysis of Big Data technologies and method - Query large Web public RDF datasets on Amazon cloud using Hadoop and Open Source Parsers. *Proceedings of the 2013 IEEE International Conference on Semantic Computing*, Irvine, USA (pp. 244-251). doi:10.1109/ICSC.2013.49

Garg, S. K., & Buyya, R. (2012). Green Cloud computing and Environmental Sustainability. In S. Murugesan, & G. R. Gangadharan (Eds.), Harnessing Green IT: Principles and Practices. Wiley-IEEE Press.

Garg, S. K., Yeo, C. S., & Buyya, R. (2011). Green Cloud Framework for Improving Carbon Efficiency of Clouds. *Proceedings of the 17th International European Conference on Parallel and Distributed Computing*, Bordeaux, France. doi:10.1007/978-3-642-23400-2_45

Garrett, J. J. (2005). Ajax: A new approach to web applications.

Gates, A., Natkovich, O., Chopra, S., Kamath,P., Narayanamurthy, S.M., Olston, Ch.,...Sristava, U. (2009). Building a high level dataflow system on top of MapReduce: The pig experience. *PVLDB, 2*(2), 1414–1425.

Ghemawat, S., Gobioff, H., & Leung, S.-T. (2003). The Google File System. *SIGOPS Oper. Syst. Rev., 37*(5), 29–43. doi:10.1145/1165389.945450

Gibson, G. A., Nagle, D. F., Amiri, K., Chang, F. W., Feinberg, E. M., Gobioff, H., & Zelenka, J. et al. (1997). File Server Scaling with Network-attached Secure Disks*Proceedings of the 1997 ACM SIGMETRICS International Conference on Measurement and Modeling of Computer Systems* (pp. 272-284). Seattle, Washington, USA: ACM. doi:10.1145/258612.258696

Gilbert, S., & Lynch, N. (2002). Brewer's conjecture and the feasibility consistent, available, partition-tolerant web services. *ACM SIGACT News*, *33*(2), 51–59. doi:10.1145/564585.564601

GitHub, Inc. (2014). *Project Voldemort - a distributed database*. Retrieved from http://www.project-voldemort.com/voldemort/

GlassFish. (2014). Retrieved from https://glassfish.java.net/

Gliem, J., & Gliem, R. (2003). Calculating, Interpreting, and Reporting Cronbach's Alpha Reliability Coefficient for Likert-Type Scales. Proceedings of the Midwest Research to Practice Conference in Adult, Continuing and Community Education (pp. 82 - 88).

Gluster, F. S. (2014). Retrieved from http://www.gluster.org/

Google App Engine. (n. d.). Retrieved from http://code.google.com/appengine

GoogleChrome. (2015). chrome.fileSystem. Retrieved from https://developer.chrome.com/apps/fileSystem

GoogleCloudStorage. (2014). Retrieved from https://cloud.google.com/storage/#pricing-calc

Gordon, D., Wirz, M., Roggen, D., & Tröster, G., & Beigl, M. (2014). Group affiliation detection using model divergence for wearable devices. *Proceedings of the 2014 ACM International Symposium on Wearable Computers*, Seattle, Washington (pp. 19-26). ACM. doi:10.1145/2634317.2634319

Gordon, J., & McNew, R. (2008). Developing the Online Survey. *Nurs Clin N Am, 43*(4), 605 – 619..

Gratton, D. A. (2013). *The Handbook of Personal Area Networking Technologies and Protocols*. Cambridge University Press. doi:10.1017/CBO9780511979132

Grolinger, K., Capretz, M. A. M., Marti, J. R., & Srivastava, K. D. (2012). Ontology–based representation of simulation models. *Proceedings of the 24the International Conference on Software Engineering and Knowledge Engineering*, San Francisco Bay, CA, USA (pp. 432-437).

Grolinger, K., Higashino, W. A., Tiwari, A., & Capretz, M. A. M. (2013). Data management in cloud environments: NoSQL and NewSQL data stores. *Journal of Cloud Computing: Advances, Systems and Applications*, 2(22).

Grolinger, K., Higashino, W.A., Tiwari, A., & Capretz, M.A.M. (2013). Data management in cloud environments: NoSQL and NewSQL data stores. *Journal of Cloud Computing: Advances, Systems and Applications*, 2(22).

Grolinger, K., Higashino, W. A., Tiwari, A., & Capretz, M. A. (2013). Data management in cloud environments: NoSQL and NewSQL data stores. *Journal of Cloud Computing: Advances. Systems and Application, 2*. doi:10.1186/2192-113X-2-22

Grolinger, K., Mezghani, E., Capretz, M. A. M., & Exposito, E. (2013). Knowledge as a service framework for disaster data management.*Proceedings of the 22nd WETICE Conference* (pp. 313-318). Hammamet, Tunisia. doi:10.1109/WETICE.2013.48

Grolinger, K., Mezghani, E., Capretz, M. A. M., & Exposito, E. (2015). Collaborative knowledge as a service applied to the disaster management domain. *International Journal of Cloud Computing, 4*(1), 5–27. doi:10.1504/IJCC.2015.067706

Gubbi, J., Buyya, R., Marusic, S., & Palaniswami, M. (2013). Internet of Things (IoT): A vision, architectural elements, and future directions. *Future Generation Computer Systems*, *29*(7), 1645–1660. doi:10.1016/j.future.2013.01.010

Gudivada, V. N., Rao, D., & Raghavan, V. V. (2014). NoSQL Systems for Big Data Management. (SERVICES). *Proceedings of the 2014 IEEE World Congress on Services* (pp. 190–197). doi:10.1109/SERVICES.2014.42

Güting, R. H. (1994, September 12-15). GraphDB: Modeling and querying graphs in databases. *Proceedings of 20th International Conference on Very Large Data Bases,* Santiago de Chile, Chile (pp. 297-308).

Guttman, A. (1984). R-trees: A Dynamic Index Structure for Spatial Searching. *SIGMOD Record, 14*(2), 47–57. doi:10.1145/971697.602266

Hadoop, D. B. Team - Yale University (2009). *HadoopDB - An Architectural Hybrid of MapReduce and DBMS Technologies for Analytical Workloads.* Retrieved from http://db.cs.yale.edu/hadoopdb/hadoopdb.html

Hair, J., Black, W., Babin, B., & Anderson, R. (2009). *Multivariate data analysis.* Upper Saddle River, NJ: Prentice Hall.

Han & Kamber. (2006). *Data Mining: Concept and Techniques.* Maurgan Kaufmann Publishers.

Han, J., Song, M., & Song, J. (2011, May 16-18). A Novel Solution of Distributed Memory NoSQL Database for Cloud Computing. *Paper presented at the 2011 IEEE/ACIS 10th International Conference on Computer and Information Science (ICIS).*

Härder, T. (2005). DBMS Architecture – the Layer Model and its Evolution. *Datenbank-Spektrum, 13,* 45–57.

Harizopoulos, S., Liang, V., Abadi, D. J., & Madden, S. (2006). Performance tradeoffs in read-optimized databases. *Paper presented at the Proceedings of the 32nd international conference on Very large data bases,* Seoul, Korea.

Harris, S., Lamb, N., & Shadbolt, N. (2009). 4store: The design and implementation of a clustered RDF store. *Proceedings of the 5th International Workshop on Scalable Semantic Web Knowledge Base Systems* (pp. 94-109).

Hecht, R., & Jablonski, S. (2011). NoSQL evaluation: A use case oriented survey. *Proceedings 2011 Int Conf Cloud Serv Computing* (pp. 336–341). doi:10.1109/CSC.2011.6138544

Hewlett-Packard Development Company. L.P. (2014). *HP Vertica Analytics Platform.* Retrieved from http://www.vertica.com/

Hewlett-Packard. (2014). HP autonomy. Retrieved from http://www.autonomy.com/

Hill, B. D. (2012). *The Sequential Kaiser-Meyer-Olkin Procedure As An Alternative For Determining The Number Of Factors In Common-Factor Analysis: A Monte Carlo Simulation* [Dissertation].

Hjaltason, G. R., & Samet, H. (2003). Index-driven similarity search in metric spaces. *ACM Transactions on Database Systems, 28*(4), 517–580. doi:10.1145/958942.958948

Hosman, L., & Baikie, B. (2013). Solar-Powered Cloud Computing datacenters. *IT Professional, 15*(2), 15-21.

Hristidis, V., Chen, S., Li, T., Luis, S., & Deng, Y. (2010). Survey of data management and analysis in disaster situations. *Journal of Systems and Software, 83*(10), 1701–1714. doi:10.1016/j.jss.2010.04.065

Hsiao H.-C., Chung, H.-Y., Shen, H., Chao, Y.-C. (2013, May). Load Rebalancing for Distributed File Systems in Clouds. *IEEE Transactions on Parallel and Distributed Systems, 24*(5), 951-962.

Huang, J., Abadi, D. J., & Ren, K. (2011). Scalable SPARQL querying of large RDF graphs. *Proceedings of the VLDB Endowment, 4*(11), 1123–1134.

Hua, X. Y., Wu, H., Li, Z., & Ren, S. P. (2014). Enhancing throughput of the Hadoop Distributed File System for interaction-intensive tasks. *Journal of Parallel and Distributed Computing, 74*(8), 2770–2779. doi:10.1016/j.jpdc.2014.03.010

Hupfeld, F., Cortes, T., Kolbeck, B., Stender, J., Focht, E., Hess, M., & Cesario, E. et al. (2008). The XtreemFS architecture—a case for object-based file systems in Grids. *Concurrency and Computation, 20*(17), 2049–2060.

Husain, M. F., Khan, L., Kantarcioglu, M., & Thuraisingham, B. M. (2010, July 5-10). Data intensive query processing for large RDF graphs using cloud computing tools, *Proceedings of the 2010 IEEE International Conference on Cloud Computing*, Miami, USA (pp. 1-10). doi:10.1109/CLOUD.2010.36

Husain, M. F., McGlothlin, J. P., Masud, M. M., Khan, L. R., & Thuraisingham, B. M. (2011). Heuristics-based query processing for large RDF graphs using cloud computing. *IEEE Transactions on Knowledge and Data Engineering, 23*(9), 1312–1327. doi:10.1109/TKDE.2011.103

Hwang, K., Dongarra, J., & Fox, G. C. (2013). *Distributed and Cloud Computing: From Parallel Processing to the Internet of Things*. Elsevier Science.

Hypertable Inc. (2014). *Hypertable*. Retrieved from http://hypertable.org/

IBM Corporation Software Group. (2013). Wrangling big data: Fundamentals of Data Lifecycle Management, 1-12

IBM. (2014). IBM enterprise content management. Retrieved from http://www-03.ibm.com/software/products/en/category/enterprise-content-management

IDC. (2014). IDC Ranking of issues of Cloud Computing model. Retrieved from http://www.idc.com/

Idreos, S., Groffen, F., Nes, N., Manegold, S., Mullender, S., & Kersten, M. (2012). MonetDB: Two decades of research in column-oriented database architectures. *Bulletin of the IEEE Computer Society Technical Committee on Data Engineering, 35*(1), 40–45.

Ilyas, A. (2014). MicroFilters: Harnessing twitter for disaster management. Paper presented at the *IEEE Global Humanitarian Technology Conference* (pp. 417-424). doi:10.1109/GHTC.2014.6970316

Infosys Labs Briefings. (2013). Big Data-Challenges-Opportunities, 11(1).

Issa, T. (2013). Online Survey: Best Practice. In P. Isaias, M.B. Nunes (Eds.), Information Systems Research and Exploring Social Artifacts: Approaches and Methodologies (pp. 1–19). Hershey, PA, USA: IGI Global. doi:10.4018/978-1-4666-2491-7.ch001

Issa, T., Chang, V., & Issa, T. (2010). The Impact of Cloud Computing and Organizational Sustainability. *Cloud Computing and Virtualization 2010*, Singapore.

Itani, W., Kayassi, A., & Chehab, A. (2012). Energy-efficient incremental integrity for securing storage in mobile cloud computing. *Proceedings of theInternational Conference on Energy Aware Computing (ICEAC10)*. Cairo, Egypt.

Jadeja, Y., & Modi, K. (2012). Cloud computing - Concepts, Architecture and Challenges. In *Computing* (pp. 877–880). Electronics and Electrical Technologies.

Jagadish, H. V., Gehrke, J., Labrinidis, A., Papakonstantinou, Y., Patel, J. M., Ramakrishnan, R., & Shahabi, C. (2014, July). Big Data and its Technical Challenges. *Communications of the ACM, 57*(7), 86–94. doi:10.1145/2611567

Jain, A., & Pandey, U.S. (2013), Role of Cloud Computing in Higher Education. *Intl. Journal of Advanced Research in Computer Science and Software Engineering*, 3(7).

Jain, A., Mishra, M., Peddoju, S.K., & Jain, N. (2013). Energy Efficient Computing-Green Cloud Computing. *Proceedings of the International Conference of the Energy Efficient Technologies for Sustainability (ICEETS)*, Nagercoil (pp. 978-982).

Jensen, M., Schwenk, J., Gruschka, N., & Iacono, L. (2009). On Technical Security Issues in Cloud Computing. IEEE ICCC, Bangalore (pp. 109-116).

Jeong, J.-S., Kim, M., & Yoo, K.-H. (2013). A Content-oriented Smart Education System based on Cloud Computing. *Intl. Journal of Multimedia and Ubiquitous Engineering, 8*(6), 313–328. doi:10.14257/ijmue.2013.8.6.31

Jiang, D., Ooi, B. C., Shi, L., & Wu, S. (2010). The performance of MapReduce: An in-depth study. *Proceedings of the VLDB Endowment, 3*(1), 472–483. doi:10.14778/1920841.1920903

Jing, H., Haihong, E., Guan, L., & Jian, D. (2011, October 26-28). *Survey on NoSQL database. Paper presented at the 2011 6th International Conference on Pervasive Computing and Applications (ICPCA)*.

Johnson, P. E. (2013). A Review of "Cloud Computing for Libraries". *Journal of Access Services, 10*(1), 71–73. doi:10.1080/15367967.2013.738572

Juan, S. (2012). *Statistical testing of random number generators ", National Institute Standards Technology*. NIST.

Juan, S. (2012). *Statistical testing of random number generators*. National Institute Standards Technology.

Juve, G., Deelman, E., Vahi, K., Mehta, G., Berriman, B., Maechling, P., & Berman, B. P. (2010). Data Sharing Options for Scientific Workflows on Amazon EC2. *High Performance Computing, Networking, Storage and Analysis*, 1-9.

Kaisler, S., Armour, F., Espinsoa, J. A., & Money, W. (2013). Big Data: Issues and Challenges Moving Forward. *Proceedings of theHawaii International Conference on System Sciences* (pp. 995-1004). doi:10.1109/HICSS.2013.645

Kallman, R., Kimura, H., Natkins, J., Pavlo, A., Rasin, A., Zdonik, S., & Abadi, D. J. et al. (2008). H-store: A high-performance, distributed main memory transaction processing system. *Proceedings of the VLDB Endowment, 1*(2), 1496–1499. doi:10.14778/1454159.1454211

Kamble, R.S., & Nikam, D.A. (2013). Green Cloud computing New Approach of Energy Consumption. *International Journal of Latest Trends in Engineering and Technology, 3*(2).

Kaoudi, Z., & Manolescu, I. (2015). RDF in the clouds: A survey. *The VLDB Journal, 24*(1), 67–91. doi:10.1007/s00778-014-0364-z

Karim, , F., & Goodwin, R. (2013). Using Cloud Computing in E-learning Systems. *Journal of Advanced Research in Computer Science & Technology, 1*(1), 65–69.

Karnouskos, S. (2013, February 25-28). Smart houses in the smart grid and the search for value-added services in the cloud of things era. *Paper presented at the 2013 IEEE International Conference on Industrial Technology (ICIT)*.

Katal, A., Wazid, M., & Goudar, R. H. (2013 August). Big Data: Issues, Challenges, Tools and Good Practices. *Proceedings of theInternational Conference on Contemporary Computing(pp.404-409)*. doi:10.1109/IC3.2013.6612229

Kaur, G., & Kumar, P. (2013). Compositional Framework of Green Cloud. *Journal of Emerging Trends in Engineering and Development, 3*(1), 670-675.

Kaur, M., & Singh, P. (2013). Energy Efficient Green Cloud: Underlying Structure. *Proceedings of the IEEEConf. on the Energy Efficient Technologies for Sustainability (ICEETS)*, Nagercoil. doi:10.1109/ICEETS.2013.6533383

Kaur, A. (2014). Green Computing: Emerging Trends in Information and Communication Technology. *Intl. Journal of Engineering Inventions, 3*(9), 42–46.

Kawade, U., & Kapse, S. (2013). Green Computing: An Integrated Approach to Cloud Computing Architecture. *Proceedings of National Conference on Emerging Trends: Innovations and Challenges in IT.*

Kelly, J. (2014). Big Data: Hadoop, Business Analytics and Beyond. *Wikibon.* Retrieved from http://wikibon.org/wiki/v/Big_Data:_Hadoop,_Business_Analytics_and_Beyond

Ke, S., Gong, J., Li, S., Zhu, Q., Liu, X., & Zhang, Y. (2014). A Hybrid Spatio-Temporal Data Indexing Method for Trajectory Databases. *Sensors (Basel, Switzerland), 14*(7), 12990–13005. doi:10.3390/s140712990 PMID:25051028

Khadilkar, V., Kantarcioglu, M., Thuraisingham, B. M., & Castagna, P. (2012). Jena-HBase: A distributed, scalable and efficient RDF triple store. *Proceedings of the 2012 International Semantic Web Conference.*

Khoshnevis, S., & Rabeifa, F. (2012). Toward knowledge management as a service in cloud-based environments. *International Journal of Mechatronics. Electrical and Computer Technology, 2*(4), 88–110.

Kifayat, K., Merabti, M., & Shi, Q. (2010). Future security challenges in cloud computing. *International Journal of Multimedia Intelligence and Security, 1*(4), 428–442. doi:10.1504/IJMIS.2010.039241

Kim, H. S., Ravindra, P., & Anyanwu, K. (2013, May 13-17). Optimizing RDF(S) queries on cloud platforms, *Proceedings of the 2013 International World Wide Web Conference,* Rio de Janeiro, Brazil (pp. 261-264).

Kim, K. H., Beloglazov, A., & Buyya, R. (2011). Power-Aware Provisioning of Virtual Machines for Real-Time Cloud Services. *Concurrency and Computation, 23*(13), 1491-1505.

Kim, S. W. (2006). Hybrid storage scheme for RDF data management in Semantic Web. *Journal of Digital Information Management, 4*(1), 32–36.

Kim, Y., & Shim, K. (2012). Parallel top-k similarity join algorithms using MapReduce.*Proceedings of the International Conference on Data Engineering,* Arlington, Virginia, USA (pp. 510-521). IEEE Computer Society. doi:10.1109/ICDE.2012.87

Kliazovich, D., & Bouvry, P. (2010). Green Cloud: A Packet-level Simulator of Energy-aware Cloud Computing Data Centers.*Proceeding of the IEEE Global Telecommunications Conference (GLOBECOM),* Miami, FL.

Kumar, R., Gupta, N., Maharwal, H., Charu, S., & Yadav, K. (2014). Critical Analysis of Database Management Using NewSQL. International Journal of Computer Science and Mobile Computing, May, 434-438.

Lai, I., Tam, S., & Chan, M. (2012). Knowledge cloud system for network collaboration: A case study in medical service industry in China. *Expert Systems with Applications, 39*(15), 12205–12212. doi:10.1016/j.eswa.2012.04.057

Lakshman, A., & Malik, P. (2010). Cassandra: A decentralized structured storage system. *ACM SIGOPS Operating System Review, 44*(2), 35–40. doi:10.1145/1773912.1773922

Lal Sahu, B., & Tiwari, R. (2012). A Comprehensive Study on Cloud Computing. *Intel. Journal of Advanced Research in Computer Science and Software Engineering,* Vol. 2(9).

Laney, D. (2001). 3D data management: Controlling data volume, velocity and variety. Meta Group, Gartner. Retrieved from http://blogs.gartner.com/doug-laney/files/2012/01/ad949-3D-Data-Management-Controlling-Data-Volume-Velocity-and-Variety.pdf

Lee, D., & Liang, S. H. L. (2011). Geopot: A Cloud-based geolocation data service for mobile applications. *International Journal of Geographical Information Science, 25*(8), 1283–1301. doi:10.1080/13658816.2011.558017

Lee, Y. C., & Zomaya, A. Y. (2012). Energy efficient utilization of resources in cloud computing systems. *The Journal of Supercomputing, 60*(2), 268–280. doi:10.1007/s11227-010-0421-3

Leloglu, E., Ayav, T., & Aslan, B. G. (2013). A Review of Cloud Deployment Models for e-Learning Systems. *Proceedings of the43rd Annual IEEE/IFIP Intel. Conf. on Dependable Systems and Networks (DSN)* (pp. 1-2). doi:10.1109/DSN.2013.6575331

Li, R., Tang, S., Guo, C., & Hu, X. (2010). Thinking the cloud computing in China. *Information Management and Engineering* (pp. 669-672).

Li, S. L., Chen, X., Yang, Z., & Chen, J. (2011). Virtualization security for cloud computing service. *Proceedings of theInternational Conference on Cloud and Service Computing* (pp. 174-179).

Liao, H., & Tao, C. (2008). An Anatomy to SaaS Business Mode Based on Internet. *Paper presented at the 2008 International Conference on Management of e-Commerce and e-Government.* http://dx.doi.org:10.1109/ICMECG.2008.16

Lim, J., & Hurson, A. R. (2002, November). Transaction Processing in Mobile Heterogeneous Database Systems. *IEEE Transactions on Knowledge and Data Engineering, 14*(6), 1330–1346. doi:10.1109/TKDE.2002.1047771

Li, R., Yang, D., Hu, H. B., Xie, J., & Fu, L. (2013). Scalable RDF graph querying using cloud computing. *Journal of Web Engineering, 12*(1 & 2), 159–180.

Liu, W. N., Ma, Q. L., Sun, D. H., & Dan, Y. F. (2010). Traffic State Identification Methods Based on Cloud computing Model. Retrieved from http://202.164.55.108/CSE/CSE/traffic%20state.pdf

Lohmosavi, V., Nejad, A. F., & Hosseini, E. M. (2013). E-learning ecosystem based on Service-Oriented Cloud Computing Architecture.Proceedings of the 2013 5th conferenceon Information and Knowledge Technology, Shiraz (pp. 24-29). doi:10.1109/IKT.2013.6620032

Lopez, V. (2014). *Big and Open data challenges for Smart City.* Researching Group at Madrid.

Ltree (2015). Retrieved from http://www.postgresql.org/docs/9.1/static/ltree.html

Luo, Y., Picalausa, F., Fletcher, G. H. L., Hidders, J., & Vansummeren, S. (2012). In R. De Virgilio et al. (Eds.), *Storing and indexing massive RDF datasets, Semantic Search over the Web* (pp. 31–60). Springer-Verlag Berlin Heidelberg. doi:10.1007/978-3-642-25008-8_2

Ma, A., & Sethi, I. K. (2007). Distributed k-median clustering with application to image clustering. *Proceedings of the 7th International Workshop on Pattern Recognition in Information System*, Funchal, Madeira, Portugal (pp. 215-220). INSTICC.

Malewicz, G., Austern, M. H., Bik, A. J. C., Dehnert, J. C., Horn, I., Leiser, N., & Czajkowski, G. (2010). Pregel: A System for Large-scale Graph Processing. *Proceedings of the /PODS*, Indianapolis, IN, USA.

Malviya, P., & Singh, S. (2013). A Study about Green Computing. *International Journal of Advanced Research in Computer Science and Software Engineering, 3*(6).

Mandeep U., & Manish T. (2012). Implementing Various Encryption Algorithm to Enhance the Data Security of Cloud in Cloud Computing. *International Journal of Computer Science and Information Technology, 2*(10).

Manoj, P. (2013). Emerging Database Models and Related Technologies. *International Journal of Advanced Research in Computer Science and Software Engineering, 3*(2), 264–269.

Manola, F., & Miller, E. 2004, RDF Primer, W3C Recommendation, http://www.w3.org/TR/2004/REC-rdf-primer-20040210/

Manpreet, W., & Rajbir, N. (2013). Implementing Encryption Algorithms to EnhanceData Security of Cloud in Cloud Computing. *International Journal of Computers and Applications*, *70*(18).

Manyika, J., Chui, M., Brown, B., Bughin, J., Dobbs, R., Roxburgh, Ch., & Byers, A. H. (2011). Big data: the next frontier for innovation, competition, and productivity. McKinsey Global Inst. Retrieved from http://www.mckinsey.com/insights/business_technology/big_data_the_next_frontier_for_innovation

MarkLogic Corp. (2014). *MarkLogic*. Retrieved from http://www.marklogic.com/

Marks, E. A. (2010). *Executive's Guide to Cloud Computing*. USA: John Wiley and Sons.

Marston, S., Li, Z., Bandyopadhyay, S., Zhang, J., & Ghalsasi, A. (2011). Cloud computing — The business perspective. *Decision Support Systems*, *51*(1), 176–189. doi:10.1016/j.dss.2010.12.006

Maskare, P.R., & Sulke, S.R. (2014). E-learning Using Cloud Computing. *International Journal of Computer Science and Mobile Computing*, 3(5), 1281 – 1287.

Massoud, P. (2012). Energy-Efficient Datacenters. *IEEE Trans. on Computer Aided Design*, 31(10).

Masud, A.H., & Huang, X. (2012), An E-learning System Architecture based on Cloud Computing. *World Academy of Science, Engineering and Tech.*, 6, 736-740.

Masud, M. A. H., & Huang, X. (2012). An E-learning System Architecture based on Cloud Computing, World Academy of Science. *Engineering and Technology*, *62*, 74–78.

Mather, T., & Kumaraswamy, S. (2012). *Cloud security and privacy; An enterprise perspective on risks and compliance* (1st ed.). O'Reilly Media.

Matthew, G. (2013). Statistical tests of randomness on QKD through a free-space channel coupled to daylight noise. *Journal of Lightwave Technology*, *3*(23).

Matthew, P., Caleb, H., Lamas, L., & Christian, K. (2008). *Daylight operation of a free space, entanglement-based quantum key distribution system*. Centre for Quantum Technologies, National University of Singapore.

McBride, B. (2002). Jena: A Semantic Web toolkit. *IEEE Internet Computing*, *6*(6), 55–59. doi:10.1109/MIC.2002.1067737

McCandless, M., Hatcher, E., & Gospodnetic, O. (2010). *Lucene in action*. Stamford, CT, USA: Manning Publications.

McGrath, M. J., & Scanaill, C. N. (2013). *Sensor Technologies: Healthcare, Wellness and Environmental Applications*. Apress. doi:10.1007/978-1-4302-6014-1

Medaglia, C., & Serbanati, A. (2010). An Overview of Privacy and Security Issues in the Internet of Things. In D. Giusto, A. Iera, G. Morabito, & L. Atzori (Eds.), *The Internet of Things* (pp. 389–395). Springer New York. doi:10.1007/978-1-4419-1674-7_38

Mell, P., & Grance, T. (2011). The NIST Definition of Cloud Computing. *NIST Special Publication 800-145*.

MemSQL Inc. (2014). *MemSQL*. Retrieved from http://www.memsql.com/

Menezes, A., van Oorschot, P., & Vanstone, S. (1996). Handbook of Applied Cryptography.

Mesnier, M., Ganger, G. R., & Riedel, E. (2003). Object-based storage. *Communications Magazine, IEEE, 41*(8), 84–90. doi:10.1109/MCOM.2003.1222722

Mircea, M., & Andreescu, A. I. (2011). Using Cloud Computing in Higher Education: A Strategy to Improve Agility in the Current Financial Crisis. *Communications of the IBIMA, 20*(11), 1–15. doi:10.5171/2011.875547

Miri, A. (2013). *Advanced Security and Privacy for RFID Technologies.* Information Science Reference. doi:10.4018/978-1-4666-3685-9

Mishne, G., Dalton, J., Li, Z., Sharma, A., & Lin, J. (2012). Fast Data in the Era of Big Data: Twitter's Real-Time Related Query Suggestion Architecture. *CoRR, abs/1210.7350.*

Mittleman, D. D., Briggs, R. O., Murphy, J., & Davis, A. (2008). Toward a taxonomy of groupware technologies. *Lecture Notes in Computer Science, 5411*, 305–317. doi:10.1007/978-3-540-92831-7_25

Mohammad, G., John, M., & Ingo, K. (2010). An analysis of the Cloud Computing Security Problem. *Proceedings of APSE 2010 Cloud Workshop*, Sydney, Australia.

Mohammad, O.K.J., Abbas, S., El-Horbaty, E.-S.M., & Salem, A.-B.M. (2013). A Comparative Study of Modern Encryption Algorithms based On Cloud Computing Environment. *Proceedings of the 8th International Conference for Internet Technology and Secured Transactions (ICITST-2013)* (pp. 536-541).

Mohammad, O.K.J., Abbas, S., El-Horbaty, E.-S.M., & Salem, A.-B.M. (2014). Advanced Encryption Standard Development Based Quantum Key Distribution, the 9th International Conference for Internet Technology and Secured Transactions (ICITST-2014), pp.446-456.

Mohammad, O.K.J., Abbas, S., El-Horbaty, E.-S.M., & Salem, A.-B.M., (2014). Cryptographic Cloud Computing Environment as a More Trusted Communication Environment. *International Journal of Grid and High Performance Computing, 6.*

Mohammad, O.K.J., Abbas, S., El-Horbaty, E.-S.M., & Salem, A.-B.M. (2014). Statistical Analysis for Random Bits Generation on Quantum Key Distribution. *Proceedings of the 3rd IEEE- Conference on Cyber Security, Cyber Warfare, and Digital Forensic (CyberSec2014)* (pp. 45-52).

Mohammad, O.K.J., Abbas, S., El-Horbaty, E.-S.M., & Salem, A.-B.M. (2015). Quantum Key Distribution: Simulation and Characterizations. *International Conference on Communication, Management and Information Technology (ICCMIT 2015)*, Prague (pp. 78-88).

Mokbel, M. F., Ghanem, T. M., & Aref, W. G. (2003). Spatio-Temporal Access Methods. *IEEE Data Eng. Bull., 26*(2), 40–49.

Mongo, D. B. Inc. (2014). *MongoDB*. Retrieved from https://www.mongodb.org/

Moniruzzaman, A. B. M., & Hossain, S. A. (2013). NoSQL Database: New Era of Databases for Big data Analytics - Classification, Characteristics and Comparison. *International Journal of Database Theory and Application, 6*(4), 1–14.

Moniruzzaman, A. B. M., & Hossain, S. A. (2013). NoSQL Database: New Era of Databases for Big data Analytics - Classification, Characteristics and Comparison. *International Journal of Database Theory and Application, 6*(4), 1–14.

Moose, F. S. (2015). Retrieved from http://www.moosefs.org/

Nascimento, M. A., Pfoser, D., & Theodoridis, Y. (2003). Synthetic and Real Spatiotemporal Datasets. *IEEE Data Eng. Bull.*, *26*(2), 26–32.

Nelson, G., Charles, M., Fernando, R., Marco, S., Tereza, C., Mats, N., & Makan, P. (2014). A quantitative analysis of current security concerns and solutions for cloud computing, Journal of cloud computing: advanced, systems and applications, 1(11).

Neo Technology, Inc. (2014). *Neo4j*. Retrieved from http://www.neo4j.org/

Netmesh Inc. (2014). *InfoGrid – the Web Graph Database*. Retrieved from http://infogrid.org/trac/

Neumann, T., & Weikum, G. (2008). RDF-3X: A RISC-style engine for RDF. *Proceedings of the VLDB Endowment*, *1*(1), 647–659. doi:10.14778/1453856.1453927

Neumann, T., & Weikum, G. (2010). The RDF-3X engine for scalable management of RDF data. *The VLDB Journal*, *19*(1), 91–113. doi:10.1007/s00778-009-0165-y

NGDATA. (2014). *Lily*. Retrieved from http://www.lilyproject.org/lily/index.html

Nguyen-Dinh, L.-V., Aref, W. G., & Mokbel, M. F. (2010). Spatio-Temporal Access Methods: Part 2 (2003 - 2010). *IEEE Data Eng. Bull.*, *33*(2), 46–55.

Nicoara, D., Kamali, S., Daudjee, K., & Chen, L. (2015). Hermes: Dynamic partitioning for distributed social network graph databases. *Proceedings of the 18th International Conference on Extending Database Technology* (pp. 25-36).

Ning, H. (2013). *Unit and Ubiquitous Internet of Things*. Taylor & Francis. doi:10.1201/b14742

Nishimura, S., Das, S., Agrawal, D., & Abbadi, A. E. (2011). MD-HBase: A scalable multidimensional data infrastructure for location aware services. In: Proceedings of the 2011 IEEE 12th Int. Conf. on Mobile Data Management - Volume 01, IEEE Computer Society Washington, pp. 7–16.

November, V., & Leanza, Y. (2015). *Risk, disaster and crisis reduction: Mobilizing, collecting and sharing information*. Springer International Publishing; doi:10.1007/978-3-319-08542-5

Nuo, D. B. Inc. (2014). *NuoDB*. Retrieved from http://www.nuodb.com/

Nurmi, D., Wolski, R., Grzegorczyk, C., Obertelli, G., Soman, S., Youseff, L., & Zagorodnov, D. (2009). The eucalyptus open-source cloud-computing system. *Paper presented at the 9th IEEE/ACM International Symposium on Cluster Computing and the Grid CCGRID'09*. doi:10.1109/CCGRID.2009.93

Odeh, A., Elleithy, K., Alshowkan, M., & Abdelfattah, E. (2013). Quantum key distribution by using RSA.*Proceeding of 3rd International Conference on Innovative Computing Technology (INTECH)*.

ODMS. org. (2013). Big Data Analytics at Thomson Reuters. Interview with Jochen L. Leidner. Retrieved from http://www.odbms.org/blog/2013/11/big-data-analytics-at-thomson-reuters-interview-with-jochen-l-leidner/

Oh, S. W., & Kim, H. S. (2014). Decentralized access permission control using resource-oriented architecture for the Web of Things. *Paper presented at the 2014 16th International Conference on Advanced Communication Technology (ICACT)*. doi:10.1109/ICACT.2014.6779062

Okabe, A., Boots, B., Sugihara, K., & Chiu, S. N. (2000). *Spatial tessellations, concepts and applications of Voronoi diagrams* (2nd ed.). John Wiley and Sons Ltd. doi:10.1002/9780470317013

Okcan, A., & Riedewald, M. (2011). Processing theta-joins using MapReduce. *Proceedings of the ACM SIGMOD International Conference on Management of Data*, Athens, Greece (pp. 949-960). ACM.

Oliveira, T., Thomas, M., & Espadanal, M. (2014). Assessing the determinants of cloud computing adoption: An analysis of the manufacturing and services sectors. *Information & Management, 51*(5), 497–510. doi:10.1016/j.im.2014.03.006

Oracle (2014a). *Oracle NoSQL Database.* Retrieved from http://www.oracle.com/technetwork/database/database-technologies/nosqldb/overview/index.html

Oracle (2014b). *Big Data Appliance X4-2.* Retrieved from http://www.oracle.com/technetwork/database/bigdata-appliance/overview/index.html

OracleNimbula. (2014). Retrieved from http://www.oracle.com/us/corporate/acquisitions/nimbula/index.html

Orient Technologies, L. T. D. (2014). *OrientDB.* Retrieved from http://www.orientechnologies.com/orientdb/

Othman, S. H., & Beydoun, G. (2013). Model-driven disaster management. *Information & Management, 50*(5), 218–228. doi:10.1016/j.im.2013.04.002

Othman, S. H., Beydoun, G., & Sugumaran, V. (2014). Development and validation of a disaster management metamodel (DMM). *Information Processing & Management, 50*(2), 235–271. doi:10.1016/j.ipm.2013.11.001

Owusu, F., & Pattinson, C. (2012). The current state of understanding of the energy efficiency of cloud computing. *Proceedings of the IEEE 11th International Conf. of the Trust, Security, Privacy in Computing and Communications (TrustCom)*, Liverpool. doi:10.1109/TrustCom.2012.270

Padmapriya, A., & Subhasri, P. (2013). Cloud Computing: Security Challenges and Encryption Practices. *International Journal of Advance Research in Computer Science and Software Engineering, 3*(3).

Palanivel, K., & Kuppuswami, S. (2014). Towards Service-Oriented Reference Model and Architecture to e-Learning Systems. *Intel. Journal of Emerging Trends & Tech. Computer Science, 3*(4).

Palankar, M. R., Iamnitchi, A., Ripeanu, M., & Garfinkel, S. (2008). Amazon S3 for science grids: a viable solution? *Paper presented at the Proceedings of the 2008 international workshop on Data-aware distributed computing*, Boston, MA, USA. doi:10.1145/1383519.1383526

Palen, L., Anderson, K. M., Mark, G., Martin, J., Sicker, D., Palmer, M., & Grunwald, D. (2010). A vision for technology-mediated support for public participation & assistance in mass emergencies & disasters. *Proceedings of the ACM-BCS Visions of Computer Science Conference,* Edinburgh, UK (pp. 1-12).

Papailiou, N., Konstantinou, I., Tsoumakos, D., Karras, P., & Koziris, N. (2013). H2RDF+: High-performance distributed joins over large-scale RDF graphs. *Proceedings of the 2013 IEEE International Conference on Big Data* (pp. 255-263). doi:10.1109/BigData.2013.6691582

Papailiou, N., Konstantinou, I., Tsoumakos, D., & Koziris, N. (2012). H2RDF: Adaptive query processing on RDF data in the cloud. *Proceedings of the 21st World Wide Web Conference*, 397-400. doi:10.1145/2187980.2188058

Paper, W. (2007). *Green Grid Metrics—Describing Data Centres Power Efficiency.* Technical Committee by the Green Grid Industry Consortium.

Parkhill, D. (1966). *Article on The challenge of the Computer Utility.* Addison-Wesley Publications.

Parwekar, P. (2011, September 15-17). From Internet of Things towards cloud of things. *Paper presented at the 2011 2nd International Conference on Computer and Communication Technology (ICCCT).*

Patil D., & Akshay R. (2012). Data Security over Cloud Emerging Trends in Computer Science and Information Technology. International Journal of Computer Applications, pp. 123-147.

Patil D., Akshay R. (2012), "Data Security over Cloud Emerging Trends in Computer Science and Information Technology", proceeding published in International Journal of Computer Applications, pp. 123-147.

Pautasso, C., Zimmermann, O., & Leymann, F. (2008). Restful web services vs. "big" web services: making the right architectural decision. *Paper presented at theProceedings of the 17th international conference on World Wide Web*, Beijing, China. doi:10.1145/1367497.1367606

Pavlo, A., Paulson, E., Rasin, A., Abadi, D., DeWitt, D. J., Madden, S., & Stonebraker, M. (2009). A Comparison of Approaches to Large-Scale Data Analysis.*Proceedings of SIGMOD/PODS'09*, Providence, RI, USA. doi:10.1145/1559845.1559865

Pawlowski, B., Shepler, S., Beame, C., Callaghan, B., Eisler, M., Noveck, D., & Thurlow, R. et al. (2000). The NFS version 4 protocol. *Proceedings of the 2nd International System Administration and Networking Conference (SANE 2000)*.

Pepple, K. (2011). *Deploying OpenStack*. O'Reilly Media, Inc.

Pfoser, D., Jensen, C. S., & Theodoridis, Y. (2000, September 10-14). Novel Approaches in Query Processing for Moving Object Trajectories. *Proceedings of 26th International Conference on Very Large Data BasesVLDB 2000*, Cairo, Egypt (pp. 395–406).

Phankokkruad, M. (2012). Implement of Cloud Computing for e-Learning System. *Proceedings of theInternational Conference on Computer & Information Science*. doi:10.1109/ICCISci.2012.6297204

Piatetsky-Shapiro, G., & Parker, G. (2006). Module on Data Mining. Retrieved from www.kdnuggets.com

Pocatilu, P., Alecu, F., & Vetrici, M. (2009). Using Cloud Computing for E-learning Systems. *Proceedings of the 8th WSEAS Intel., Conference on Data networks, communications, computers*, Baltimore, USA (pp. 54-59).

Pocatilu, P. (2010). Cloud Computing Benefits for E-learning Solutions. *Economics of Knowledge*, 2(1), 9–14.

Pokorny, J. (2011). NoSQL Databases: A step to database scalability in Web environment. *Int J Web Info Syst*, 9(1), 69–82. doi:10.1108/17440081311316398

Pokorny, J. (2011).NoSQL databases: A step to database scalability in web environment. *Proceedings of the 2011 International Conference on Information Integration and Web-based Applications and Services* (pp. 278-283). doi:10.1145/2095536.2095583

Porter, S. (2004). Pros and Cons of Paper and Electronic Surveys. In *New Directions for Institutional Resaerch* (Vol. 2004, pp. 23–38). Wiley Periodicals, Inc. doi:10.1002/ir.103

Pritchett, D. (2008). BASE: An ACID alternative. *ACM Queue; Tomorrow's Computing Today*, 6(3), 48–55. doi:10.1145/1394127.1394128

Prud'hommeaux, E., & Seaborne, A. (2008). SPARQL Query Language for RDF, W3C Recommendation. Retrieved from http://www.w3.org/TR/2008/REC-rdf-sparql-query-20080115/

Qayyum, J., Khan, F., Lal, M., Gul, F., Sohaib, M., & Masood, F. (2011). Implementing and Managing framework for PaaS in Cloud Computing. *International Journal of Computer Science Issues*, 8(5), 474–479.

Qirui, Y. (2012). Kaas-based intelligent service model in agricultural expert system.*Proceedings of the 2nd International Conference on Consumer Electronics, Communications and Networks,*Yichang, China (pp. 2678-2680). doi:10.1109/CECNet.2012.6201763

Quercia, D., Lathia, N., Calabrese, F., Lorenzo, G. D., & Crowcroft, J. (2010, December 14-17). Recommending Social Events from Mobile Phone Location Data. *Proceedings of the 10th IEEE International Conference on Data Mining ICDM 2010, Sydney, Australia* (pp. 971–976). http://doi.org/ doi:10.1109/ICDM.2010.152

Rahman, H. A., Armstrong, M., Mao, D., & Marti, J. R. (2008). I2Sim: A matrix-partition based framework for critical infrastructure interdependencies simulation.*Proceedings of the Electrical Power and Energy Conference*, Vancouver, BC, Canada (pp. 1-8). doi:10.1109/EPC.2008.4763353

Rajaman, A., & Ullman, J. D. (2011). *Mining of Massive Datasets*. Cambridge University Press. doi:10.1017/CBO9781139058452

Rasetic, S., Sander, J., Elding, J., & Nascimento, M. A. (2005, August 30 - September 2). A Trajectory Splitting Model for Efficient Spatio-Temporal Indexing.*Proceedings of the 31st International Conference on Very Large Data Bases*, Trondheim, Norway (pp. 934–945).

Ratnasamy, S., Francis, P., Handley, M., Karp, R. M., & Shenker, S. (2001). A scalable content addressable network. In: *Proceedings of SIGCOMM*, ACM, pp. 161–172.

Rawal V., Dhamija A., Sharma S. (2012). Revealing New Concepts in Photography & Clouds. *International Journal of Scientific & Technology Research*, 1(7).

Rawson, A., & Pfleuger, J. (2008). *Cader*. Green Grid Data Center Power Efficiency Metrics. Consortium Green Grid.

Redis (2014) *Redis*. Retrieved from http://redis.io/

Reeves, D. (2009). *Enterprise Cloud Computing: Transforming IT*. Whitepaper Platform Computing.

Ren, L., Tian, F., Zhang, X., & Zhang, L. (2010). DaisyViz: A model-based user interface toolkit for interactive information visualization systems. *Journal of Visual Languages and Computing*, 21(4), 209–229. doi:10.1016/j.jvlc.2010.05.003

Report, A. M. (2010). Cloud computing and Sustainability: The Environmental Benefits of Moving to the Cloud. Retrieved from http://www.wspenvironmental.com/media /docs/newsroom/ Cloud_ computing_ and_ Sustainability_-_Whitepaper_-_Nov_2010.pdf

Revolution Analytics White Paper. (2011). Advanced 'Big Data' Analytics with R and Hadoop.

Rosado, D. G., Mellado, D., & Piattini, M. (2013). *Security Engineering for Cloud Computing: Approaches and Tools*. Information Science Reference. doi:10.4018/978-1-4666-2125-1

Roselli, D., Lorch, J. R., & Anderson, T. E. (2000). A comparison of file system workloads. *Paper presented at theProceedings of the annual conference on USENIX Annual Technical Conference*, San Diego, California.

Rouse, M. (2009). Traffic State Identification Methods Based on Cloud computing Model). Public Cloud. Retrieved from http://searchcloudcomputing.techtarget.com/definition/public-cloud

Saha, D., & Sridhar, V. (2012). *Next Generation Data Communication Technologies: Emerging Trends*. Information Science Reference. doi:10.4018/978-1-61350-477-2

Sakr, S., & Al-Naymat, G. (2009). Relational processing of RDF queries: A survey. *SIGMOD Record*, 38(4), 23–28. doi:10.1145/1815948.1815953

Sakr, S., Liu, A., Batista, D. M., & Alomari, M. (2011). A survey of large scale data management approaches in cloud environments. *IEEE Communications Surveys and Tutorials*, 13(3), 311–336. doi:10.1109/SURV.2011.032211.00087

Sarojadevi, K., & Jeevitha, R. (2011). Uncloud the Cloud of Cloud Computing. Retrieved from http://www.caesjournals. org/spluploads/IJCAES-AISC- 2011-174.pdf

Satoh, F., Yanagisawa, H., Takahashi, H., & Kushida, T. (2013). Total Energy Management system for Cloud Computing. *Proceedings of the IEEE International Conference of the Cloud Engineering (IC2E)*, Redwood City, CA. doi:10.1109/ IC2E.2013.46

Sawyer, S. M., O'Gwynn, B. D., Tran, A., & Yu, T. (2013, September 10-12). Understanding query performance in Accumulo. *Proceedings of theIEEE High Performance Extreme Computing Conference HPEC 2013*, Waltham, MA, USA (pp. 1–6). http://doi.org/ doi:10.1109/HPEC.2013.6670330

ScaleArc. (2014). *ScaleArc*. Retrieved from http://scalearc.com/

Schram, A., & Anderson, K. M. (2012). MySQL to NoSQL: Data modeling challenges in supporting scalability.*Proceedings of the 3rd Annual Conference on Systems, Programming, Languages and Applications: Software for Humanity*Tucson, AZ, USA (pp. 191-202). doi:10.1145/2384716.2384773

Schubert, L. (2010). Traffic State Identification Methods Based on Cloud computing Model). The Future of Cloud Computing-Opportunities for European Cloud Computing Beyond 2010. Retrieved from http://cordis.europa.eu/fp7/ ict/ssai/docs/cloud-report-final.pdf

Schuh, M. A., Angryk, R. A., Pillai, K. G., Banda, J. M., & Martens, P. C. (2013, *September 15-18*). A large-scale solar image dataset with labeled event regions. *Proceedings of theIEEE International Conference on Image Processing, ICIP 2013*, Melbourne, Australia (pp. 4349–4353). http://doi.org/ doi:10.1109/ICIP.2013.6738896

Schulz, W. (2009). What is SaaS, Cloud Computing, PaaS and IaaS? Retrieved from http://www.s-consult.com/2009/08/04/ what-is-saas-cloud-computing-paas-and-iaas/

Sen, R., Farris, A., & Guerra, P. (2013, June 27-July 2). Benchmarking Apache Accumulo BigData Distributed Table Store Using Its Continuous Test Suite. *Proceedings of theIEEE International Congress on Big Data, BigData Congress 2013* (pp. 334–341). http://doi.org/ doi:10.1109/BigData.Congress.2013.51

Seong Hoon, K., & Daeyoung, K. (2013, June 28-July 3). Multi-tenancy Support with Organization Management in the Cloud of Things. *Paper presented at the 2013 IEEE International Conference on Services Computing (SCC)*.

Sharma, S., Shuman, M. A. R., Goel, A., Aggarwal, A., Gupta, B., Glickfield, S., & Guedalia, I. D. (2014). Context aware actions among heterogeneous internet of things (iot) devices: Google Patents.

Shekhar, S., & Chawla, S. (2003). *Spatial databases - a tour*. Prentice Hall.

Shinde, S., Nalawade, S., & Nalawade, A. (2013). Green Computing: Go Green and Save Energy. *International Journal of Advanced Research in Computer Science and Software Engineering*, 3(7).

Shon, T., Cho, J., Han, K., & Choi, H. (2014). Toward Advanced Mobile Cloud Computing for the Internet of Things: Current Issues and Future Direction. *Mobile Networks and Applications*, 19(3), 404–413. doi:10.1007/s11036-014-0509-8

Shute, J., Vingralek, R., Samwel, B., Handy, B., Whipkey, Ch., Rollins, E.,… Apte, H. (2013). F1 A Distributed SQL Database That Scales. *PVLDB*, 6(11), 1068-1079.

Shvachko, K., Hairong, K., Radia, S., & Chansler, R. (2010, May 3-7). *The Hadoop Distributed File System*. Paper presented at the 2010 IEEE 26th Symposium on Mass Storage Systems and Technologies (MSST).

Shvachko, K., Kuang, H., Radia, S., & Chansler, R. (2010). The Hadoop Distributed File System, *Proceedings of 2010 IEEE 26th Symposium on Mass Storage Systems and Technologies (MSST)*, Lake Tahoe, Nevada, USA doi:10.1109/MSST.2010.5496972

Silva, T., Wuwongse, V., & Sharma, H. N. (2011). Linked data in disaster mitigation and preparedness.*Proceedings of the Third International Conference on Intelligent Networking and Collaborative Systems*Fukuoka, Japan (pp. 746-751). doi:10.1109/INCoS.2011.113

Simmhan, Y., Kumbhare, A. G., Cao, B., & Prasanna, V. (2011, July). Analysis of Security and Privacy Issues in Smart Grid Software Architectures on Clouds. *Proceedings of theIEEE Conference on Cloud Computing* (pp. 582-589). doi:10.1109/CLOUD.2011.107

Singh, A., & Malhotra, M. (2012). Agent Based Framework for Scalability in Cloud Computing *International Journal of Computer Science & Engineering Technology,* April, 41-45.

Singh, D., & Reddy, C.K. (2014). A Survey on Platforms for Big Data Analytics. *Journal of Big Data*, 8.

Sintek, M., & Kiesel, M. (2006). RDFBroker: A signature-based high-performance RDF store, *Proceedings of the 3rd European Semantic Web Conference* (pp. 363-377).

Smith, J., & Nair, R. (2003). *Virtual Machines: Versatile Platforms for Systems and Processes*. Los Altos, CA: Morgan Kaufmann.

Smith, R. (2007). An overview of the Tesseract OCR engine.*Proceeding of the Ninth International Conference on Document Analysis and Recognition*Curitiba, Brazil. doi:10.1109/ICDAR.2007.4376991

Smith, S., & Marchesini, J. (2007). *The Craft of System Security*. Pearson Education.

Snow, D. (2012). *Dwaine Snow's Thoughts on Databases and Data Management*. Retrieved from http://dsnowondb2.blogspot.cz/2012/07/adding-4th-v-to-big-data-veracity.html

Solange, G., & Mohammed, A. (2014). Applying QKD to reach unconditional security in communications. European research project SECOQC. Retrieved from www.secoqc.net

solid IT (2014). *DB-engines*. Retrieved from http://db-engines.com/en/ranking

Son, N. H. (2012). Module on Data Preprocessing Techniques for Data Mining on Data Cleaning and Data Preprocessing. Retrieved from http://elitepdf.com/

Song, Z., & Roussopoulos, N. (2003, January 21-24). SEB-tree: An Approach to Index Continuously Moving Objects. *Proceedings of the4th International Conference, MDM 2003*, Melbourne, Australia (pp. 340–344). http://doi.org/doi:10.1007/3-540-36389-0_25

Son, I., Lee, D., Lee, J.-N., & Chang, Y. B. (2014). Market perception on cloud computing initiatives in organizations: An extended resource-based view. *Information & Management, 51*(6), 653–669. doi:10.1016/j.im.2014.05.006

Soren, B., Sven, B., & Hugo, I. (2013). Consumer –controlled cryptography-as-a-service in the cloud.*Proceedings of 11th International Conference, ACNS 2013*.

Spaccapietra, S., Parent, C., Damiani, M. L., de Macêdo, J. A. F., Porto, F., & Vangenot, C. (2008). A conceptual view on trajectories. *Data & Knowledge Engineering, 65*(1), 126–146. doi:10.1016/j.datak.2007.10.008

Sperka, S., & Smrz, P. (2012).Towards adaptive and semantic database model for RDF data stores. *Proceedings of the Sixth International Conference on Complex, Intelligent, and Software Intensive Systems* (pp. 810-815).

Stantic, B., & Pokorný, J. (2014). Opportunities in Big Data Management and Processing. *Frontiers in Artificial Intelligence and Applications, 270*, 15–26.

StarWind Virtual SAN- Quick Start Guide. (2014). *StarWind Software*. USA.

Stavroulakis, P., & Stamp, M. (2010). *Handbook of Information and Communication Security*. Springer. doi:10.1007/978-3-642-04117-4

Stevens, J. (1992). *Applied multivariate statistics for the social sciences. NJ*. Hillsdale: Erlbaum.

Stonebraker, M. (2014). *No Hadoop: The Future of the Hadoop/HDFS Stack*. Retrieved from http://istc-bigdata.org/index.php/no-hadoop-the-future-of-the-hadoophdfs-stack/

Stonebraker, M., Abadi, D. J., Batkin, A., Chen, X., Cherniack, M., Ferreira, M., . . . Zdonik, S. (2005). C-store: a column-oriented DBMS. *Paper presented at theProceedings of the 31st international conference on Very large data bases*, Trondheim, Norway.

Stonebraker, M. (2010). SQL databases v. NoSQL databases. *Communications of the ACM, 53*(4), 10–11. doi:10.1145/1721654.1721659

Stonebraker, M., & Rowe, L. A. (1986). The design of Postgres: Vol. 15. *No. 2* (pp. 340–355). ACM.

Stonebraker, M., & Weisberg, A. (2013). The VoltDB Main Memory DBMS. *IEEE Data Eng. Bull., 36*(2), 21–27.

Stuart, J., & Barker, A. (2013). Undefined By Data: A Survey of Big Data Definitions.

Stuart, J., & Barker, A. (2013). Undefined By Data: A Survey of Big Data Definitions. *CoRR*, abs/1309.5821. Retrieved from http://arxiv.org/pdf/1309.5821v1.pdf

Sumathi, C. P., Santhanam, T., & Gayathri Devi, G. (2012). A survey on various approaches of text extraction in images. *International Journal of Computer Science and Engineering Survey, 3*(4), 27–42. doi:10.5121/ijcses.2012.3403

Sun, E., Zhang, X., & Li, Z. (2012). The internet of things (IOT) and cloud computing (CC) based tailings dam monitoring and pre-alarm system in mines. *Safety Science, 50*(4), 811–815. doi:10.1016/j.ssci.2011.08.028

Sunita, M., & Seema, S. (2013). *Distributed Computing* (2nd ed.). USA: Oxford University Press.

Sun, J. L., & Jin, Q. (2010). Scalable RDF store based on HBase and MapReduce. *Proceedings of the 3rd International Conference Advanced Computer Theory and Engineering* (pp. V1-633-V1-636).

Swaminatha, T. M., & Elden, C. R. (2003). *Wireless Security and Privacy: Best Practices and Design Techniques*. Addison-Wesley.

Syam, P., Subramanian, R., & Thamizh, D. (2010). Ensuring data security in cloud computing using sobol sequence. *Proceedings of the 1st international conference on parallel, distributed and grid computing (PDGC)*.

Tatebe, O., Hiraga, K., & Soda, N. (2010). Gfarm Grid File System. *New Generation Computing, 28*(3), 257–275. doi:10.1007/s00354-009-0089-5

Tauro, C., Aravindh, S., & Shreeharsha, A. B. (2012). Comparative Study of the New Generation, Agile, Scalable, High Performance NOSQL Databases. *International Journal of Computer Applications, 48*(20).

The Apache Foundation. (2013). Apache Tika toolkit. Retrieved from http://tika.apache.org/

The Apache Software Foundation. (2014a). *Hadoop*. Retrieved from http://hadoop.apache.org/

The Apache Software Foundation. (2014b). *Apache HBase*. Retrieved from https://hbase.apache.org/

The Apache Software Foundation. (2014c). *Cassandra*. Retrieved from http://cassandra.apache.org/

The Apache Software Foundation. (2014d). *Apache CouchDB™*. Retrieved from http://couchdb.apache.org/

The Apache Software Foundation. (2014e). *Mahout*. Retrieved from http://mahout.apache.org/

The Apache Software Foundation. (2014f). *Apache Solr™ 4.10*. Retrieved from http://lucene.apache.org/solr/

The Article from Dataconomy. (2014). Big Data Complexity and India's Election. Retrieved from http://dataconomy.com/big-data-complexity-and-indias-election/

The NIST Definition of Cloud Computing. (n. d.). *National Institute of Standards and Technology*.

The University of British Columbia. (2011). DR-NEP (disaster response network enabled platform) project. Retrieved from http://drnep.ece.ubc.ca/index.html

Thusoo, A., Sarma, J. S., Jain, N., Shao, Z., Chakka, P., Anthony, S., & Murthy, R. et al. (2009). Hive - a warehousing solution over a map-reduce framework. *PVLDB, 2*(2), 1626–1629.

Tsuchiya, S., Sakamoto, Y., Tsuchimoto, Y., & Lee, V. (2012, April). Big Data Processing in Cloud Environments, FUJITSU Sc. *Tech Journal, 48*(2), 159–168.

United States Environmental Protection Agency. (2008). EPANET - water distribution modeling. Retrieved from http://www.epa.gov/nrmrl/wswrd/dw/epanet.html

Vaidya, M., & Deshpande, S. (2013). Study of Hadoop-based Traffic Management System, IJCA Proceedings of ICRTITCS (Vol. 3, pp. 38-42).

Vasseur, J. P., & Dunkels, A. (2010). *Interconnecting Smart Objects with IP: The Next Internet*. Elsevier Science.

Vattani, A. (2011). K-means requires exponentially many iterations even in the plane. *Discrete & Computational Geometry, 45*(4), 596–616. doi:10.1007/s00454-011-9340-1

Velte, A. T., Velte, T. J., & Elsenpeter, R. (2010). *Cloud Computing - A Practical Approach*. USA: McGraw Hill.

Vernica, R., Carey, M. J., & Li, C. (2010). Efficient parallel set-similarity joins using mapreduce.*Proceedings of the ACM SIGMOD International Conference on Management of Data*, Indianapolis, Indiana, USA (pp. 495-506). ACM.

Vinayak, R., Borkar, V., Carey, M.-J., & Li, Ch. (2012). Big data platforms: What's next? *ACM Cross Road, 19*(1), 44–49. doi:10.1145/2331042.2331057

Viswanathan, P. (2012). Cloud Computing – Is It Really All That Beneficial? Retrieved from http://mobiledevices.about.com/od/additionalresources/a/Cloud-Computing-Is-It-Really-All-That-Beneficial.htm

VMware. (2010). Public Cloud Service Definition (Technical White Paper). Retrieved from http://www.vmware.com/files/pdf/VMware-Public-Cloud-Service-Definition.pdf

Volt, D. B. Inc. (2014). *VoltDB*. Retrieved from http://voltdb.com/

Vouk, A. (2008). Cloud computing–issues, research and implementations. *CIT. Journal of Computing and Information Technology*, *16*(4), 235–246. doi:10.2498/cit.1001391

W3C. (2015). File API: Writer. Retrieved from http://dev.w3.org/2009/dap/file-system/file-writer.html

Wang Q., Cong X., Min S. (2012). Protecting Privacy by Multi-dimensional K-anonymity. *Journal of Software*, 7(8).

Wang, L., Zheng, Y., Xie, X., & Ma, W.-Y. (2008, April 27-30). A Flexible Spatio-Temporal Indexing Scheme for Large-Scale GPS Track Retrieval. *Proceedings of the9th International Conference on Mobile Data Management (MDM 2008)*, Beijing, China (pp. 1–8). http://doi.org/ doi:10.1109/MDM.2008.24

Wang, Y., Lin, J., Annavaram, M., Jacobson, Q. A., Hong, J., Krishnamachari, B., & Sadeh, N. (2009). A framework of energy efficient mobile sensing for automatic user state recognition. *Paper presented at the Proceedings of the 7th international conference on Mobile systems, applications, and services*, Kraków, Poland. doi:10.1145/1555816.1555835

Wang, F., Oral, S., Shipman, G., Drokin, O., Wang, T., & Huang, I. (2009). Understanding Lustre filesystem internals. *Oak Ridge National Lab technical report. ORNL. U. S. Atomic Energy Commission, TM-2009*(117).

Wang, J. (June), Young, K., Hock, T., Lauritsen, D., Behringer, D., Black, M., … Zhang, J. A. (2014). A Long-Term, High-quality, High Vertical Resolution GPS Dropsonde Dataset for Hurricane and Other Studies. *Bulletin of the American Meteorological Society*. doi:10.1175/BAMS-D-13-00203.1

Wang, J., Wu, S., Gao, H., Li, J., & Ooi, B. C. (2010). Indexing multi-dimensional data in a cloud system. In: *Proceedings of SIGMOD*, ACM, pp. 591–602.

Wang, Y., Du, X. Y., Lu, J. H., & Wang, X. F. (2010). FlexTable: Using a dynamic relation model to store RDF data. *Proceedings of the 15th International Conference on Database Systems for Advanced Applications* (pp. 580-594_. doi:10.1007/978-3-642-12026-8_44

Waugh, W. L., & Streib, G. (2006). Collaboration and leadership for effective emergency management. *Public Administration Review*, *66*(1), 131–140. doi:10.1111/j.1540-6210.2006.00673.x

Wei, X., Zhang, J., & Zeng, S. (2009). Study of the Potential SaaS Platform Provider in China. *Proceedings of the 2009 WRI World Congress on Software Engineering, 4*, 78-80.

Weil, S. A., Brandt, S. A., Miller, E. L., & Maltzahn, C. (2006). CRUSH: controlled, scalable, decentralized placement of replicated data. *Paper presented at the Proceedings of the 2006 ACM/IEEE conference on Supercomputing*, Tampa, Florida. doi:10.1109/SC.2006.19

Weil, S. A., Leung, A. W., Brandt, S. A., & Maltzahn, C. (2007). RADOS: a scalable, reliable storage service for petabyte-scale storage clusters. *Paper presented at the Proceedings of the 2nd international workshop on Petascale data storage: held in conjunction with Supercomputing '07*, Reno, Nevada. doi:10.1145/1374596.1374606

Weil, S. A., Brandt, S. A., Miller, E. L., Long, D. D. E., & Maltzahn, C. (2006). Ceph: A Scalable, High-performance Distributed File System*Proceedings of the 7th Symposium on Operating Systems Design and Implementation* (pp. 307-320). Seattle, Washington: USENIX Association.

Weiss, C., Karras, P., & Bernstein, A. (2008). Hexastore: Sextuple indexing for semantic web data management. *Proceedings of the VLDB Endowment*, *1*(1), 1008–1019. doi:10.14778/1453856.1453965

White, T. (2009). *Hadoop: the definitive guide: the definitive guide*. O'Reilly Media, Inc.

Wilder, B. (2012). *Cloud Architecture Patterns: Using Microsoft Azure*. O'Reilly Media, Inc.

Wilkinson, K., Sayers, C., Kuno, H. A., & Reynolds, D. (2003). Efficient RDF storage and retrieval in Jena2. *Proceedings of theSemantic Web and Databases Workshop* (pp. 131-150).

William, S. (2012). Cryptography and network security (5th ed.). Prentice Hall.

Windows Azure (software). (n. d.). Microsoft. Retrieved from www.microsoft.com/azure

Winkler, J. (2011). Securing the cloud: cloud computer security techniques and tactics.

World Wide Headquarters, B. S. A. (2012). *BSA Global Cloud Computing Scorecard*. Washington, DC.

Wu, S. & Wu, K. (2009). An indexing framework for efficient retrieval on the cloud. IEEE Data Engineering Bulletin, 01/2009, 32:75-82.

Wyld, D. (2010). The Cloudy Future of Government It: Cloud Computing and the Public Sector around the World. *International Journal of Web & Semantic Technology*, *1*(1).

Xi, C., Jianming, L., Xiangzhen, L., Limin, S., & Yan, Z. (2011, October 14-16). Integration of IoT with smart grid. *Paper presented at the IET International Conference on Communication Technology and Application (ICCTA 2011)*.

Xia, C., Lu, H., Ooi, B. C., & Hu, J. (2004). Gorder: an efficient method for knn join processing.*Proceedings of the International Conference on Very Large Data Bases*, Toronto, Canada (pp. 756-767). Morgan Kaufmann. doi:10.1016/B978-012088469-8.50067-X

Xiao, Z., & Xiao, Y. (2014). Achieving accountable MapReduce in Cloud Computing. *Future Generation Computer Systems*, *30*, 1–13. doi:10.1016/j.future.2013.07.001

Xu, X., Jager, J., & Kriegel, H. (1999). A fast parallel clustering algorithm for large spatial databases. *Data Mining and Knowledge Discovery*, *3*(3), 263–290. doi:10.1023/A:1009884809343

Yaghob, J., Bednárek, D., Kruliš, M., & Zavoral, F. (2014). Column-oriented Data Store for Astrophysical Data.*Proceedings of 25th International Workshop on Database and Expert Systems Applications*, Munich, Germany.

Yamini, R. (2012). Power Management in Cloud Computing Using Green Algorithm. *Proceedings of the IEEE-International Conference on Advances in Engineering, Science and Management ICAESM '12)*, Nagapattinam, Tamil Nadu.

Yao, B., Li, F., & Kumar, P. (2010). K nearest neighbor queries and kNN-joins in large relational databases (almost) for free.*Proceedings of the International Conference on Data Engineering,*Long Beach, California, USA (pp. 4-15). IEEE. doi:10.1109/ICDE.2010.5447837

Yau, S. S., & An, H. G. (2010). Confidentiality Protection in Cloud Computing Systems. *Int J Software Informatics*, *4*(4), 351.

Ye, X. (2011). Cloud Computing Era Dawns for China's Navigation Industry Retrieved from http://english.peopledaily.com.cn/90882/7455078.html

Zaheer. (2012). China has the largest number of internet users with more than 500 million people. Retrieved from http://www.americanlivewire.com/china-has-the-largest-number-of-internet-users-with-more-than-500-million-people/

Zhang, C., Li, F., & Jestes, J. (2012). Efficient parallel kNN joins for large data in MapReduce.*Proceedings of the International Conference on Extending Database Technology*, Berlin, Germany (pp. 38-49). ACM. doi:10.1145/2247596.2247602

Zhang, Q., Cheng, L., & Boothbay, R. (2010). Cloud Computing: State-of-the-Art and Research Challenges. *J Internet Serv Appl, The Brazilian Computers & Society*, 2010.

Zhang, Q., Cheng, L., & Boutaba, R. (2010). Cloud computing: State-of-the-art and research challenges. *Journal of Internet Services and Applications*, *1*(1), 7–18. doi:10.1007/s13174-010-0007-6

Zhang, S., Han, J., Liu, Z., Wang, K., & Xu, Z. (2009). SJMR: Parallelizing spacial join with MapReduce on clusters. *Proceedings of the IEEE International Conference on Cluster Computing*, New Orleans, Louisiana, USA (pp. 1-8). IEEE Computer Society. doi:10.1109/CLUSTR.2009.5289178

Zhang, X., Ai, J., Wang, Z., Lu, J., & Meng, X. (2009). An efficient multi-dimensional index for cloud data management. In *Proceedings of CloudDB* (pp. 17–24). ACM.

Zhang, Y. (2010). Cloud Computing Assisted Instructions in China. *Education and Information Technologies*, *2*, 438–440.

Zhao, W., Ma, H., & He, Q. (2009). Parallel k-means clustering based on MapReduce. *Proceedings of the First International Conference CloudCom*, Beijing, China (pp. 674-679). Springer.

Zhou, M., Zhang, R., Xie, W., & Qian, W. (2010). Security and Privacy in Cloud Computing: A Survey. *Proceedings of the 2010 Sixth International Conference on Semantics, Knowledge and Grids* (pp. 105-112).

Zhou, P., Zhang, D., Salzberg, B., Cooperman, G., & Kollios, G. (2005, November 4-5). Close pair queries in moving object databases. *Proceedings of the 13th ACM International Workshop on Geographic Information Systems, ACM-GIS 2005,* Bremen, Germany (pp. 2–11). http://doi.org/ doi:10.1145/1097064.1097067

Zhou, H. (2013). *The Internet of Things in the Cloud: A Middleware Perspective*. Taylor & Francis.

Zhou, M., Mu, Y., Susilo, W., Yan, J., & Dong, L. (2012). Privacy enhanced data outsourcing in the cloud. *Journal of Network and Computer Applications*, *35*(4), 1367–1373. doi:10.1016/j.jnca.2012.01.022

Zissis, D., & Lekkas, D. (2011). Securing e-Government and e-Voting with an open cloud computing architecture. *Government Information Quarterly*, 2–13.

Zissis, D., & Lekkas, D. (2012). Addressing Cloud Computing Security Issues. *Future Generation Computer Systems*, *28*(3), 583–592. doi:10.1016/j.future.2010.12.006

About the Contributors

Zongmin Ma received a Ph. D. degree from the City University of Hong Kong and is currently a Full Professor of College of Computer Science and Technology at Nanjing University of Aeronautics and Astronautics, China. His current research interests include intelligent database systems, knowledge representation and reasoning, the Semantic Web and XML, knowledge-bases systems, and big data processing. He has published over 100 papers in international journals, conferences and books in these areas since 1999. He also authored and edited several scholarly books published by Springer-Verlag and IGI Global, respectively.

***

Safia Abbas received her Ph.D. (2010) in Computer science from Niigata University, Japan, her M.Sc. (2003) and B.Sc. (1998) in computer and information sciences from Ain Shams University, Egypt. Safia is interested in research regarding data mining augmentation, intelligent computing, and artificial intelligent. She has published around 15 papers in refereed journals and conference proceedings in these areas which DBLP and springer indexing. She holds the first place in the international publication with honor from the president of Ain Shams University.

Vijay Akkineni is currently a doctorate student in the Department of Computer Science at Georgia State University, and a member of the Data Mining Lab. He received his M.Sc. degree from the Department of Computer Science at Texas Tech University in 2007, and his B.Tech degree from the National Institute of Technology, Warangal in 2003. His research interests are big data, data mining, and parallel computing.

Bashar Alohali is a PhD research student in Network Security at Liverpool John Moores University. His fields of interest are smart grid and cyber security, computer forensics, computer networks and security, sensor-based applications for smart cities, critical infrastructure protection and cloud computing. He obtained his master's degree in computer systems security from the University of Glamorgan in 2011.

Rafal A. Angryk received his M.S. and Ph.D. degrees in Computer Science in 2004 from Tulane University. Dr. Angryk also holds two other master's degrees, which he obtained from universities in Poland. In 1999, Dr. Angryk received a M.A. in Business Management from the University of Szczecin and three years later a M.Eng. degree in Computer Science from the Technical University of Szczecin. Dr. Angryk is currently employed as a 2CI Associate Professor in the Computer Science Department at Georgia State University (GSU). Before joining GSU in August 2013, he spent almost a decade as a faculty member at Montana State University. Dr. Angryk is the founding director of MSU/GSU Data Mining Laboratory (http://dmlab.cs.montana.edu/), and holds the title of Affiliate Professor of Physics at MSU due to the interdisciplinary research he is conducting on massive repositories of solar data. Prior to arriving at MSU, he was involved for four years in the National Geospatial-Intelligence Agency (NGA) research project on Intelligent Database Agents for Geospatial Knowledge Integration and Management, administrated by the Center for Computational Sciences in the Stennis Space Center (NASA). Before that, he was an instructor at the Institute of Computer Science at the University of Szczecin. Dr. Angryk's research and teaching interests lie in the areas of Very Large Databases (Spatial and Spatio-temporal Databases, and kNN Indexing of High Dimensional Data), Data Mining (Frequent Patterns Discovery, Clustering and Classification of real-life large-scale data), and Information Retrieval (Text and Image data). He has published about 90 journal articles, book chapters and peer-reviewed conference papers in these areas. His research has been sponsored by the federal agencies: NASA (as a major contributor), NSF, NGA, and industry: Intergraph Corporation, RightNow Technologies (now Oracle), with a successful grant history exceeding $9M.

Berkay Aydin is currently a doctorate student in the Department of Computer Science at Georgia State University, and a member of Data Mining Lab. He received his B.Sc. degree from the Department of Computer Engineering at I.D. Bilkent University in 2012. His main areas of research interests are spatiotemporal pattern mining and information retrieval.

Miriam A. M. Capretz is a Professor in the Department of Electrical and Computer Engineering at Western University, Canada. Before joining Western University, she was an Assistant Professor in the Software Engineering Laboratory at the University of Aizu, Japan. She received her B.Sc. and M.E.Sc. degrees from UNICAMP, Brazil and her Ph.D. from the University of Durham, UK. She has been working in the software engineering area for more than 30 years and has been involved with the organization of several workshops and symposia as well as has been serving on program committees in several international conferences. Her current research interests include cloud computing, Big Data Analytics, service oriented architecture, and privacy and security.

Vanessa Chang's research activities and interests in Information Systems are focused in the areas of leadership, governance and processes of ICT and the use of systems, applications, and data in organisations. In addition to her Information Systems research, she is an active researcher in immersive learning in 3D virtual worlds environment, mobile learning, e-learning ecosystems and learning analytics. She has also worked on a number of experiments in 3D virtual worlds in Second Life, OpenSim, and OpenWonderland. She has also collaborated with international researchers in teaching ERP/SAP enterprise systems business process in a globalized context using 3D virtual worlds. She developed the Web-based Learning Environment instrument (WEBLEI) and this instrument is active in use and adopted by researchers and institutions around the world to assess the use and effectiveness of the on-line learning environments. She has published in ranked international journals and conference proceedings.

Yuchao Duan is studying for a PhD at Curtin University, and is currently employed as a software tester for Dynamic Digital Depth Australia Pty Ltd.

El-Sayed M. El-Horbaty received his Ph.D. (1985) in Computer science from London University, U.K., his M.Sc. (1978) and B.Sc. (1974) in Mathematics from Ain Shams University, Egypt. His work experience includes 25 years as an academic in Egypt (Ain Shams University), Qatar (Qatar University), and Emirates (Emirates University, Ajman University, and ADU University). He worked as the Deputy Dean of the faculty of IT, Ajman University (2002-2008). He is working as a Vice Dean in the faculty of Computer & Information Sciences, Ain Shams University (2010-2012), and he is working as a head of computer science dept. at the same college (2012-now). Prof. El-Horbaty's current areas of research are parallel algorithms, combinatorial optimization, and image processing. His work appeared in journals such as Parallel Computing, International Journal of Computers and Applications (IJCA), Applied Mathematics and Computation, and the International Review on Computers and Software. Also he has been involved in more than 26 conferences.

Ernesto Exposito is Associate Professor at INSA Toulouse and researcher in the SARA team (Services et Architectures pour les Réseaux Avancés) at LAAS-CNRS, France. In 2004, he worked as a Researcher in the National ICT Australia Limited (NICTA) research center in Sydney, Australia. In 2003, he earned his PhD in computer science and networking from the Institut National Polytechnique de Toulouse. His research interests include autonomic communication services aimed at satisfying the requirements of new generation distributed applications in heterogeneous networked environments. His research activities include designing, modelling and developing service-oriented, component-based and ontology-driven autonomic transport and middleware communication services. He has served as chairman and member for many Program Committees. He has participated in several European and French research projects (GCAP, EUQoS, NetQoS, Feel@home) and currently he is the coordinator at LAAS of the IMAGINE European project (FoF/2011-2014) in the domain of Dynamic Manufacturing Networks. He is author of more than 80 publications including international journals, regular and invited international conference papers, books and book chapters.

Katarina Grolinger is currently a Postdoctoral Fellow at Western University, Canada. She received her Ph.D. and M.Eng. Degrees in Software Engineering from Western University. Previously, she obtained her M.Sc. and B.Sc. in Mechanical Engineering from the University of Zagreb, Croatia. She is also a Certified Oracle Database Administrator with over ten years of industry experience in database administration and software development. Her research interests include Big Data, NoSQL data stores, cloud computing, data management, software integration and interoperability.

Tomayess Issa is a senior lecturer at the School of Information Systems at Curtin University, Australia. Tomayess completed her doctoral research in Web development and Human Factors. As an academic, she is also interested in establishing teaching methods and styles to enhance the students' learning experiences and resolve problems that students face. Tomayess Issa Conference and Program Co-Chair of the IADIS International Conference on Internet Technologies and Society and IADIS International Conference on International Higher Education. Furthermore, she initiated the IADIS conference for Sustainability, Green IT and Education. Currently, she conducts research locally and globally in information systems, human-computer interaction, usability, social networking, teaching and learning, sustainability, green IT and cloud computing. Tomayess participated in a couple of conferences and published her work in several peer-reviewed journals, books, book chapters, papers and research reports Tomayess Issa is a Project leader in the International research network (IRNet-EU (Jan2014 – Dec 2017)) to study and develop new tools and methods for advanced pedagogical science in the field of ICT instruments, e-learning and intercultural competences. Finally she is a senior research member of ISRLAb (Information Society Research Lab) from International Association for Development of the Information Society.

Theodora Issa is a Senior Lecturer, a member of Systems Change Working Group at Curtin University, and a recipient of multi awards and grants from the faculty, university and external bodies. She has published on business ethics, sustainability and higher education, social media, cloud computing, and is currently conducting her research on ethical mindsets. Member of editorial committees of international journals, reviewer of Journals, and has recently been appointed co-editor in chief of the Journal of Electronic Commerce in Organizations. Theodora is one of the webmasters of http://soca.cjb.net and is one of the editors of the weekly bulletin http://noohro.cjb.net. In November 2013, at the 10th Assembly of the World Council of Churches in Busan, South Korea, Dr Theodora Issa was elected as a member of the Central Committee (CC) of WCC representing the Syrian Orthodox Patriarchate of Antioch and all the East. It is worthwhile noting that this is the first time a female member was elected to this position on behalf of the Syrian Orthodox. In July 2014, the WCC CC approved the appointment of Dr Issa as a member of the WCC Commission on Ecumenical Formation and Education (EEF).

Omer K. Jasim received his PhD. (2015) from the Faculty of computer and information sciences, he received his M.Sc. (2009) and B.Sc. (2007) in Computer Science from College of Computer at Al-Anbar University, Iraq. He got the first ranking in two studies with honor grade. As academic filed, Omer has experience includes 3 years in Iraq-Private college(Alma'arif University College). He occupied a Head of the Computer science department at such College (2010-2012). He is a member of IEEE and Cyber security council. Omer works as organizer, technical,scientific, and reviewer in the different International conferences. The interesting fields of Omer are: cloud computing, quantum cryptography, cryptography and network security, and artificial intelligence.

S. Kuppuswami received a M.Sc. degree in Applied Electronics from the University of Madras and a PhD degree in Computer Science from Universite' de Rennes I, France. He was a Professor in Department of Computer Science, Pondicherry University. He was awarded an Indo-French Research Fellowship for the year 1983 and CNRS (France) Best Thesis Award for the year 1986 (Prix de These CNRS - 1986). Currently he is working as a Principal at Kongu College of Engineering, Perundurai. His research interests are object oriented systems, neural networks, multimedia and Tamil computers.

Emna Mezghani is currently a PhD student in Software Engineering at the University of Toulouse. Previously, she obtained her MSc degree and her BSc degree in Computer Science from the National School of Engineering of Sfax, Tunisia. Her research interests include service-oriented architecture, collaborative systems, cloud computing, big data, semantics and knowledge management.

K. Palanivel received his B.E in Computer Science & Engineering and M. Tech. in Computer Science & Engineering from Bhrathiar University, Coimbatore and Pondicherry University, Puducherry in 1994 and 1998 respectively. He joined as Technical Assistant in 1995. Presently, he is working as a Systems Analyst in the Computer Centre of Pondicherry University. His field of interest is software engineering, computer networks and design patterns. He has more than 15 years of experience in the field of computer applications, teaching and research at Pondicherry University.

Jaroslav Pokorny is a full professor in the Faculty of Mathematics and Physics, Charles University in Prague. He has published more than 300 papers and books on data modeling, relational databases, query languages, XML technologies, and data organization. His current research interests include semi-structured data, Web technologies, database architectures, indexing methods, Big Data, and social networks. He was involved as a chair and co-chair in the organization of many international conferences and workshops. He was also a member of many PC committees. He is a member of the ACM and the IEEE. He also works as the representative of Czech Republic in IFIP.

Abdel-Badeeh M. Salem is a Professor of Computer Science in the Faculty of Computer and Information Sciences, Ain Shams University, Cairo, Egypt. He has been Professor Emeritus since 2007. Previously he was Director of the Scientific Computing Center at Ain Shams University (1984-1990). His research interests include intelligent computing, expert systems, biomedical informatics, and intelligent e-learning technologies. He has published around 250 papers in refereed journals and conference proceedings in these areas. He has been involved in more than 300 conferences and workshops as an International Program Committee member, organizer and Session Chair. He is author and co-author of 15 Books in English and Arabic Languages. His work has appeared in more than 100 journals.

Bela Stantic is Director of "Big Data and Smart Analytics" lab within the Institute for Integrated and Intelligent Systems, Griffith University, Gold Coast, Australia. He is also Deputy Head of the School of Information and Communication Technology within Griffith University. His area of research is the efficient management of complex data structures including Big Data, Spatio-temporal and High dimensional data. He has published more than 90 peer reviewed conference and journal papers and presented many invited and Keynote talks at prestigious conferences. He has supervised many PhD students to their graduation and served on the Program Committees of more than 100 conferences and was/is doing the editorial duties of many Journals in area of his research.

Madhavi Vaidya is working as an Assistant Professor in Mumbai, India. Her research area is Data Analytics. She is a teacher at heart and teaches in the areas of Databases, Operating Systems and Software Engineering. She has published and presented research papers at National and International conferences. She has published and presented research papers at National and International Conferences with She has published and presented various research papers at National and International Conferences and reviewed some papers. She is a member of ACM and IEEE.

Dan Watson is an associate professor and head of the Department of Computer Science at Utah State University. He holds a Ph.D. in Electrical Engineering from Purdue University. Dr. Watson's recent work includes the efficient parallel implementation of algorithms for hydrological analysis of large digital elevation maps. He is a member of the ACM.

Li Yan received her Ph.D. degree from Northeastern University, China. She is currently a Full Professor in the College of Computer Science & Technology at Nanjing University of Aeronautics and Astronautics, China. Her research interests include database modeling, XML data management, as well as imprecise and uncertain data processing. She has published over 50 papers in international journals, conferences and books in these areas since 2008. She also authored and edited several scholarly books published by Springer-Verlag and IGI Global, respectively.

Wei Yan received his Ph. D. degree from Northeastern University, China. He is currently a lecturer at Liaoning University, China. His research interests include big data, massive XML data management, XML personalized and flexible query, as well as XML fuzzy queries.

Ahmet Artu Yildirim received his Ph.D. degree in Computer Science in 2015 from Utah State University. His research interests include algorithms, parallel and distributed computing, and data mining.

Index

Become an IRMA Member

Members of the **Information Resources Management Association (IRMA)** understand the importance of community within their field of study. The Information Resources Management Association is an ideal venue through which professionals, students, and academicians can convene and share the latest industry innovations and scholarly research that is changing the field of information science and technology. Become a member today and enjoy the benefits of membership as well as the opportunity to collaborate and network with fellow experts in the field.

IRMA Membership Benefits:

- **One FREE Journal Subscription**
- **30% Off Additional Journal Subscriptions**
- **20% Off Book Purchases**
- Updates on the latest events and research on Information Resources Management through the IRMA-L listserv.
- Updates on new open access and downloadable content added to Research IRM.
- A copy of the Information Technology Management Newsletter twice a year.
- A certificate of membership.

IRMA Membership $195

Scan code to visit irma-international.org and begin by selecting your free journal subscription.

Membership is good for one full year.

www.irma-international.org